THE LIFE OF NICCOLÒ MACHIAVELLI

THE LIFE OF NICCOLÒ MACHIAVELLI

◇◇

by

ROBERTO RIDOLFI

Translated from the Italian by

CECIL GRAYSON

◇◇

The University of Chicago Press

Originally published in Italy as
VITA DI NICCOLÒ MACHIAVELLI
Copyright 1954 by Angelo Belardetti Editore, Rome

THE UNIVERSITY OF CHICAGO PRESS, CHICAGO

The University of Toronto Press, Toronto 5, Canada
Routledge & Kegan Paul, London, E.C. 4

*English translation © 1963 by The University of Chicago. All rights
reserved. Published 1963. Printed by* THE UNIVERSITY OF
CHICAGO PRESS, *Chicago, Illinois, U.S.A.*

Library of Congress Catalog Card Number: 62-15048

CONTENTS

◇◇

CONTENTS

PLATES

PREFACE

CRIPTURE tells us that Man is made of clay; but every man is in another sense made of clay, that of his own land, where he was born and where over the centuries the remains of his ancestors have returned to dust. We Florentines are made of a fine stony gravel, shifting and difficult to work; and because it seems easier for men to understand each other when they were born on the same soil and beneath the same sky, I conceived the ambition to write this book about that quintessential Florentine, Niccolò Machiavelli.

Indeed I had had the desire in mind for some time, perhaps ever since my youth when I was first struck by that unattractive portrait sketched by De Sanctis in the remarkable pages he dedicated to the great Secretary in his *History of Italian Literature*: 'He strongly resembles Lorenzo de' Medici. Pleasure-loving and merry, and equally at ease with fraternities and bands of revellers . . .' Long study and great affection, and the devilish goading of my friend Giovanni Papini did the rest.

Another book about Machiavelli! Yes, but this one is not going to contain the usual fog of words about the concepts of 'virtù' and 'fortuna' or the land he loved 'more than his own soul'. It may seem a paradox, but the fact is that amid the flood of works about the Florentine Secretary there existed no life of Machiavelli, no real straightforward biography. The monumental and fundamental books of Villari and Tommasini are not biographies; in them the biographical part disappears and is lost beneath a great mass of adipose exegesis, history and criticism, so that in a continuous reading one cannot follow the course of his life (always supposing, that is, a continuous reading of these works to be possible!), and it is difficult to use them for rapid consultation on biographical points. It is enough to say that Villari begins to mention Machiavelli after about 300 pages, and that in other parts of his three fat volumes we find occasional biographical fragments floating in a vast whirlpool of other material and hundreds of pages apart. In addition, these two overcrowded monographs often leave much to be desired not only on the score of order and proportion, but also in their interpretation of the sources (particularly in Tommasini's book). Other lesser biographies bring no fresh light to the subject.

With the aid of a few new documents and the better use of those already known, this book brings some new order into Machiavelli's house; the chronology of his works emerges slightly changed here and there; certain important facts have come to light and corrected errors solemnly repeated by scholars for years; windows have been opened to let in the air, the dust has been brushed off, and one or two things have been restored. I felt that this work of cleaning and restoring was needed, and I have tried to do it to the best of my ability, not, I think, without some new positive results. Those who enjoy the foggy discussions I mentioned above, can find a great variety anywhere around, constantly changing with the changing times as such things always do.

In short, I have tried to write the book I have always wanted to read: a straightforward human narrative of the life of this man, in which his own deeds and his own words should speak for themselves. I would add that these pages would have seemed too austere to me as the story of a poet—which indeed Machiavelli was, though not so much in his poems, and not, as some have unkindly suggested, when it came to politics—if they had remained closed in their historical discipline to any breath of poetry.

R. R.

La Baronta,
3 December 1953

PREFACE TO THE ENGLISH EDITION

◇◇◇

T HE first Italian edition of this book was published seven years ago. Since then, despite the somewhat unusual fortune it has enjoyed in Europe and in America, I have not made additions or changes of any kind apart from a few corrections of minor significance in the second Italian edition; nor have I concerned myself at all with the translations that have already been made of the work into other languages. I have made an exception for the first time in the case of this present translation into English: the importance of the translation itself, the reputation and skill of the translator and the prestige of the publishers, inspired me with the wish to correct my book and bring it up to date in various respects. In this way it has the advantage over the existing Italian editions.

The already considerable body of literature on Machiavelli has been much increased even in these intervening years, but no discovery of texts or new documents, no fresh conjecture produced by the fertile and subtle minds of scholars has made necessary major changes in the biographical pattern of my narrative. Nonetheless, here and there, especially in the notes, I have taken account of recent studies by well-known specialists in this field like H. Baron, F. Gilbert and J. H. Whitfield.

The most important work to appear in these years has been the volume written by Gennaro Sasso, who (and I cannot note the fact without a certain personal satisfaction) accepts all, or nearly all my conclusions on biographical, chronological and textual matters. As it is the first study to appear after my own work of cleaning and restoring (as I called it in the Preface to the Italian edition), Sasso's book is the first to take advantage of it, and may be regarded as a very useful complement to my biography as far as Machiavelli's political thought is concerned. The reader is referred to Sasso's well-informed study especially for the most recent bibliography on Machiavelli: as it contains no items which contribute to his biography, no account has been taken of them in this edition.

The well-known Italian scholar J. H. Whitfield, to whom I must be grateful for the warm admiration of my biography he has expressed in various essays and reviews, has vigorously criticized Sasso's study, and Sasso has replied with equal if not greater vigour.* Their discussion, which turns in part on the interpretation of my views, or at least has been provoked by this biography of mine, is flattering to my self-esteem; and I feel that students of Machiavelli will not be sorry it has taken place, because it is from the collision of opposing views that rise the sparks of truth.

La Baronta, Florence,
    February 1961.

* J. H. WHITFIELD, *Il caso Machiavelli*, in *Le parole e le idee*, I (1959), pp. 80–94; G. SASSO, *La polemica sul Machiavelli, ovvero il 'caso Whitfield'*, in *Nuova Rivista Storica*, XLIV (1960), pp. 297–330.

Chapter I

EARLY LIFE AND EDUCATION

◇◇◇

WHILE the Arno was still carrying away the remains of the pyre which had consumed the body of Savonarola, a revolution which had begun immediately after the Friar's arrest, had quietly been accomplished in the Florentine Republic. The 'piagnone' magistrates had all been dismissed from their offices and replaced by men of the opposing faction. The first to be deposed were the Ten (*Dieci*), the Eight (*Otto di guardia*), and the Councils (*Collegi della Signoria*); then right down to the lowest officials of the commune, they had to give up their jobs to men who had had nothing to do with the Friar unless it were to oppose or harm him; and the more openly they had done so, the better for them.[1]

Among the 'piagnoni' dismissed from the chanceries was, besides the humanist Ugolino Verino, author of the poem *De illustratione urbis Florentiae*, that Alessandro Bracci or Braccesi, head of the second chancery, who as the Republic's envoy at the Papal Court had laboured until the end to avert the Pope's anger from the city's prophet while steering a difficult course between a Signoria hostile to Savonarola and a Council of Ten favourable to him. In place of Bracci, author of Italian poems in the manner of Burchiello and of good Latin verse,[2] an almost unknown young man was nominated: Niccolò di Bernardo Machiavelli.

His origins were not at all obscure, though the Machiavelli had never been among the most influential in the city. They had moved into the town from the Val di Pesa, where they owned a good deal of land; and whether or not it is true that they were related to the former lords of

I

Montespertoli, they had soon become good middle-class citizens. They figure among the 'middle-class, noted families' of the district of Oltrarno, together with the Barbadori, Canigiani and Soderini, in Villani's list of the most important Guelph families who had left Florence after the great defeat by the Ghibellines in 1260, and later returned from every quarter. They held many offices in the city, and provided twelve gonfaloniers and fifty-four priors; but the only one who made a name for himself in the history of Florence was a certain Girolamo, who suffered torture, exile and finally death in imprisonment for having expressed himself openly against government by oligarchy.[3]

Their decent prosperity as 'popolani grassi' (rich commoners) was supported less by trade than by the family properties in Val di Pesa. Less prosperous than the rest at that time was Bernardo di Niccolò di Buoninsegna, whose fortunes had fallen so low that he was generally thought to belong to some spurious branch of the family. Later on this gave rise to the belief, rightly or wrongly, that his must really have been an illegitimate branch.[4] His fortunes improved slightly with an inheritance from Totto Machiavelli, but even with this help Bernardo would have had difficulty in maintaining his family without his own industrious efforts and the strictest economies. He was a doctor of law, and seems to have held the post of treasurer in the Marches,[5] although we do not know when. In Florence he exercised his profession but seldom and with small profit, while he managed his other slender resources with the greatest of care.

A most valuable *Libro di Ricordi*, a kind of diary kept by Bernardo and unknown until a short time ago,[6] reveals him as a somewhat miserly man, perhaps from necessity rather than by nature, meticulous and pernickety, but not without culture, giving much thought to money matters, but not insensible to the consolations of study. Messer Bernardo cannot afford luxuries, sometimes he lacks the wherewithal to maintain a standard of living verging rather on poverty than on modest prosperity, and yet from time to time he finds a few florins to buy books. It is his only vice, his one passion. Most of his books he buys loose and has them lovingly bound, sometimes illuminated. If he cannot buy, he borrows, and not only law books but books in Greek and Latin.[7] When these memoirs of his begin, printing has been introduced into Florence only four months before, but unlike the rich and disdainful bibliophiles of his day he eagerly takes advantage of it. From one of the earliest Florentine printers Niccolò della Magna he received a volume of Livy to compile its index of place-names; and as a reward for his long labour, which took nine months and used up twelve quires of paper, he kept the book he longed to possess.[8]

Bernardo had first two daughters, Primavera and Margherita,[9] and then Niccolò, who was born in Florence on the 3rd of May 1469.[10] A second son was called Totto in memory of the uncle from whom Bernardo had received the inheritance. The mother of these children was Bartolomea de' Nelli, to whom a later member of her family attributed some religious verses which have not come down to us.[11] But the fact of such attribution is enough to explain in the light of modern genetic theories on qualities inherited from the mother's side, the source of the poetic gift which inspired the whole of Machiavelli's life. From his father he derived by heredity or example a love of study. His father's memoirs now tell us something of Niccolò's early studies, of which hitherto nothing was known.

On the 6th of May 1476 Niccolò began to learn the 'Donatello', that is the first elements of Latin, from a certain maestro Matteo. He was then seven years old, which was just the right age for this beginning according to current educational precepts. The following year he was given a new teacher of grammar, one ser Battista da Poppi of the church of S. Benedetto.[12] *Multa fecit tulitque puer* . . . During this period of early studies he would go off to play in the woods at Sant'Andrea around his father's modest villa, or on the ruined castle walls of Montebuiano in the Mugello, that surrounded a property belonging to his mother's family. In 1480 he began to study arithmetic as well.[13] In the same year messer Bernardo, who had been struck down by the plague the previous year and had miraculously survived when many had perished in Florence, among them two of his own relatives, declares his meagre income, and numbers among his diminished dependants: 'Niccolò aged 11, Totto aged 5, going to school.'[14] In fact the following year we find the two boys being taught by a certain ser Paolo da Ronciglione. While Totto gets to grips with the 'Donatello', Niccolò '*fa de' latini*',[15] that is writes short compositions in Latin. This gives the lie to Giovio (but he must be used to it by now!), who would have us believe that Niccolò learned Latin when old enough to be married.

On the other hand, proofs accumulate that he never learnt Greek.[16] His father never intended to make him a learned man, nor did Machiavelli ever think to become one. Money was lacking perhaps as

3

well as the thought. The authors he read were undoubtedly those on which every youth exercised himself in those days, learning a good part of them by heart. But one can imagine and understand that that 'constant reading' of histories, of which Machiavelli will write in later life, must have begun like all great vocations from those early years. Justin, the first history book that children read,[17] was not among his father's books, but Bernardo borrowed a copy and gave it back when Niccolò was twelve years old and already doing Latin compositions. He did possess the *Decades* of Biondo and, more important, those of Livy, which he sent to the binders in 1486, probably together with a manuscript copy of his painstaking index. Niccolò then aged seventeen went to collect that favourite book from the binders, and as his father was in the country, it was he who paid for the work with 'three bottles of red wine and a bottle of vinegar'.[18] Reading these paternal memoirs it is easier to understand the words Niccolò wrote later in life: 'I was born poor, and I learned to know want before enjoyment.'

This, then, must have been the 'constant reading of ancient events' that nourished Machiavelli until the middle of his life. The other half was spent more in a 'long experience of modern affairs', through which the coming chapters will follow him. But first we must consider the events of which he was witness from the moment he opened his sharp eyes upon the world. He was later to remark that those things heard and seen in early years 'cannot help but make an impression on a young man', which will 'guide his actions for the rest of his life.'[19] It is likely that in setting down this universal truth he was thinking of his own experience.

Machiavelli was born just in time to know the ancient way of life of Florence both from what he saw himself and from the memory of it preserved by others. The government of the Ottimati founded in 1382, when the power of the lesser guilds was weakened, reformed in 1387, better organized and strengthened in 1393 by Maso degli Albizzi, had led the Republic to unprecedented happiness and greatness. If it were not as sober and decent as Dante pictured the commune at the time of Cacciaguida, the Florence of Niccolò da Uzzano and Maso degli Albizzi, before the Medici and the passing years brought corruption with them, was still a moral city. Abounding in wealth, in trade, in fine skills, and in clever and brilliant men, knowledge and well-being were there more evenly distributed than elsewhere. There was no other ostentation than that of great buildings public and private, sacred and profane, even though the latter may have been built in order to place upon them the family arms, as Savonarola was later to remark with sarcasm. Cosimo de' Medici the Elder said: 'I know the temper of this city; we shall be thrown out before fifty years have passed, but these buildings will still remain.' This sober wealth was refined by literature and the arts. Public ceremonies displayed a certain magnificence, but in private life the appearance was one of great civilization and propriety, greater than in any other city in Italy.

The ruling force was not the excellence of the laws but the virtues of the leaders. And although in political life many were elected to office, few to government, even injustice and usurpation of power were given such an appearance of justice, were done with such scruples, such care not to overstep the established forms, that few felt themselves aggrieved. Before they reached the Palazzo della Signoria, these difficult manœuvres in which men of government learned their craft, were conducted with the simplicity typical of this bourgeois city, in the shops and offices of the principal citizens, who were distinguished more by wisdom than by wealth—offices and shops to which men were not ashamed to return after performing the duties of the highest public positions, after the most grave deliberations, truly resembling in their austere simplicity 'those ancient Romans' to which one of them was compared by the biographer Vespasiano da Bisticci.[20] In fifteenth-century Florence where a contemporary poet praised its Roman liberty and culture, there appears more justification than elsewhere for the temptation to which Machiavelli so often gave way, to compare men and affairs with those of ancient Rome.

These leading Florentine citizens bore no resemblance to the nobles of the republic of Venice. They were plebeian nobles, deeply respectful of certain outward shows of popular sovereignty. The people regarded them almost as *primi inter pares*, and felt free beneath their rule, proud of their wisdom and happy to follow from the market-place, from stores and wine-shops the game of government going on in the Palazzo, which seemed the finer the more subtly it was conducted. Satisfied with its nominal sovereignty like a constitutional monarch of our own times, it left the business of government to the few.

The Medici too, in the first fifty years of their rule observed the complicated rules of this game, and the more closely they followed them the more successful they were. Thus the contentment and way of life which had been enjoyed under the government of an oligarchy,

B

survived for some time even under the rule of one man, whether he were called Cosimo, Piero or Lorenzo. Rulers in fact and not by right, and armed only with constant vigilance, they remained in power not by force but by the common consent of those who were their fellow-citizens, not their subjects. The subtle means by which these popular princes maintained their rule included finding seats in the magistrature for their own favourites, and holding the balance of wealth and favours by marriages and gifts of offices. But even more important for them was the art of avoiding jealousies and suspicion, the careful study of affairs that enabled them to hold the city in their grasp almost man by man.

Machiavelli was born in the same year in which Piero de' Medici died. He had followed Cosimo as ruler of the city, and this role was to pass after him to his sons Lorenzo and Giuliano. Machiavelli was too young to remember the cruel revenge and broken faith to rebel Volterra in 1472, but he was already studying his Latin authors when the Pazzi conspiracy occurred in 1478. He then saw the jealousy and resentment of certain principal citizens disguise themselves under the name of freedom, and conspire with the excessive greed of the nephews of Sixtus IV, who had given his consent to this attempt to overthrow the Medici. Among the conspirators were the Archbishop of Pisa and the young cardinal Riario. The place and time chosen for the slaughter was in the cathedral at the elevation of the Host. Giuliano was murdered, but Lorenzo escaped. The Archbishop and many of his accomplices were hanged from the windows of the Palazzo they had vainly attempted to make their own, and their bodies and those of others torn to pieces by the mob in the streets made a dreadful sight for many days.

The Pope sent his hypocritical condolences for the death of Giuliano, and then began his complaints, less on account of the Archbishop than on behalf of his young nephew the Cardinal who had been held prisoner. He was finally sent back by the Florentines, 'and as a result the Pope attacked them without compunction with all his own forces and those of the King of Naples', as Machiavelli was later to remark, drawing from this episode a machiavellian lesson.[21]. But before he resorted to temporal arms, Sixtus had attacked with spiritual ones, excommunicating Lorenzo and the magistrates, and placing the city under an interdict. Niccolò observed that the citizens paid little heed to these measures, since such weapons had long been blunted by the ill use made of them and by the wretched example of the man who used them.

But if the spiritual offensive mattered little to the Florentines, the war of armies drained their resources and eventually defeated them, with the rout of Poggio Imperiale. The cause of this was the extraordinary cowardice of the mercenaries, which was long remembered in the city, and made a deep impression on Niccolò, who seems to have recorded the fact in his own mind long before writing it down in his *Histories*. Florence, or rather the house of the Medici, was saved by the bold decision of Lorenzo, who, having borne manfully the great responsibility of the war, went to throw himself on the mercy of the King of Naples, and brought back an honourable peace, much to the annoyance of the Pope who later on gave his agreement to the treaty. After these events, Niccolò wrote in later years, Lorenzo's reputation was vastly increased in Florence, 'a city greedy for gossip, and judging things by results not by theories'.[22]

Events from then on proved favourable to Lorenzo, whose political wisdom had already begun to balance the powers of Italy. No other wars of the period impinged on the territories of the Rebublic: not the war of Lombardy that came to an end with the death of Sixtus (he died, it was said, at the sound of the word 'peace'), nor the war of the Barons (1486), which found the Florentines in league with King Ferdinand of Naples against the new Pope Innocent VIII. Niccolò, now seventeen years of age, was able to gather fresh material for observation from this war on the subject of the appalling conduct of mercenaries. He also learned from the actions of the King how a 'wise' prince may 'not care if he were famed as cruel if he thus held his people together',[23] and pledge and break his faith to suit his convenience. This latter art, however, was to be demonstrated to Machiavelli more clearly by another Pope, the successor of Innocent VIII, as he tells us in his *Prince*: 'Alexander VI never thought of anything but deceit, and he never failed to find those he could deceive. There never was any man better able to assert and swear to things or who more consistently failed to keep his word; and yet his deceptions were always successful'.[24] Lessons in similar arts he was to have daily from the various courts of Italy, and from the family massacres habitual in nearby Romagna (1488).

At that time Lorenzo's iron hand within the velvet glove was quietly extinguishing the liberty of Florence. At ten-year intervals, in '70–'71,

'80 and '90, reforms had gradually restricted the governing power in ever fewer hands faithful to Lorenzo, which ensured the security of his personal rule. As freedom ebbed away, there went also the old way of life of the city which we have described, surviving only in the regrets of those who had enjoyed its last moments. The corruption of morals, beginning with the corruption of political life, which arose inevitably from the changing times and was imported from other courts, was favoured by Lorenzo as an instrument of government. These were precisely the years in which the generation of Machiavelli was at an age most susceptible to corruption. Writing in later years of these changes in Florentine life, he noted in his contemporaries also a greater and more unbridled mordacity: 'The one who could rend his fellows most cleverly, was deemed the wisest and most estimable'.[25] It would seem that he owed something himself to this background as well as drawing conclusions from it.

In those years simple living gave place to luxury and gambling, and lechery and sodomy (the 'Florentine vice') unashamedly increased. As is always the case (and Machiavelli remarks on it) the relaxation of morals was accompanied by the decay of religion. The vices of laymen were part cause and part effect of the vices of priests and monks. The worst example was set by Rome, and especially after Alexander VI became Pope. At that moment, against both layman and cleric and against Lorenzo's encouragement of corruption the terrible voice of Savonarola was raised.

The great Friar had been in Florence from '82 to '87 without arousing much controversy. He returned in the summer of '90, fortified by constant preaching, meditation and prayer, confirmed in his mission by voices and visions; emboldened by the success his new manner of preaching enjoyed on his return, he set to, to do battle with vice and with those who set the example of viciousness in high places. Lorenzo failed either with flattery or with threats to silence him. Savonarola boldly denounced his latest political reforms. In the end, Lorenzo died in '92, and when Piero and his supporters were driven out after the invasion of Charles VIII, Savonarola remained alone in the field. He had become an object of veneration to the people who saw him as a prophet and a man of saintly life, and were grateful to him for saving them from being sacked by the French and from civil war, and for giving them freedom and the new popular government inspired and promoted by him.

Such a new government should have pleased Machiavelli, who was now twenty-five years old, because it was a people's government. But he could not have liked its founder, a friar and a foreigner, or his conception of the state dedicated to the service of religion, that is of God, while Machiavelli at least in his writings wanted religion to serve the state, that is mankind. Although he was certainly never a piagnone and it is easier to imagine him among the Arrabbiati,[26] we do not find his name among those of the most fervid followers of this sect. Besides the Friar's political achievement, Machiavelli must have approved his battle with the corruption of the Church, with the bad prelates of Rome, with the wicked monks. And if according to his own nature and that of his fellow Florentines he was to jeer at the fallen hero, yet as soon as he gave the subject mature and serious thought he did not hide the reverence in which he held Savonarola.

One of the first dated writings which we possess of Machiavelli, and one of the first documents in his biography, is a letter he sent to Ricciardo Becchi on the 9th of March 1498 to tell him of two sermons delivered by Savonarola. At that moment, 'giving way to the Pope's anger', Savonarola had removed himself from the pulpit of the Cathedral and was preaching in San Marco. These first two sermons given in the church of his own convent were among the last he was ever to pronounce. The 'unarmed prophet' was soon to succumb beneath the Pope's spiritual weapons, the temporal arms of the League, the mercantile prudence and forgetful instability of the Florentines. When we read Machiavelli's letter today, remembering as we do the great goodness of Savonarola and the ideals which inspired his sermons and led him with serenity to the scaffold and the fire, it will always seem an unworthy letter, for in it the great Friar is judged a fraud, 'a trimmer and an ingenious liar'.[27]

However, it would be a mistake to take Machiavelli too seriously when he is writing half in jest these letters to friends, where he lets loose his biting Florentine temperament for his own amusement and theirs. Besides, he was twenty-nine, he liked a free and easy life, he was fond of all those luxuries and frivolities that the Friar had suppressed. One should not ask of such a young man more than one asked of the very Vicar of Christ, that Rodrigo Borgia who, within less than two months from that letter, and in full agreement with the Florentines, was to have burnt at the stake the man who had dreamed of reconquering Rome and Italy for Christ with no other weapons than his own words. That funeral pyre was the last lesson Machiavelli received from men before passing from private to public life.

We have summarized briefly the dismal teachings of Machiavelli's own times. If it seems that he benefited from them more than his contemporaries did, albeit only in his writings, that should be attributed to his greater powers of observing closely men and affairs and of drawing conclusions from them with the rigour of a syllogism, unimpeded by sentimental or moral considerations. It should not be imagined that the almost scientific conclusions he draws from observation and reasoning necessarily coincided with his own feelings. In his theories intellect almost dominates sentiment; in his actions it rarely does so. Reason and feeling constantly brought yet another conflict into a character which was full of them.

For that matter the Florentine character was full of contrasts; Dante called one of them 'bizzarro', and the epithet has had wide currency in general application. One might compare the character of the Florentine people to that of the land which engendered and ripened it, varied and yet always the same, harsh and at the same time kindly; where the earth is hard rock tamed by the heat of the sun and even more by men's labour, compelled to constant arduous effort. Thus the Florentine character has a harsh and bitter core beneath its outward amiability, and perhaps too a spark of cruelty beneath its urbanity. Their brilliant irony and the practical jokes for which they are famous, are not all kindly or free from malice.

As a proof and symbol of the joyful and carefree nature of this people, the refrain from Lorenzo's *Trionfo di Bacco e di Arianna* has been quoted, *ad nauseam*, without it being realized that this invitation to the enjoyment of life has that same sad and bitter core beneath its merry aspect:

> *Quant'è bella giovinezza*
> *che si fugge tuttavia!*
> *Chi vuol esser lieto, sia:*
> *di doman non c'è certezza.*

[How beautiful is youth that is for ever fleeting! Let him be gay who will be: there is no certainty in the morrow.]

In seeking to understand the character of the Florentines, we must not forget either that at this time, besides the most sensual carnival songs, they sang to the very same tunes, merely changing the words but often keeping the same rhymes, sacred hymns, composed in greater numbers and with greater devotion than in any other city at any time. Thus no one should be astonished or still less regard it as a joke that Machiavelli should have written lewd songs and the *Mandragola*, and also an *Exhortation to repentance*. In this city piety and impiety constantly mingled, exactly as they do in the very typically Florentine *Morgante* of Pulci. Here we find the pages of history recording the wonderful Savonarolan reformation interleaved with those of the paganizing age of Lorenzo and those which describe the excesses of the Arrabbiati and the Compagnacci after the burning of the Friar, when one of the signori could exclaim: 'God be praised, now we can all commit sodomy again'.[28]

In Florence political life too bore the impress of this same character, moved by bitter conflicts, constantly changing. It may seem a strange coincidence, and yet it is really the logical consequence of such conditions, that the three greatest political writers of the sixteenth century should have been produced by a city where the system of government was bad, and the leaders were, as we have seen, better than the laws they administered. Behind the unfortunate constitution, inherited from the days of the ancient free commune and reformed or patched up over the years on no other system than the day to day suspicions and jealousies of intolerant and capricious men, there lay the acute experience of a political school which trained men to rule and rule themselves under conditions of the utmost difficulty. Here were rulers hampered by bad laws, offices as ephemeral as the laws themselves, ambassadors without authority, with ambiguous and restricted mandates. Even the 'tyrants', as we have seen, had to accommodate themselves to the city's temper, maintaining their rule with constant effort, controlling it day by day, guiding their actions not merely with art but with artifice. The motto *Non sine labore* adopted by one ancient Florentine family, is admirably suited to everything having its origins between Fiesole and the Arno, and especially to that school of the art of statesmanship which was the Florence of the fifteenth century. Such was the school in which Niccolò Machiavelli grew up.

To complete this chapter I would like here to sketch a portrait of Machiavelli at the beginning of his thirtieth year, but I am overwhelmed at the thought of attempting to portray an intellect as difficult to understand and to reproduce, I would say, as the expression on his face which artists have endeavoured to represent. Here is a mind which people have been striving to understand for four centuries and a half, and which has never been properly understood. Machiavelli has often been accused of cynicism, which was in fact only the 'faith of one who sincerely believed in his own logic'.[29] It is not surprising if we find those who have attempted to analyse his character speaking of dualism in his make-up, when faced with the cold realism of this great idealist, the pessimism of this optimist. He was something like his own idea of politics, which he conceived in the form of a centaur, 'half man, half beast'.[30]

I shall begin by quoting those words which Gino Capponi wrote of him: otherwise, since they are the simple truth, I should only have to paraphrase them, and as they are admirable words, they would be spoiled by a paraphrase: 'His intellect was elegant and abundant, his morals lax; he was marvellously acute in comprehension, but without his actions corresponding to his thought; he felt about politics as Italy felt: his aims were high, his ideas lofty, but here were energies misused, greatness corrupted, that for lack of means and hope lay in the mud like the Roman eagles in defeat. Religion was not extinct in his thought any more than in Italy at large: he revered religion as a noble thing, and loved it as part of Italy. Then despising the bad government which led religion into disrepute, he attacked it with scorn and drove it from his heart. Thus was Machiavelli, and thus was Italy itself'.[31] Italy was indeed like that, but not all Italy, and Machiavelli was the expression and image of his native Florence more than of any other part of Italy —an enlarged image in which the virtues and the vices necessarily appear larger than life.

For that matter, he had no outstanding vices, if we except that of lusting after women,[32] whereby he gave relief to an exuberance of vitality and perhaps also of affection. He was, for all his poverty, extremely generous, a most loving father, scrupulously honest, a lover of his country and of freedom. To his contemporaries he appeared exceptionally corrupt because, being a great man, he did not seek to hide that which others hid; he hid his good qualities and displayed the less good. Indeed he liked to be thought worse than he really was, to shock his equals and show he was equal to the great. He noted with some bitterness that certain cynical precepts 'would not be good', if only men were good. Having drained the cup of human wickedness and seen the good always overcome by the bad, and having formulated

I. Portrait of Machiavelli by Santi di Tito. Palazzo Vecchio, Florence

II. Bust of Machiavelli, Florentine School, 16th century. Palazzo Vecchio, Florence

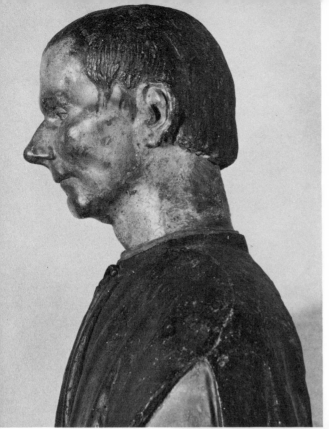

III. (a) Bust of Machiavelli
(Plate II) in profile.
Galleria Doria,
Rome

(b) Portrait of Machiavelli
by an unknown artist.
Galleria Doria,
Rome

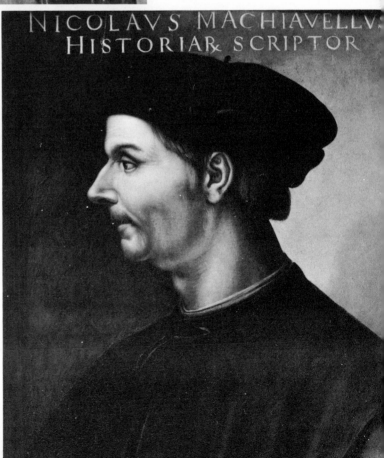

NICOLAVS MACHIAVELLVS
HISTORIAR SCRIPTOR

IV. Bust of Machiavelli, Florentine School, 16th century.
Formerly in the Accademia Colombaria, Florence

this experience into one of his rules of life, he liked to be thought of as belonging to the wicked, though his place is rather with the good.

Capponi says that Machiavelli loved religion and pursued high ideals; there is hardly a page of his however cynical in which we do not catch a glimpse of a poet's sensitive and impassioned spirit, and there can be no real wickedness where there is poetry. But looking about him, he was overcome by the desperate state of the good and the immanence of evil, and his spirit rebelled. Then he either gave expression to his feelings in those bitter maxims or in laughter. He hid behind his laughter; he laughed at his own emotion, he laughed because he had looked for and believed in the noble and the good, he laughed at himself for not laughing before.

Some of these characteristics of his nature are preserved in a self-portrait which he sketched in an eight-line stanza:

> *Io spero, e lo sperar cresce 'l tormento:*
> *Io piango, e il pianger ciba il lasso core;*
> *Io rido e il rider mio non passa drento,*
> *Io ardo e l'arsion mia non par di fore;*
> *Io temo ciò che io veggo e ciò che io sento;*
> *Ogni cosa mi dà nuovo dolore;*
> *Così sperando, piango rido e ardo,*
> *E paura ho di ciò che io odo e guardo.*[33]

[I hope, and hope increases my torment: I weep and weeping feeds the weary heart; I laugh and my laughter does not touch my soul; I burn and no one sees my passion; I fear what I see and what I hear; everything gives me fresh pain; thus hoping, I weep and laugh and burn, and I fear what I hear and see.]

A son of Humanism, but a prodigal son who never returned, he differed from the humanists in spirit even more than in his studies.[34] He was extremely fond of music, which he cultivated 'with the lute' and 'by the book'; but once only do we find in his pages an allusion to the place of the figurative arts in that marvellous renaissance: when he speaks of 'this province . . . born to revive the things that were dead, as we have seen, in poetry, painting and sculpture'; and it was he who longed for the revival of ancient virtue and order.

In his person he was well proportioned, of middle height, thin, erect and bold in his bearing. His hair was black, his skin pale but slightly sallow. His head was small with bony features and a high fore-head. His eyes shone very bright, and his thin compressed lips seemed always to bear an ironical smile. We have several portraits of him,[35] but only Leonardo, with whom he came in contact in his better days, could have reproduced for us in line and colour the real meaning of that slight, ambiguous smile.

Chapter 2

NICCOLÒ MACHIAVELLI
SECRETARY

◇◇

IT was the 28th of May 1498 when the council unexpectedly desig-
nated as second Chancellor the young Niccolò Machiavelli, barely
five days after the execution of Savonarola.[1] Biographers have not
up to now realized that it was the fall of the 'unarmed prophet' that
opened this career to Machiavelli. It was another lesson for him to add
to the teachings of modern times. Indeed, in this connection it is not
without significance that when his appointment had gone through the
Council of Eighty on the 15th of June and they passed it on to be
debated, according to the law, in the Great Council, Niccolò had as
his rivals Francesco Gaddi,[2] teacher of rhetoric at the University,
Andrea di Romolo a notary, and that Francesco di ser Barone notorious
for having manipulated the record of the martyr's trials.[3] It was truly
a miracle that two mediocre people of long experience in the Chanceries, and a proved scoundrel with his part in that peaceful revolution
to recommend him, should all three have been passed over in favour
of a young man of no reputation, very little experience, and brilliant
intellect. Thus on the 19th of June Machiavelli was elected head of the
second chancery.[4]

The office was an important one, although not comparable in dignity
and authority with that of the first Chancellor of the Republic. Some
have out of ignorance confused the two, others have supposed them
to be of equal consequence. Under the new young secretary were men
of maturer years and long experience of the work. At the age of

twenty-nine, so totally unknown that up to then there is not the slightest trace or mention of him either in chronicles or in private or public documents, Machiavelli issued forth like a figure in a myth, full-grown and armed, from the bosom of his people.

The offices of the Chancery, even the assistantships, were normally filled by doctors of law, notaries or literary men of some reputation, and this tradition was maintained even after the reforms of the 13th of February 1498, according to which anyone could be elected.[5] Such qualifications were possessed not only by his colleagues and pre-decessors, but also by his successors and subordinates. Many of these left written works which are remembered in the histories of literature or at least in the pages of other scholars. He on the other hand was neither doctor of law nor notary, and this is confirmed by the form of his name in public documents, where he is never given the title of 'messere' or 'sere'. Nor do we know of any writings of his either in prose or verse which can safely be attributed to the first half of his life. Quite definitely, not only his major works, but all the minor ones of any merit belong to the second half of his life after he left the Chancery. Possibly one or two of his very few carnival songs,[6] or a love poem might be attributed to the period of his youth, but only because there is nothing actually against such an attribution, and not for any stronger reason.

On the other hand, that he had a reputation as a man of letters, perhaps even a certain authority in the restricted circle of his family, is proved by a letter he wrote on the 2nd of December 1497, on behalf of all the 'Malclavellorum familia', to Giovanni Lopez cardinal of Perugia, in support of their claims to the rich Pieve di Fagna against those of the Pazzi. This is the first dated writing of his which we possess.[7] It seems in fact strange that all the Machiavelli should have entrusted this task to the young Niccolò during the lifetime of his father Bernardo, head of the family, doctor of law, and not at all an unlettered man. We might add in passing that this letter is not lacking in address, and beneath the legal language there is already visible the firm, distinctive style of the great writer. And what is more important, the letter was successful, with the help of the Signoria which also wrote to the Cardinal on the subject,[8] in preserving to the family the owner-ship of that church.[9]

But the literary reputation that Niccolò had among the Machiavelli does not show that he had any at all among the citizens at large. On the contrary, we possess, down to the very last and least of them, the names of those who were citizens of Florence and of the republic of letters, and the fact that we do not find among them either his name or any trace of writings of his at this age is almost a certain proof that he had none. From the second half of his life we may form a conjecture which might serve to throw some light on the obscurity of the first half. He loved things more than words; he preferred life to letters. Unlike so many of his colleagues and contemporaries, who were dried-up men of letters, he was never a literary man. He wrote his works after 'long experience' had fertilized that 'constant reading' on which his youth was nourished, and supplied him with material for comparison. He could not have done so before. Without the experience that reading would have been sterile; without the reading he would not have sought its evidence in experience.

Though this may be the key to the secret of his obscurity in youth, and to a better understanding of the works of his maturity, it gives us no clue to the lesser secret of his election to the Chancery. It would all be explained if there were any proof of what several scholars of the nineteenth century wrote[10] : that he had served in the Chancery from 1494 or 1495 as an assistant or even in some lesser capacity. Unfortunately those who made these assertions made no attempt to prove them, or accompanied them with so many errors as to destroy any value which they may have had.[11] The historian of the Florentine Chancery who attempted to support them with a document he totally misunderstood, really fell into an error 'worthy of laughter and compassion'.[12]

Therefore we must set aside the hopeful conjecture of a period of apprenticeship, which might explain the secret of his election, until more valid proofs are available. All the more so, since Machiavelli himself contradicts this in a well-known letter, when he counts the years he spent 'in the study of the art of statecraft',[13] which must include all those passed in the secretariat. Furthermore, the historian of the Florentine Chancery[14] suggests the hypothesis that the spirit of a decision made on the 30th of April 1498 had some influence in the election of Niccolò. According to this, a young man was to be sent with ambassadors abroad, in order that the younger generation should learn statecraft. This provision, which according to the chronicler Parenti 'gave hopes to worthy young men', could have had no influence in the matter; but it does not seem impossible that Machiavelli may have gone abroad with some ambassador even before this decision was taken, as was to be the case with one of his successors in the secretariat Donato Giannotti.[15]

Setting these hypotheses aside, only one most likely conjecture remains: that he obtained this office—so humble in comparison with his talents, and so exalted in comparison with his status—by the influence of a prominent citizen, or of someone associated with the Chancery who had authority with the Signoria. One thinks immediately of Marcello Virgilio Adriani,[16] first secretary of the Republic, head of the first Chancery, in which he had succeeded Scala on the 13th of February of that same year 1498; and it was he whom Giovio[17] states was Machiavelli's teacher—a striking coincidence!

It is well known that Giovio cared little for the truth, and in fact often deliberately wrote what was not true, and Machiavelli received from him his share of malice and calumny. However, this scrap of information that now concerns us, can hardly have been falsified (though it may be inaccurate); and we should not be in a hurry to discard it, because Giovio did have quite close contacts with Florence and the Florentines,[18] at least up to the time when his *Historiae sui temporis* brought him into disrepute with many of them. At any rate, the principal biographers of Machiavelli believed it to be true—pruned of the more imaginative details—that Machiavelli learnt a great deal from Marcello Virgilio, though they rightly rejected the implication that he may have learnt Latin with him, for this seemed an absurd conjecture for several reasons even before the memoirs of messer Bernardo were available to controvert it.

The same biographers were, however, wrong in assuming that the relationship between Marcello Virgilio and Machiavelli could not have been in any sense that of master and pupil, or have gone beyond an informative intercourse between friends of unequal preparation. I do not wish to assert too definitely that Adriani was his teacher, but I do say that other biographers rejected the idea for the wrong reason—that of their respective ages. They say that Machiavelli was only five years younger than Adriani (nine years in point of fact), and so could not be his pupil.[19] A stupid assertion as one can see, and all the more so in that, as Adriani is known to have been teaching in the University of Florence, one cannot see why Machiavelli, nine years younger (and even if he were five years younger), could not have attended his lectures.

It is all conjecture based on the passage from Giovio, but it is reasonable conjecture, and if we accept it, it gives us the key to the election to the Chancery which I have so far been seeking. Actually no one more than Adriani, who was inside the camp and in fact its keeper, was in a better position to bring into it the man who is said to be his pupil, no one had a better authority to propose him to the Signoria. They could not deny him some say in the matter when it came to electing his closest collaborator and lieutenant. We now know from a recently discovered document that Machiavelli was a candidate for a post in the Chancery as early as the 19th of February 1498.[20] Adriani had entered on his office on the 16th of that month, so that once he had won over the Signoria and they had persuaded the 'consiglio dei Richiesti' (which made its decision on the 28th of May), it cannot have been difficult to push through such an election in the Council of Eighty, even 'ex plurimis nominatis et scrutinatis', who perhaps were there only for the form, and still less in the Great Council, particularly as amongst his rivals in this final test the best qualified was Gaddi, and after him, ser Ceccone. Of these the first was suspect as a fanatical Medici man, and the second despised even by those who had despicably made use of him.

Of course, Adriani could have favoured Machiavelli's election if he had had only the friendly relationship with him which the biographers suppose, and not those of master and pupil indicated by the words of Giovio. There does not, however, seem to be evidence of a real friendship between the two during the time when they both worked in the Palazzo della Signoria. Even though the first-born of the head of the second Chancery was held at the font by the first Chancellor (as the custom was), the letters which he wrote to Machiavelli show no sign of a close or confidential relationship, of which the letters of other colleagues are so eloquent. The fact is that one of them loved things, the other words. The solemn and grave Adriani could not have been at his ease with his wild and womanizing young colleague, who lived and wrote in the vulgar tongue, to the great scandal of Adriani's academic gravity.

Now Machiavelli is made secretary, whether by luck or by cleverness or both, and it remains for us to explain what the office of secretary implied. At that time, as we already know, the Florentine Republic had a first and second secretary in charge respectively of the first and second Chanceries, although the authority, or at least the shadow of the first extended over the second. Originally the first dealt with foreign affairs and correspondence, the second with home affairs and war, but as time went on and their business changed and overlapped, part of their functions was handed over to the secretariat of the Ten when there was one, and with this office the second Chancery was eventually combined or confused. Since the Ten corresponded with ambassadors abroad as did the Signori themselves through the first Chancery, one can see how confused the matter was. One even finds registers of foreign correspondence begun by the Signori and carried on by the Ten. Both the secretariats had their own minute books and copy files divided into external and internal affairs.[21] At any rate, the division between them was rather of particular transactions and registers: the offices and officials were often the same.

It is enough to say that the two chanceries between them managed all home affairs, foreign affairs and war, and that, by virtue of the brief tenure of the magistrates, they alone held the thread of affairs in their hands. The Chanceries were reformed several times and most recently in January 1498 after the death of the chancellor Bartolomeo Scala when the principal offices were distributed as follows: in the first Chancery, messer Marcello Virgilio Adriani, first chancellor, with an annual salary of 330 *fiorini di suggello*, assistant ser Antonio della Valle, with 80 florins; in the second Chancery Niccolò Machiavelli, 'secretary to the Signoria', with the functions of head of the Chancery and a salary of 192 *fiorini di suggello* equal to a little more than 128 gold florins;[22] his assistants ser Agostino Vespucci and ser Andrea di Romolo, with respectively 96 and 60 *fiorini di suggello*. These and other assistants, among them ser Biagio Buonaccorsi, we find attached sometimes to the secretariat of the Signoria, sometimes to that of the Ten. This Chancery of the Ten was shortly afterwards, by a decision of the 14th of July, given to Machiavelli,[23] though the additional office brought him no change of function, salary or staff. All he had, nominally, was ten additional masters to serve.

The attributes of the office which Machiavelli held were never thoroughly defined even in his own times, and varied according to need. Their definition is a difficult and controversial matter, and it is not to be wondered at if today these attributes vary from biographer to biographer and from author to author. Some have confused his office with that of the first chancellor of the republic, and put him on a level with Salutati, Bruni, Poggio and Scala. Others, correcting this error to excess, fell into the opposite one of denying importance and dignity to the office filled by Machiavelli, even that recorded in the official registers of the second Chancery, '*cuius caput est Nicolaus Macla-vellus*', as we read in one dated 1500,[24] or more explicitly in one of 1502 where he is actually called '*secundus cancellarius*'. The historian of the Florentine Chancery was, therefore, in error when he reproved a very learned historian of Italian literature for writing that 'of the second Chancery Machiavelli was head more in fact than of right', and denied that he was ever 'continuously' head even in fact.

Once again common knowledge instinctively corrected the many learned follies written on this subject. The title 'Florentine secretary' is historically correct, and in fact translates literally some of his signatures: it is the title under which he was long referred to and quoted, and under which his works were published when that great name was persecuted. Neither Salutati nor Bruni, both famous chancellors and greatly honoured in their lifetimes by the city and by the courts of Italy, enjoy the honour of such antonomasia. That was to be the lot of the obscure young man whom we now find occupying the second place in the Chancery, poor in everything but intelligence and confidence; and even now he seems to be uttering to Florence and to Italy his famous '*eccomi*'.

Chapter 3

THE FIRST COMMISSIONS

◇◇◇

A T the time when Machiavelli first took office, the Florentines'
main preoccupation was the recapture of Pisa, and one could say
that every internal or external piece of business which passed
through the Chancery bore the mark of that war. Since the city had
rebelled in the presence and with the consent of Charles VIII, all efforts
had been directed first at getting Pisa back from the King, who was the
cause of its loss, and then, after a long history of illusions and disillusions,
of temporizing and betrayals, they sought to retake it by military action.
This would have been simple, had it not been for foreign greed and the
Florentines' tenacious friendship for France, which gained them the
enmity of the Italian states in league against Charles VIII. They had been
held firm to this friendship by ancient tradition, by commercial
interests, and by Savonarola's sermons. The latter had thereby brought
upon himself the wrath of the power that wielded spiritual as well as
temporal arms under the banner of the League. In consequence there
had been a hard duel between the Florentine government and the
court of Rome, which wished to make them pay for Pisa with the
French alliance and the Friar's life.

I shall now explain briefly what were the relations of Florence with
the more important states of Italy and what their policies were on the
death of Savonarola. Charles VIII had died on the day before the Friar
was taken prisoner, but this did not lessen the threat of French arms to
the peace and future of Italy. The new sovereign Louis XII declared his
intentions promptly by taking the title not only of King of the Two

Sicilies like his predecessor, but also of Duke of Milan, to which he laid claim through his grandmother. Everyone on the Italian side of the Alps thus looked towards him with fear or hope. Now that the League against Charles had been disbanded, the Italian powers had to decide how best to adapt themselves to his successor. Among those who sent ambassadors, the least enthusiastic were the Florentines, as though their new government wished to detach itself from the wholehearted Francophile policies of the Friar's government, and seek more reliable alliances nearer home.

The Pope, however, having won the game in which the Friar's life had been at stake, and no longer fearing either the Concilium or Charles, was now turning his thoughts to the aggrandisement of his family in Italy. To this end he needed the help and friendship of Louis XII. Knowing that the King wished to dissolve his marriage in order to wed his sister-in-law, the widow of the dead king—an ambition fraught with difficulties and complications—the Pope planned to 'sell him spiritual favours in exchange for temporal powers'.[1] He now professed friendship towards the Florentines, and showed himself ready to favour them in the reacquisition of Pisa, and even to persuade the Venetians to agree. The latter persistently opposed the Florentines, although Lodovico Sforza himself was now urging them to give in.

Lodovico, out of suspicion and jealousy of his neighbours, the Venetian Republic, fearing that Pisa would be for them a stepping-stone to greater things, had changed his policy to the point of not only agreeing to the Florentines' ambition, but of wanting to help them to achieve it. This was particularly true since the removal of the Friar and his faction had left power in hands which he felt better able to trust. He may also have hoped that the republic might mitigate the hostility of the French King towards him, or help to oppose his might, or if need be, that of the Venetians.

Having mentioned the obstinate hostility of the Venetians to the Florentines' retaking of Pisa, little more remains to be added about the relations of Florence with the other states of Italy. The neighbouring republics of Genoa and Siena were old enemies of the city. Lucca too was an enemy on her borders, though remaining apparently neutral through the influence of Lodovico. In Romagna, Bentivoglio lord of Bologna, and Caterina Sforza, mistress of Imola and Forlì, were friendly; Faenza was with the Venetians.

These then were the feelings with which Italy, not at that moment involved in any other disturbances, watched the war going on in the area around Pisa. We must give some account of this war, since it became Machiavelli's daily concern at the Chancery. The Florentines had suffered a minor defeat at San Regolo in May, and had then called to the rescue as their Captain General Paolo Vitelli, a famous condottiere, at the same time seeking assistance from Sforza. He came out openly on their side with reinforcements, money and promises, and asked the Pope to do likewise. The Pope stopped short at promises.

The new Captain took up his command with solemn ceremony on the 1st of June, and at once set the war moving. Buti, Vicopisano and Librafatta, places strongly held by the Pisans, he either took by storm or by treaty. The Venetians were determined to help Pisa either directly or by a diversion, and having failed in their attempt to enter the Garfagnana, and not had much success in Romagna, they sought free passage for their troops from the Sienese and the Perugians. Their request being refused, they carried the war into the Casentino via Faenza, and there occupied Bibbiena and various castles. To meet this threat to the heart of the Florentine state, Vitelli was brought up from Pisa, and there followed a sad winter for the Venetians, who had with them the exiles Piero and Giuliano de' Medici, caught in those in- hospitable places between a strong enemy force and an even tougher and more hostile nature.

Finally the Venetians agreed to accept the arbitration of the Duke of Ferrara, being tired of expending their strength in a distant war with- out being supported as the Florentines were by the hope of gain. The Duke published a decision which displeased both parties. It gave the Florentines in Pisa a limited sovereignty, which was nonetheless re- garded as an insult by the Venetians. It obliged the Florentines to pay the Venetians a large sum which seemed to the latter too small a price for their dishonour, and to the former neither just nor bearable. In the meantime, the Republic of St. Mark had joined the league with the King of France against Lodovico Sforza, and was turning its attention to a nearer and more profitable task. Although rejecting the proposed treaty, it withdrew its forces at the time stipulated, so that the Florentines were able to bring all their weight to bear on Pisa now abandoned to its fate by all its allies.

Though it is easy to follow the course of this war in the letters which Machiavelli wrote with his own hand in the minute books, and in those he dictated to his assistants or had them write, which fill the second

chancery's registers and those of the council of Ten, it is very difficult
to follow in those same minute books and registers the labours of the
chancellor himself. This could not have been limited solely to this day
by day correspondence, although the letters are numerous. Furthermore, it is hard to discern in these letters how much is his and how
much the magistrates' in whose name they were written. Sometimes it
may be the form alone which is his, sometimes the content too; only
occasionally is he responsible for neither.[2]

Where the mind of Machiavelli shines out with a brilliance all its
own, even from the privacy of the secretariat, is in the reports written
to inform or advise the magistrates on particular military or political
matters. An example is the *Discorso della guerra di Pisa* (Discourse on the
Pisan war) written at this very time, in May in fact,[3] when the Florentines having removed the dagger plunged into their flank by the
Venetians, returned with fresh impetus to the retaking of that city.
Lucid, vigorous, and closely argued, this, the first political work of
Machiavelli's which has come down to us, already shows the lion's
claws. Perspicacious in expressing the views of the military leaders and
his own, acute in judgement, and robust in style, it is not difficult to
understand, as one reads, why the Secretary's influence with the Signoria increased daily.

Secretaries could also be used in other ways. Sometimes they were
entrusted with commissions and even embassies, when to save expense
or because of the nature of the business or for some other reason they
did not wish to send a real ambassador. The chancellors sent on such
missions were not called ambassadors or orators, but envoys (*mandatari*).[4] They were not sent to negotiate peace treaties or alliances but
to observe and report, or to negotiate matters of moderate importance
where speed was essential, or to prepare the way for duly elected
ambassadors, or sometimes to accompany, assist, advise or supervise
them.

The first time Machiavelli had an appointment of this kind, it was on
a matter of small moment and one connected still with the endless
Pisan war. He was sent to Jacopo d'Appiano, lord of Piombino, who
was one of the republic's captains and was demanding an increase of
pay and of command. What took place between Machiavelli and this
petty chieftain, who, according to Machiavelli's judgement, 'spoke
well, judged ill, acted worse',[5] we know from the results, which were:
for the first request, that he agreed to be content with what he already

received, and for the second, that Machiavelli satisfied him with promises.

He had a second commission of rather greater importance on the 12th of July, and the Pisan war was again its subject. He was sent to Caterina Sforza, countess of Imola and Forlì and Ludovico's illegitimate niece, to negotiate the commission of her young son Ottaviano Riario, who had fought the year before for the republic with a salary of 15,000 florins. At the end of that year he had declined to serve another term which was optional. The Countess, however, seeing the storm-clouds gather over her own as well as her uncle's head, but not revealing her motives, had asked what was to be done about her son's commission. The Florentines, to keep the mother on their side, wanted to employ the son for a further year but at the expense of 10,000 florins only. They wanted Machiavelli to negotiate, to obtain 500 good foot-soldiers under good officers, and to buy, if there were any, munitions for the artillery to send to the Pisan campaign. But above all they wanted to preserve the friendship of the Countess who, standing on their borders, could be a fortress to defend or to attack their state.[6]

Leaving Florence on the 13th he stopped at Castrocaro whence he reported to the Signoria on certain munitions and on the factions of that place.[7] Reaching Forlì on the 16th, he presented himself to the Countess. Before the great but as yet unknown politician stood a woman famous for her beauty and her courage, hardened in the government of her small and difficult state. The lands of Romagna were notoriously turbulent. Virile in spirit as any man, yet lacking nothing in femininity, she had lost her first husband, Girolamo Riario, at the age of twenty-six, and had not only revenged his murder but kept the state for herself and her children. When her second husband was also killed, she again took harsh revenge. Now at thirty-six she was again a widow: her third husband had been Giovanni de' Medici, by whom she had a son who perpetuated his father's name and inherited his mother's courageous ferocity with the warlike virtues of his Sforza ancestors. That Florentine secretary, who in the next room was negotiating a matter of small importance, was one day to propose that the young Giovanni de' Medici raise a standard round which Italy's last hopes might rally.

Meanwhile the Secretary stood before the great lady, and with her was the envoy of her powerful kinsman, whether to advise, to supervise or to direct her, we do not know. The Duke of Milan, abandoned by the Pope, and indeed by the Florentines too, who showed short memories for his recent benefactions, felt the avalanche of the French armies rushing down on him from the Alps. Since he was in dire need of soldiers and every other kind of war material, he was a strong competitor in this field with Machiavelli. When the latter had explained his commission to the Countess, he received a reply with which the Florentines must by then have been familiar: that 'she had always liked what the Florentines said, and disliked what they did'.[8] He also heard that she was being offered better terms from Milan, and that he should soon have an answer. This promise was generously fulfilled, for in the following days he received several answers, all of them different, and justified with the comment that 'the more things are discussed, the better they are understood'.[9]

Machiavelli wrote to Florence that the Countess ' was standing on her dignity'; she had the Milanese agent constantly at her side, and soldiers were continually leaving for Milan; according to her, she had no munitions to spare. Meantime Adriani from the Chancery was asking for soldiers and his assistant Buonaccorsi wanted 'the Countess's head drawn on a piece of paper'.[10] Machiavelli felt it quite enough to have that devil of a woman before him in flesh and blood. Having finally agreed to a salary of 12,000 florins, when it came to signing the agreement she made a new demand at the last moment that the Florentines should undertake in writing to defend her state. They, however, would only commit themselves verbally. Hearing of this sudden change, Machiavelli did not restrain himself 'in words and gestures', and at once departed leaving the matter unfinished.[11]

In Florence they were very pleased with him and his letters.[12] Perhaps they had extracted from them what appears to us to be their essence: if the Countess wished to temporize, this suited the Florentines even better, as their best allies in the contest for the lady's arms and favours were time and the King of France. Machiavelli must have thought, while she appeared to be playing cat and mouse with him, that she would no longer stand on her dignity once her uncle the Duke was caught between the Venetians and the powerful armies of France now on the move. And while he bowed before that handsome woman, his ambiguous smile surely never left his lips.

Having returned to Florence on the 1st of August he again took up his usual work in the Chancery, where, if we are to believe the letters that Buonaccorsi sent him at Forlì, his absence had been felt and work had piled up as their efforts in the Pisan war were intensified. The Florentines camped beneath the walls of Pisa on the very day of Machiavelli's return; on the 6th they broke down with cannon-fire forty yards of the wall, and on the 10th took the Rocca di Stampace. The taking of this fortress, which laid the city open to the Florentines, so frightened the inhabitants that they elected their representatives to negotiate the surrender. But Vitelli who did not realize what straits the enemy were in, did not feel prepared to give battle, and withdrew his soldiers at the very moment of victory, when the war was virtually over. The Pisans took heart after a day and a night had passed without their assailants putting in an appearance. Through the breach in the walls the way was still open for Vitelli to seize his lost opportunity. Yet, although urged on by the Signoria in pressing letters, among them an 'exhortatoria pulcherrima', which, since it is in the registers of the second Chancery, we must attribute to Machiavelli, though it is not in his hand[13]—Vitelli still preferred to temporize. Finally malaria decimating his forces obliged him to raise the siege on the 14th of September.

Grave discontent then broke out in Florence. For some time the city had been feeling weary, exhausted by the expense of war. From the preceding May it had proved impossible to elect in the councils the new Ten to serve for the second half of that year, 1499. Such was the odium which that council had incurred, for it was felt that the Ten had squandered public money on the war which it was incapable of running. In the end the Signoria had been obliged to assume the functions of the vacant council. This in no way altered Machiavelli's functions, since, if the Ten were not there in person, their office remained in existence and their secretariat was more in evidence than ever; and, as we have already explained, this was practically the same thing as the second chancery.

Besides this, the patient prudence of Paolo Vitelli was unpopular with the impatient Florentines. If in the past they had complained of him without reason, after the Stampace incident even a less suspicious people would have accused him of incompetence and cowardice. This was Florence, and they began to talk of treachery. So after the letters of exhortation to Vitelli come those of reproof, these also perhaps dictated by Machiavelli. Anger and mistrust were at such a pitch that when Vitelli finally gave signs of life and wanted to lay siege to Pisa again, the plan was coldly received. On the other hand, the new Signoria with Giovacchino Guasconi at its head, deciding that something must be done and that an exhausted city could not be expected to spend more money to carry on the war under an untrustworthy captain, determined to have him removed.

The matter was discussed in the Palazzo with the greatest secrecy, but it seems abundantly clear from his letters that our Secretary was present at every stage. One should not forget either that one of the Signori was a blood relation of his, another Niccolò Machiavelli, son of Alessandro.[14] It would be too bold a conjecture, however, to attribute the machiavellian method of punishing Vitelli to Machiavelli himself. Having called him to Cascina, the commissioners had him taken prisoner: his brother Vitellozzo, who was to meet the same fate at more expert hands, managed on this occasion to escape. Paolo was brought to Florence, tortured with ferocity, and although, whether because he was innocent or because he was brave, he confessed nothing, his head was cut off.

This pitiless justice, if one may so call an obvious injustice, pleased the Florentines very much. The gonfalonier and those who were responsible with him won praise for their action. A cruel streak (as I have said before) existed in the character of this civilized and urbane people. The greatness of the example was agreeable to this popular republic, which was glad to have inflicted exemplary punishment on an aristocrat, the most famous captain in Italy, just as the aristocratic republic of Venice had done to Carmagnola. Finally, the manner in which it had been done seemed to them a work of art, such things 'increased the reputation' of a state, they said. This was perhaps Machiavelli's opinion too, but whatever he thought, regarding himself as the spokesman of the republic according to chancery tradition, he wrote in no uncertain terms to a certain Luccan Secretary whose letter condemning the dreadful incident had been intercepted.[15]

It seems to me that with different persons and in different circumstances the Florentine people were mercilessly repeating the iniquitous treatment meted out to Savonarola. The axe which cut off the head of Paolo Vitelli was intended not so much to do justice as to sever a knot that bound the whole city. Once it was done, everything concerning the war must be begun afresh. At this moment the French army had arrived in Italy and had made such rapid and easy progress that Lodovico Sforza could find no better defence than prompt flight, while the rich cities of Lombardy fell one after the other into the invaders' hands.

Thus the Moor was finally overcome by that avalanche which four years before by calling the French into Italy he had set in motion with his own hands. Not twenty days after the flight of the Duke, Milan and the entire Duchy were in the King's hands. Then the Florentines, who up to that time had played a double game with the Moor and the King, were prompt to give public demonstrations of rejoicing and to ally themselves with the victor on terms which were the worse for being so late. These, in short, bound the King to lend troops to help retake Pisa, and obliged the half-ruined Florentines to dig deeper in their purses for a large sum of money.

But before helping the Florentines in the Pisan enterprise at their own expense, the King had engaged himself to assist Caesar Borgia, the new Duke of Valentinois, free and for love in his campaign against Caterina Sforza. This was the price of the Pope's dispensation for the King's divorce. Strong in the forces of the Church and in his French auxiliaries, and even more in the name and arms of the King, Borgia (or Valentino as he will henceforth be called) easily took Imola and then Forlì. The courage of the Countess was not sufficient to defend them, though 'among the many womanish defenders, she alone bore a manly spirit'.[16] For the Florentines who had her under their protection, it was a grave blow;[17] but much graver was the inconvenience of having acquired such a dangerous new neighbour.

French greed gave them little respite, since the King now demanded those monies which had been lent to them by the dispossessed Duke. Because of this dispute the Signoria decided to send Machiavelli to Milan. In letters of the 27th of January his arrival had already been announced to the governor Trivulzio and to the Bishop of Luchon, Secretary to the all-powerful Cardinal of Rouen, and on the 5th of February the envoy's credentials had been made out,[18] when on that very same day news reached Florence that Cardinal Ascanio Sforza, the Duke's brother, had been joyfully received by the Milanese, and that the Duke himself was on his way there with a strong army of Swiss and Germans. Machiavelli's departure was therefore put off till they could see how things went.

The Moor, having recaptured with marvellous speed almost all his states, lost them again even more rapidly on the return of the King, through the treachery of his Swiss mercenaries, and lost his own freedom along with his state. 'The thoughts and ambitions of this man, which the whole of Italy could scarce contain, were now bounded by the confines of a narrow cell.'[19] Nothing now prevented the Florentines from proceeding with the Pisan enterprise; nothing now prevented the French from obtaining from the Florentines the conditions and monies which they desired. The Swiss soldiery came, once famous and now infamous, the Gascon foot-soldiers, the King's men-at-arms, leaving Piacenza in the first days of June under the command of Beaumont. First, however, they decided to milk the lord of Bologna at the expense of the Republic—an episode which caused Machiavelli to write, with a pun on the red saw on the arms of the Bentivoglio, that in passing

> *Beumonte*
> *trasse alla Sega più di un mascellare.*[20]

[Beaumont extracted more than one tooth from the Saw.]

At Florence in the meantime provisions of money for the enterprise were being made. The city had less money than it had hopes, for it was felt that an army with such a reputation of ferocity, which had taken the whole of Lombardy with ease in a few days, would need merely to appear before the walls of the exhausted city for its resistance to be at an end. On the 10th of June they sent to Beaumont who had entered the Lunigiana, two commissioners general: Luca degli Albizzi and Giovambattista Ridolfi, a wise man, who had held the highest rank in the republic, and had been alone in opposing the enterprise. Machiavelli was attached to them, and he seems to have played a double role, as one day we find him in the field writing the commissioners' letters to the Ten, and the next day in his office writing the letters of the Ten to the commissioners. Thus on the 22nd of June he was dictating letters in Florence,[21] while on the 24th he was writing a letter with his own hand, signed by Albizzi *ex terribilibus Gallorum castris* (from the terrible camp of the French).[22] They soon proved terrible indeed, not for the Pisan enemy but for the Florentines who employed them.

The Moor had recently discovered to his cost what the Swiss mercenaries were capable of doing to those who paid for their services. With an undisciplined and delinquent army led by a captain lacking ability and authority,[23] a scarcity of victuals increased by the greed and malice of the soldiers who spoiled or hid them,[24] soon gave rise to disorders that became an almost daily occurrence. As they became more frequent, Ridolfi, who had fallen ill and, as he told Beaumont, was sore in mind and body, returned to Florence, where he had occasion to show how right he had been in dissuading them from this adventure. Albizzi and Machiavelli remained alone in the field to stand up to these madmen.[25]

While time and pay were wasted in slow preparations for battle, ambassadors from Pisa came to the camp to offer the surrender of the city on condition that its handing over to the Florentines should be postponed. Similar terms had already been offered when the army was on its way, but whereas at first they had asked for an interval of four months, now with the army at their walls they asked only for one month's delay. Beaumont was inclined to accept the surrender, but as the Florentine commissioner utterly rejected this proposal with angry words, though Machiavelli did not approve,[26] they began on the 30th of June to bombard the walls. A large part of these were destroyed, but no further advance was made, as those 'ferocious' soldiers had not the courage to enter the city with the same spirit they had shown in assaulting the supply trains. Thus, after all their reputation for invincibility, Machiavelli remarked:

conobbesi il vero:
come i Franzesi possono esser vinti.[27]

[The truth was out, how the French may be conquered.]

Their poor showing before the walls, instead of diminishing the insolence of the soldiers, increased it, and every day the disorders and riots grew worse. Finally, the Gascons left through unfounded complaints about their pay; then on the 9th of July some of the Swiss mutinied abetted by the rest, and held the commissioner captive. Machiavelli was with him in that infernal tumult, and tried courageously to follow him, but Albizzi 'ordered him to go back and report this incident to Florence';[28] which he did at once in a brief and agitated letter.[29] A few hours later, the commissioner ransomed himself at a cost of 1300 ducats. After this last excess the Swiss departed, and thus an enterprise which had seemed likely to be easy and rapid, ended with dishonour to the King, but with derision and scorn to the Florentines. While the Pisans, encouraged and given a new lease of life by this discomfiture of their assailants, carried out occasional successful skirmishes, the Florentines could do nothing but send representatives to France to give a true account of the events, to complain, and to see how matters could be mended. For this mission they chose to go with Francesco della Casa, who had succeeded Albizzi in the camp before Pisa, the man who had the best first-hand knowledge of the affair, Niccolò Machiavelli.

Chapter 4

THE FIRST MISSION TO FRANCE

◇◇

O N the eve of Machiavelli's departure on the Pisan commission on the 10th of May, his father had died.[1] His mother
died four years earlier on the 11th of October 1496. His
sisters were married, one to Francesco Vernaccia, the other to Bernardo
Minerbetti. He was therefore alone with his brother Totto, who had
chosen or was about to chose a career in the Church, and Machiavelli
must have felt more than commonly the loss of his father, and heavier
the seal that such a loss sets on the earlier and easier portion of our life.
Messer Bernardo and his son, besides being fond of one another, got
on very well together. Their cheerful and companionable natures
formed an almost brotherly bond between them, and they often teased
one another verbally or in writing, in prose or in verse. After his
father's death, as he sorted out old papers and the well-loved books of
his childhood studies, Machiavelli found, among other similar things, a
sonnet written by him to messer Bernardo on the occasion of his
father's having sent in from the country the gift of a fat goose, because
he worried about his busy son's city diet (if we can believe him) of
dried meat and dried fruit or even just 'bread and the taste of the knife'.

> Costor vissuti sono un mese e piue
> a noci, a fichi, a fave, a carne secca;
> tal ch'ella fia malizia e non cilecca
> el far sì lunga stanza costà sue.
>   Come 'l bue fiesolan guarda a l'ingiue
> Arno, assetato, e' mocci se ne lecca,

34

*così fanno ei de l'uova ch'hà la trecca
e, col beccaio del castrone, e del bue.*

*Al fin del giuoco poi,
messer Bernardo mio, voi comprerete
paperi ed oche e non ne mangerete.*[2]

[They have lived a month and more on nuts, figs, beans and dried meat, till it's no joke to stay here all this time. Just as the Fiesolan ox looks down at the Arno thirstily and licks his nose, so they at the eggs of the market-woman and at the butcher's mutton and beef. . . . In the end you, messer Bernardo, will be buying ducks and geese and not eating any yourself.]

Poor messer Bernardo! His famous son was to address yet another joke to him beyond the grave, and with the same affectionate intimacy. When around 1504 a monk from Santa Croce went to speak to him about other bodies fraudulently buried in the Machiavelli tomb, and urged him to have them removed, Machiavelli's reply to the friar's pleas was simply: 'Well, let them be, for my father was a great lover of conversation, and the more there are to keep him company, the better pleased he will be.'[3] In such a jest we see not impiety but pity for the dead; not irreverence or indifference, but a liberal tolerance, a generosity and open-handedness commensurate with his greatness— qualities which he was to demonstrate some years later when he ratified a pious donation made verbally by his father.[4]

In the meantime public affairs kept Machiavelli busy, leaving him little time for grief, for emotion, for memories, and even less to settle his private affairs and come to an arrangement with his brother Totto over their meagre inheritance. At the very time of Bernardo's death the Chancery was in the thick of its preparations for the Pisan expedition, and shortly afterwards Machiavelli had to set out with the commissioners. Hardly had he returned before he was being sent away again, this time to France.

It was his first foreign mission, and marked a notable stage in his life. One may say that the real reward of his Pisan adventure was not the six gold florins he received 'in payment of his labours on this occasion and of the dangers he ran',[5] but this journey. Before this, he had hardly been outside Tuscany except in the pages of books; and now he was off abroad with Caesar's *Commentaries* in his saddle-bags. Rarely can foreign peoples have been revealed, just like an opening book, to a more avid observer. His native Florence had taught much and had still more to teach to the peoples beyond the Alps, but those nations which were still described as 'barbarous' by Italians had now something to teach Florence and Italy and especially the political genius of Machiavelli. Their strength lay in their unity, they were better able to command other nations because they themselves had a greater capacity for obedience, had arms of their own, and were united in the name of a prince.

The Florentine republic had already in France as ambassadors Francesco Gualterotti and Lorenzo Lenzi, one of whom it was intended should remain after the arrival of Della Casa and Machiavelli. Theirs may be called an extraordinary legation, for it is described as a legation in the decision taken on it on the 18th of July,[6] even though the two envoys were referred to as *mandatari*. There was no distinction of rank or authority between them, although Della Casa who was the senior in age and standing was named first in the official documents and signed first at the end of the legation's letters, which were, however, entirely composed by Machiavelli. This point has not been thoroughly understood by biographers and literary historians, led into error by the difference in their salaries. Della Casa drew eight lire a day (equivalent to one gold florin and a third), and Machiavelli had four lire. The latter, according to Villari, 'was of lower rank'.[7] And so he received half pay? The truth is that Della Casa had no other emoluments from the state, whilst from Machiavelli's 'extraordinary salary' the republic avariciously deducted, as is clearly stated in the document concerning his election, '*eius salarium ordinarium*', according to the custom of the Chancery.

The Signoria felt it to be of the greatest importance that its own justifications and complaints should reach the court before anyone else's complaints and accusations. Thus their exhortations to haste, placed as always before their instructions to their ambassadors, were on this occasion more pressing than ever: 'You will go with all possible speed, riding post while you have strength to do so.'[8] They set off, therefore, on the 18th of July, but their rate of travelling was not as rapid as was desired. They stopped at Bologna, since they had to consult with Bentivoglio on behalf of the Signoria. Between Parma and Piacenza they found a thousand or so of those Swiss who had abandoned the siege of Pisa. This should have been a cause for haste rather than delay after Machiavelli's earlier experience of them, unless he was forced to make a detour to avoid them. Whatever the cause, some 'disorder and accident'[9] compelled the two envoys to lose time on the way.

They arrived at Lyons on the 26th of July, 'very tired but in good spirits'.[10] Of the two ambassadors who had been there before, they found that Gualterotti had already set off for Italy, and Lenzi who had remained gave them certain information in writing on the feeling at court and on the best way to carry out their instructions.[11] He should have accompanied them into the presence of the King, but as the latter had left Lyons before Machiavelli and his colleague got there, Lenzi refused to embark on any journey that would take him farther away from home. And in fact he set off for home shortly afterwards, since now there had arrived, as he wrote to Florence, 'those who are well able to attend to any major affair'.[12]

In the meantime, the zeal of the new arrivals was being wasted at Lyons. There, since they had arrived on post horses without luggage, they were obliged to provide themselves with horses, servants and clothes. The republic was not generous towards its ambassadors. Machiavelli and his colleague had received before they left an advance of eighty florins apiece, and in one week they had already spent thirty each: the salary for twenty-two days! In those first few days in Lyons they exhausted the ready money they had been given and used a good part of what they had brought of their own money. No, they were not to get rich in the territories of France! Finally, on the 30th of July they went off to seek the court. It was a long labour, since the horses they had bought were spirited only in proportion to the length of their purses, while the King moved rapidly with frequent detours motivated by the plague which infested the country. On the 5th of August they were in St. Pierre Le Moutier, and had almost caught up with the court which was at Nevers; and from there they wrote a joint letter to the Signoria.[13] Machiavelli added a letter of his own to demand a salary equal to that of his colleague since their expenses were the same. He wrote boldly: 'If it seems too much to you to spend, I think that either it is as well spent on me as it is on Francesco, or that the twenty ducats you give me each month are wasted: if the latter be true, I beg Your Excellencies to recall me.'[14]

The following day, 'ignoring all discomfort and fear of contagion', the envoys joined the court at Nevers. As soon as they arrived, they presented themselves to 'Roano', as Machiavelli called the all-powerful Georges d'Amboise, cardinal of Rouen. The first greetings of both the Cardinal and the King, to whom the Cardinal at once accompanied them, were cheerful and pleasant. However, neither King nor Cardinal showed much interest in the tale of the disorders which had taken place at the siege of Pisa, which was the core of their message, as the subject was to their discredit and of no advantage to them. They said that the Florentines must share part of the blame, that they regretted the affair, but that these were things that were over and done with: it was necessary now to think of the present and the future, and to continue the enterprise in order to restore the King's honour and repair the harm done to the Republic. This they said in French or in court Latin, but in plain Florentine it meant maintaining the royal troops at the expense of the city.

The envoys' troubles began where their message ended. They had come solely to exculpate themselves and lay the blame on others. They knew that the Republic had no funds to carry on the war and no desire to do so with such soldiers. They therefore replied ingeniously that the King might carry out the Pisan enterprise himself, and that when Pisa was taken, the Florentines would reimburse him for the expenses incurred. But the King and his chorus of ministers were quick to reject the proposal. They also reminded the envoys that a prompt decision was necessary, since in the meantime the pay of the ill-famed mutinous and fugitive Swiss was still the responsibility of the Florentines.[15] With this sting in the tail the audience closed with more coolness than it had begun.

Dismissing the Florentine envoys, the King had said that he hoped to hear better proposals from them at Montargis where he would be in three days' time, and in fact they were at Montargis on the 10th of August. There they immediately had an altercation with Roano which was to be repeated unchanged in subsequent discussions, and almost the whole of this embassy was to resemble an exchange between deaf men, in which each repeats the same things *ad nauseam* without regard for the arguments of his interlocutor. The King reproached the Florentines on three main points: for not being willing to go on with the Pisan war to restore his honour with their money, as Machiavelli sarcastically remarked; for refusing to take responsibility for the pay of the Swiss after their departure from the siege; and for their unwillingness to allow other forces of the King to enter their territory after the experience they had already had. Machiavelli warned the Signoria: 'Your Excellencies should not imagine that good letters or good arguments are any use, because they are not understood. It is useless to recall the fidelity of our city towards the Crown of France and what was done in the reign of the former king, the money that was spent, the dangers that were faced, how often we have been paid with vain hopes, the recent events and their ruinous expense to the city, the advantage to His Majesty of our prosperity, the security He would gain from your greatness, how little the other Italian states can be relied on: all this is superfluous, because such matters are considered by them in quite another way and seen with a different eye from that of anyone unfamiliar with conditions here, because they are blinded by their own power and the thought of immediate advantage, and esteem only those who are well armed or those who are prepared to give money.'[16]

Between the anvil of an exhausted republic which did not wish to go beyond what was reasonable, and the hammer of a king, who was not interested in reason but only in his own profit, between an impatient court demanding an answer and a Signoria which replied inadequately or not at all, without authority and with a limited and unrewarding mandate, the embassy had become a hell for the two envoys and seemed likely to end in the ruin of their native city. In vain Machiavelli wrote that fresh ambassadors should be sent, 'because our rank and quality, without any commission agreeable to them, are not such as to be able to refloat an affair which is about to sink altogether'. And he added: 'It will be of little use if they do not come with some new proposal.'[17] The discomfort of the envoys was increased by their restricted means, which prevented them from sending a special messenger when necessary.

However, Machiavelli at last had his allowance increased, as he had again urgently requested,[18] partly through the efforts of his brother Totto, and partly through the favour in which he stood with the Gonfalonier. Totto sent him the first news of this.[19] Thus while seeming to have been given equality with his colleague, in fact, when one takes into account his ordinary salary, he received considerably more. He deserved it too. He wrote those splendid letters of the legation, all in his own hand, though Machiavelli is recognisable in them even more by the style than by the writing. In Florence they were greatly admired, and the faithful Buonaccorsi, hearing them praised one day, was able to describe with what ease and facility they were written.[20] The improvement in his finances and the praise of the Florentines were some small recompense for the bitterness of his experience in France. His friends' letters were a consolation too, particularly those of his dear friend Buonaccorsi, who swelled with pride when Machiavelli showed him by his letters that he esteemed him better than 'the rank and file of the Chancery'.[21] But he also received letters or postscripts from the other assistants, devoted and merry letters which affectionately wished him 'a thousand plagues' for the austerity and frowning severity into which the office had fallen as a result of his absence.[22]

In the meantime the court had gone from Montargis to Melun, and our envoys with it. Places changed, but their situation remained the same. As they could give no satisfactory answers, they promised that the new ambassadors would bring them. These, however, were never forthcoming, as in Florence no one could be found who was willing to take on the job, and probably also because they could not think of a satisfactory message to send. First Francesco Pepi had been elected; then instead of him Luca degli Albizzi. As soon as this appointment had been announced to the court by our envoys, he too found some excuse for not going. The reasons he gave in a private letter to Machiavelli were the trouble and expense involved. After him, Bernardo Rucellai and Giovanni Ridolfi were chosen, and like him they refused.[23]

The situation of Machiavelli and his colleague now became untenable. On the 3rd of September they lacked funds even to send urgent letters by special messenger, and they threatened to leave immediately without permission 'and to face the vagaries of fortune in Italy rather than in France'.[24] The anger and threats of the French increased; Roano uttered grave warnings, and it seemed as though the King were intending an open break with Florence. Machiavelli wrote that he would not like 'to be present at the break-up of a friendship which has been sought and nourished at such great expense and maintained with such high hopes'.[25] In the meantime from Florence the replies continued to be unsatisfactory if they came at all. In a letter of the 20th of September the Signoria frankly admits that an ambassador has not been found 'nor a basis for his commission', perhaps because they had been unable to get people to agree to accede to the King's demands, or collect enough money to satisfy them. Indeed, the envoys are told that they cannot have the small sum which they so insistently request, on the grounds that 'money is short'.[26] And all they asked was a few score florins. So low had the Florentine republic fallen!

Matters being in this state, Francesco della Casa, alleging some indisposition or other went to Paris to restore body and soul, while Machiavelli still following the nomadic court moved on to Blois. Now left on his own he seems to be doubly zealous, and does miracles to temporize with the King and Roano. Forced to repeat one ridiculous refrain without any material for negotiation, he tries to make himself useful by summarizing the humours of the court in those acute and succinct judgements of which he is master. A few days before, he had written that the King was going ahead slowly with the Neapolitan expedition, 'particularly since he has seen recently from the example of Pisa, that where strength is needed, chalk and reputation are not enough.' And he adds: 'The secretary from Naples is here, and is continually negotiating for an agreement; and here when they begin to listen to a man who makes promises and gifts, it is difficult to believe they will not take him up.'[27] Recently, however, he had received new food for thought from the preparations for a fresh expedition which Valentino was making with the Pope's money and in the Pope's name. Some said it was to be against the Colonnas, some said against the rulers of Romagna: Faenza, Rimini and Pesaro. Machiavelli wrote: 'Everything is allowed to the Pope, more because His Majesty is unwilling to oppose openly any of his inordinate ambitions, than because he really wishes him to achieve victory.'[28]

It was soon clear that the Borgias' appetites were turned towards Romagna, but not so clear that Romagna alone would suffice to satisfy them. The enterprise at once aroused the suspicions of the Florentines, and their suspicions turned to fear when the Pope's son was seen to be flirting with the Medici, and he openly boasted that he wished to put Piero back in power. These storm-clouds were gathering on the Florentine borders at the very time when the friendship with the French which alone could have protected the Republic, was on the point of turning into open enmity. On the 11th of October Machiavelli was repeating his usual story that fresh ambassadors would bring an answer on the subject of the mercenaries' pay, and Roano replied sourly: 'That is what you said, it is true; but we shall all be dead before the spokesmen come. However, we shall see to it that others die first.'[29] The Florentines were playing with fire.

While Borgia was besieging Rimini and Pesaro, which immediately surrendered, fear suddenly gave the Florentines wisdom, and at once ambassadors and money were found. Thus Machiavelli, who had gone to Nantes with the court, was at last able to announce that the ambassador Pierfrancesco Tosinghi had left on the 16th of October and was bringing a satisfactory message. It was very little, but enough for him to obtain the sending on the 4th of November of royal letters to the Lieutenant in Italy with orders to advise Borgia not to attempt anything to the detriment of Florence. To these very days and these discussions on the ambitions of the Borgias belongs a famous reply of Machiavelli's to the Cardinal. The latter having observed that the Italians did not understand war, Machiavelli promptly answered that the French knew nothing about the state or they would not have allowed the Church to become so powerful.[30]

But if the Florentine Secretary did not lack daring and a ready tongue before the all-powerful minister, neither did he lack prudence in advising his government in almost every letter that it would be wise to forget their resentments, their rights and their reasons, in the face of the King's power which alone could protect them in such a situation. Thus they at last made up their minds to promise the pay for the Swiss: ten thousand straight away and the rest in instalments. Although the King did not care for this delay, their differences had now been reduced to manageable proportions, and Machiavelli had a better time at court.

He was also filled with hope of soon seeing home and friends again, and perhaps more anxious to be back in the Chancery, full of occupation and good companions, than in his home, now empty of affections. During that long sojourn of his in France, his sister too had died —the one who was married to Francesco Vernaccia. This fresh loss added to that of his father whom he had been almost too busy to grieve for, caused him to ask permission to return to settle his private affairs, which, as he wrote, 'were in some confusion and disorder'.[31]

But there was something else as well which incited him to seek his return. First the faithful Biagio, perhaps in letters now lost, then certainly his other assistant Agostino Vespucci in a long and amusing letter in Latin, had written to him about certain manœuvres which, if his return were too long delayed, risked losing him his place in the Chancery.[32] Perhaps this was true, perhaps not. Of that second Chancery, which had come to be so much part of his life and soul, he was the very life and soul. As we gather from the letters of his assistants and from this last letter from Vespucci, the absences of their chief were felt almost physically; they missed his conversation, his amusing sallies and jokes, which gave fresh inspiration to the clerks.

From Nantes the court moved to Tours and Machiavelli followed, arriving there on the 21st of November. There he fulfilled his last obligations to the Republic. He wrote his final warnings about the machinations of the Pope, 'worthy of His Holiness', and gave his last

advice, insisting, as he had often done, on the necessity to make themselves *amicos de mammona iniquitatis*, which was the only way of making
friends at the court of France.[33] Finally, while the new ambassador was
journeying north in a leisurely fashion, a letter of the 12th of December,
which must have reached him about Christmas, brought him the long
desired permission to return.[34] He came home by easy stages and without hurrying too much, but certainly more rapidly than Tosinghi who
had taken more than a month and a half for the journey. Machiavelli
arrived in Florence on the 14th of January 1501.[35] He had been abroad
for six months.

From that long stay in France he brought back nothing which could
make his saddle-bags heavy, perhaps not even a book printed in Lyons
or Paris. French literature had as yet little to say to an Italian humanist
in that last year of the 15th century, nor could the ballads of Villon
have had the attraction for him that they have for us. Machiavelli may
not even have learnt to appreciate the beauties of the French language,
though he certainly acquired a superficial knowledge of it. It is true
that at the court they spoke to him in that rough and ready Latin of
which we have already seen some examples, but a man as curious and
quick as Machiavelli was, could not live for six months in a country
without learning to understand and make himself understood. He was
always eager to converse even with the simplest people, to question
and to understand, even though the ordinary Frenchman was not to
be compared with the educated and subtle Florentines. At any rate, in
the correspondence of the legation, when he was describing discussions
which took place at court, he put in the occasional French or Frenchified
word.[36]

Such an acquisition of the language, however imperfect, if it was of
no value to the man of letters (which, in fact, he was not), may perhaps
have been of some use to the political observer; an enrichment of the
spirit at all events, and a useful adjunct to the baggage of observations
he brought back stored in his mind rather than written down on
paper. The *Ritratti delle cose di Francia*, and even the brief notes *De
natura Gallorum*, which German scholarship incorrectly attributed to
this period,[37] found material but not form during this first mission to
France. Its fruits did not ripen at once; but rather than of fruits we
should speak of seeds, which together with others gathered in other
similar experiences will one day germinate in the thought and spirit
of Machiavelli.

Chapter 5

THE REBELLIONS OF SUBJECT STATES AND THE CAMPAIGNS OF CAESAR BORGIA

◇◇◇

To hold Pisa with fortresses, that is by force, and Pistoia by factions was an ancient rule of the Florentines, but now it appeared that force had not been enough to hold Pisa, and the factions seemed about to dispossess them of Pistoia. During Machiavelli's mission to France, in August 1500, the hatreds of the ancient factions dividing that city, finding in the weakness and disunity of the Florentine government a favourable occasion, had broken out in violent conflict. The Cancellieri rose in arms and drove out the Panciatici, burning, looting and killing. In the surrounding country the same thing happened, 'almost as in an ordered war, with aid from outside'.[1] Such disorders were not to the Republic's credit and not without danger while beyond her frontiers the greedy Borgia champed at the bit. Internally, the city was already weary of war, suspicious, and financially impoverished; and now the division of minds, which had nourished the divisions of the Pistoiese, was in its turn fomented by them. As the Panciatici were supporters of the Medici and the Cancellieri supporters of the popular state, so the principal citizens of Florence favoured or openly took sides with one faction or the other. In addition, outside Florentine territory, Giovanni Bentivoglio, lord of Bologna, favoured the Cancellieri, while the Vitelli and the Orsini, soldiering under Caesar Borgia, sided with the Panciatici.

The disease, not prevented earlier, nor remedied when it became apparent, simply got worse. Pistoia itself, and even more the plains and hill-country around the city, had almost slipped from the control of the Republic. Rebel bands overran the countryside. One of these came nearly as far as Carmignano, and Machiavelli was sent there as 'commissioner with full powers' to see and do what was necessary. It was the 2nd of February, barely a fortnight after his return from France. This time, however, the hours spent on horseback to get there were few, and those spent on the spot to settle the affair were not many more.[2]

The troubles of Pistoia were more or less patched up in April when the Florentines sent in commissioners with sufficient forces to get the city under control again.[3] Among them was our Secretary's cousin, Niccolò di Alessandro, whom posterity finds it hard to forgive for bearing the same great name, Niccolò Machiavelli, at the very same period. While, however, the commissioners were doctoring this wound, a much greater peril came to threaten the Republic.

In spring Caesar Borgia had again come to besiege Faenza, which had been fiercely defended the year before by its citizens, helped by the rigours of winter. When the good weather came, only the citizens remained to defend the city, and they were obliged to come to terms with so powerful an assailant. After this victory, having received from his father the title of Duke of Romagna, he promptly turned against Bologna with great hopes of taking the city. He was stopped on the borders of the territory, not by Bentivoglio's men, but by a warning from the King of France who had Bentivoglio under his protection, and full of rage and mortification he had to obey. Then he asked the Florentines for free passage to go and besiege Piombino, and thereupon entered their territory without waiting for their reply. He was conciliatory while the road through the Appennines was closed to him, harsh and insolent as soon as he had crossed them. He wanted no less than that the Florentines should ally themselves with him, undertake to pay him a large sum for his military services, and change their government for one more pleasing to him. To give force to these demands he advanced with his army to Campi almost under the city walls. Piero de' Medici was waiting on the Bolognese border, while his supporters, Vitellozzo and the Orsini, were with the Duke Valentine who, as Machiavelli wrote *in nomine publico* to the Pistoia commissioners, was advancing with his terrible host, 'favoured by heaven and fortune'.[4]

With the enemy at the gates and even within the gates, as there were not a few partisans of the Medici and discontented Ottimati, weak and divided as it was, the government of Florence was obliged to accept those conditions which it could with least shame: the league with Borgia and the payment he asked. The ink was hardly dry on this agreement when the city began to think of not observing it, because just at that time a fresh order came from the King of France to Borgia, that he should cease from persecuting the Florentines, and he was obliged to move off on the 17th of July without having received a penny. He moved on with his troops to besiege Piombino, leaving a trail of ruin and destruction.

The passage of Borgia had reduced the affairs of Pistoia to a worse state than they were before, and the Florentines had to see about bringing them under control again. On the 23rd of July Machiavelli was again sent there, but he only remained two or three days.[5] Shortly before this, he had been sent to Cascina; and soon after, on the 18th of August, he went to Siena with a commission of which we know nothing, though it was certainly connected, like the other one, with the Duke's movements.[6] In October he was again in Pistoia, when he prepared for the return of the Panciatici and a short period of peace to that unhappy city.[7] Thus he divided his efforts between these outside commissions and the constant demands of the Chancery.

Such, then, were Machiavelli's occupations at this period. They were not, however, his only ones, although they are the only ones which we know of. Though we have not yet mentioned it, his life had taken another turn since his father's death. When he came back to his empty home from the mission to France, he had begun to think of taking a wife. I do not know whether at the period we have now reached in these pages, Totto was still at home with him, but if he was, Niccolò now thought of the pair of them what he would one day write in his most famous comedy: 'they have no women in the house, and they live like beasts'.[8] So he married Marietta, daughter of Luigi Corsini.[9] The dowry and the family were appropriate to his own modest means and origins. This marriage had already taken place or was about to do so in August 1501, even though we find no trace of it in documents until somewhat later.[10] For the biographer it does not bring about any very notable change in his story, nor perhaps did it alter much at that time for our hero. Niccolò, who was to be a loving father and certainly nourished a quiet affection for Marietta, was not the sort of man to bother too much about his wife; and even had he wanted to, he was too busy.

At that time Caesar Borgia was attacking Piombino and the French were occupying the Kingdom of Naples without much effort, having first treacherously agreed to divide it with the Spaniards. This was the evil seed of many future wars and of much misfortune for Italy. After Piombino had surrendered to Borgia's troops on the 3rd of September 1501, the Florentines found themselves trapped more and more between his forces and his ambitious greed. Their suspicions grew as they saw increasing signs of his father, the Pope's, ill disposition towards the city. From the 25th of August, the coadjutor Vespucci in Rome as Florentine envoy, in some of his mordant private letters to Machiavelli on the subject of the immoral Papal court,[11] had hinted at Borgia's future campaigns against Camerino and Urbino, and there was no foreseeing where they would stop. This drove the Florentines to buy a new confederation with the King of France, and they obtained it more cheaply than they expected, on the 16th of April 1502, for the King had begun to fear that they would join against him with Roman Emperor Maximilian, who showed signs of intending to descend into Italy.

Encouraged by this pact, the Florentines decided to lay waste the land around Pisa and to send artillery there. But almost at once they had to give up these renewed ideas of conquest, and struggle to preserve what they already had. During the night of the 4th of June Arezzo rebelled in complicity with Vitellozzo Vitelli. He had been on the borders of the Valdichiana since the beginning of May with some of Borgia's armies, and he was able to march straight into the rebel city with the few troops he had. Too late the Florentine government recalled the forces from Pisa; the Pisans drew breath again, and the Aretines were not intimidated, being daily reinforced by further troops from Borgia. In the meantime too Piero de' Medici had entered the town.

Even more than these blows abroad, it was the internal weakness, the suspicions and ineptness of the popular government, and the fears and discontent of the leading citizens, that had now brought the Republic to the verge of disintegration. The rich lands of the Valdichiana gave in to the enemy one after another without waiting to be attacked. Monte a San Savino, Cortona, Castiglione, Anghiari and Borgo San Sepolcro likewise surrendered, the latter before enemy artillery had even come in sight. The entire territory was crumbling away. Landucci's comment in his popular style was: '*E così pareva ch'e' Fiorentini avessin le budella in un catino. Ognuno vicino si rideva dei Fiorentini.*' [Literally: 'So it seemed the Florentines had their bowels in a basin. All the neighbouring towns were laughing at them.']¹²

Borgia showed no sign of fearing the growing fury of the French king. He swore that he had no part in the Aretine rebellion, and that 'his man' Vitellozzo—who, however, dated his letters from Arezzo *ex pontificiis castris*—was engaged in a private revenge. Perhaps Borgia was not involved in the rebellion, but he certainly was in the war with the Florentines. Besides, all his actions were a complex web of deceit and treachery. The entry into Arezzo had been carried out by part of the forces assembled ostensibly for the attack on Camerino; and he besieged Camerino while 'his man' looked after this substantial diversion. Then, when everyone thought the Duke was entirely absorbed in that enterprise, suddenly, with incredible rapidity, 'without stopping to eat or drink', he moved on to Urbino and with equal rapidity took possession of that small state; an easy task, for he had first employed the ruse of emptying it of artillery and troops by asking in the name of friendship for their loan against Camerino. He took Camerino, too, immediately afterwards with equal good fortune; but before he did so, and before the commands of the King of France came to spoil his plans, he wanted to test whether all his successes and all the Florentines' reverses had opened the way to a much bigger gamble for power. On the eve of leaving for Urbino he wrote to Florence that they should send him someone with whom he might discuss matters of great moment.

The Florentines were extremely anxious to find out what were the intentions of the man who had started such a conflagration in their territory and could either extinguish it at one blow or send it raging further. It was of the greatest importance to watch him and delay him until the arrival of French aid. So they at once sent the Bishop of Volterra, Francesco Soderini, and with him, more as a discreet reinforcement than as a secretary, Niccolò Machiavelli.¹³ They left in haste on the 22nd of June, and riding at top speed reached Ponticelli the same day, whence they wrote to the Signoria. That is, Machiavelli wrote, as usual, and Soderini signed. They had heard on the way, at Pontassieve, the news of the lightning capture of Urbino and the stratagem used to achieve it. The letter ends on this machiavellian note: 'Your lordships should take note of this stratagem and of this remarkable speed combined with extraordinary good fortune.'[14] It was a lesson for the dilatory Florentine government which was for ever losing itself in argument and drowning in petty considerations.

They reached Urbino in the evening of the 24th and were received at the second hour of the night. After the envoys' congratulations on his latest victory and the somewhat sarcastic thanks of Borgia, the contest of accusations and excuses began. The accusations went back to the Duke's arriving beneath the city walls, the agreements extorted by him and not observed, the embassies and letters sent to him at that time. Here Machiavelli's presence was of the utmost value, for he held the thread of all these affairs, having dealt with them himself or been present when they were decided, and written all the letters. Borgia's concluding words were threatening: 'This government of yours does not please me, and I cannot trust it; you must change it and give me a pledge that you will observe everything you promised; otherwise you will soon realize that I have no intention of going on like this, and if you do not want me as a friend, you will find me your enemy.' They replied that the city had the sort of government that it considered best, and that as they were satisfied with their government, so their friends could be satisfied with it too. After two hours of argument, it was decided to go on with the discussion the following day, each side urging the other to maturer thoughts. Thus the two envoys took their leave exceedingly dissatisfied, reflecting that the Duke's method was 'to instal himself in someone else's house before anyone noticed it'—as had happened to the Duke of Urbino 'whose death was heard of before he was known to be ill'.[15]

The following day they were visited and artfully worked on by the Orsini, who did their best to persuade them that the King of France had given Borgia leave to maltreat the Florentines provided it were done rapidly, while he would send the assistance he was committed to give, with deliberate slowness. The envoys realized that these seeds of doubt were being sown on the orders of the astute Borgia, but they were nonetheless worried by them. They were then received by the Duke at the third hour of the night, heard the same story repeated as the night before, and were given four days in which to reply. They were more worried than ever by this, and although they had earlier planned to return to Florence together, they decided that to gain time Niccolò should go alone as he was better able to ride fast, and in this way save one day of the Duke's four. In the same letter in which these incidents are related, sent off immediately by special messenger, we find this description of the Duke by the hand of Machiavelli: 'This prince is very splendid and magnificent, and in war he is so bold that there is no great enterprise that does not seem small to him, and to gain glory and territory he never rests or knows danger or weariness: he arrives at a place before anyone has heard that he has left the place he was in before: he wins the love of his soldiers, and has got hold of the best men in Italy. These things make him victorious and formidable, and are attended with invariable good fortune.'[16] When one sees the usual signature of Bishop Soderini below this pen-portrait, it looks like an error or a forgery.

As it was written, so it was done. Machiavelli, having talked with Borgia that evening and discussed the affair at length with Soderini, wrote that long letter before dawn, mounted his horse and rode with all speed to Florence. The Bishop stayed behind to plough the hard furrow, but the minds of the one who went and of the man who stayed behind were equally dominated by the image of the terrible Duke.[17]

In the meantime, however, the days passed, those last days so precious for the Pope's son, who, while pretending not to be worried by the communications of the royal heralds or by the famous French troops who were marching up the Arno valley to the rescue of the Florentines, hastily fell back on more modest and reasonable demands, merely asking that the old agreement for his commission should be honoured. The Florentines haggled over these terms with an avarice all the greater as their credit with the King increased and their adversary's diminished. In the end, Soderini had instructions to break off negotiations and return, leaving Borgia in suspense and empty-handed.

Thus the Florentines had checkmated their dangerous adversary with their King, who by now had had enough of both father and son and finally realized that what Machiavelli had said to his minister in Nantes was true. He announced that he intended to come in person to punish the Borgias, 'saying openly that it was as pious and holy an expedition as any against the Turk'.[18] In consequence, Borgia who could see the arms and the wrath of the King descending upon him, ordered Vitellozzo to retire, while the French forces under Imbault advanced towards Arezzo, and others, coming down from Asti, were about to move from Parma into Tuscany. The Florentines promptly got their lost territories back, with the exception of Arezzo, where Imbault, who had taken it by negotiation from Vitellozzo, still hung on. They received it only when Mgr. de Lancres was sent there by the King with the express order that it should be handed over. The storm had passed, and it was very fortunate for the Republic that they had at the helm an able Signoria led in name by a man of little worth, but in fact by Alamanno Salviati. To him and to the gallant commissioner Antonio Giacomini the city owed no small part of that happy outcome of events.

No one would expect that in all these affairs Machiavelli, '*equitandi, evagandi ac cursitandi tam avidus*' [so greedy of riding, wandering and running about], as his assistant Vespucci wrote of him,[19] would be sitting in the Chancery writing letters, even if at that time letters were needed more than ever.[20] He went three times to Arezzo: from the 15th to the 19th of August, or thereabouts, to accompany, entertain and assist Lancres; again on the 11th and 17th of September with various messages for Lancres.[21] As we find him in that city on the 13th with no suggestion that he meant to leave the next day,[22] one can safely say that between the second and third excursions he had barely a moment to stop in Florence.

These commissions, like nearly all the others within Florentine territory, do not seem to have been of great moment. In the recent internal affairs of the Republic, the factious disturbances of Pistoia and the rebellion of Arezzo, Machiavelli made his most valuable contribution through the anonymous labours of the Chancery, where the continuity of his work beside the ephemeral magistrates could be of some influence either through discreet reminders or in the composition of letters. His biographers and the commentators on his works are unanimous in saying that Machiavelli used his influence to persuade the magistrates to punish the subject cities of Pistoia and Arezzo with just severity.[23] There is no doubt that he would have been in favour of such severity. It is said to be probable that he advised it, though this cannot be proved; and history shows that, if he did give such advice, it was not entirely followed.

In all Machiavelli's experiences we do not so much seek their effects in Florentine politics as in the maturing of his own intellect, even if, as I have said of the French mission, we must so far speak of seeds rather than of fruits: seeds which will germinate later in inactivity and grief. That organic weakness of the Florentine government, which he had to reckon with every day, was a continual lesson to him, especially when he compared its causes and effects with the causes and effects of Borgia's strength.

The rebellions of the subject cities afforded him no less valuable material for observation and study. His *De rebus pistoriensibus*[24] is merely one of the many official accounts which he wrote for the information of new magistrates or commissioners, and one of the barest and driest of them all into the bargain. Quite another matter, however, is the discourse, perhaps incomplete, *Del modo di trattare i sudditi della Valdichiana ribellati* [How to deal with the rebellious subjects of the Valdichiana]. Written a year after the retaking of the city,[25] it is generally accepted as the first of his political writings of a retrospective character.[26] It does not seem to me to be purely retrospective, although the time for punishment was past, because it discusses the need to make sure of Arezzo while the external danger from Borgia persists. But certainly it is the first work not arising out of the immediate needs of the Chancery; the first with an almost literary flavour, distinguishing it from earlier office reports; the first in which the 'constant reading of ancient events' is applied by the Secretary to contemporary affairs with the proposition which will be one of the fundamental principles of his new science: 'the world was always inhabited, as it is now, by men who have always had the same passions.' Hence, this brief work which foreshadows and contains *in nuce* so much of Machiavelli's writings,[27] has a unique importance beyond and above its political content. The essence of it is what one may expect from Machiavelli: that rebellious peoples must either be favoured or crushed; any middle way is disastrous. The virtuous mean of the old philosophers was not, at least in politics, made for him.

Chapter 6

THE MISSION TO CAESAR BORGIA

◇◇

FLORENCE had always made up for the shortcomings of her laws with the ability of her citizens, but at this period its best citizens held aloof from public office. Disaffected, malcontent, and frightened by the jealousies of the populace, they were no longer willing to serve the Republic with their wisdom or their money. The Republic was hampered by old forms ill-suited to modern times and to the new conflict of interests and forces. Their curious way of electing the Signoria by lot for very short periods regularly brought to power men without experience or ability, and removed them from office before they gained any experience of public affairs. The consequences of these and other abuses had been seen in the Republic's latest tribulations.

Having escaped so great a danger, all were at last agreed on the need to reform the government, but not on the way of doing it. No one, not even those whose purpose it would most have served, thought of abolishing the *Consiglio grande* [the Great Council], foundation and symbol of the Florentine state. There was talk of introducing a smaller number of magistrates, almost like a council of *ottimati* [principal citizens] within the framework of a popular government, to deal with the most important business of state, like the Venetian system of the Pregati. But it was feared that the people would never accept such a proposition, and it was decided meanwhile to appoint a gonfalonier for life, who should in time and with mature consideration perfect the reform of the government.

This too was a compromise; and the choice of the first 'perpetual

E   53

gonfalonier' likewise fell between the wishes of the *ottimati* and those of the populace, and brought to power a man of moderate calibre. As the election had to be in the Great Council, it was not necessarily the ablest who was called but the man most acceptable to the people, probably because he was the one who had most courted their favour. This was Piero Soderini, a good citizen and a man of good family, who would have done very well in times of peace. As he had never refused a commission or an embassy, he was assumed to be a strong supporter of the popular state; and the people, 'seeing his services used more than anyone else's, and not considering that the reason was that his equals avoided office, thought that he must be more able than the others'.[1] It was not a choice to please the *ottimati*, but, all things considered, it was good for the Republic.

It was also good for Machiavelli. Hardworking, devoted servant of the state as he was, Soderini took to him at once, being himself just such another. Machiavelli also pleased him by his perception, intelligence and resolution—all qualities needed by the gonfalonier and possessed in not too generous measure by him. And then, Niccolò, with his flaunted vices and hidden virtues, with his bold and jesting manner, with an intelligence that at first encounter shocked the mediocre and made him appear to them presumptuous or eccentric, had qualities which made him unpopular with the majority and greatly loved by those few who knew him well and appreciated his courtesy, his humour and his talent[2]. We shall see him later winning the friendship of men far more touchy and difficult than Soderini.

Machiavelli had had many dealings with Soderini in the Chancery when the latter had been constantly employed in various offices. Also, when he had accompanied the Bishop, Soderini's brother, on the recent mission to Urbino, he had at once gained his esteem; and this too proved a key to the heart of the new gonfalonier. It is likely that Machiavelli at once wrote privately to congratulate him, as well as sending him an official letter on behalf of the Ten. Certainly he wrote to his brother, the Bishop, in Latin, that is, with all ceremony; and the Bishop hastened to reply, thanking him for his 'most elegant' letter expressing devotion to the Soderini family and to Florence.[3]

At that time Borgia, who had gone with all speed to justify himself with the King, had returned in glory and triumph, bringing back not only a pardon conceded with typical French irresponsibility, but also with *carte blanche* to take Città di Castello from Vitellozzo, now become a scapegoat, and even Bologna from Bentivoglio, till recently a paying protégé of the King. The Florentines feared this return of Borgia, but even more afraid were the petty princes who until now had been the instruments of his success—Vitelli, the Orsini, the Baglioni, Oliverotto da Fermo, and Pandolfo Petrucci. They all realized that they had helped Borgia to dig the pit of their own destruction, and began to think how they could forestall him.

A common hatred and fear should have brought together the Florentine Republic with its recent enemies, who did in fact make some overtures through Pandolfo Petrucci. Florence, however, was determined not to depart in any respect from the wishes of the French, and decided to remain neutral until these were made clear, and in the meantime to watch Borgia's every move. And so, when Borgia asked them to send an ambassador to Imola to negotiate an alliance, the Florentines did not approve the idea of a league any more than they liked the perfidious, erstwhile cardinal son of Alexander VI; but they did wish to maintain contact and keep a close watch on him. For this they needed someone who would understand everything and not commit them at all. They sent Machiavelli.

He left on the 6th of October with orders to ride hard,[4] and he took his instructions literally, because at Scarperia, finding that his horses did not go as fast as he would like, he rode post to Imola,[5] leaving behind baggage and servants. Arriving on the following day, he at once presented himself just as he was, 'in his riding clothes', before the Duke;[6] and after friendly greetings explained his commission. The gist of this was that the Florentines had been invited to take part in a conference called by the Orsini, the Baglioni, Vitelli and their supporters at Magione, but they had refused, being determined to remain firm in their friendship with the King of France and the Duke.

Borgia thanked Machiavelli, and then did his best to throw upon those who had been his accomplices and were now his enemies, all the blame for the harm, depredations and betrayals, which they had jointly inflicted on the Republic. He showed contempt for that 'assembly of bankrupts', and said he cared little for the rebellion of the duchy of Urbino, which they had fostered. If he lost it, he said, he had not forgotten the way to take it again. While the King was in Italy and the Pope was alive, these two 'kindled so great a fire beneath him that it would need quite different water than those conspirators had to quench him'. He therefore asked that the Republic should join with him, once the Orsini and Vitelli, who had been the cause of their enmity, had been removed. As for any details of the proposed alliance, however, he 'avoided committing himself', although Machiavelli 'pressed him hard to discover them.'[7]

The following day, the Duke called Machiavelli to him and made great play with certain letters from France promising him the King's assistance. Machiavelli, knowing what Borgia was like, was careful to assure the Ten that he had recognized the signatures of the letters from having seen them before in France. He also communicated to them the new pressing proposals for an alliance which the Duke had made to him, and gave details of the few forces now remaining to Borgia after the defections of the condottieri, in terms of foot-soldiers, horse and artillery, and of the fresh troops he was now collecting, and of his relations with other powers and with his subjects.[8]

From these very first letters they were pleased with him in Florence, and praise came thick and fast. Niccolò Valori was the first to praise him. Machiavelli had gained his respect, as he well knew how to do, during the mission to Pistoia; and now that he was one of the Signori, he wrote to the young secretary that he was all on his side.[9] What is more, he proved it with his actions. He was never tired of praising Machiavelli's letters and his judgements, and wrote: 'Would to God that every man would do as you do, they would make fewer mistakes!'[10] Valori used his influence also with the new gonfalonier, who was to take office on the 1st of November, and having obtained a grant of thirty ducats for Machiavelli, he wrote to him at once to say that, although the money was not much, he had supplemented it with public and private praise for the way he had handled the Duke and for his letters full of vigour and good sense.[11]

Praise came too, as we would expect, from Buonaccorsi, who, as enamoured as ever of his Niccolò, sometimes wrote to him with the jealousy of a lover.[12] Once he even risked a criticism: in his letters Machiavelli should limit himself to facts, and leave out his concise and definite conclusions.[13] And those were precisely the things that Valori had been praising! But the worthy Biagio criticized Machiavelli because he feared for him, he feared because he loved, and love served him better than reason when he added ingenuously: 'God bless you and bring you greatness.'[14]

Day by day Niccolò was acquiring greatness, at least for the eyes of posterity, by his acute observation and judgement of everything that went on at the school of that unscrupulous prince. Luigi della Stufa was right when he wrote to him from France where he was ambassador: 'A change of climate and the sight of different faces, especially of this quality, sharpens the mind.'[15]

Machiavelli liked this prince. His name was Caesar, and his fortune was as great as his name. On his banners was written: *Aut Caesar aut nihil*. He had dazzled Machiavelli's imagination from the time when, with conquest after conquest, and ruse after ruse, he had come to the gates of Florence, 'favoured by the heavens and by fortune'; he had fascinated Machiavelli when he had seen him in the magnificent fortress of the Montefeltro at Urbino, still flushed with his recent victory. He liked him no less now, when captains, states and fortune rebelled against him. On the 17th of October his enemies routed his few remaining forces; he was within an ace of losing all he had usurped. Machiavelli sees him bear it all with fortitude, dissimulating, temporizing, and meanwhile striving with all his powers to hold his subjects firm, strengthen fortresses, provide himself with everything needed for war; and in the intervals, 'to lure some of them away', lending a sympathetic ear to the rebel captains who are already making timid overtures of peace. He spends vast sums on couriers which he sends off continually to France, Rome, Ferrara, to negotiate, to obtain armaments, favours, soldiers. Machiavelli contrasts the means employed and the results obtained by him with those of his own parsimonious republic. Before he had been in Imola a fortnight, he wrote back: 'Since I have been here, he has spent as much money on riders and messengers as another government spends in two years.'[16] It does not strike him that his compatriots have to pay from their own purses, while Borgia spends the money of a Pope who creates cardinals for a low price, then, like chickens in a coop (the image is suggested by the Venetian ambassador), fattens them with benefices ready for the kill.[17]

In spite of everything, the prince pleases him; even though a Florentine ten times less wicked would only have pleased him hanging from the gallows. He likes him as the creator and the symbol of a strong state; he admires him for his indefatigable industry in war and diplomacy, for his temerity and prudence, his secretiveness and dissimulation, his mature counsel and lightning execution. His fortune dazzles Machiavelli, and even more his faith in his fortune. Machiavelli studies him, scrutinizes him, reports back to Florence what he says, takes note of his every deed. One day he asks his faithful Biagio to send him

Plutarch's *Lives*: an indication perhaps that his imagination was already tempted by a new parallel between present experience and the record of the past.[18]

The Duke, from the heights of his greatness and of his Spanish and Roman pride, did not dislike the humble secretary. If it is foolish to believe, as some have written and believed, that Machiavelli in the course of this mission inspired the machiavellianism of Borgia, yet the unusual ease with which audiences were granted,[19] their length, the nature of their conversations, all show us quite definitely that Borgia found to his liking the intelligence and the acute and freely spoken judgements of this lively, open-minded Florentine.

In the meantime Borgia continued to press for an agreement with the city. Florence, as usual, was generous with words, and extremely chary of action. The excuse was that they had to wait for royal consent, which they had written to obtain. Weeks passed and the answer did not come. The Duke again insisted, courteously however, in accord with his new manner and with a certain magnanimous insouciance. What really mattered to him was his military commission, that is, the fine gold florins with the imprint of John the Baptist on them. Machiavelli now had the task of jousting with this clever soldier on behalf of the Florentines, and he did so as only he knew how, and with those blunt and rusty weapons his masters, the Signori, gave him. One day they were talking about the Marquis of Mantua, lately commissioned by the Republic. Borgia asked: 'And what commission will the Signori give to me?' Machiavelli jokingly replied that he would have thought His Excellency should expect '*piuttosto condurre che a esser condotto*'[20]

When the pretext of the King's consent was no longer valid, the Florentines said they wanted to have the Pope's opinion, and then again that they were sending Bishop Soderini to France, and that everything depended on that mission. Borgia wanted to press them, saying that he had almost reached agreement with the Orsini and Vitellozzo, and after that, the Florentines would be in an awkward position. Machiavelli would gladly have gambled some 10,000 ducats on that venal friendship with the Duke, if the responsibility had been his own, but as his Signori thought otherwise, he had to tell him one day that, as they were not able to give him a handsome commission, they did not wish to give him a small one. When a minister proposed to him that they might turn the commission into a grant, he replied that it would be changing the name but not the thing itself.[21]

The Florentines were right not to want to spend a single ducat on Borgia' s friendship, because, as he observed, that friendship became more worthless every day. The latest decision of the Signoria removed any further possibility of negotiation or discussion with the Duke. His friend Biagio teased Machiavelli in a letter from Florence: 'Niccolò, you'll draw a blank; and you thought you would reach a conclusion there which would please the Duke . . .'[22] This led him to ask to be given leave to return more urgently than before. He had no lack of good reasons for wishing to come home, besides those given in his letter to the Ten. He had no one to see to his affairs in Florence which were going badly; for while he was away his capital was diminishing, as he had to spend for his own honour, and that of the Republic, more than he earned. He wrote, with a pride which his miserly Signori may not have appreciated: 'I could have had my expenses and could have them now from the (Duke's) court. I do not want them, and in the past I have taken little advantage of the possibility, feeling it is to my own honour and that of the Signoria to act thus. Your Excellencies may imagine how much I enjoy going begging four ducats here and three ducats there.'[23]

Among other reasons, which he did not mention in his letters, were the angry complaints of poor Marietta, whom he had told, to keep her quiet, that he would be away a week; and now, after eight weeks, she was 'fit to tie'.[24] So as not to be on her own, she had gone to stay with her brother-in-law Piero del Nero, where, without husband or money, 'she curses, and feels she has thrown away her life and her property'.[25] There was something else too, of which we know less, and which perhaps caused him greater anxiety. The date for his reappointment was near, and knowing that the absent are always wrong, he feared that his being away might lose him his job. His friends were never tired of telling him that the gonfalonier liked and esteemed him particularly, and Soderini's letters prove the same thing. As for his reappointment, Alamanno Salviati wrote to him: 'Your conduct has been and is such that people will come begging you (to accept office) rather than you having to beg them'.[26] However, he knew human nature too well, and that of the Florentines in particular, to trust to others without making an effort on his own behalf. He was not encouraged either by certain reports from Buonaccorsi: first, that the new government wanted to reduce the salaries of the secretaries, and second, to reduce their numbers.

But he was the soul of the two secretariats he directed. In his absence, the second Chancery was looked after by the head of the first, Marcello Virgilio, but he did very little according to the assistants. He also had his work in the University, and wrote almost in despair to Machiavelli: 'Here I am with my own affairs and yours on my hands as well as my teaching.'[27] His friend Biagio substituted for him with the Ten, and told him: 'I am mostly managing this office of yours, and I'm getting along nicely.'[28] He sent him news of the work and of his colleagues, who always had some quarrel or misfortune on hand. Now it was ser Andrea di Romolo who had played backgammon all day; now ser Antonio della Valle and ser Andrea had come to blows in the office over some gambling dispute, and the latter had kicked ser Antonio and hurt his back. Not to mention the obscenities with which these office pleasantries were larded. Gossip of a more respectable and witty kind was sent to him by the other assistant Agostino Vespucci, who related among other things his misadventure when one of the magistrates, a silly man, rushed into the room crying: 'Ho there, ho, write'; and as all his colleagues had fled, he had to sacrifice himself and take dictation from this bore.[29] To these letters, which brought him in the gloomy court of Caesar Borgia a breath of sparkling Florentine air, Machiavelli replied in kind with letters of his own which 'made everyone die of laughing'.[30] Unfortunately, these are all lost, and judging by the others he wrote to friends, it is a serious loss to Italian literature.

Finally, on top of all the other reasons for asking leave to return, he fell ill. I do not know whether he pretended it was worse than it really was to strengthen his other arguments which up to then had had no effect, but on the 22nd of November he wrote: 'Two days ago I had a high fever, and I still feel rather ill.'[31] On the 6th of December he added: 'For about twelve days now I have been feeling very unwell, and if I go on like this, I fear I may have to come back in a cart.'[32] But even so, they would not give him leave to return! If he had to go in a cart, then it would be in the train of the Duke, who was about to move with all his forces, certainly to the detriment of someone, but no one knew who. The Florentines wanted to keep an eye on his movements, and, if possible, on his secret thoughts, and they urged Machiavelli to watch him. When they pressed him too hard, he grew impatient with them: 'Your Excellencies must excuse me, and bear in mind that one cannot guess such things and that we have to do here with a prince who takes all his own decisions; anyone who does not want to write mere fantasies and fairy-tales, has to collate the facts, and this takes time. I am doing my best to spend my time usefully and not to waste it.'[33]

At Florence they read his letters and remained in suspense, no one being able to guess where Borgia's first blow would fall. One thing only was certain: he had built up his forces, while temporizing, to such an extent that he could harm his enemies and not they him. This was what Machiavelli had predicted to the incredulous Signoria right from the beginning, when Borgia was defeated and without troops. On the 19th of November, conversing privately with the Duke as he often did, he could tell him with more pride than flattery that he had always predicted his victory, and that if on the first day of his mission he had put his thoughts on paper, 'it would look to him like a prophecy'. He also gave the reasons which had inspired his forecast, but principally 'that he was one man, and had against him many, and could easily break such chains'.[34]

In fact peace was now made, and not only with Bentivoglio, whom the King of France, changing his mind, had once again taken under his protection, but also with the incautious Orsini, whom Borgia had cleverly 'lured away from his companions',[35] and the other rebels had been obliged to follow. Fear of the King and of the Pope had indeed broken the chains which bound together the conspirators of Magione, but the patient dissimulation of the Duke had done even more to that end; and it was going to be easy for him too before long to break the links astutely forged with these enemies of yesterday. That this was the way things were going, Machiavelli foresaw when he wrote to the Ten 'of the preparations of this prince for war in these days of peace-making', 'especially considering how little good faith can be relied on these days'.[36] In a later letter to the Ten telling them of the 'very submissive and pleasing letters' written by Vitellozzo to the Duke, he added: 'His Lordship accepts everything; and one does not know what course he intends to pursue, for it is difficult to understand and discern it. If one has to give an opinion on the matter . . . one can only expect the worst'.[37] The next few weeks showed him to be a true prophet.

On the 9th of December Borgia moved with his forces towards Cesena, and Machiavelli followed him two days later, rather unwillingly however, because of weakness of purse and body which caused him to threaten the Ten that he would have 'to obey necessity'. But Soderini wrote to him: 'I think it more urgent than anything else to supply your needs', and he had them send him twenty-five ducats. Having thus cured more than half his troubles, he gave him the following instructions: 'You will go on watching how things go there and write often, and when we see what turn things take, you will get your leave and we will nominate someone to take your place, as we have decided to keep a representative with that illustrious Prince. In the meantime you will maintain the diligence you have exercised up to now.'[38] Machiavelli did continue to be very diligent. The Gonfalonier's medicine had done him good.

However, at Cesena matters seemed no clearer than at Imola. Some said that the Duke intended to march into the Kingdom of Naples, some that he would go to Ravenna and Cervia against the Venetians. Machiavelli, on the other hand, was convinced that he would first 'make sure of those who had played him false and very nearly lost him his state'.[39] In Rome the Pope—whether merely a spectator or a moving force in his son's enterprises—became indignant at this long delay, and urged him on exclaiming loudly so that he was heard by those present: 'Ah, son of a whore, bastard!'[40] Anger, like wine, brings out the truth.

On the 26th of December Borgia moved with the whole army, less the French lancers which had left suddenly four days earlier, thus multiplying conjecture and confusion in the minds of those who wanted to make prophecies. On his departure, he left on the town square the quartered body of the powerful and terrible Ramiro Lorqua, who had been his instrument in holding down the peoples of Romagna. So with this bloody Christmas present he discharged the hatred of his subjects on his minister and assumed the mantle of the just prince, 'who shows he can make and unmake men at will according to their merits.'[41] Machiavelli also noted this memorable deed to draw from it a lesson and a conclusion.

It was the 26th of December, and in those last five days of the year events followed one another thick and fast like moves on a chessboard. The Orsini and Vitelli took Senigallia by the order and in the name of the Duke. He, having moved his army to Fano in small detachments to hide his true strength, went from there to Senigallia with remarkable speed. He was met respectfully on the way by Vitellozzo, Paolo Orsini and the Duke of Gravina, and entered the city with part of his forces, conversing affectionately with them. Once inside the city, he sent also for Oliverotto da Fermo, and at a given signal his guard leaped upon the captains and took them prisoner. Borgia then ordered his men to disarm the Orsini and Vitelli troops.

At Fano Machiavelli had received from the Duke some dark hints of this,[42] had followed him, and was present at this scene of violence. When it was at its height, he wrote in great agitation to the Ten: 'The town is still being sacked, and it is 11 o'clock at night. I am extremely worried. I don't know if I shall be able to find anyone to take this letter. I will write at length later. My opinion is that they will not be alive tomorrow.'[43] In actual fact that last day of the year was for Vitellozzo and Oliverotto the last day of their lives. The execution of the other two was put off until the Pope could sieze cardinal Orsini and the rest of the family. The deed was criminal, but it was a master stroke. In the eyes of the Florentine Secretary the Duke's stature became immense.

At about the second hour of the night Borgia sent for him and 'with perfect good cheer' congratulated himself on what had happened. Then he added words 'exceedingly wise and kindly' towards the Florentines, indicating that they ought to be grateful to him for exterminating their principal enemies, when they would have readily paid two hundred thousand ducats to dispose of them, 'and then it would not have been such a clean sweep'[44] as he had achieved. Finally he asked them to send troops to join his own in an expedition to Città di Castello and Perugia.

Machiavelli wrote to Florence, but the Duke's movements were more rapid than those of the messengers carrying the letters.[45] On the 1st of January he was already at Corinaldo with the whole army, on the 3rd at Sassoferrato, on the 5th at Gualdo. There he found waiting for him the ambassadors of Città di Castello who offered him their surrender; and the next day those of Perugia arrived to offer him theirs. They said that the populace had risen with cries of 'duca duca', and that Giampaolo Baglioni with a few remnants of the Orsini and Vitelli supporters had fled hastily to Siena. But at Siena Pandolfo Petrucci did not feel any safer than they did from the claws of Borgia:

> Sentì Perugia e Siena ancor la vampa
> de l'idra; e ciaschedun di que' tiranni
> fuggendo innanzi la sua furia scampa.[46]

[Perugia and Siena too felt the hot breath of the hydra; and each of those tyrants flees to escape his fury.]

Thus wrote Machiavelli long after the events. In the meantime, the hydra went on without respite. On the 8th he was in Assisi, on the 10th at Torciano, where the Duke sent for him and spoke at length about the affairs of Siena, stating that he had no designs on that city: he simply wished to chase out Petrucci, suggesting the Florentines might help him. The army was on the point of moving towards Chiusi, a Sienese possession, when at Città della Pieve, where he again had a long discussion with Borgia, Machiavelli learned from a letter of the Ten that the Republic had at last taken the advice he had repeatedly given, and chosen an ambassador to the Duke. He was one of the leading citizens: Iacopo Salviati. And so, on the 20th, while Pandolfo too was fleeing before the hydra, Machiavelli left the Borgia camp and set off for Florence.[47] He reached home on the 23rd.[48]

For him the legation, begun at a time when the plan for revenge was first taking shape in the inscrutable mind of Borgia, had ended during the tragic night which set the seal of blood on that revenge and on the year 1502. The only fruit of the legation is his famous *Descrizione del modo tenuto dal Duca Valentino nell'ammazzare Vitellozzo Vitelli*, etc.,[49] which is the story from conception to epilogue of that vengeance, written not as an official chancery report but as a brief work of purely literary intention. Some critics have compared it with the official letters, found divergences which do not in fact exist, exaggerated those which do, and have been in too much of a hurry to show it up as an idealized account.[50] I do not think it is true to say that Machiavelli idealized Borgia; what is true is that, admiring strongly in him certain qualities and conditions, like a painter who takes some features from life for an ideal painting, he lent these characteristics to an abstract portrait of a prince, and sought them in vain in other princes of his time.

Many other people have written, and we have hinted at the fact in these pages, that the Florentine Secretary learned a good deal during this mission, at the school of Caesar Borgia. By this we mean, that placed before actions which were certainly great and memorable and fired his imagination, he learned to draw from them scientific theories. We do not mean to suggest, as is commonly thought, that only there and then Machiavelli learned machiavellianism.

Chapter 7

THE FIRST ROMAN LEGATION

◇◇

H E had spent all his time as envoy in Romagna trying to reach an agreement with Borgia, and on his return this was still to be one of his principal tasks as secretary. Where he had failed, the envoy who followed him did not succeed either. Besides the coldness of the Florentines, the changeable climate of relations between the Pope and the King of France, and the uncertainty of the outcome of the war between the Spanish and the French in the Kingdom of Naples, were hardly propitious to such an agreement. The Pope felt that he could derive little advantage from being allied to the King, who had several times thwarted his ambitions, and seeing the fortune of French arms in decline, he thought it was time to transfer his forces and his projects to the side of the Spaniards. The King, on his side, guessing something of these thoughts, was plotting another league to balance the forces of the Pope and his worthy son against those of Bentivoglio and the republics of Florence, Lucca and Siena. He began, meantime, by restoring the expelled Petrucci to Siena in spite of the Borgias.

At that time the Florentines, not feeling very safe from Borgia, and wishing to get the Pisan war going again, decided to raise an army; but first they had to think of the financial implications. Any attempt in the Council to get new taxes voted by the very people who would have to pay them, was attended with a storm of protest. This time too, things did not go easily. Many proposals were put forward by the Gonfalonier, against whom the first malcontents were beginning to stir, and none of them was accepted. Finally a tithe was approved to be imposed on the clergy as well, if they could get the permission of the Pope. On this occasion Machiavelli wrote (not spoke) his *Parole sopra la provvisione del denaio*,[1] intended for the use of whoever was to speak in favour of the law. It was a short, vigorous discourse to move the Florentines to defend their liberty and arm themselves with their own forces, because 'one cannot always rely on someone else's sword, and so it is a good thing to have one at hand, and put it on when the enemy is approaching'. In these early writings we see his powers as a thinker and writer constantly increasing.

In mid-April, either on account of the tithe on church property or for some other reason, an agreement with the Pope was again under discussion; and so that Pandolfo Petrucci, lately returned to Siena, should not be made suspicious, Machiavelli was sent there on the 26th of April 1503 to inform him of the conditions agreed on.[2] It was a short and simple commission, and moreover a useless one, since the agreement came to nothing, and the Florentines dropped it altogether. The city gained nothing from Borgia but the cardinal's hat for Bishop Soderini —whether this was done to win over his brother, the Gonfalonier, or to gain favour in France where the Bishop was ambassador, or for twenty thousand other reasons worth a gold ducat apiece.

The principal reason for breaking off the negotiations between the Florentines and the Pope was the latter's wish to exclude the clauses in favour of the King of France. The more the French sustained defeats and reverses in the Kingdom of Naples, the more the old Pope felt the urge to draw closer to the victorious Spaniards. Only his prudent cunning still held him back, as he wished to be absolutely certain of the result. First peace had been negotiated between the two kings, then when Gonsalvo, peace or no peace, had again routed the French in Puglia and Calabria, the Pope was restrained by fear of the armies which the French were sending to the rescue. Meantime he went on negotiating with the French, and Caesar Borgia with the Spaniards. In Rome the proverb was current that of the two of them, the son never said what he would do, and the father never did what he said.[3] In these great and obscure projects, both then seemed at the height of their ambitions. But on the 18th of August, after three days of tertian fever, the Pope was dead; and Caesar Borgia was as good as dead, having fallen ill of the same disease on the same day as his father. The Borgia star began to set in the sky of that heavy Roman summer.

The Duke, as he was later to tell Machiavelli, had long prepared himself against his father's death. He had thought of everything, foreseen everything, except that he might himself at that same moment be more dead than alive.[4] His states suddenly fell apart like a house of cards, and at Perugia, Città di Castello, Urbino, Camerino, Senigallia, their former rulers returned, while his own forces dwindled around him. Nevertheless, he reconciled himself with the Colonna family so that they should not ally themselves with the Orsini against him, and sought to defend himself against hatred, danger and misfortune. Although because of the imminent Conclave he was being wooed, despite his reduced condition, both by France and Spain, he looked to the French rather than to the far-off Spaniards. The French could much more easily defend or attack him with that great army which, on its way to the Kingdom of Naples, lingered now at the walls of Rome to make its influence felt in the election of the Pope. So in the end, he made an agreement with the Cardinal of Rouen, placing himself once again under the King's protection.

With this agreement Rouen thought he had acquired the papacy for himself with the votes of the cardinals following Caesar Borgia. Meanwhile, having failed in his first ambition to create the Pope he wanted through force of arms, Borgia had also to abandon his hope of achieving this through the ballot. The two opposing factions of cardinals, French and Spanish, both despairing of victory, fell back on electing Piccolomini. Because of his age and infirmity, this was understood to be no more than a truce. In fact, barely twenty-six days after, Pius III also died; and they were back where they started.

The news arrived in Florence on the 20th of October. On the 21st it was decided to send Machiavelli to Rome 'until the election of the new Pope'.[5] The same decision had been taken after the death of Alexander VI, on the 28th of August, when Niccolò was just returning in the heat of the summer sun from having met Sandricourt coming with a large part of the French army from Fivizzano towards Siena, and from having met and accompanied a good part of the way Cardinal Soderini who was going to Rome from Volterra for the Conclave.[6] On that occasion the Secretary's departure had been delayed and finally cancelled, but this time, after the death of the second Pope, it was not a false alarm, and on the morning of the 24th of October he left for Rome.[7]

He carried credentials and letters to the leading cardinals favoured by the Republic, to whom he was to express the wish that a new Pope should be elected, suitable to the needs of Christendom and Italy.

Besides these general instructions he had the particular duty to ratify under certain conditions the commission of Giampaolo Baglioni issued by the King of France in the name of the Republic. For this and every other affair the legate was first to refer to Cardinal Soderini. There was in Rome another Florentine cardinal, Giovanni de' Medici, but it was tacitly understood that he was to pretend not to see him.

He reached Rome on the 27th. We must restrain our imagination on the subject of his first encounter with the remains of the ancient city. In his writings we do not find a word about it, not even an allusion; and yet we cannot do otherwise than think of him dwelling on those ruins, as he did on the pages of Livy. But if at all, this certainly would not have been in the first days of his legation, as it was neither pleasant nor safe to walk through the city packed with armed men. There had flocked in more peasants and thieves than soldiers, followers of the Roman barons who were once more a force to reckon with. The Prati and the Borghi were held by Valentino's men. Suspicion and riots were rife.

This is how Machiavelli first saw Rome, and this is the picture he gave to the Signoria in the first letters of the legation.[8] He wrote about Giampaolo Baglioni's commission after having discussed it with Cardinal Soderini, and he wrote about the forecasts on the Conclave. The shadow of Caesar Borgia still looms over him: 'The Duke is in the Castle, and has better hopes than ever of doing great things.'[9] He soon observed that the Duke's hopes depended on others, he who had never done anything but harm to others: 'Duke Valentino is much cultivated by those who wish to be Pope, because of the Spanish cardinals his favourites, and many cardinals have been to talk to him every day in the Castle, so that it is thought that whoever becomes Pope will be indebted to him, and he lives in the hope of being favoured by the new Pope.'[10]

The belief grew daily that the new Pope would be San Pietro in Vincula, that is, Cardinal della Rovere; and this growing favour could be seen in the progress of the betting. On the 28th of October, when Machiavelli wrote his second letter, the Banks were taking thirty-two per cent on him, and on the 30th, sixty per cent; on the 31st, before the cardinals went into conclave, the rumour went round that Rouen was behind della Rovere as well as Borgia, having sought in vain to promote his own election, and his price went up to ninety per cent. Disease and misfortune must have turned Borgia's brain if, believing in promises, he was willing to give the Borgia votes to a man who had spent ten years in exile out of hatred for the name of Borgia. Often extreme necessity drives men to strange resorts, and, as our envoy wrote, the cardinals needed to be made richer and the Duke to be resuscitated.[11]

Thus the impetuous nephew of Sixtus IV went into the Conclave with the result in his pocket; and there, before the doors could be locked, he was at once elected. Writing that night to Florence, Machiavelli was able, from the rumours that were going around, to announce the election before it was published, and also to state that the new Pope would take the name of Julius II. The following morning he confirmed the news with these simple words, which one might not have expected of him: 'In the name of the Lord I notify your Excellencies that this morning the Cardinal of San Pietro in Vincula was elected the new Pope. May God make him a useful leader of Christendom.'[12] That was all he wrote.

But the Florentine Secretary, on great occasions when his words needed to have wings, was unlucky with his letters. His wings were clipped by the miserly Republic, which did not give him the means to send by special messenger;[13] and just as had happened with the events at Senigallia, the creation of the new Pope was known in Florence from other sources several days before the arrival of their envoy's letters, although he had been among the first to know of it.

Machiavelli's ambiguous smile, which had disappeared for a brief moment in the presence of the Vicar of Christ, reappears in the last of the four letters written by him to the Ten on that same 1st of November, when he passes from the divine aspect to the human and very temporal details of the election: 'He will have difficulty in keeping the promises he has made, for many of them will be at odds with each other; nevertheless he is Pope, and we shall soon see to whom he made genuine promises.'[14] Three days later, enlarging further on the 'miraculous favours' Julius II had enjoyed in his election, he added: 'The reason for these favours was that he promised whatever was asked of him, and so it is felt that the difficuty will come in the keeping of these promises.'[15] It was said that he had promised Borgia not only the restitution of the whole state of Romagna, which, after having been more faithful to him than the others, was now being divided between its former rulers and the greed of the Venetians, but also other minor favours such as Ostia for his personal safety, and the post of Gonfalonier of the Church. However, the subtle Florentine, believing it to be impossible that the Pope could have forgotten his old hatreds and his exile, concluded with a touch of irony: 'The Duke allows himself to be carried away by his brave confidence, and believes that other people's words are more to be relied upon than his own were.'[16]

Immediately after the publication of the name of the new Pope, the envoy hastened to assure the Ten that the election was judged to be excellent for the Florentines. They needed it, for the Republic was in greater anxiety than ever about what was happening in Romagna, where after the decline of Borgia, a new neighbour had appeared even more unwelcome and dangerous. As soon as the Duke's cause seemed to be doomed, Romagna had fallen to pieces, some parts going back to their allegiance to the Church, others recalling their former rulers. The Ordelaffi, for example, had re-entered Forlì with the help of the Florentines, who also had some understanding with Faenza, where they eventually called in a bastard son of the Manfredi, after having remained faithful to Borgia for longer than most other cities. But the Venetians, having already acquired Rimini and taken many castles by force or enforced treaties, finally attacked and took Faenza. The Duke Valentino was a new prince, grown up like a poisonous fungus in the shadow of a short-lived Pope, but Venice was a republic as old as its own lagoon, powerful and extremely rich, sister and enemy of Florence. The relations between the two cities were always fraught with jealousy and suspicion. *Inde irae*. Hardly had the news of Julius's election arrived, than the Ten rained down letters on Machiavelli demanding that he should complain to the Pope about these Venetian usurpations.

On the 5th of November he presented himself with fresh credentials to perform the due ceremonies at the feet of the Pope; and the next day he returned with these complaints. He also spoke to some of the leading cardinals, 'reminding them that it was not a question of the freedom of Tuscany but of the freedom of the Church, and that the Pope would become the chaplain of the Venetians if their power were further to increase, and that it was up to them to make provision against this as it was a question of their rightful inheritance'.[17] He also went to stir Borgia to action, but he began to complain bitterly about the Florentines, saying that they had always been his enemies. This was quite true; and he also went on to threaten that he would take his revenge for this by placing himself at the disposal of the Venetians. And he continued to expatiate on the subject with words full of venom and passion. The envoy was strongly tempted to answer him in the same terms, but he restrained himself, and having said a few words to calm him down, took his departure as quickly as he could.[18] Gone were the days of the mission to Romagna and the fine though machiavellian conversations between Machiavelli and the Duke.

However, five days later the Duke sent for Machiavelli, appearing much calmer, for he now had need of him. He talked at length about his affairs, saying that the Pope was helping him and the Florentines too must help him against the common danger of the Venetians. He was in effect simply trying to promote his cause with words, having no other means at his disposal. Machiavelli listened to him patiently; and perhaps it was that very day that Machiavelli heard from Borgia's own lips the explanation of his ruin which we noted above.[19] But the magic had faded, and Machiavelli observed him with other eyes, like an anatomist looking at a corpse: no, no one could now revive him. Machiavelli now laughed inwardly at his varied and vain hopes, seeing only too clearly that the Pope was temporizing with him to avoid keeping his promises and to avoid telling him so too soon. The Duke went on hoping that he would be made Gonfalonier of the Church; he believed in the King of France, and in the Pope, who was pressing him to go to Romagna so as to remove him from his own vicinity. Yet he saw that everyone was really breaking their promises to him—and no one had been less faithful in this respect than he—and he could not understand it. He began to feel the ground give way beneath his feet; he was astonished and did not know what to do.

He had demanded a safe conduct from the Florentines, and they had refused it, their long-standing hatred being greater than their present fear of the Venetians. Borgia then sent his forces all the same towards Tuscany led by the wicked don Michele and himself went to Ostia to take ship. But before doing so, he sent for Machiavelli and protested violently to him about the safe-conduct refused by Florence, threatening to ally himself with Pisa and the Venetians against the Florentines.[20] Yet he felt his own threats ring false, and calmed down. At one time he never said what he was going to do; now he says things which he is incapable of doing. The Florentine Secretary manœuvred cleverly, and gave him some slight encouragement so that he and his forces should hasten towards their downfall; and then he wrote to the Ten describing the forces which were on their way to Tuscany, and explaining that it was within their power to stop them or let them pass. A few days later he prophesied that 'don Michele and his troops who set off for the north will not make much of a success of it'.[21]

It seems that someone in Florence disliked these conversations of Machiavelli with the Duke and the importance he gave them in his letters. At least this is what Buonaccorsi told him with some concern.[22] This is surprising, because if the city hated Borgia, there was all the more reason to watch and parley with him; and if this were done, the envoy could not help but give an account of his discussions. It is still less true that he wrote about them *gagliardamente* [with enthusiasm], because in these very letters he writes that the Duke's affairs 'have suffered a thousand changes; and it is true that they have continuously gone from bad to worse'.[23]

From that very moment they were going downhill at breakneck speed. At Ostia he was joined by two cardinals sent by the Pope to demand the surrender of those fortresses in Romagna which were still faithful to him, with the promise that they would be handed back when the threat from the Venetians was past. When he refused, the Pope had him arrested and brought a prisoner to Rome. Almost at the same time, his forces which had entered Tuscany without a safe-conduct were attacked and stripped of their arms and baggage in the Florentine dominion. Don Michele, Borgia's lieutenant, strangler, and devilish disciple, also fell into their hands.

The Pope, who had been glad to hear of the refusal of the safe-conduct, learned with much greater pleasure, in Machiavelli's presence, of the rout of these last remnants of Borgia power, and sent a brief to Florence demanding that the villainous don Michele be handed over to him, 'thinking that his capture would give him the opportunity to discover all the cruelties, robberies, murders, sacrileges, and other end-less crimes perpetrated in Rome against God and against men in the past eleven years'.[24] Thus every day Borgia descended another rung. He was to descend the last rungs the day he fell on his knees before that Duke of Urbino whom he had betrayed and despoiled, abjectly begging his forgiveness and cursing his own father's soul.[25] His son's curses were probably the only ones that had not yet fallen on Alexander VI. No one ever prayed for his soul, except possibly a Dominican friar when he climbed the scaffold and the pyre by order of that Pope.

Of his hero's final steps to ruin, Machiavelli ironically remarks: 'We see that this Pope is beginning to pay his debts honourably; he wipes them out with the cotton-wool from the inkstand. Nevertheless his hands are blessed by all.'[26] And two days later, speaking again of Borgia's fortunes: 'One can see that his sins have brought him little by little to penance.'[27] Finally he wrote: 'And so, inch by inch, the Duke slips into the tomb.'[28] Amen.

There are those who, scandalized, have reproached the Florentine Secretary with this pitiless attitude towards the fallen hero. They have misunderstood him. He had admired only certain aspects of the prince, while good fortune filled his sails. A villain of that kind, once fallen, does not arouse anyone's pity, least of all if he falls without showing any spark of cleverness or boldness. Machiavelli was to write later in the *Discorsi:* 'In any action one may gain glory: for it is generally acquired in victory, and in defeat it is acquired ... by performing immediately some courageous action which wipes out that defeat.'[29] But Valentino performed no bold deed in those last wretched and irresolute days in Rome, when

in altrui trovar credette
quella pietà che non conobbe mai.

[he hoped to find in others that compassion he had never felt].

These words from the first *Decennale*[30] and others like them in the same poem and elsewhere, show that Machiavelli as a man recognized Borgia's abject moral qualities, even if as a writer of political science he did not object to them. It is true that, as a political writer, he must also have learned something from the sad end of this wretch—and not merely that one should never trust those whom one has betrayed and injured. To Machiavelli this must have seemed a fault no less unpardonable than all Borgia's other crimes.

While the Duke of Romagna was thus disappearing from the scene, the latest events in that region had become the principal affair our envoy had in hand. He made every effort to rouse the Pope against the Venetians. He found him well disposed in conversation, but tardy and chill as the north wind in action, and this did not seem quite in character for him. Machiavelli therefore suspected that he might have made certain promises to the Venetians at the time when he was promising everyone something in order to gain their support for his election to the papacy. In that case it was to be hoped that he would keep them as he had kept his promises to Borgia. However, on closer scrutiny of the Pope's words and deeds, he found them unambiguous, and came to the conclusion that one should attribute his moderation to the fact that he was a new Pope, without arms or money, who was obliged to temporize and go carefully until he had 'settled into the saddle'. Machiavelli concluded with his usual acuity: 'There is only one thing one can put one's trust in, and that is his honourable and choleric nature.'[31] Four days later he prophesied of the Venetians: 'Either this will be a gateway that will lay the whole of Italy open to them, or it will be their ruin.'[32] The second alternative proved him a true prophet.

November passed. Machiavelli had been in Rome more than a month, and what was most unusual for him, always so restless, he neither asked for leave nor voiced any complaints. Only once during this time did he write home to ask for funds and seek an increase in salary to meet his heavy expenses. If they could not raise his salary, he asked that they should pay the expenses of his messengers. Protesting that he could not endure such a lack of satisfactory arrangements, he concluded: 'and even if I could, men labour these days to get ahead, not to retreat.'[33] Our Secretary never lacked bold words! When one of the Signori, a man of low birth, asked to be personally informed on the Pope's policy in Romagna, and made a fuss because he did not get a quick reply, Machiavelli answered sharply: 'I will write in the vulgar tongue, if it so happened that I used Latin in my dispatch to the office, which I do not think I did.'[34] He objected no less boldly once when reproached with laziness in writing: 'I am sorry that after much discomfort and danger and extreme diligence, and with expenses far greater than the salary Your Worships give me, and beyond my own means, I should be told I am slow.'[35]

But, apart from these irritations, it is evident that Machiavelli was happy in Rome in spite of the plague. Tommasini was wrong in saying that this Roman sojourn was 'joyless' and 'unpleasant'. On the contrary Machiavelli enjoyed it so much that, when in mid-December the Ten ordered him to return, he turned a deaf ear, and the excuse that he was indisposed, which used to support his requests for recall, was now used to delay it.[36]

Yet now he should have had the strongest reasons to wish to go home. At Rome there was the plague, in Florence his young wife whom he had left on the eve of giving birth to their second child, the first having been a girl. Even if, wild as he was, he did not make much difference between his wife and the plague, he must surely have longed to see his child just born, and a son! He was christened on the 9th of November and named after his grandfather Bernardo; his godfathers among others were the first chancellor of the Republic, Marcello Virgilio, and Machiavelli's friend Buonaccorsi.[37] The latter sends him the usual news about the office, where Marcello 'scamps the work';[38] he recounts the caprices of one of the Signori, and reproaches Machiavelli with coldness in their friendship; but he never fails to tell him about his son: 'We shall do our best to ensure that this sprig shall turn out well and do us credit, do not doubt it; but he looks like a little crow, he is so dark.'[39] His wife also wrote him an affectionate letter about the little boy as soon as she was able: 'He looks like you, his skin is as white as snow, but his head looks like black velvet, and he is hairy like you, and because he looks like you he seems handsome to me . . . he opened his eyes as soon as he was born and filled the house with his cries.'[40]

However, as though all this and the orders of the Ten counted for nothing, Machiavelli did not budge. He is often at the house of Cardinal Soderini, with whom he has renewed his old friendship, and he seeks to influence him in favour of some great scheme for the benefit of Florence. Meantime, he continually sings the Cardinal's praises in his letters to the Ten, and the Cardinal is equally assiduous in writing to Florence in praise of Machiavelli; so much so that there are some among the Signoria who are not pleased with this friendship. Those who object most are probably the enemies of the Gonfalonier, who are becoming daily stronger and more numerous. The Cardinal too had stood god-father to Machiavelli's little boy,[41] and it was he who encouraged the envoy to resist the first recall of the Ten. When at last Machiavelli decided to obey, Soderini wrote to the Ten regretting that Machiavelli had been taken away from him, and begging them to take good care of him because of his quite extraordinary prudence and diligence.[42]

On the 18th of December the envoy set off,[43] unwillingly bringing to an end that sojourn in Rome which to one of his biographers seemed 'joyless'. With more imagination, Tommasini might have been nearer the mark if he had shown us a Machiavelli contemplating the ruins of Rome, frequenting the papal rooms crowded with ambassadors, the inns with their fine food, and the beautiful Roman women.

Chapter 8

THE SECOND MISSION TO FRANCE
THE FIRST *DECENNALE*. THE MILITIA

◇◇◇

THE war which was being fought in the far-off Kingdom of Naples was of close interest to the Florentines, attached as they were to the fortunes of the French. During his Roman mission Machiavelli was continually being pressed for news of this campaign. At that time there were in fact no battles, but shortly after his departure, on the 28th of December, the French suffered a heavy defeat on the Garigliano through the superior discipline and bravery of the Spanish infantry and the boldness of their commander Gonsalvo. The vanquished had also to contend with the rigours of the winter weather. Piero de' Medici met his end there, not in the fighting, but drowned in the river in flood: a fitting conclusion to a foolish and unhappy life.

In Florence the government would have celebrated that timely death if their displeasure and fear at the defeat of the French had not outweighed their enthusiasm. Having lost everything he held in the Kingdom of Naples, defeated by the Spaniards, uncertain of the intentions of the Swiss and of Maximilian, King Louis would have too much to do to defend himself from the next attacks to be able to do anything to protect his allies. It was feared that Gonsalvo intended to drive the French out of Lombardy too, and that the first blow would fall in Tuscany, where he already had some support in Pisa and was preparing others in Siena and Lucca. With the affairs of Romagna going as they were, the Florentines felt that they were between the

76

hammer of the Grand Captain (Gonsalvo) and the anvil of the Venetians.

It is understandable, therefore, that they wanted to get a clear view of the situation at once, and to know what were the King's preparations and intentions. So, at the beginning of 1504, they sent to see him Niccolò Valori, who at that time was in Firenzuola. Before he left, Valori received his instructions from Machiavelli, sent to him for that purpose.[1] A much longer journey was in store for Machiavelli, however, for hardly had Valori reached the court than the Republic, having received further information of Gonsalvo's intentions and none about the King's, decided to send Machiavelli to France in great haste; and he for his part (so great was the urgency) boasted that he would be there in six days:[2] no mean feat!

Machiavelli's mission may seem strange in view of the fact that the Florentines had an ambassador at court, only recently sent there with fresh instructions. They could simply have written to him. But apart from the unreliability of letters, Machiavelli was sent on this occasion also because of his knowledge of all these negotiations and above all because of the faith the Florentines, and particularly the Gonfalonier, had in his judgement. This is clearly evident in the instructions given to him on the 19th of January: 'The purpose of your journey is to observe the preparations which are being made and to report them immediately to us with your own comments and conjectures.'[3] It appears that they did not rely on the ambassador's judgement.

Leaving on the 20th of January, he reached Milan on the 22nd. As he had been instructed, he spoke with the French lieutenant, Charles D'Amboise, and told him that, if they received no help, the Florentines must either wait to be conquered or come to an agreement with those who sought to conquer them. Amboise replied that he did not believe that Gonsalvo would invade, but that if he did, the King would not abandon his friends. However, he promised to write a pressing letter on the subject to the court, which was all the envoy wanted. When Machiavelli took his leave, Amboise said loudly: '*Non de rien doutez.*' And Machiavelli reported these words to the Ten, rather boasting of his knowledge of the French language.[4]

He left Milan on the next day, and on the 27th reached Lyons where the court was.[5] He had kept his promise to get there in six days, if we discount the time wasted in Milan. As soon as he had dismounted he went to see the ambassador. These two Niccolòs were old friends, and in these pages we have already said something of the affectionate letters which Valori addressed to Machiavelli: none more affectionate than this one which ends with the words: 'As I have no brothers, I propose to regard you as a brother and that you do the same to me; and you may take this in lieu of a bond.'[6] The two must therefore have got on well together, and I do not think that Valori could have taken offence at a man so discreet as Machiavelli being sent to him by the Ten. The ambassador, who was something of a literary man, wrote the letters of the mission himself and signed them alone. Machiavelli, since he had a separate commission and orders to express his own opinion, could have written on his own account. Instead, in all that time he wrote no more than two letters, in the first of which, the only one of any importance, he merely confirmed and ratified what Valori had written.[7] He may perhaps have written more frequently to the Gonfalonier.

The following day, being unable to gain audience of the King, who was physically and mentally ill as a result of all these setbacks, the two Niccolòs went to Cardinal Rouen, where Machiavelli presented his credentials and explained the reason for his coming. He spoke about Gonsalvo and the Venetians, about the hostile neighbouring republics and about Pisa. Amid so many dangers the Florentines' only hope was the King; he was sent to find out what help he would give, and trusted that it would be such that the city could rely upon it. 'And here he spoke emphatically, as the occasion required', and added that, if friends failed, it would be necessary to come to terms with the enemy. The Cardinal 'listened to him with displeasure, visibly angered', and in his reply he complained that the Florentines should express themselves thus when times were so difficult for the French. Valori then intervened. 'And Niccolò Machiavelli, with the greatest dexterity . . . added that, if they wished to save Tuscany, they must think of preserving its defences, and that its defences against Gonsalvo were the Pope, Siena and Perugia.' Replying that he felt he could rely on the Pope and Siena and that Perugia belonged to the Pope, the Cardinal broke off the conversation.[8]

The following day, Valori and Machiavelli had milder words from the Cardinal. He spoke of the truce which was being prepared between the kings of France and Spain; he said that peace or war would be decided that week, but that, whichever it was, the Florentines could feel safe. Machiavelli replied that he would delay his departure until he could take back to Florence the certainty either of a truce or of substantial assistance.[9] Finally on the 30th they had an audience with the King to whom they spoke as they had done to Rouen, and received similar answers. Very much the same exchanges took place between the two Florentines and other representatives at the court. One of these was Robertet, another, Claude de Seyssel the translator of Thucydides, to whom Valori boasted of the promptness of the Florentines in sending 'some of their first secretaries post haste'.[10]

This promptness, however, turned out to be of little avail, for on the 11th the ratification of the truce arrived. It was to be for three years and each side could name its allies in the pact. France, as was to be expected, named the Florentines. Machiavelli, although 'constantly ready to ride',[11] still put off his departure for various reasons until the beginning of March. Then in short stages and at a leisurely pace he set out for home.

We do not know when he reached Florence. We know that he did not stay there long, because on the 2nd of April he was sent to Piombino. He was to discuss with the local overlord certain suspicious warlike preparations being made in the territory of Siena, explain to him that the Florentines, desiring his preservation, were ready to assist him in their common interests, and exhort him to renew his old friendship with them. It was true that it was of great importance to the Republic that others should not take over his small state; and so the overtures entrusted to Machiavelli were perfectly sincere. But the principal aim of his journey must have been that mentioned at the end of his instructions: to find out which way the wind was blowing in those parts. 'During your stay there you will observe all the qualities of that prince, how the people are disposed, what influence the Sienese have and what influence we have.'[12]

The importance of this legation, as Passerini pompously terms it, was no greater than that ruler and his state were. The Secretary finished his task in a few days, and was back in the Chancery writing letters. A sudden calm had fallen on Italy after the truce between the two kings who had been fighting over her territory. In Romagna the Venetians now contented themselves with what they had taken. Julius II, the warlike nephew of a belligerent Pope, was not yet 'firmly in the saddle'. If it had not been for that interminable Pisan war, now turned into a long siege, it would have seemed like the peace of Octavian.

At this period our interest is drawn, rather than to his official correspondence, to certain military ideas that Machiavelli began to put into practice. He had been brooding over these for many years. Ever since his youth, wars had shown him the baseness, sedition and faithlessness of mercenary troops, and he had seen Florence and Italy ruined by them. Now he had gained greater experience in the Chancery, in the courts, in the disorders of military camps, an idea came to him and left him no peace: to abolish that plague, to make true the words of Petrarch

che l'antico valor
negli italici cor non è morto.

[that ancient valour is not yet dead in Italian hearts].

He had seen the peasants of Romagna, conscripted 'one per house', become soldiers under the hard discipline of don Michele; he had seen the Pisans defend themselves bravely against the mercenaries of Italy and France.

Although the memory of the glorious communal militias was not altogether dead, the idea of a citizen army was so alien to the Florentine mind after a lapse of nearly two centuries, as to appear extravagant and fantastic. Nor, among so many novelties catalogued in the *Riforma santa e preziosa* of the piagnone Domenico Cecchi,[13] would the suggestion of having all able-bodied citizens trained in arms have seemed the least strange to the few contemporary readers of that popular fable. It is true that *comandati* (conscripts) were at that time recruited from the country districts for the Pisan war and other needs, but these could more aptly be called pioneer companies than soldiers, and they were only used for particular occasions. The Florentine Secretary was the first to make political theory of the national militia, the first to give it practical application with regular levies and stable ordinances under the control of a government official.

Such great novelties were extremely difficult to introduce, but faith gave Machiavelli courage, as well as the increasing favour shown him by the Gonfalonier and his brother the Cardinal. I believe that he spoke to the Cardinal on the subject for the first time during his mission to Rome. It is certain that it was discussed between them at that time, and that the Cardinal's response was prompt, enthusiastic and strongly favourable. When he returned to Florence and discussed the matter with the Gonfalonier and some of the leading citizens, it was felt to be almost impossible to overcome the suspicions of the cautious Florentines. Those who seven years earlier had opposed the plan to give the

Signoria an armed guard, would be hard to convince that this new devilish suggestion was not a plot by the Gonfalonier-for-life to make himself into a tyrant-for-life.

Amid so much opposition Machiavelli wrote to the Cardinal half in despair on the 24th of May 1504, and the latter replied five days later: 'The argument against the militia is invalid *in re tam necessaria et salubri*; and suspicion is not justified *de vi, quae non paretur ad commodum privatum sed publicum.* Do not desist in your efforts, for perhaps one day you shall have the glory of it, if nothing else.'[14] Indeed he had no other reward, but one day he did have the glory. These prophetic words must have been balm to the soul of Machiavelli. The Cardinal's affectionate regard gave him new hope, for in the same letter he calls him 'very dear fellow godparent', and protests his intention to give him other proof of his friendship besides that of being godfather to his children.

Machiavelli combined these military cares with the tasks of the Chancery, which were then largely military too. The Florentines were fighting around Pisa where they had begun their operations with the usual destruction of crops, retaking Librafatta and employing measures to cut off the city from the outside aid which kept it alive. Because such aid could only come from the sea up the Arno, they began by setting a guard on the mouth of the river with narrow galleys, and then they planned to leave the Pisans high and dry by diverting the course of the river. The Gonfalonier took a particular interest in this scheme which Florentine and foreign experts assured him was possible. However, all they achieved was the sinking of 7000 of the Signoria's ducats in the ditches that were dug, and the wearing out of many pens by the Secretary without any tangible result.[15] Opinions have differed as to whether Machiavelli approved the plan or not. Tommasini says not, for no great man may make mistakes, especially for his biographer. I would not care to state this definitely without more evidence. The relations between the Secretary and Soderini who was the guiding spirit of the enterprise, cause me some suspicions, and the nature of the plan itself, more daring and ingenious than practical, seems wonderfully to accord with the genius of Machiavelli.

The last hopes of this watery enterprise were washed away in the first autumn floods. At that time, towards the end of October, Machiavelli completed a poem in 550 lines representing 'the labours of Italy for ten years and *his* own for a fortnight',[16] and starting from the descent of Charles VIII. As to the *terminus a quo,* which was clearly the beginning of many new things, one cannot speak of coincidence, while for the *terminus ad quem* fortune served the poet well in the last deeds of Caesar Borgia (still his fateful prince!), who having freed himself from the claws of Julius II, was first welcomed and then betrayed by Gonsalvo, when

> *gli pose la soma*
> *che meritava un ribellante a Cristo*

[he dealt him the punishment deserved by a rebel against Christ].

Machiavelli was not to discuss him again in prose or verse. Borgia was sent a prisoner to Spain and died there fighting: once he had stepped out of the history of Italy, he had really for Machiavelli 'slipped into the tomb'. Thus the story of ten years could be ended in a manner suited to a popular ballad, with the sad end of an evil-doer.

The first *Decennale*[17] tells us many things which the biographer is obliged to reduce to a few and to deal with in a short space. First, his long study and great affection for the *Divine Comedy*, which here appears for the first time, not so much in the choice of *terza rima* as in the use of expressions, forms and verses taken from Dante.[18] Secondly it tells us that Machiavelli was more a poet when he wrote in prose than when he wrote in verse, and that if verse is hardly suitable for the discussion, as in this case, of historical and political matters, still less can his robust, realistic style adapt itself to the rhythm of verse. There are a few fine lines, and many pungent sayings which became so popular that they passed into proverbial use. Because of these sayings, some vigorous thoughts and its patriotic sentiments, the poem is not unworthy of Machiavelli, who has here given us a true self-portrait with his inner fire and his perpetual ambiguous smile.

The dedication of the *Decennale* to Alamanno Salviati is of political origin: it was he who had saved the Republic at the time of the Arezzo rebellion. In fact the great military innovation Machiavelli planned and dreamed of, had to reckon with Salviati, who with Giovambattista Ridolfi and others had placed himself at the head of the faction opposing Soderini. This plan was meeting with so many difficulties that at the end of October the Gonfalonier himself had cooled off almost completely. Even the Cardinal, who had stood godfather to yet another child born to Machiavelli exactly nine months after his return from Rome,[19] had given up the cause, and was offering excuses for his brother.[20]

But the Florentine Secretary did not lose courage, and made up for the coldness of others with his own burning enthusiasm,

tanto che si consuma a dramma a dramma,

[so that he is consumed drop by drop],

while he still exhorts the Florentines and particularly the dissident Salviati to support his military plans:

ma sarebbe el cammin facile e corto
se voi el tempio riapriste a Marte

[but the road would be short and easy, if you would reopen the temple of Mars].

These are the last two lines of the *Decennale* that close its political forecast almost like a popular horoscope. But the forecast is by Machiavelli, and so it is well worth following the poet as he enumerates the causes which led him to prophesy wars soon to break out on the fair fields of Italy:

'l Papa vuole
guarir la Chiesa delle sue ferite.
L'Imperator con sua unica prole
vuol presentarsi al successor di Pietro.
Al Gallo il colpo ricevuto duole

[the Pope wishes to cure the wounds of the Church. The Emperor with his only child wishes to present himself to the successor of St. Peter. The Gaul is smarting from the blow].

The Florentines too, and the Venetians, had their share:

Marco, pien di paura e pien di sete
fra la pace e la guerra tutto pende;
e voi di Pisa troppa voglia avete . . .

[St. Mark, fearful and greedy, hesitates between war and peace; and you have too great a desire for Pisa].

'Between war and peace', St. Mark, pressed by the Pope who wished 'to cure the wounds of the Church', reached a short-lived agreement with him. Between war and peace, Venice subsidized Bartolomeo d'Alviano who had left the banners of Gonsalvo and allied himself with Petrucci, the Vitelli and Giampaolo Baglioni, nominally in defence of their own states, but in fact against the Florentines. They in their turn through their 'too great desire for Pisa', suffered on the 27th of March 1505, near Ponte a Cappellese, a tiresome if not too serious defeat.

At that time Machiavelli was doing his usual work in the Chancery, writing letter after letter. More important to us than this official correspondence[21] are the very few remaining private letters of this period. There is a letter from his brother Totto, still hunting after ecclesiastical benefices;[22] there is a very affectionate one from Niccolò Valori, who laments (like all our author's correspondents) that he has had no reply to several letters, so much so that, having also stood god-father to Machiavelli's latest child, he had the impression of having made an enemy not a friend by accepting to do so. Weary of the French legation Valori turned to the man who held both keys to the heart of Piero Soderini to obtain his return. He felt that at the French court they needed 'a man of great ability and few words', and he wanted Machiavelli to take his place in France when he left.[23]

But Machiavelli did not go to France. He only went to Castiglione del Lago to see Giampaolo Baglioni, lord of Perugia, who after ratify-ing the renewal of his commission with Florence, had given it up with the excuse that he could not defend anyone else's territory while he had to protect his own. Baglioni's commission was one of the most im-portant for the Republic, and the Florentines already weakened by the defeat at Cappellese were in some danger from his sudden defection, particularly if it had been plotted with their enemies. As always when they needed to see clearly in troubled waters, they sent Machiavelli. His instructions were to press Giampaolo not so much to bring him back to his agreement as to find out whether his withdrawal was due to greed or to some less evident cause.[24]

He set off, therefore, arriving on the 11th of April at Castiglione del Lago, where before and after dinner he conversed with Baglioni for more than three hours. In this lengthy skirmish Machiavelli 'scored hits right and left', and made him 'change countenance' several times. At one point, Baglioni said that he had consulted many Perugian lawyers; to which Machiavelli replied 'that these matters were not to be decided by lawyers but by men of honour; and that those who held arms in high regard and wished thereby to attain glory had nothing so precious to lose as their good faith; and that it seemed to him Baglioni was gambling with his at this moment': everyone would look on him as 'a stumbling horse'. Although Baglioni stood firm in his resolve, as though it were no longer in his power to change, Machiavelli with feints and thrusts twice made him betray himself and utter words which, combined with information picked up on the spot, sufficed to show Machiavelli and the Ten that there was a secret agreement between Baglioni, the Orsini, Pandolfo and the Luccans. Giampaolo knew the dangers of his situation, and had been 'for two months as though distracted, and never once smiled spontaneously'—so Machiavelli was told. He must have smiled even less after Machiavelli had warned him 'that he should think well on the choice he was making which was weightier than all Perugia'.[25]

The troubles of the Florentines were now aggravated since they were at the same time ill-provided with forces and fully aware of their enemies. They gave up the idea of enlisting Alviano, which would have been a cunning but misguided plan to protect themselves by employing the very man they feared might attack them—and turned instead to the Marquis of Mantua. As negotiations with him were meeting with difficulties, Machiavelli was sent to Mantua with instructions drawn up on the 4th of May. But neither he nor anyone else was able to bring the negotiations to a successful conclusion.[26] Hardly had he returned when the Gonfalonier discussed sending him to Naples to negotiate with Gonsalvo who was sending troops from there by sea to Pisa and might possibly be trying to implicate Alviano. However, the plan was wrecked by those leading citizens whose opposition to Soderini and to anyone who enjoyed his confidence was growing daily. Someone else was sent in his stead.[27] It is true that Machiavelli could not get out of going to Siena, but that was forty miles instead of four hundred and must have seemed to him a good exchange.

This was how matters stood: Pandolfo Petrucci had warned the Florentines that Alviano had decided to attack them and was already on the move. This did not surprise anyone because it was known that the storm would come from that direction, and soon. What was surprising was that Pandolfo, who was the originator and partner in all these plots, should suddenly have become so solicitous for the safety of Florence. The envoy was therefore, while apparently there to thank him, to find out the cause of this miraculous conversion.[28]

Reaching Siena on the 17th of July before the city gates opened, he talked with Pandolfo 'on his rising'. Pandolfo was a cleverer adversary than Giampaolo Baglioni: it was not difficult to discover that his object was to extort from the Florentines in their present danger the abandonment of their rights in Montepulciano. What faith one could have in the help and in the contradictory advice he offered was hard to judge. Machiavelli tried to make him understand who he was dealing with. He wrote to the Ten: 'So that he should understand that others were alive to these equivocations whether natural or accidental, I thought it well to tell him that these negotiations left me so confused that I did not know if I was coming or going'; and he then went on to confront him with all his contradictions. He wrote seven letters to the office in a week on the subject.[29] Finally, on the 24th of July, being at the end of his patience and his money, he asked permission to leave, but by then his friend Buonaccorsi had already obtained from the Gonfalonier both his leave and his money.[30]

For some months past in fact, first the negotiations with Alviano and then his military movements had given food for thought and action to the chanceries and the gossips. The smoke was not without fire, but in the end the fire turned out to be a small one. Having reached San Vincenzo on the 17th of August, Alviano was met there by the Florentines led by Ercole Bentivoglio, and after a long struggle defeated. Practically all his men were captured or disarmed, and his standards and transport were lost. The Florentines were emboldened by this victory: it went to the Gonfalonier's head, and gave fresh courage to Bentivoglio and the commissioner Giacomini. It was decided to attempt to take Pisa. Preparations were put in hand with great speed to forestall the rainy season and the arrival of reinforcements from Gonsalvo. Machiavelli too was sent to the scene of operations.[31] But the fortunes of the enterprise were not equal to the hopes they had cherished. The army arrayed itself before the walls on the 6th of September, and in the following days two great breaches were opened in the walls by the artillery, but the infantry lacked courage for the assault. They were obliged therefore to quit the field in a way that brought little glory to the Florentines and still less credit to the reputation of Italian arms.

The poor performance of those mercenaries gave Machiavelli new courage and new arguments in support of his military plan, and persuaded the Gonfalonier and his friends to listen to it with greater favour. When they had overcome their doubts and got down to discussing the means, it was considered necessary 'for the reputation and preservation of so great a measure', to debate and decide the matter in the Council, particularly as Soderini, remembering the recent opposition and suspicion and doubting whether some of the leading citizens would ever give their consent, preferred as usual to rely on the agreement of the people. But then 'considering that as it is a new and unusual matter the people would not agree if they had not first seen some sample', he began without consultation and on the sole authority of the Signoria to recruit men in the most military-minded areas like Mugello and Casentino.[32]

First it was necessary to think of a way of educating these people in the discipline of arms, and Machiavelli who was now conducting the whole affair, found someone suitable for his purpose. The notorious don Michele, Borgia's lieutenant, whom the Florentines had captured and sent to the Pope, had finally been set free. Under this 'extremely cruel, terrible and much feared man' Niccolò had seen the peasants of Romagna become soldiers. This was the man he needed to transform into soldiers the peasants of Mugello and Casentino.

Looking to the ends rather than to the means, it was easy enough to persuade the Gonfalonier. It was more difficult to overcome the resistance of the citizens since don Michele's name was infamous and Borgia's memory hated. There were even some who suspected Soderini of wishing to tread in Borgia's footsteps! Machiavelli carefully sounded Giovambattista Ridolfi, Piero Guicciardini and others on the matter and found them all hostile. So, without taking other advice, the Gonfalonier put the commission to the vote in the Council of Eighty and got it accepted. The opposition, in the circumstances, could only express its displeasure and await the outcome.[33]

It was yet to be seen whether this militia would win battles, but Machiavelli had certainly won his. There was no holding him back now. He went in person to conscript the men from Mugello; and the first day of the year 1506 found him happily impatient to begin this new institution. He was not put off by the rigours of the season, and on the 2nd of January, reporting to the Ten on the men chosen and conscripted, he ended his letter facetiously: 'I commend myself to your Lordships and to these north winds, that teach me to go about on foot.'[34]

The Ten replied with letters of praise and encouragement, but he needed no urging on. Here we find him overcoming the resistance of the subjects, willing enough to take arms, but afraid that under it all there was some devilish plot concerned with taxes; here we find him holding the balance between the enmities of different villages and of different factions. He returned to Florence for a few days, and then he is back again in Mugello inscribing and collecting troops. On the 27th of January he is in Pontassieve enrolling the men of that area; from there he goes to Dicomano and San Godenzo, then back to Pontassieve to review the fresh troops.[35]

These soldiers had 'a white doublet, a pair of trousers half white, half red, a white cap, and shoes, an iron breastplate and lance, and some with guns'.[36] Machiavelli made them 'exercise and drill in the Swiss manner',[37] that is, in the German fashion. In Florence the first parade took place on the 15th of February 1506, a carnival day, in the Piazza della Signoria. The surly and cautious optimates 'condemned it terribly', but the common people were delighted. Reflecting their view, Landucci showed himself wiser than the wise when he wrote of it in his Diary: 'It was the finest spectacle that has ever been organized in the city of Florence.'[38]

Chapter 9

THE FLORENTINE HISTORIES
THE SECOND LEGATION TO JULIUS II

◇◇◇

A<small>T</small> the sight of Machiavelli the man of the pen suddenly becoming the man of military affairs, historians and biographers alike proclaim his patriotism. I shall certainly not be the first to deny him that virtue. Beyond the love for his own small city state and its liberties, which has been recognized in him since his own times, there is no one today who does not see in him more clearly than in any other Italian of his age the glimmerings of a loyalty to a wider nation.

But fairness requires us to make a distinction and to admit that the fervour and preoccupation of the Florentine Secretary for the Militia were primarily the fervour and preoccupation of a man for the favourite child of his own mind, for the success of an idea vigorously attacked by its opponents. Not only his pride was at stake: this was the ship in which Machiavelli and his future embarked together. Nor must we forget the ardour of his passionate nature: for him a theory, an idea were the same as a flag.

Besides, this restless spirit yearning for new things, '*equitandi, evagandi ac cursitandi tam avidus*', was perhaps happier recruiting soldiers than writing letters in the Chancery. Among the small joys of those days in which everything for him had the taste of victory, came the first edition of the *Decennale*—just at the time when he had finished conscripting in Mugello and was on his way to Casentino. His assistant Agostino Vespucci had it printed at his own expense with a dedicatory letter to the Florentines which is of greater importance than has hitherto been believed.[1] In this letter the work is praised and described not as a payment but as an earnest of the author's debt to his native Florence—'which (i.e. the payment) is being made in his workshop on a larger scale and with more expense of sweat'. It is clear that the reference is to a broader historical work by Machiavelli, not in vague and hypothetical terms, but as a present reality. What was being made in his workshop was already more than a determination to continue the traditional annals of the Florentine chancellors: the work was already well ahead with the collection of source material. Here at last we have the explanation of the many copies and extracts of office documents, mostly belonging to that decade, which are partly in Machiavelli's own hand or apograph, partly written by his assistants: copies and extracts certainly made at this period and not *post res perditas* when he was to write his Florentine histories commissioned by a Medici cardinal.[2] His friend Agostino was something of a prophet when he concluded that the author destined his *Decennale* to contemporary readers and his forthcoming histories to posterity.

Posterity must also be grateful to the *Decennale* for all that Machiavelli put into it for himself, for the affection he had for it, and also for the little consolation his first printed work brought him. He at once gave copies to his friends and to the public figures with whom he had official dealings, receiving from them real praise, not mere polite compliments. Among others, Ercole Bentivoglio, captain general of the Florentines, wrote to him on the 25th of February 1506 a long letter praising the elegant brevity of the work.[3] No such praises can give an idea of the popularity and wide diffusion of the poem better than a pirated edition which appeared about three weeks after the original publication.

Machiavelli heard of it while he was in Casentino enlisting soldiers, having reached Poppi on the 28th of February.[4] At once he informed his assistant and editor Vespucci, who after strenuous efforts discovered that the competition came from the printer Andrea Ghirlandi da Pistoia, who was in partnership with ser Antonio Tubini—two names more familiar to modern bibliographers than they can have been to Vespucci. He got hold of a copy of their edition and wrote to Machiavelli about 'the wretched thing it is'—'a complete fraud, with no spacing, and the quires very small, with no blank page in front or behind; the type is bad with many misprints'.[5]

Brandishing the *corpus delicti*, and full of indignation and zeal for his friend's honour and interests, Vespucci went to the Eight and lodged a complaint against Ghirlandi, then to the Archbishop's Vicar to put his case against the priest Tubini. In both places victory was complete; the sale of the edition was forbidden. The Vicar strongly rebuked Tubini, expressing the desire to 'punish this priest and make him repent of other vices which he has'.[6] But all these things and others it is best to read in Vespucci's amusing letter, from which the bibliographer may also derive some profit, not only for what one may learn of those two little-known editions of the *Decennale* but also for certain information about the two printers, although our curiosity about the 'other vices' of Antonio Tubini still remains unappeased.

Thus revenged, Machiavelli continues to collect soldiers in Casentino in the cold season among the snow-covered mountains with his head-quarters in Poppi. He gets worried, and storms if they delay in sending him arms for the new soldiers. Never can the armourers have worked so hard in Florence. On the 5th of March he writes to the Ten to urge them to speed up deliveries, 'for I can do nothing more here if the arms do not come, and I am wasting my time'. Impatient with these difficulties, he gives up for the time being the idea of conscripting from the Chiusi district which was very large and 'so best tackled after the snows had passed'.[7]

So leaving the mountain snows he returned to manage the affairs of the Chancery. March had now come to an end, and it seemed as though the peace of Italy, which had been strengthened by the treaty concluded in the previous October between Spain and France, was now heading in the same direction. The Archduke Philip had gone to Spain to take possession of Castile and share the kingdoms with Ferdinand of Aragon, who was to come to Italy to take over the kingdom of Naples. These movements were discussed and feared, but more imminent dangers of war seemed to lie, as Machiavelli had foreseen in his *Decennale*, in the arrival of the fickle and foolish Maximilian, and in the enterprises of Julius II, who wanted to 'cure the Church of its wounds'. Julius before his elevation 'had always been full of vast and immeasurable designs',[8] but since he had attained high office he appeared less formidable. Yet he had not changed: he was merely 'settling into the saddle', making his preparations and collecting funds.

These were the matters which gave the chanceries most to write about in the spring of 1506; and as an example one should see how subtly Machiavelli writes of them in a long 'bible' which he sent in mid-June to Giovanni Ridolfi, commissioner general against Pisa.[9] We know that in the end pens always succeed in setting arms to work, unless and until the opposite happens. The first movements of troops, as everyone expected, were those of the Pope, and Machiavelli was sent to observe these movements at close quarters.

Julius II had informed the Florentines that he wanted to 'clear of tyrants' the lands of the Church, and asked that their captain Marcantonio Colonna with his troops should serve him in his expedition against Bentivoglio. The Republic disliked this request for various reasons, and not only because it diminished their forces before Pisa. When the matter was discussed, the opinion of the Gonfalonier prevailed, supported by Giovambattista Ridolfi, not to oppose the Pope's demand but to play for time as long as possible.[10] The commission was therefore entrusted to Machiavelli, who was by now accustomed and resigned to temporising missions. In compensation he bore to Julius II a small store of fine words to 'praise his good and holy intent.'[11]

Leaving on the night of the 25th–26th of August,[12] he met the Pope at Nepi on the 27th, the latter having started from Rome the day before with a great following of cardinals, courtiers and soldiers. He obtained an audience in Civita Castellana and made a fine speech,[13] in which after compliments and congratulations he stated the difficulties over Colonna's participation more strongly than had been done in his commission, which he finally drew from his bosom and read to the Pope. Julius listened 'attentively and cheerfully', and then he replied that from what he had heard it seemed that the Florentines feared three things: that France was not a partner to the enterprise; that he himself was going into it without enthusiasm; that he might come to an agreement with Bentivoglio without driving him out, or that having ejected him, he might allow him to return.

It was quite true that the Florentines feared these three things, and regarded them as a much greater obstacle to participation than the loss of their troops, for as to the first point, they could not go against the wishes of the King who had Bentivoglio under his protection. As for the other two, it could not please them very much to have to come out against a neighbour with whom until then they had maintained friendly relations, if he were later, through the Pope's clemency or lack of zeal, to be left in his state. The Pope reassured the envoy as to the first matter, showing him letters from the King which encouraged him in his enterprise and promised his aid. As for the second, he assured Machiavelli that he could not be more enthusiastic for the campaign, for he was leading it himself and was already on his way. And as for the third objection, he said that Bentivoglio would be mad to remain in Bologna as a private citizen, which was the only capacity in which he would permit him to stay.

In the evening as Machiavelli followed behind the Pope, 'who was viewing this fortress and marvelling at its construction', His Holiness called him and repeated what he had told him in the morning. The envoy assured him that the help offered by his Republic would not be the last to reach him, and the Pope thereupon told him how many men he had and how many he would eventually have, 'and his pockets were full of soldiers'. He said that he did not wish to take advantages of the great offers made him by the Venetians, so as not to be obliged to concede to them what they had already taken from the Church to his own and the Florentines' loss. The Pope's words suggested that Colonna would be asked for before the French reinforcements came,[14] and this did not please the Florentines.

However, things went off quietly, and Machiavelli led a very peaceful life as he followed this travelling court. Through Viterbo, Orvieto, Castel della Pieve, and Castiglione del Lago, the Pope came by easy stages to Perugia where the first account was to be settled, with Giampaolo Baglioni. This account, in fact, appeared to be already closed, since Giampaolo had come to meet his creditor at Orvieto, placing himself in his hands and giving him hostages and fortresses and anything else he could ask for. But Machiavelli thought it was the Pope who was putting himself in the hands of the villain Giampaolo when he entered Perugia on the 13th of September. Writing to the Ten as he did nearly every day,[15] and observing that Baglioni had in his power Pope and College, he concluded: 'If he does no harm to the man who has come to take away his state, it will only be out of kindness and humanity. How this affair will end I cannot tell.'[16]

It ended happily. It is easy to say to those who held up their hands in horror at these famous words, that Machiavelli was a politician reasoning coldly on the political relations between two princes: for such appeared to him a Pope who behaved as a prince not as a Pope—a prince who had come at the head of his army to dispossess another prince. Guicciardini too, writing after the affair was long over and with mature consideration, was surprised that on that occasion Giampaolo had 'been unable to make resound throughout the world in so great an affair the perfidy which had already blackened his name in much smaller things'.[17] A parricide such as he was, was held back by cowardice, not by conscience or respect of those who did not deserve respect. Machiavelli and Guicciardini do not say that this smaller edition of Caesar Borgia would have done well to take the Pope prisoner: they say that it was in his power to do so, and that the Pope had been unwise to trust him. What Giampaolo did not do then with Julius, the Colonna faction were to do with less provocation with Clement VII, and on that occasion too Machiavelli was to mock the Pope, reproaching him with having 'believed more in a penful of ink than in a thousand soldiers'.

The Pope enjoyed his first triumph and remained in Perugia until the 22nd of September. In almost a month he had made little progress. He lingered, waiting for help from the French who would draw in with them the Florentines. But the King, hearing that Maximilian had revived his plans and preparations for entering Italy, instead of soldiers sent advice, which proved very unwelcome to the enthusiastic and impatient Julius. As early as the 12th of September in one of his frequent conversations with Machiavelli he had told him that if France had played him false and the Emperor's coming was not genuine or imminent, 'he might well place his own honour before any consideration of danger or damage to the Church or to anyone else'.[18]

In this state of mind, followed by the court and his troops, Julius moved to Cesena passing through Gubbio and Urbino. Machiavelli followed too. Finally the news came that the King was sending his forces and this 'so encouraged the Pope that, imagining himself already victor of Bologna, he began to think of some other greater enterprise'.[19] On the 3rd of October he made a boastful speech to the ambassadors of Bentivoglio saying among other things that he had 'forces to make all Italy tremble let alone Bologna'.

While the French were on the way, he held a review of the forces he had with him at Cesena on the 5th of October. Machiavelli, immersed as he was in military matters, could not fail to be present at the parade. He watched with expert eye and reported to the Ten, concluding with these words: 'If you could see these soldiers of the Duke of Urbino and those of Nanni, Your Lordships would not be ashamed of your own conscripts or think them of little worth.'[20] His friend Buonaccorsi in a letter written at that time commented humorously on these words spoken *pro domo sua*: 'You brought a bit of tallow to the ship on the subject of the soldiers.'[21]

The ship of the militia continued to sail along happily during these long absences of its steersman, and Biagio did not fail to send him from time to time some extracts from the log book.[22] Information of all kinds was packed into his letters which he very often enclosed with official communications: political news, about the King of Castile who had died almost as soon as he had begun to taste the honey and the gall of his kingdom, or about Maximilian who, with his eternal see-sawing, gave the impression of throwing the dice every day to see whether he should come or not; news of the city and of the office, where there was now talk of recalling Machiavelli, seeing that in the Papal court 'he was not killing himself with work',[23] and so his lieutenant was already looking forward to having less work to do and to sitting 'in a corner dreaming'; he also related that Alamanno Salviati when dining with some friends had called Machiavelli a rogue,[24] for he was now included with the Gonfalonier in a common hatred. This was Salviati's thanks for the dedication of the *Decennale*.

The letter of the 'tallow for the ship' is dated the 11th of October and is humorously addressed 'to Forlì or wherever the devil he may be'. In fact Machiavelli was in Forlì from the 9th, and from there the Pope followed up the interdict ordered on the 7th in Cesena with a powerful bull against Bentivoglio. Suspecting that bulls alone would not suffice to take Bologna, when the French forces were quite near, he called for Machiavelli and told him that he was now ready to use Marcantonio Colonna and his men: the Florentines had promised that they would not be the last to send him help, but if they did not want to be the last, they had better hurry up. Machiavelli should therefore send a messenger riding post to tell them this in Florence. The envoy counted up the days that would be needed. They 'seemed too many' to the impetuous pontiff.[25]

When Machiavelli came to him again on the 16th of October with the news that Colonna had already had his orders to set off, and with his orders had received the money needed for the time he had to serve, Julius's joy was boundless. Being then at table he called all those around him to hear the letter from the Ten. As he had decided, in order to avoid Venetian territory, to travel over that of the Florentines, Machiavelli told him that he would at once ride ahead to make provision for the Pope, his court and troops in their journey through this ill-provided country.[26]

This he did. The tireless Secretary became quartermaster, and through Castrocaro, Modigliana, Marradi and Palazzuolo he preceded or accompanied the court. His letters to the Ten were few and brief, more concerned with victuals than with politics; but from Palazzuolo he again discussed the actions of Julius II: 'If he succeeds at Bologna, he will lose no time in attempting something greater; and it is felt that now or never Italy will defeat those who have designed to swallow her up.'[27] Reaching Imola on the 20th, the Bolognese ambassadors complained to him 'politely', while waiting in the Papal antechamber, of those troops which the Florentines were sending against their master. To which he replied laughing that their master had taught the Florentines 'to swim with the current', and that he should complain not of the ways of the Florentines but of those which the Florentines had to their cost learnt from him.[28] After what Bentivoglio had done in the days of Caesar Borgia, this reply was a master stroke, delivered in a style that, with its blunt humour, is typical of Machiavelli.

It was a Parthian shot. Several days earlier Francesco Pepi had been elected ambassador to the Pope, and he arrived in Imola on the 26th of October. He was to see the surrender of the city after Bentivoglio's departure, and the Pope's solemn entry on the 11th of November. Machiavelli, who had remained in Imola another two days after the ambassador's arrival, was back in Florence for All Saints' day.[29]

Here, while waiting for the birth of another child—a yearly event[30]— he entirely immersed himself in the affairs of his dear Militia. The ship— to go on with Buonaccorsi's image—instead of tacking, now suddenly made for the open sea under full sail. On the 6th of December were created the *Nove ufficiali dell'ordinanza e milizia fiorentina* [the nine officers of the Florentine ordinance and militia], then the first magistrature to be set up to govern permanently the military affairs of a state. Everything great or small was inspired and sustained by Machiavelli, who at that time, when the order for setting up the Nine was going through (and it was he who drew up the order too),[31] wrote a *Discorso dell'ordinare lo stato di Firenze alle armi* [Discourse on the military organization of the state of Florence][32], a lucid and remarkable work in which he goes into the minutest details of the new order after having begun from general principles: 'To speak of men who command . . . implies the possession of judicial authority and arms: you have little of the former and none at all of the latter.'

The new office of the Nine required a Secretary, and this could only be Machiavelli,[33] while he remained of course chancellor of the second Chancery and secretary of the Ten. This meant that he had several jobs for one salary, but unlike what happens today, progress had not yet suggested any alternative. Besides, although the Secretary liked money, if only to spend it, he was no less fond of praise and reputation, and he got so much of both for this achievement of his that he regarded himself as well paid. The most enthusiastic of all was cardinal Soderini, who wrote from Bologna in the warmest of terms: 'We do not believe that in Florence anything as worthy and well-founded as this has been done for some long time' in defence of its new freedom, 'a divine gift not a product of men.'[34]

Agostino Vespucci also wrote to him from Bologna where he had recently been sent. Offering his congratulations he begged Machiavelli to get him the job as his assistant with the Nine, as he was already for the Ten. He also told him of certain gossip according to which Pepi had asked to be recalled and Machiavelli was coming back to the Papal court.[35] I cannot say whether this went further than gossip, but Machiavelli was too keen to organize the new office in those early days not to have resisted anything which might have distracted him from the work he had begun. Progressing with his usual enthusiasm he spent thirty-four successive days from the 14th of March to the 17th of April conscripting soldiers in the areas of Pieve Santo Stefano, Anghiari, Val di Chiana, Chianti, Poggibonsi, Colle, San Gimignano and Pomarance.[36] He went back to San Gimignano, and possibly also to the other places in May for the review of troops.[37]

The Gonfalonier was more than ever devoted to Machiavelli, and the Secretary would have had no difficulty in persuading him to any measure that this work required, but he also had the assistance of cardinal Soderini, who had always been generous to him in this way and promised him yet greater things in a letter of the 4th of March 1507.

In this letter the Cardinal aptly wrote: 'Your satisfaction cannot be small that so worthy an institution has been begun through your efforts', *pro salute et dignitate patriae*. Machiavelli had sent him his *Discorso dell'ordinare lo stato di Firenze alle armi*,[38] to which the Cardinal replied: 'The things which you have written are such as may be read by every man of discrimination; and if, as you say and we believe, you have not put all your energy into this work, consider of what great merit will be the works to which you devote all the power of your intellect.' He could hardly have hit the nail more squarely on the head.

97

Chapter 10

THE GERMAN LEGATION
THE WAR AND
THE RETAKING OF PISA

◇◇◇

U NDER the rule of the Gonfalonier Soderini, and in more prosperous times, Florence was again flourishing and tasting that happiness which nations enjoy when their leaders are good, wise, and moderate. When he was elected he found the city practically ruined, and he therefore devoted his attention to administering her finances with the utmost diligence, exercising that extreme parsimony which he applied in his own private affairs. In four years he had restored the city's economy, revived the government's credit and lightened the taxes. He trusted the people and they trusted him. On the other hand, the hatred and suspicion which some of the Optimates felt for him, had increased. It seemed to these few leaders of great families, among whom were Alamanno Salviati and Giovambattista Ridolfi,[1] that he did not take enough heed of them. This was quite true, for the Gonfalonier, seeing that in the small councils he was overshadowed by their wisdom and reputation, preferred to govern through the Signoria and the Colleges or the Council of Eighty, where men of lesser stature were in the majority and readier to give way to the authority of his office and his greater experience of public affairs. The suspicions and displeasure of the Optimates therefore increased, so that eventually they opposed all his plans simply to annoy and humiliate him, while Soderini, when one of his proposals was checked by them, would turn to those with whom he more easily found favour, and with obstinate perseverance usually succeeded in carrying them with him.

Machiavelli, as we have already said, was identified with the Gonfalonier in these hatreds, and was referred to as his 'mannerino',[2] meaning his tool and go-between—a description that has affinities with the 'ribaldo' applied to him earlier on by Alamanno Salviati. It is not surprising that in this battle the squire received a few blows as well as his master. In the space of a few pages we have already noted more than one, and another is just about to fall.

Julius II for a while had been quiet, but the peace of Italy had been broken at the beginning of 1507 by an insurrection at Genoa, promptly subdued by the King of France, whose subsequent meeting with the King of Aragon promised nothing good. After the departure of the two kings from Italy, the fears of Maximilian's coming increased once more. By reviving the ghost of the Holy Roman Empire and playing on the theme of German honour at the Diet of Constance he had managed to secure promises of large quantities of troops and money to invade Italy, drive the King of France out of Lombardy and receive the Imperial Crown in Rome.

Maximilian's reputation could not have been lower with the Florentines: it was a matter of ridicule. They were too far away both in distance and spirit to appreciate his qualities as a good and generous and noble prince, and only saw his unhappy enterprises, his vain and varied efforts to reconcile grand designs and continual lack of means. But when they heard of the promises made to him at the Diet, they began to fear that German pride might have suddenly knit together those divided members, and that the acquisition of so much power would give Maximilian greater force and determination.

They decided, therefore, to send to him an envoy who should watch his preparations and movements, and try to find out how much his friendship would cost the city should he enter Italy. It was a matter of some importance, since it also affected their friendship with France. The Gonfalonier, who wanted someone he could rely on, had Machiavelli chosen for this mission. 'As he was making his preparations to leave', an outcry arose from the usual opposition 'that someone else should be sent, there being in Florence many worthy young men suitable to go, who ought to have the experience'. As a result Soderini had to give way. The nomination was altered, and on the 27th of June Francesco

Vettori was sent with the general commission, 'to observe and report, not to negotiate and conclude agreements'.[3]

The defeat was certainly greater for the Gonfalonier than for the Secretary. But the commissioners Filippo da Casavecchia and Alessandro Nasi wrote at once to Machiavelli to sympathize with him and console him. The former, writing from Fivizzano, exhorted him 'to be patient over the German triumph', and not to mind those who prided themselves on having stood in his way. The latter, from Cascina, congratulated his 'dear and by no means unlucky Machiavelli' on his recovery, as if from some unspecified disease, by having 'got the imperial commission out of his system', and offered his opinion that it was much more to his advantage and that of the city that he should stay in Florence instead of going to Germany.[4]

However, it was for German affairs that Machiavelli had to travel again on the 9th of August. The Pope was sending as legate to Maximilian Cardinal Carvajal, and as he had to pass through Florence, the Ten commissioned their secretary to go and see how large his suite was and how they were received by the Sienese. So he went, first to Siena and then, to save time, to San Quirico d'Orcia. He wrote three letters to the Ten, in which having spoken of the number of men and beasts, he criticized the quality of the courtiers, 'who for the most part look as though they come from the *Stinche*'.[5] He also added news which he had picked up: the Legate had instructions to advise against Maximilian's coming, unless it were peacefully; the astute Pandolfo did not believe he would come anyway. Then 'by the most direct road, and slowly', the Secretary returned.

As the news of the imperial arrival grew more urgent, the tempers and differences of the citizens also grew warmer. The Gonfalonier, who was strongly for the French alliance in the old tradition of the Florentine people, would not hear of sending a solemn embassy to Germany as the opposition was demanding (among them Alamanno, who was thereby being true to his name). Amid these disputes and with Francesco Vettori's letters becoming more and more pressing, it was decided to send him fresh instructions as to the tribute to be offered to Maximilian, who after his first volley at 500,000 ducats had lowered his sights.

The Gonfalonier, who had not much confidence in Vettori, protested that it was an affair of the greatest importance and that someone should be sent who could report verbally if letters should go astray. With this, he succeeded in getting them to send his Machiavelli,[6] who at that time was busy looking for a successor to the villainous don Michele as commander of the Militia.[7] The same pretext as he had used to send Machiavelli to France to support Valori now gave Soderini this small revenge over his enemies. His commission briefly was this: to offer up to 50,000 ducats, beginning with 30,000, with certain conditions of payment, and to ask in return for the reintegration and preservation of all the territory of the Republic without any limitation of authority.

It was a bad journey in a bad season. Leaving on the 17th of December and travelling as fast as he could over terrible roads, he reached Lombardy where he already found the smell of war. The French were on the alert, and the envoy, who had been 'examined closely', and feared an even closer investigation, tore up the instructions and the letters he carried.[8] On Christmas Day he was in Geneva, and wrote briefly to the Ten.[9] Then he went on to Bolzano where the court and Vettori were, arriving on the 11th of January 1508. He justified the time it had taken by the length of the journey, the inclemency of the weather and the roads, the weariness of the horses and lack of money, having spent on the way all the 110 ducats he had been given on leaving.[10] He asserted that by making such a wide detour he had not lost more than three days; but they were not wasted since they enabled him to discover in the course of four nights spent on Swiss soil, 'how they lived and what sort of people they were', particularly from a military point of view, and to report on them with great perspicacity to the Ten in his first letter from Bolzano. He also recounted what he had picked up on the way about the Emperor's plans, by constantly exercising with all he met, great and small, his insatiable curiosity. At Constance he talked 'with two Milanese in the Cathedral', sought out the famous musician Ysaach whose wife was in Florence, conversed and dined with an ambassador of the Duke of Savoy who told him: 'You want to know in two hours what I have not been able to find out in many months.'[11]

At Bolzano, having told Vettori what was in the commission he had torn up, he at once sought an audience with the Emperor. The Italians, always inclined to be generous with titles, had been referring thus to the King of the Romans for some time. At the interview, he offered 30,000 ducats in three instalments; and when this offer was immediately refused as unsuitable, he went up to 40,000. Then Maximilian began to show some satisfaction and said he should have an answer the next day.

H   101

Calling one of his courtiers on one side, 'he asked who was this Secretary who had just come'.[12]

The following day went by, ten more days passed, and still no answer came from the King. At last, on the 24th of January Vettori was summoned into the presence of Maximilian to be told that the money was too little and he could not accept it. He wanted 25,000 ducats at once on loan, the price of the tribute to be negotiated with the Florentine ambassadors when he eventually reached the Po. It was a certain payment for a very uncertain return. Vettori refused and asked Florence for new instructions. It was always hard to reach an agreement with the Florentine government over a question of money, and this time the ambassador's task was rendered even more arduous by the immense distance, which often served the Ten to temporize and get out of a difficulty. More than ever this resembled a dialogue between deaf men.

The letters of this legation are almost all written by Machiavelli and in his own hand. Vettori merely signed them, alone, simply adding at the most a few lines in his own hand. He himself was not without merit as a writer,[13] and it is hard to say whether he allowed his companion to wield the pen out of laziness or because he enjoyed using the services of a secretary, or because he felt that Machiavelli could do it better than him. Obviously the two Florentines consulted one another on their attitude and what they would write, and this is quite clear from the correspondence of the legation. 'Niccolò and I had discussed both these matters',[14] Vettori writes at one point; and on another occasion he confesses that without his companion (and what a companion!) 'he would have understood less'.[15] I am aware that it is easy to lose the right perspective in these matters, but I would risk the conjecture that by his greater subtlety of mind, age and experience, the man who took the greater share in these deliberations was the one with the lesser appointment. On other occasions Machiavelli had the functions if not the name of an ambassador. This time he had not even the functions, but he was inclined by nature to lead others, and these letters, in which there are passages which would be recognizable as his even if they were written in Vettori's hand, show that he contributed more than the mere writing.

But because in this kind of joint effort it is not possible to distinguish how much is due to each of the participants, this legation in itself is not of great importance for anyone writing about Machiavelli. It is significant only for his meeting with the Germanic world. Even if it was a fleeting encounter made more difficult by the barrier of the language as well as by the greater difference of customs and way of thought, it was still another window opened to his mind.

If he went to France with Caesar, he went to Germany with Tacitus.[16] A man of his times and education could not do otherwise. Of a country which to a Florentine born in the fifteenth century must have appeared completely barbarous, not least in its immense size, he saw only a part of Switzerland and the Tyrol which was nearest in its alpine ruggedness to Tacitus' description. He knew nothing of the wealth and culture of the great northern cities, and it would not have been of much help to him to do so, reasoning as he did mostly in political and military terms. But in his *Rapporto delle cose dell'Alemagna* [Report on the state of Germany],[17] written the day after his return to Florence, we find, together with errors, omissions, and prejudices natural to its author and the conditions in which he wrote, marvellous flashes of intuition. It is these brilliant moments, not particular facts or truths, that we must seek in Machiavelli. This *Rapporto* was later developed into the *Ritratto delle cose della Magna*,[18] in which he added nothing except improvements to the style and the structure, although after his departure he was still having inquiries made by German booksellers, in search of what I do not know.[19]

It has been said that the Venetian ambassadors' reports are superior to those of Machiavelli. The truth is that the Venetians portrayed with greater diligence and detail the outer appearance of things, while Machiavelli caught the inner spirit in a flash of intuition. In this way, inquiring and speculating from his small observatory in the Tyrol, he might really see in two days what the ambassador of the Duke of Savoy had not seen in two months, and understand at once the eternal contrast between the strength of that nation and its political weakness, thereby anticipating its tragic inability to discover its equilibrium and its road in life.

Meantime the unfortunate Maximilian was bearing the burden of these unhappy political conditions, unable to collect even a part of the money and troops promised by the Diet. Our two Florentines were also in some difficulties, caught between the parsimony of the Republic and the Emperor who was 'at sea with few provisions', between the vague instructions of the Ten and the even greater uncertainties of the Emperor. From Florence they were told they could go up to 50,000 or 60,000, if they thought Maximilian would in fact invade; but whether he would or not, neither Vettori nor Machiavelli knew, nor even Maximilian.

Fresh troops would arrive and encourage the Emperor in his design, whereupon others would leave him and his enthusiasm would cool off. One of his ministers said that anyone could deceive the Emperor once, but never a second time if he had realized the deception. To which Machiavelli sarcastically observed that there were so many people and so many affairs that he might well be deceived every day even if he did notice it every time. It was not surprising, therefore, that the wind changed daily in that court, blowing now hot and now cold for the Italian expedition. The Florentine who was used to French loquacity was further disconcerted by the almost ridiculous secrecy with which everything there was surrounded.

All these secrets added to the vast size of the country and the difficulty of communicating with Florence made Machiavelli and Vettori feel 'as though they were on some lost island'.[20] From Trent where all the ambassadors had followed the Emperor, the two Florentines were sent back with the others to Bolzano and then to Merano in order, it was said, to conceal the movement of troops. The first such move, however, was 'more like a small captain's than a king's'[21]—after which the Venetians gave him a good beating in Cadore.

Maximilian then summoned a diet at Ulm to get help, and as Vettori had fallen ill, it was decided that Machiavelli should go there alone.[22] Unfortunately he did not go, and apart from a trip from Bolzano to Trent where the court was staying, he remained to keep Vettori company, which is a loss to posterity. However, they got on well together, and that legation was the beginning of a friendship which lasted to the end of the Secretary's life:[23] if he drew no other advantage from this, it did give rise to one of the most memorable pages he ever wrote. At that moment the Secretary's company was precious to Vettori. Machiavelli had been asking the Ten for leave to return from the very day of his arrival, but Vettori wrote in his own hand to the opposite effect: 'I beg Your Lordships to have him stay until everything is settled: his presence is necessary.'[24] Meantime, on the 13th of March they both moved to Innsbrück, and from there back to Bolzano and to Trent where they heard the Emperor's final requests: 60,000 ducats in three instalments with short intervals only between them. Machiavelli took up his epistolary labours again to obtain from the Ten a definite commission and the money to back it up. On the 30th of

May he wrote: 'With all respect, Your Lordships have spun this thread so fine that it is impossible to weave it'; and further on, 'I have said before that no one can prevent him from invading in the face of any opposition, because Germany has the power and has only to take the decision to do so; on the other hand no one can be sure he will invade, because Germany has never made up her mind, nor shown any signs of doing so up to this day.' And finally, 'it is essential to choose one way or the other . . . and decide where lies the least danger, and take that road, and make up one's mind on this in God's name, because by trying to measure these great events with a pair of compasses, men only make mistakes.'[25]

But once again events proved right those in Florence who took, as they said, 'the advantage of time'. The Emperor was again thoroughly beaten by the Venetians, and having left in their hands Gorizia, Trieste and the whole of Friuli, and finally Fiume, he made a truce with them. The terms were, briefly, that each side should keep what it had taken, the Venetians all the territory, and the Emperor all the shame and the loss. The invasion of Italy, the coronation in Rome, the punishment of the French, the restoration of Imperial authority, all again took on the inconsistency of dreams. Nor were the Florentines in the habit of taking shadows for reality, or paying for them more than they were worth.

On the 10th of June, while Vettori was getting ready to rejoin the court, Machiavelli who had had his fill of German affairs, and was suffering from gallstones, left Trent with the declared intention of returning home for treatment.[26] Travelling faster than he had done on the way out, he reached Bologna on the 14th, and by the 16th was in Florence.[27]

He must have been suffering from homesickness more than gall-stones if he could ride so rapidly, and shortly after his return endure the hardships of life in the field. In fact, as the Republic was now determined to deal with Pisa once and for all, the ubiquitous Secretary went first to raise the troops of his battalions at San Miniato and Pescia, then accompanied them to Pontedera, and from there on the 21st of August began to lay waste the countryside around the besieged city.[28]

After the King of France and then the King of Aragon had generously taken up the cause of the poor Pisans but only to be able to set a price on them and make a profit of 150,000 ducats in all, the Florentines became even more enthusiastic in their plans for a siege. The moment had come to put the new militia to the test and to profit from it.

Machiavelli was filled with joy, but also with trepidation. First in October, then in November and December he went to raise levies and carry out inspections at San Miniato and in Valdinievole, in the vicariate of Chianti and in Valdicecina.²⁹

At the end of January 1509 he was already on guard with his troops at Mulina di Cuosa; and in mid-February we find him leading a thousand men to the mouth of the Fiumemorto to prevent outside help from reaching the besieged city. The Arno and all the canals were closed with bridges, piles, bastions, while Machiavelli kept his eye on discipline, guard duties, works and everything else. His letters at this time were necessarily brief,³⁰ and as they were read in the council of Eighty, Buonaccorsi begged him, but in vain, to send some of his usual kind.³¹ To their Secretary, 'who hovered everywhere throughout the armies',³² the Ten wrote: 'We have placed on your shoulders the responsibility for all this.'³³

But as all that responsibility was too heavy for these shoulders, 'Niccolò Machiavelli being the only representative of the government in the field',³⁴ Alamanno Salviati and Antonio da Filicaia were sent as commissioners. Before their arrival, on the 4th of March Machiavelli had gone to Lucca on his own initiative to remind that republic of its undertaking not to assist the besieged.³⁵ When the commissioners did arrive, he was sent by the Ten to the Lord of Piombino who had made it known that he had been asked by the Pisans to act as mediator for an agreement with the Florentines. There he was to find out whether there was any truth in this, or whether it was a ruse in order to enjoy 'the advantage of time', for there were movements of war afoot in Italy, from which men without hope might at least hope something. For the Florentines, on the other hand, who nearly had success in their grasp, this was no time for delays.

He went therefore, and on the 14th of March he met Jacopo d'Appiano and the Pisan envoys. The latter began with general remarks, and added that they could not reach any firm decision without the presence of their Signori; whereupon the exchanges became embittered. We must read Machiavelli's report of these: 'To the first part I replied as I thought best; to the second I said that I could not reply as they had said nothing, and if they wanted me to reply, they should say something. They answered that they had said a great deal by asking for guarantees of their life, honour and property. I replied that they should say what guarantees, if they wished me to answer; and if the guarantees were reasonable and honourable, they should not be lacking, since Your Lordships wanted their obedience, not their life, property or honour.'[36] The negotiations broke off, not without Machiavelli making some effort to sow discord among the envoys. He reported to the Ten by letter from Piombino, then personally in Florence; after which he returned to share the life of his soldiers in camp.

On the 16th of April, having heard that the Ten wished him to go to Cascina where the commissioner Niccolò Capponi was looking after the rearguard services and the supplies for the whole army, he wrote: 'I know that being stationed there would be less arduous and dangerous, but if I had not wanted danger and hard work, I should not have left Florence. So may it please Your Lordships to leave me here in the field to work along with the commissioners on matters that arise, for here I can be of some use, but there I should not be doing any good and I would die of despair.'[37] Here one may really speak of patriotic feeling in Machiavelli. And how much more attractive is his passionate nature when it is suddenly revealed beneath that other crude and sarcastic side of his character.

So 'he hovered everywhere throughout the armies', going from one to another of the three camps into which the battalions of the Militia were divided. The soldiers recognized his authority more than that of the commissioners, and this fact on one occasion moved Salviati to utter in anger, when speaking to a constable, words like those he had used about him on another occasion. When Machiavelli wrote to him protesting, Salviati replied denying the insult and justifying his anger by the lack of respect shown to the authority of a commissioner: 'Although they wish to recognize your authority, you are not always present everywhere to command them. I approve that they should love and esteem you because being with you every day, they will be the more obedient and know what they have to do.'[38]

In mid-May Machiavelli left the camp for two or three days, and went to Pistoia to improve the organization of supplies.[39] But the war was now over. On the 20th of May he was with the commissioners negotiating with certain Pisan envoys for the first stages in the surrender of the city. There are some letters in his own hand written to the Ten to give an account of these moves.[40] An embassy of the conquered city went to Florence, and the ubiquitous Machiavelli with it. When agreement was reached and the treaty signed, his name appeared below that of the first Secretary Marcello Virgilio in the act of surrender of the city on the 4th of June.[41] On the 8th, after a war that had lasted fifteen years, the Florentine commissioners entered Pisa, and with them went Machiavelli and his battalions.

Amid the joy of victory which then possessed the Florentines, I cannot say how many remembered the humble Secretary to recognize the part he had played and give him the praise he deserved; but there were certainly some who did. Agostino Vespucci wrote to him that same day: 'congratulations on having been present on such a glorious occasion, and having had no small part in the affair.' And he goes on: 'I would make bold to say that you, with your battalions, have produced so fine an institution that, not slowly but rapidly, you have restored the dominion of Florence. I do not know what to say. I swear to God, we are so happy that I could write a Ciceronian oration for you.'[42] And Filippo da Casavecchia: 'A thousand congratulations on the great acquisition of this noble city, for it may be truly said to have been your work, or at any rate the greater part of it.' He goes on further: 'I do not think that your philosophy can ever be understood by stupid people, and there are not enough of the clever ones, you understand me. . . . Every day I see more clearly that you are the greatest prophet the Jews or any other people ever had. Niccolò, Niccolò, truly I tell you that I cannot express all that I would like to say.'[43]

Machiavelli never saw his own name carved in marble as a perpetual memorial to that triumphal entry into Pisa, as were the names of Salviati (who, soon after, died there of malaria), Filicaia and Capponi. He was satisfied with these praises simply written on paper, where the passage of time, which usually does the opposite, has transformed into simple truth what was at that time probably exaggeration and adulation.

Chapter 11

MISSION TO MANTUA AND VERONA
THE THIRD MISSION TO FRANCE

◇◇◇

W HILE the small fire of the Pisan war was dying down
quietly, a far worse conflagration was burning up in Italy.
At Cambrai the league between the King of France and
Maximilian was formed against Venice, and joined with some reluc-
tance by Julius II and the King of Aragon, so that in the spring of
1509 all were attacking the Venetians. In Lombardy they were defeated
on the 14th of May between the Mincio and the Adda, and lost Ber-
gamo and Brescia. In Romagna, Faenza was lost on the 24th and immediately afterwards Ravenna, and giving way before the armies of the
Pope, they handed over Rimini and Cervia without a struggle. Overwhelmed by the victory of French arms, Verona, Vicenza and Padua
fell too, and the Emperor was able to take possession of them in virtue
of the agreements signed at Cambrai, not through any prowess of his
own troops.

After the worst was over, the Emperor came down from his mountains with a large army put together at the expense of the Pope and the
King of France. His arrival, tardy, irresolute and ridiculous, only re-
sulted in his losing part of what the arms of others had won; for Padua
was regained by the Venetians, and though Maximilian surrounded it
with a large army and a remarkable array of artillery, he had to withdraw with the usual humiliation. He first retired to Verona, and thence,
having vainly sought help from the French and asked the Venetians for
a truce which the vanquished refused him, the victor, he withdrew still
further to safer territory.

However, before leaving Verona he had entered into an agreement with the Florentines over the famous tribute, by which they were to pay him 40,000 florins in four instalments. It was a smaller sum than that which he might have had from Vettori earlier on, and now they would not even have given him that without the instances of the French. At any rate it was one of the few things he had gained by coming into Italy! The first payment was made straightaway in October, and he then greeted the ambassadors with the words: 'Here one cannot live without money.' With the second instalment, which was to be handed over in Mantua in mid-November, they sent Machiavelli.

He left on the 10th of the month with two horsemen carrying 10,000 gold florins.[1] He reached Mantua on the 15th almost at the same time as the news that Vicenza had rebelled and expelled the Imperial garrison. He had been charged with observing the developments of the war as well as looking after his consignment of gold.[2] And so, having got rid of the money, he went on the 21st to Verona where the storm was gathering: if he had lingered another day, he would have found the roads cut. This was the way he expected the war to go, and there he planned to await the Emperor.[3]

In his first letter, having described the situation in the city, where the common people, unlike the nobility, were all on the side of the Venetians, he drew these conclusions: 'On one side it is believed the Veronese have a strong desire to imitate the people of Vicenza; on the other it seems reasonable to suppose that the fortresses and the French forces near by will hold them back. Nevertheless peoples sometimes wish to satisfy a desire without considering what the consequences will be.' He reported on the state of the Imperial forces and on those of the Venetians encamped five miles away, and he described the position and the walls of the city.[4]

He seemed to take pleasure in the prospect of the battle that was at hand, although in writing to Buonaccorsi he had earlier shown some disquiet about the trap he was running into.[5] However, days went by and nothing happened. The Venetians left Verona; the Emperor was in low water having vainly sought help from the King, who felt he had already given him enough. The Venetians were getting their second wind. Machiavelli wrote: 'If these kings stand watching one another and do not make this a short sharp war, something might happen which would bring back these lands to their rightful owners faster than they lost them.'[6] And on the 1st of December: 'Of these two kings one can fight, and doesn't want to, the other would like to and can't.'[7] The 'other' was, of course, Maximilian.

At Verona, therefore, Machiavelli had nothing to do. 'And yet, to show willing,' he went on 'scribbling homilies to the Ten'.[8] He also composed some 'frivolous tale',[9] which he then sent to Luigi Guicciardini who from Mantua was urging him to write one;[10] and it has been thought that this was the second *Decennale*,[11] which was interrupted in fact at that very point of the year 1509. It may be so. Besides this strange coincidence of the *terminus ad quem*, there are other arguments in favour, as for instance certain lines which seem to echo words from his letters written at that time. But there is no lack of arguments to the contrary, as for example the epithet 'old' applied to Giacomini in the generous and heartfelt eulogy of that great citizen, who in 1509 would have been barely fifty-three.[12] This consideration would suggest that the poem, was written after 1514. It is much more likely that it was in this or the following year that the author thought of writing the history of the decade 1505–1514, not to mention the fact that he might then have called Giacomini 'old' with more justification, and have described himself, *post res perditas*, as 'lost in grief'.[13]

Be this as it may, in Verona he had leisure, and leisure inspired him to write. Among what he wrote I would place a letter to that same Luigi Guicciardini, who always suffered from a tiresome literary impulse and had written to Machiavelli recounting certain of his amorous delights and describing some female beauties. This gave Machiavelli the idea of a reply in contrast, something like the parody of a famous sonnet by Bembo later written by another eccentric Florentine. So he describes to his friend an incident which had happened to him 'for lack of a wife', when he was deceived by the dark and an old procuress. How the matter went we need not repeat here. Suffice it to say that having promptly assuaged his desperate hunger, he sought by the light of a lamp to see what kind of supplies had averted famine. Alas! She was a squalid old hag. No similar description attempted before in literature is better than Machiavelli's; and he nonetheless manages to introduce into the awfulness of it some comic aspects all his own ('. . . her mouth was like Lorenzo de' Medici's, but it was twisted on one side, and there it dribbled'). At the sight of such a monster he was sickened, and so is the reader.[14] The anecdote probably has some basis of truth; the details are too forced to be likely, too realistic to be real.

However, after three weeks of these scribblings and this leisure, the Florentine Secretary had had enough. On the 1st of December he writes to the Ten: 'If the Emperor stops at Trent, I may go up there'[15]; but later, when he had received news that the Emperor had gone to Innsbrück and was going on from there to Augsburg for the Diet, he came back on the 11th to Mantua and wrote the following day asking leave to return home, 'because it is not absolutely necessary to go to Augsburg . . . and the Emperor does not share the liking of other princes to have with them men from other powers'.[16] He was given leave on the 17th and it must have reached him on the 21st or 22nd; but he did not leave until after Christmas and he travelled slowly because he did not reach Florence until the 2nd of January.[17]

I do not know what can have been the cause of this delay, nor whether he wished to recoup himself in Mantua and Bologna for the famine suffered in Verona. But his return was not a happy one. On the way he received a letter from Buonaccorsi dated the 27th of December addressed to him 'wherever he may be', in which in the greatest agitation and anger he tells him that a masked man accompanied by two witnesses had presented to the notary of the 'Guardians of the law' a statement to the effect that Machiavelli, 'being born of a father who, etc.', could not hold the post he had. Buonaccorsi adds that, although the law was in favour of his friend, 'a great number of people have taken up the affair and shouted it everywhere and threatened that if something is not done, etc., so that the matter is not in a very good way and needs powerful assistance and delicate handling'. Continuing in this vein the letter does its best to exaggerate the dangers, the number and bitterness of the adversaries and the lack of support.[18]

It is immediately obvious what this supposed incapacity of Niccolò to exercise office on account of his father involves; but Tommasini, excited by that 'etc.', which to him seemed 'tactful and respectful'— without noticing that all the letters of Buonaccorsi are full of etceteras that are neither tactful nor respectful—was moved to imagine that Bernardo must have been illegitimate. It is quite clear, however, that Bernardo was 'a specchio',[19] that is, an insolvent debtor of the commune. This was the condition and not his father's illegitimacy which also disqualified the son from holding public office.[20] Tommasini need only have stopped to consider that the same letter goes on to state that there were other colleagues in Machiavelli's situation; and while there were several thousand citizens on the 'specchio', it hardly seems likely that the Chancery could be full of the sons of fathers of illegitimate birth.

Buonaccorsi wrote that he had taken defensive action, but it was most important that Machiavelli should put off his arrival for a few days, and he begged him to do this. The letter must have reached Machiavelli somewhere on this side of Bologna round about the 29th of December, so it would seem that he did linger on the way following Buonaccorsi's advice, but only a day or two. His assistant's alarm must have seemed exaggerated. He knew him to be timid and excitable and used to tease him about it.[21] He knew he had many enemies, but also powerful friends, beginning with the Gonfalonier himself. I do not believe that even his enemies thought Soderini would let them take away his 'mannerino'. The deposition was simply one of many insults devised more to annoy the Gonfalonier than the humble Secretary.

Machiavelli had other and possibly greater troubles of his own. From his private correspondence we know of a suit which at that time was being carried on for him in Rome.[22] Conjecture is uncertain and useless; but I do not think one would be far wrong (and it would not matter a great deal if one were) in believing that it had something to do with ecclesiastical benefices connected in some way with the transactions between him and his brother, who at that same time, on the 5th of January 1510, was ordained priest.[23] By this transaction, approved by Francesco Nelli and Piero del Nero, Totto had given up his share of their father's estate consisting primarily of the house in Florence and the property at Sant'Andrea in Percussina.[24]

We do not know how the Roman suit ended, but we do know the outcome of that laying of information in Florence from the results, because Machiavelli went on being Secretary of the Signoria, of the Ten and of the Nine. For the Ten he went from the 12th to the 23rd of March to Monte San Savino to settle a dispute between the inhabitants of Gargonza in the Florentine dominion and those of Armaiolo in the territory of Siena.[25] For the Nine he went to the vicariates of San Miniato and Valdinievole to enlist troops from the 25th of May to the 3rd of June.[26] He had been back in Florence for only a few days when for the third time he had to go to France.

There was no holding Julius II now. He had settled his accounts, old and new, with the Venetians, and did not wish to take further action against that glorious republic. This did not please Maximilian whose accounts were still open and very difficult to settle, or the King of

France who had as many reasons for wishing to dismember Venice as the Pope had for wishing to preserve her. One wanted to tame the Lion of St. Mark to strengthen his position in Italy, the other wanted to use it to get rid of the French. Julius tried to raise the other powers against the French while engaging Swiss mercenaries and preparing to besiege Ferrara in spite of its being under the King's protection. With their mutual suspicions and jealousies, the Pope's hatred and the King's resentment grew daily, and it seemed that only the worst could come of it, particularly since the Cardinal of Rouen had died the previous May, and he had always acted as an intermediary between his spiritual and his temporal masters.

The Florentines were gravely concerned: they wished to keep in with France and could not make an enemy of Julius, because, as Soderini said, 'although a Pope is not very useful as a friend, as an enemy he may do much harm'. For this reason, on the departure of the ambassador they had with the French court, they sent Machiavelli to justify their cautious prudence in their dealings with the fiery pontiff. He also had a private commission from the Gonfalonier, who wished to assure the King in this present crisis of his own loyalty and that of his brother the Cardinal.[27] When the latter heard of Machiavelli's departure, he sent after him from Rome a letter recommending, as the Gonfalonier had done, that the Pope and the King should make their peace.[28]

Reaching Lyons on the 7th of July,[29] after having met on the way the returning ambassador (Alessandro Nasi, a very good friend of his), Machiavelli went on two days later, and on the 17th arrived at Blois where the court was. Rubertet told him at once that he had come just in time, as the King was thinking of sending a man post-haste to Florence, his suspicions having been aroused by the ambassador's departure in the very midst of his own difficulties with Rome, and even more by the fact that the Republic had given way to the Pope's requests and allowed a safe conduct to Marcantonio Colonna, who had left the King's service and was on his way to attempt a *coup de main* against Genoa. The Florentine did not find himself short of words on this occasion either.

The King, receiving him in audience shortly afterwards, quickly got down to facts and asked that the Republic should declare 'without any delay' what it would do if the Pope attacked him. It was not enough for the envoy to reply that the Florentines had treaties with His

Majesty, which they would never infringe. 'He replied that he felt
fairly sure of this, but wished for still further reassurance', and enjoined
Machiavelli to write at once in these terms to the Signoria and give the
letter to Rubertet who would send it by the royal post.[30]

Machiavelli did so, and while waiting for the answer—in any case
realizing already what it would be, knowing his Florentines as well as
he did—he went to visit the gentlemen of the court. Everywhere he
met the strongest antagonism to the Pope. 'Withdraw obedience, con-
voke a concilium against him, ruin him in his temporal and spiritual
power, these are the least of the threats against him.'[31] However, the
papal nuncio was at court too, 'a really good man, very prudent and
well versed in matters of state'; and when Machiavelli visited him, he
found him distressed 'and completely astonished at the way things have
so suddenly turned to hostilities'.[32] At court there was also the agent of
Cardinal Soderini, one Giovanni Girolami, who gave him daily reports
on his patron's attitude. With him Machiavelli at once began negotiations whereby the Florentines might act as intermediaries and peace-
makers in those developments which boded ill for Italy, for Florence
and for the Cardinal's own private interests.[33]

On the 8th of August while riding near a place where the King had
gone hunting, Machiavelli and Rubertet discussed 'all the affairs of
Italy' over a distance of three leagues. The essence which Machiavelli extracted from this talk for the Ten, was this: 'Your Lordships
may believe as you believe the Gospels, that if the King and Pope make
war, you will be obliged to declare for one side or the other'; and as
this involved danger, he judged it wise 'not to run that danger without
the compensation of some gain'. When Rubertet had asked him if the
Duchy of Urbino would suit the Florentines, Machiavelli had avoided
answering, but he suggested to the Signoria that this might be the time
to think about Lucca. All the same, he had not failed to point out the
dangers in which a war with the Pope would involve the French,
'showing him all the implications that were in it'; 'because if they made
war alone, they knew what it would bring in its train; if they do so
jointly with some other power, they will have to divide Italy with their
ally, and later on they will have to fight a fresh war with him, far more
dangerous than the one they fought with the Pope'. Finally he had
persuaded Rubertet and almost persuaded himself that he could influence the minds of the French 'who knew nothing about politics':
'One might hope to impress these implications on their minds if there

were more than one Italian of authority here who took the trouble to do so.'[34] But there were no other Italians like him in France, and probably not even in Italy.

Meanwhile matters were taking their inevitable course. To the King's pressing demand that they should declare for him, the Florentines replied that they would always observe their written agreements but could offer nothing definite to help him. Machiavelli took their answer to the King, 'who was very satisfied with it'; but then, as though none of this had taken place, he was called before the Council and told that the Republic must assist Chaumont with her troops if the Pope, 'actuated by a diabolical spirit which has entered into him', should make any attempt against Genoa. When he replied that the city would thereby at once draw down on itself the wrath and the armies of Julius, the gentlemen of the Council, 'practically all with one voice', exclaimed that it would simply be a question of holding off an attack for a few days, because the King was preparing to make in Italy *coelum novum et terram novam*. There was nothing for it, therefore, although this time too he knew the answer in advance, but to refer the royal demands to the Ten; and this he did, again concluding: 'These people wish at all costs to involve you in this war; and so one must think . . . how to win where one expects to lose.'[35]

The days pass, the envoy's assiduous reports continue, but things do not change. The King goes unwillingly towards that war with the Pope, and yet he goes. He says: 'What would you have me do? I do not want the Pope to defeat me.' He plans to temporize throughout the coming winter, and while temporizing calls together the Gallican *concilium* against Julius. The latter collects troops, carries on the war against Ferrara, and takes Modena by treaty. But the Swiss troops hired by the Pope are halted and dispersed at the passes into Lombardy, and at the French court fine words are uttered about the spring offensive: 'indeed it will not be a war, but an excursion to Rome.' Machiavelli notes that this would be a desirable thing, 'so that these priests should have to swallow some bitter pill in this world'.[36] Evidently he had good hopes for their future in the next.

At that time France was afflicted by whooping-cough, and Machiavelli too was infected. On the 24th he writes excusing himself, saying: 'for five days I have spoken to no one, having had to stay indoors with a cough'; and even when the cough was cured, he complained: 'it has left my stomach in such a wretched state that nothing agrees with me.'[37] Furthermore, he was, as usual, short of money, and this increased his general dissatisfaction. He urged the Ten to send him some, reminding them of what he had written some days before, 'if you do not want me to sell the horses and return on foot'.[38]

His illness made him long for home and perhaps also for the care of his loving wife, whose place had been taken to some extent by a certain Jeanne with whom he was later reproached.[39] His return did not seem far off, now the new ambassador, Roberto Acciaiuoli, was already on his way, if slowly, to France. Francesco Vettori wrote: 'I have asked Roberto to send you back soon, so that while losing him we will at least have you back ... Filippo [Casavecchia] and I long for you every day.'[40] Vettori, since the German legation, has become so great a friend that he signs his letters to Machiavelli simply with his Christian name, and of course he too has become godfather to one of his children. I do not know which of these was Vettori's godchild; perhaps it was one born early in the year 1510, who then died in February 1511.[41] It is impossible to keep track of Machiavelli's children and their godparents.

But in the meantime the mother and children are well, and when Machiavelli complains to the Chancery that they have never sent him news of his family, Buonaccorsi replies briefly and humorously: 'Your wife is here and she is living; the children are on their feet; no smoke has been seen from the house, and the grape harvest is likely to be poor at Percussino.'[42] The secretary of the Signoria, the Ten and the Nine, the Republic's envoy to the Most Catholic monarch, now has, besides his political and military cares, his rural pre-occupations for his small property at Sant'Andrea. The harvests, the bad seasons, the perpetual misfortunes which attend those peasants and woodsmen of his, fill him with mixed feelings: at times he is worried, at others he takes pleasure in them, and on occasions he shows off about them in complaints to his office companions.

But this is no time for peasants and woodsmen. Here he is at the French court and has to handle the difficulties of his Republic, caught like an earthen pot between two great vessels of bronze. In this legation he really shows his powers. Visiting Rubertet, who like the King has also got whooping-cough and is confined to his house, he talks to him with good sense and firmness. He tells him that if the war goes forward, the King must show 'great respect' for the city, which simply by defending itself without seeking his assistance would be doing a great

deal for him. Therefore, when in council 'people ask that the Florentines should do and say all sorts of things', they should 'thoroughly
consider and discuss such demands and designs as are made on the
Florentines'.[43]

The French appear to appreciate these arguments, then they go back
to the beginning again. The difficulty is with Chaumont, who has no
Machiavelli at his side, and finding himself bearing the whole weight
of the Italian war, presses for assistance to be sent. Machiavelli, returning
to the Council, again speaks at length, and at length discusses those
arguments. The Florentines, he said, were prepared to observe their
treaty, but it did not seem wise to them, surrounded as they were by
the states of the Church, to send their soldiers abroad and remain without protection in the midst of enemy forces: their troops, if kept at
home, would be for the Pope 'a more effective restraint than if they
were elsewhere.' The Council not only listened carefully but praised
the Secretary's words.[44] At last he had won them over.

His success was partly ensured also by the bragging of Julius who
had begun to speak openly of his intention to change the government
of Florence because it was too French.[45] The terrible Pope had not
allowed the Florentine ambassadors to utter a word when they met
him at Montefiascone on his way to Bologna, intending to offer the
services of the Republic in negotiations between the Church and the
King, and bearing words of peace to one who was bent on war. In his
rage he threatened excommunication, the sacking of Florentine possessions and worse. Even so the ill-used ambassadors felt they had got off
lightly, since an envoy of the Duke of Savoy sent on the same errand
had been thrown into prison and tortured; and not long before, at
Ostia, he had threatened to have the Ferrarese ambassador thrown into
the sea, and this was no less a person than Ariosto.

At the height of his anger the hot-tempered Pope had talked of
'delivering Italy from servitude and out of the hands of the French'.[46]
These words were recorded without comment by Machiavelli, who
was later to write his famous exhortation against the 'barbarous
dominion'. Villari and others have expressed surprise that Machiavelli
after being so enthusiastic about Caesar Borgia, should have shown no
taste at all for the great Julius.[47] It is not really surprising, since Julius
was the destroyer of Florentine freedom and the author of Machiavelli's
long misfortunes, during which he wrote his most memorable pages,
including that exhortation. Even before that time he could not like the

man, since his model of the prince could not be built on rages and impulsiveness; because he did not like the rule of priests, who had ruined both the religion of Christ and his other religion, the State; finally because, as a Florentine and an Italian, he hated the temporal power of the Church. Besides, even that famous cry against the barbarians sounded strangely in the mouth of Julius, who had himself contributed so much to bringing them into the country, and was indeed 'the fatal instrument of the ills of Italy'.[48]

It was not therefore to please the French whom he really did not like, that when the King's letters to Chaumont were read to him on the lines of the principles he had put before the Council, he urged Rubertet 'to take positive action and make a show against that Pope, otherwise things would go ill'. He wrote to the Ten: 'He replied that they knew that they must strike a heavy blow against the Pope; and with these words he laughed and clapped me on the shoulder as though to say: let it be soon.'[49]

His mission was now drawing to a close. At Tours, where he had gone with the court early in September, letters were already arriving addressed to the new ambassador whom the Ten, spoilt by their Secretary's promptness and zeal, imagined to have arrived already or at least to be due to arrive very soon. Instead he was still at Lyons on the 31st of August, and their envoy went on opening and answering his letters. He did not arrive until mid-September, but Machiavelli stayed on a few days to explain the situation to him. We do not know at what precise date he left Tours or when he left Lyons on his way home to Italy. We do know, however, that he reached Florence on the 19th of October.[50] On the 13th of November he was off again on a new task. This was of such a nature that he really could have said of it, even more than of his perpetual journeying on horseback, what Ariosto was to write of his own labours of those years: '*E di poeta cavallar mi feo.*'

Chapter 12

THE TWELFTH HOUR

‹◇›

MACHIAVELLI came back from France sure of two things: that there would be a great war between the Pope and the King, and that the Florentines would be involved in it in spite of themselves. So it is not surprising that his first thoughts were military ones. His basic conviction was that battles are won by the infantry, but he knew that they could also be fought with cavalry, and since his militia had no cavalry, he devoted his attention to persuading the Gonfalonier and the Ten to make a new provision for them. He was not thinking of heavy cavalry; it was to be light horse, armed with guns and crossbows, which could be drawn from the people of the Tuscan countryside.

They did not require much persuading. On the 7th of November 1510 the Ten elected their secretary 'to raise a detachment of light horse'.[1] It had evidently been decided to proceed by experiment, as had been done for the infantry, before making firm provision by law. The first levies were to be made in the Valdichiana, and Machiavelli went there twice, first from the 13th to the 29th of November, and then from the 3rd to the 19th of December. At the beginning of his second trip he had orders to go as far as Siena to cancel the truce between that republic and Florence which was shortly to lapse.[2]

As that year closed under the sign of Mars, military cares increased for Machiavelli with the new year 1511. On the 5th of January he goes to Pisa for six days with orders to look over the citadel with Giuliano da San Gallo and report. On the 14th he goes to Arezzo to do the same with its fortress, and on the 15th of February to Poggio Imperiale, which was a Florentine stronghold against Siena. From being Secretary he has now become the Republic's military technician! On the 14th of March for the whole of that month he goes to Valdichiana again to enlist a hundred light horse, 'giving ten gold ducats per man for their services with horses for the month of April'. Returning there on the 21st he brought a hundred light horse to Florence and paraded them for the first time on the first Sunday after Easter.[3] In this way the militia goes on developing: a fine, noble thing, but entirely new and in need of a long period of peace to become firmly established.

Instead, the free Florentine republic was approaching its twelfth hour. Under Soderini's government, a good helmsman in calm weather, navigation became difficult now that the waters stirred up by the fiery Julius were rising stormily. This pressure from outside gave courage and strength within to the enemies of the Gonfalonier and the supporters of the Medici, who in recent years had grown more numerous and more confident. The death of Piero had brought to his family's cause as many followers as his life, his political behaviour and his exile had lost them. The courtesy and generosity of his surviving brothers, Cardinal Giovanni and the noble Giuliano, had likewise contributed to the revival of their fortunes. The Cardinal in particular had overwhelmed with kindness, favours, and every kind of assistance, the Florentines who lived in Rome or went to stay there, and this behaviour of his, compared in Florence with that of Cardinal Soderini who was 'extremely mean and wrapped up in himself',[4] had brought him and his family remarkable popularity.

The Gonfalonier was deeply displeased by this sort of thing, but he did nothing to remedy it. Only when Cardinal Giovanni, in pursuit of his policy, arranged to marry Piero's daughter Clarice in Florence by offering a large dowry to Filippo Strozzi, one of the leading young men in the city, did Soderini become very annoyed and do his utmost to have Filippo punished. He was so angry about this that it was even said that he had ordered Machiavelli to draw up an accusation, 'composed with great skill and deliberation',[5] to be presented secretly, according to the law, before the Eight. But the power of the Strozzi was considerable, and the punishment was light.

The climax of this affair came at the beginning of 1508. At the end of 1510 the conspiracy of Prinzivalle della Stufa was uncovered through the zeal or the astuteness of that same Filippo Strozzi. This conspirator boasted that he had been entrusted with the task of assassinating the Gonfalonier by Cardinal de' Medici or even by the Pope himself. This gave Soderini the opportunity to take action, and on the 3rd of January 1511 the Eight issued a proclamation to the effect that anyone who lodged in the house of Cardinal de' Medici or his brother or even had any dealings with them, would be held a traitor.

Meanwhile in Romagna, French arms were victorious. At the beginning of 1511 Julius II took Mirandola, an achievement remarkable less for the importance of the place than for the personal bravery shown there by the ageing Pope, more to his own honour than to that of the papal habit. Shortly after, he was defeated near Ferrara, and on the 21st of May he lost Bologna, the Church's principal city after Rome. Even the spiritual arms which he ought to have been able to rely on and regard as invincible, were turning against him. In the cities of the Church bills were posted announcing the convocation of the Concilium to be held from the 1st of September in Pisa, and citing the Pope to appear there in person. He withdrew to Ravenna and then to Rimini, full of grief and sickness, and for the first time his indomitable spirit seemed to incline to thoughts of peace.

The war would have ended with the total defeat of the Pope, if only the King had taken proper advantage of his victory. Instead, out of respect or prudence he withdrew his army, showing himself ready to humble himself before the Apostolic See as though he were the attacker not the attacked, not the victor but the vanquished. This softness of the King hardened the heart of the Pope, who quickly resumed his former aggressiveness. In this he was encouraged by the incitement and hopes given to him by the King of Aragon who was jealous of the French victories. His first moves were with those spiritual arms which he could still use after the defeat of his armies, and he began by announcing for the following month of May a universal Concilium to be held in Rome. He thought that he had thereby dissolved the Concilium called by his adversaries, and won the war at least on that front.

However, when the time came, the procurators of the schismatic cardinals published in Pisa some documents concerning the opening of their concilium. The Pope was angry at this and threatened to punish the Florentine merchants and to place the city under an interdict. The first of these threats caused the Florentines greater concern, and they were extremely disgruntled because they had conceded under pressure from the King that the Concilium should take place at Pisa, at a time when Julius's fortunes were at a low ebb, when the Emperor was enthusiastic about such a gathering, and when there promised to be a large concourse of Gallican and German clergy. Now, however, they found Julius revived in body and soul after his many defeats and an illness which had caused rumours of his death, while the Emperor had as usual cooled off, and the Concilium was about to be opened in a far less reputable fashion by three solitary procurators.

The Florentines thus felt themselves to be in the greatest danger and an easy target for the Pope's anger. Therefore, having ordered the procurators to proceed no further until the arrival of the cardinals, they decided to send someone to persuade the cardinals not to come, and also to the French court to persuade the King to keep this plague away from their territory. Machiavelli was sent, because the envoy had to be able and trustworthy, but above all rapid and prompt.

The Secretary had not been idle in the meantime, as these last pages may have led the reader to suppose. On the 5th of May he had been to see Luciano Grimaldi, lord of Monaco, on account of certain reprisals and to negotiate a treaty. However, later instructions which reached him on his way there, reduced the importance of his mission, because the Republic had decided that it could not honourably connive at certain activities of the other contracting party which savoured too much of piracy. So the document signed in Monaco was of little importance for the Republic,[6] while for Machiavelli's career (apart from the small satisfaction of hearing himself called 'ambassador'!) it is notable only for the considerable time it took and for the long and difficult journey. After his return on the 5th of June he had a hand in the new treaty with Siena. This was a bargain struck by Petrucci to his own advantage with the mediation of the Pope and at the expense of the Sienese who paid for the agreement with the restitution of Montepulciano.[7] Then, from the 24th of August to the 7th of September he had been in upper Val d'Arno, Valdichiana and Casentino to select a hundred more horsemen for the new militia.[8] Hardly had he returned when he set out for the fourth time for France.

He left on the 10th of September[9] and arrived on the 12th at Borgo San Donnino between Parma and Piacenza where were four of the six rebel cardinals: Carvajal, Saint Malo, Cosenza, Sanseverino. He first spoke with Carvajal who was the most important. They were then joined by Cosenza and Sanseverino, and finally all went together to see Saint Malo; so that the Secretary had to repeat the same things three times over: the Pope's indignation, the danger to the Florentines, the plea that they should not come any nearer to Florence, and this 'they could do without upsetting the Concilium, as all the things needed for it had not yet been got ready, nor were they prepared with the necessary spiritual and temporal arms'. After two very long discussions among themselves, during which Machiavelli had to wait outside, the cardinals' reply was that they would not come to Florence, but within ten or twelve days they would go to Pisa by way of Pontremoli. The Secretary felt, however, that their enthusiasm for the trip had been moderated by his words.[10]

Machiavelli then went on to Milan and gave his message to the Viceroy, which consisted merely in explaining the dangers which threatened the Florentines without touching in any way on what he was to tell the King about the Concilium. On the 15th he left again at a late hour on his way to France,[11] and rode so fast that by the 22nd he was at Blois where the court resided. Roberto Acciaiuoli, the ambassador who had replaced him the year before, was still there representing the Florentines; and with him Machiavelli appeared before the King the following day. On that very same day the Pope issued his interdict against Florence. 'After Machiavelli's preliminary greetings', the two Florentines read to the King a document in which they had 'summarized all the arguments which might persuade His Majesty', drawn up under three principal heads.

In the first he was urged to avoid war and bring the Concilium to an end with a reasonable agreement for which the Florentines would be willing to act as mediators. But the King, although showing himself eager for peace ('would to God', he said, 'that you could bring it about!'), objected that the Concilium was designed to force the Pope to an agreement: to call it off would be to remove this restraint from him. The second point they put forward was that the Concilium might be removed from Pisa to some other place; but the King replied promptly and resolutely that this too was impossible since the Concilium had been announced for that city, and if it were moved elsewhere it would damage their case. The third and last argument, to which they resorted when the other two were rejected, was that the sessions of the Concilium should be postponed for two or three months to give the Republic time to strengthen its position. This is what they said, but they meant the usual Florentine policy of gaining time, in the hope that the death of the Pope or some other accident might rescue them from that danger. In the end this argument partly convinced the King. Letters were ordered to be sent to the cardinals telling them that they should put off their sessions until All Saints.[12]

The only advantage the Florentines gained was that of time. It was no great gain but better than nothing, and they should have been grateful to their Secretary who had paid for it with the discomforts of that journey. To recover, before undertaking the difficulties of the return trip, he remained at court about three weeks although he had no further business to transact. During this time he wrote one short letter of his own to the Ten.[13] We have two originals of the long account of the discussions with the King, both signed by Acciaiuoli, one written in Machiavelli's hand, the other by a secretary. But even if we only had this second copy, the style would be enough to show who was the author. In mid-October he had permission from the Ten to leave,[14] and he set off again to return to Florence, arriving there on the 2nd of November. He barely had time to dismount, because they gave him a fresh commission the very day he arrived, and early the next morning he was already on his way to Pisa.[15]

The schismatic cardinals had finally arrived at Pisa to hold the first session of their Concilium on the 5th of November. Deprived of their title by the Pope, unpopular with the people, disobeyed by the clergy, their sojourn there was not very agreeable or very safe under the guard of M. de Lautrec and fifty French archers, for they had abruptly been refused any larger escort. The Florentines objected even to these few, and no less to the escort than to those they escorted. Hence their haste in sending Machiavelli with the task of placing three hundred soldiers from his battalions alongside those fifty French, and of persuading the prelates to transfer elsewhere their persons, grievances and ambitions.

A few hours after he had left, the Ten heard from their commissioners Rosso Ridolfi and Antonio Portinari that everything was quiet, and sent after him a letter to say that he could do without the soldiers.[16] He therefore went directly to Pisa, and there, after being present at the council's first session, he presented himself to Cardinal Carvajal. Approaching the subject by a roundabout way, he said, as though to apologize on behalf of the Signoria, that in Pisa there was a great scarcity and difficulty with all supplies. The Cardinal replied that there certainly was no abundance or comfort there, but they did not complain; if, however, the Florentines meant that it would be a good idea for them to move on, this was a matter for discussion. Seeing that Carvajal had taken the hint, Machiavelli followed up by pointing out how much better it would be for them to go to France or Germany, where 'they would find the people more disposed to obey them than the Tuscans are likely to be', etc. When the Cardinal answered that he would talk to the others and that he would have to write to France and Germany, Machiavelli went still further and boldly recalled certain words spoken by the Cardinal and his companions at San Donnino to the effect that after two or three sessions they might be able to move elsewhere. Carvajal replied wearily that they would think about it. To make them think about it more seriously the Secretary gave him to understand that they should not expect assistance or favour from the Signoria, and as for bringing the disobedient Pisan clergy to reason, 'they must see to that themselves'.[17]

Machiavelli's suggestions, the hostility of the clergy, and perhaps most of all the disturbances among the people, persuaded the cardinals, who in the meantime on the 7th had held another session, to move on and take their ghost of a Concilium to Milan. Machiavelli returned to Florence on the 11th. On the 12th the cardinals departed. But this did not placate the Pope who was determined not to rest while the city remained under the rule of Soderini. On the 1st of December he raised the interdict: on the 15th he restored it, though the people of Florence received the news with indifference. These were discredited weapons, but he had meanwhile prepared others. He had concluded a pact with the King of Aragon, which was a master-stroke for his own battle, although it opened the way for more serious battles and made him once more 'the fatal instrument of the ills of Italy'. More effective than interdicts, the formidable Spanish infantry, scourge of the French as the French had been of the Italians, were to help him recapture Bologna. After that he intended to subdue the Florentines.

In Florence all were aware of the danger but not all were sorry, and there were none who prepared to put up a vigorous defence. The optimates who were the Gonfalonier's enemies were not sorry, though they were not all friends of the Medici. The friends of the Medici were delighted, for they were all the Gonfalonier's enemies. And even those who were neither friends of the Medici nor enemies of the Gonfalonier were extremely averse to spending money, and preferred to remain neutral, not understanding that, as Guicciardini observes, neutrality is only for the strong.

These matters and this atmosphere Machiavelli found to have developed during his legation in France, and he could only foresee that ill would come of them. On his return from Pisa he found that a thunderbolt falling on the tower of the Palazzo the second night after his departure had gone right through the Chancery and destroyed three golden lilies over the door. This was immediately interpreted as a sinister omen for the French King and the Florentine government. Machiavelli, like other great men, believed in celestial omens and was filled with foreboding.[18] On the 22nd of November in the presence of his colleagues he made his first will.[19] Soon afterwards the Gonfalonier followed his example.

The Florentines, hindered by their internal divisions, by their avarice and their passion for delay, did nothing. Early in 1512 they sent to the King of Aragon a young man by the name of Francesco Guicciardini. It might have been the way of saving themselves, but as usual his fellow citizens 'gave him no instructions which might in some way mitigate the ill-will of the allies'.[20] The instructions were written and handed over by the Secretary, so that the two great politicians must then have come face to face; but it was Soderini and his faction who dictated them. Hence this legation 'gave great displeasure to the King of France', and did nothing to placate the allies. Florence became more and more displeasing to God and to her enemies.

Machiavelli in the meantime was doing all he could and all he was allowed to do; it was too little to save the Republic and less than his talents warranted. After his return from Pisa, on the 2nd of December, he went off to enlist soldiers in Florentine Romagna. On the 19th of February he organized a great parade of 300 horse levies in the Piazza della Signoria.[21] On the 30th of March he had his reward when the bill he had prepared providing for the mounted militia was passed.[22] Early in May he was busy with the infantry; on the 6th he was in Pisa reorganizing the garrison of the citadel; and he was still working in the lower Valdarno for the infantry, when he was instructed to go to Siena to offer condolences for the death of Pandolfo Petrucci.[23] From Siena he went to Pisa arriving on the 6th of June, and he did not reach Florence again until after the 15th of that month after having seen to the organization of the cavalry in Pisa.[24]

In the meantime things were coming rapidly to a climax. Whilst the

Republic was spending time on preparations suitable for a war in the distant future, the menace of Julius II was already at hand. On the morrow of the great battle of Ravenna, which saw the death of the brilliant soldier Gaston de Foix, France, hard-pressed by the Swiss, abandoned by the Emperor, lost in spite of her great victory and in less time than it takes to tell, both the war and Lombardy. In that same reversal of fortune, Piacenza, Parma, all the lands of Romagna and even Bologna returned to the Church. Julius II triumphed, and Florence stood alone before that fearsome, ageing pontiff.

Lorenzo Pucci came from the Pope to demand that the city should enter the league against France and contribute to the expenses of the war. The Florentines offered to pay a certain sum of money, but hesitated over joining the league, which was the usual way of refusing to do so. Shortly afterwards, the confederates meeting at Mantua resolved to attack Florence in order to change her government. Then the Spanish troops commanded by Raimondo da Cardona, Viceroy of Naples, entered Tuscany. They were accompanied by Cardinal de' Medici as papal legate. He had recently been set free by the French who had taken him prisoner at Ravenna, and was now the favourite of the Pope and of fortune.

Too late the city woke up to the danger. Hurriedly an improvised army was raised from every corner of the dominion, to reinforce the inexperienced conscripts of the militia. She had few soldiers and not a single able captain. Machiavelli, who had spent June following the movements of armed forces belonging to the Pope, to which the Republic had not dared to refuse a safe passage even though they were on the way to swell the ranks of their enemies,[25] and in July had been raising troops in Mugello where there was already the hint of war,[26] was sent to face the enemy. He was to raise a thousand foot-soldiers and with them meet the enemy at Firenzuola; but while he was carrying out this order, a letter from the Ten, dated the 24th of August, recalled him in great haste.[27] The Spaniards, coming by way of the Stale, were at Barberino. The captains of the Florentine forces had insisted that the main body of their troops should encamp near the city walls. This, now the twelfth hour had come, was the place where Machiavelli must be.

There he received a letter from Buonaccorsi, in which, now that the Spaniards had reached Campi, he begs Machiavelli on behalf of the Gonfalonier 'to do something about it', for 'he is astonished and displeased' to find the enemy drawing so near.[28] Did he think they had crossed the Appenines on manœuvres? The poor man did not know which way to turn, and he hoped that his Secretary's fertile brain might work some miracle. However, when he heard the Viceroy's demand that he should abdicate from the government and that the Medici should return to Florence as private citizens, he replied courageously that his office could be taken from him only by the people who had given it to him. And the people, with equal courage, rejected the demand.

The Viceroy then came up to Prato which was defended by 3,000 men. The first assault was driven off, and as the enemy was then hungry and lacked supplies, the Gonfalonier might perhaps have struck a better bargain with a hundred bushels of bread, which is what, according to Machiavelli, 'wise men' (perhaps himself) 'urged him to do'.[29] But the Gonfalonier growing suddenly over-bold as timid men will, refused. Neither the walls of Prato nor the spirit of the conscripts could withstand the second attack. They had never seen an enemy before, and they had to face those fearful Spanish soldiers who had come almost like victors through the defeat at Ravenna.[30] Prato was put cruelly to the sack. Under the very eyes of the papal legate, countless murders, sacrileges and rapes were committed.

Then in Florence there were no longer any who were not afraid; and yet the Gonfalonier, according to Machiavelli who was with him, still had faith in 'certain vain opinions of his'.[31] To disillusion him four young noblemen came to see him on the 31st, among them Paolo Vettori, brother of Francesco, who spoke to him in such a way that he at once sent Machiavelli to fetch Francesco Vettori,[32] who found him 'alone and afraid', and ready to leave the Palazzo immediately if he were given a safe conduct. Francesco took him to his own house and at nightfall accompanied him to Siena. This was more of a flight than an abdication, and coming at a time when the fate of the city and of the Gonfalonier were neither of them quite hopeless, gave rise, probably from the time of the event itself, to Machiavelli's sarcastic reflections.

With the removal of Soderini agreement was sought and easily obtained. The Medici returned to Florence as private citizens, and the government was reformed. The new Gonfalonier was to be elected not for life but for a term, to hold office for fourteen months and be elected by the Great Council. They elected Giovambattista Ridolfi, 'head of the optimates, wise, courageous, of high birth and venerable aspect, certainly an ideal steersman for that almost foundering ship on so stormy a sea'.[33]

However, whether the sea was too stormy and the ship too battered, or whether, as was suggested, his family connection with the Medici had dazzled and corrupted him, Ridolfi did not persevere in the firmness and rigour which he had shown at the beginning of his term of office.[34] In the Medici household a plot was prepared by the Cardinal; on the 16th of September Giuliano and some conspirators entered the Palazzo with hidden weapons, at a given signal the square filled with soldiers and populace, and the Palazzo was quickly occupied. *Palle!* *Palle!* In short, violence dictated and fear agreed that liberty be extinguished by the usual method of calling a parliament. The Friar's warning to the Florentine people,

> *e sappi che chi vuol far parlamento*
> *vuol torti dalle mani il reggimento,*

might just as well have been written in sand instead of carved on marble in the great hall.

Elected in the piazza according to the old abusive custom, the resultant committee, chosen from among the most violent partisans of the Medici, undid piece by piece the system of magistrates and all the popular liberties. To begin with, on the 18th of September, the Nine in charge of the militia were dismissed, and the military organization created by Machiavelli was dissolved. Soderini was banished and the Great Council abolished. The Gonfalonier Ridolfi 'did not want to stay more than two months',[35] and he gave up his office or rather was forced to resign. The city went back to its condition under Lorenzo and Piero de' Medici, and nothing was done but what the Cardinal de' Medici wanted.

In all this upheaval no one was concerned about Machiavelli, and even these pages of ours seem to have neglected him. We do not know what he did under Ridolfi's régime; public and private documents are silent on the matter, and biographers have not tried to fill the gap with probable explanations. Yet it is obvious that the grave leader of the optimates, former follower of Savonarola and rival of Soderini, could not feel sympathetic or kindly towards the plebeian and not very moral 'puppet' of the deposed Gonfalonier. Nor do I think it is stretching imagination too far if I see the Secretary forgotten and fallen from favour, withdrawn into a corner of the Chancery and into his own abasement. There he ruminates on 'his troubles which are endless',[36] and dispatches what little he is given to do. Everything around him is changed, faces are no longer the same. He once had authority in the Palazzo, greater than his rank warranted. Now he is in a position of inferiority.

But there was still the poet in him, fond of dreaming, and perhaps at times he deludes himself into thinking that he can keep this office which for him is his livelihood and his vocation. The magistrates may change, but he is a man of letters who uses his pen and his wits on behalf of those in power: this is what artists, soldiers and poets do. He is the servant of the state, not of a faction; he has served the Republic faithfully under the popular government, he will serve it just as faithfully under the Medici. Therefore, if he is not among those who exert themselves to flatter and court the new powers, nor among those who, as he will shortly write, 'prostitute themselves to the people and the Medici', he certainly does not look askance at the new masters. In an account of these recent events which he writes to a mysterious 'lady', a friend of the Medici, he speaks of them with obsequious respect.[37] But in a *Ricordo ai palleschi* [memorandum to the Medici supporters][38] he demonstrates frankly that it is foolish to strive to discover and censure the misdeeds of Soderini in order to flatter the new masters. And on the 29th of September, when five officials were elected to inventory and recuperate the possessions confiscated from the Medici in 1494, he writes even more frankly and freely to the Cardinal advising him to adopt a wise and politic magnanimity[39]—advice which would have been appreciated, at least verbally, by a Lorenzo de' Medici.

The Cardinal, however, showed no appreciation of this advice either in words or deeds. The Secretary, if he were under the illusion of still living in times when the good sense and the style of his writings could bring him praise and favour, was soon to be disillusioned. The Medici kept on the neutral first secretary Marcello Virgilio, but they could not forgive the man who had done and written so much against them, the 'puppet' of Soderini, nor forget the coldness he had shown to them— as indeed he was obliged to do—as exiles in the courts of Rome and France. Besides, they had their own creatures to reward.

So, on the 7th of November, a decision of the Signoria 'dismissed, deprived and totally removed' Niccolò Machiavelli from the post of chancellor of the second Chancery and from the functions of Secretary to the Ten.[40] The same fate befell his assistant Biagio Buonaccorsi. The removal of a Secretary was a matter of no significance. Among the numerous Florentine chroniclers and diarists of the time, not one of them mentions it. Today, however, Machiavelli's misfortune seems a greater matter than the collapse of Florentine liberty.

Chapter 13

'SORROWFUL MACHIAVELLI'

◇◇

I N the writings of the Secretary the passages which speak of his grief at losing his job are few and bitter; but none seems more heartfelt than the brief but eloquent note '*post res perditas*' which he wrote to signify the period which followed his dismissal,[1] almost equating in those words his own downfall and that of the free republic, his misfortunes and those of his country. The blow was a bitter one, the injustice flagrant, after he had served the state with such faithful zeal; beset by anxiety for the future, he found unbearable those first days of an idleness to which he was totally unaccustomed. After he had been used to spending the whole day in the rooms of the Palazzo, his own home must have seemed all the poorer and smaller, now that he had to stay within its walls. Outside, he was depressed by the baseness of some and the changed attitude of others. Many who once were friendly towards the Secretary of the Republic, now avoided or looked askance at him.

This was only the beginning of his troubles: he had barely begun to go downhill. By itself, the loss of his office might have signified merely that the new government wanted someone more trustworthy or acceptable to themselves: governing through the chancellors was an old Medicean art. Instead it was to mean blame, punishment, revenge; and this was soon made clear. On the 10th of November the Signoria sentenced him to be restricted within Florentine territory for a year, obliging him to pay a caution of 1,000 gold florins,[2] a huge sum which three friends, whose names have not come down to us, found for him. This was another sharp sword-thrust into his heart.

After the sword-thrusts came the pinpricks. On the 17th of November (the brevity of the intervals made them all the more cruel) another resolution of the Signoria forbade him to set foot for twelve months in that Palazzo where he had done so much for fourteen years.[3] And would that he had not been forced to return for the reasons which shortly afterwards brought him there! Recently he had handled large sums of money to pay the battalions, and he was repeatedly called upon to account for these, being given permission on each occasion to cross the forbidden threshold.[4] It must have been no small torment for him to have to attend with his former assistants now in inquisitors' guise to those complicated accounts; to see in his old place his successor Niccolò Michelozzi, former secretary of the Medici who now served and spied on the Signoria for the benefit of the Medici; to look at the doubtful face and hear the evasive words of Marcello Virgilio. This went on until the 10th of December. It was a sad Christmas for Niccolò and his family in the humble dwelling beyond the Arno.

Even a brief letter from Piero Soderini must at that time have made the wound smart and given him some pain as well as some pleasure. The exile wrote from Ragusa where he had found a safe refuge from the claws of Julius II. But his former Secretary was not in a safe place, rather was he more than ever exposed to revenge. Soderini's feeble actions had brought him to this pass, and now his imprudence in writing threatened him with worse, because, although the letter had come disguised beneath the mask of another signature and another hand, even this procedure was not without its dangers, nor was it safe to answer. Nevertheless Machiavelli did answer.

In his reply, resentment allied with suspicion made his 'fantasies', as he called them, even more fantastic and obscure. Of great importance (more so than has hitherto been thought) for the origin of certain machiavellian ideas which are on the point of taking shape, they philosophize at length with a sententious irritability.[5] But neither suspicion nor resentment can hide a certain affectionate familiarity, which if it is not merely due to the misfortune that placed them on the same level, sheds no little light on the relationship between the two men *ante res perditas*: 'Your letter was short, and I in reading it, made it long. I was glad to have it, for it gave me the opportunity to do what I hesitated to do and which you warn me not to do;[6] and only that part of your letter did I feel was unreasonable. This would astonish me, if my fortune had not shown me so many and varied things that I am forced either to be seldom astonished at anything or to admit that I have not properly understood, in reading or experience, the actions of men and their behaviour. I know you and the guiding compass of your navigation; and if it could be condemned, which it cannot, I would not condemn it when I see to what haven it has led you[7] and with what hopes it may nourish you.'

Those hopes had not much to feed on. There was the Pope's anger with Cardinal de' Medici whom he had sent to get rid of Soderini, not to make himself a tyrant,[8] and there was his declared intention of changing the government of Florence again;[9] there was too the citizens' discontent, increased by bitter mistrust of the new régime.[10] Soderini may have been hopeful, but it cannot have been much consolation to Machiavelli. Others tried to achieve something more substantial.

Among the malcontents were Agostino Capponi and Pietropaolo Boscoli. A paper which one of them dropped bearing eighteen or twenty names was taken to the Eight, who finding that they were all of persons already suspect, decided to investigate further. Capponi and Boscoli were arrested at once and confessed that they had wanted to assassinate the Cardinal, or, according to others, Giuliano. It was one of the usual conspiracies like so many others that the times produced, which were more literary than bloodthirsty. In this particular one the classical inspiration was made the more innocuous by a certain candid simplicity. In Pietropaolo, a kindly and studious man, devoted to the memory of the Friar, Brutus was at odds with Christ.[11] In the fatal list they had put down the names of some friends whom they knew or considered to be enemies of the Medici. Among all these the only ones they had approached were Niccolò Valori and Giovanni Folchi, who received them coldly. The affair, therefore, had no firm basis or following, but the Eight did not hesitate to have all the people mentioned in the list arrested. The seventh name was that of Niccolò Machiavelli.

When they went for him, the officers of the jail did not find him at home. Perhaps, warned by some friend in the Palazzo still faithful to him, he had first thought of going into hiding. Perhaps, as seems more likely, he was elsewhere and knew nothing about it. Then a proclamation was issued stating that 'whoever knew or sheltered, or knew who sheltered Niccolò son of messer Bernardo Machiavelli', should denounce him within the hour under pain of being declared a rebel and forfeiting his goods.[12] He presented himself at once, was imprisoned, and tried with the rest. They could find nothing against him except some acquaintance with Boscoli, his friendship with Valori and Folchi,[13] and certain jibes with which he probably repaid the Medici for some of the harm they had done him in recent months.[14] But the things which he had not done counted for little in comparison with what the other accused said under torture. Four drops on the rope were usually enough to subdue any body and any spirit, and if they did not suffice, the torture went on even though their limbs were dislocated and their flesh torn. Niccolò had six drops, which he bore with such courage and patience that 'he thought the better of himself for it'.

Shut up in his prison and in his thoughts, the Secretary is slow to realize where he is, to recognize himself, to raise himself up in that dark pit where he had fallen guiltless and unawares. The agony of limbs torn by torture and confined in handcuffs and shackles increases the agony of his mind and is made more unbearable by it. He thinks of his own and his family's future. He knows his own powers and is sickened to see them humiliated by such undeserved misfortune. For himself he can foresee nothing but ill. He knows that a new régime is deeply suspicious and must maintain itself with strict measures. He knows that he has behaved well under torture, but not whether others have accused him under similar pressure. He knows that his brother Totto has at once dispatched a courier to Rome[15] (a luxury the Signoria had always been too mean to allow him on his legations!) to inform Francesco Vettori, ambassador to the Pope, of what has happened and to ask his help. But he knows that Vettori is 'all for himself', and even if he wanted to, he could not help much.

Just before dawn on the 23rd of February [16] he is woken by the funeral hymns which accompany Capponi and Boscoli to the scaffold. The Secretary is not very pious, and perhaps his resentment towards those whose thoughtless folly has brought him to ruin, does not leave him much room for thoughts of Christian piety. Suddenly his despair is lit up by a new ray of hope. He has heard the kindness, urbanity and magnanimity of Giuliano greatly praised—a man of fine manners who seeks the company of learned men and poets, and has some acquaintance with the Muses. Machiavelli, therefore, wishes to try what writing to him might do, and he is given permission and the materials to do so. But he is a man for writing sonnets not tearful supplications: he has always defended himself with laughter, always hidden behind

laughter. So with aching limbs and facing death he produces his famous
smile again and writes:

> Io ho, Giuliano, in gamba un paio di geti
> e sei tratti di fune in sulle spalle;
> l'altre miserie mie non vo' contalle,
> poichè così si trattano i poeti.
> Menon pidocchi queste parieti
> grossi e paffuti che paion farfalle,
> nè fu mai tanto puzzo in Roncisvalle
> o in Sardigna fra quegli arboreti,
> quanto nel mio sì delicato ostello.
> Con un romor che proprio par che 'n terra
> fumini Giove e tutto Mongibello,
> l'un s'incatena e l'altro si disferra,
> combatton toppe, chiavi e chiavistelli;
> un altro grida: — Troppo alto da terra!
> Quel che mi fa più guerra
> è che dormendo, presso all'aurora,
> io cominciai a sentir: Pro eis ora.
>   Or vadano in buon'ora
> purchè la tua pietà ver me si volga
> che al padre ed al bisavo el nome tolga[17]

[Giuliano, I have a pair of shackles on my legs and six drops of the strappado
on my back; my other misfortunes I shall not tell, since that is the way they
treat poets. These walls are full of lice so big and fat they seem like butterflies,
and there never was such a stench in Roncesvalles or in Sardinia amid those
groves, as in this fine dwelling of mine. With a noise that sounds as if Jove and
all Etna were hurling thunderbolts to earth, one prisoner is chained up and
another unbound, padlocks, keys and bolts rattle together, and another cries:
Too high from the ground! What worries me most is that, as I slept, near
dawn I began to hear: *Pro eis ora*. Now let them go, I pray, if only your
mercy may turn towards me, and surpass the fame of your father and your
grandfather].

One sonnet calls for another, and he sent the second one off together
with this, or some days later. In this he pretended that a muse had come
to visit him in his prison asking him who he was to complain so much;
but when he had told her his name, she beat him, saying:

> Niccolò non se', ma il Dazzo,
> poichè hai legato le gambe e i talloni
> e ci stai 'ncatenato come un pazzo[18]

[You are not Niccolò, but Dazzo, for you have your legs and heels tied together, and are chained up like a lunatic].

Andrea Dazzi was a pupil of the first chancellor, Marcello Virgilio, and was trying desperately to keep afloat in the then rather stagnant waters of Florentine letters. The joke was not without savour, and must have pleased the quick-witted Giuliano.

On the 7th of March the trials were over, Valori and Folchi were sentenced to two years imprisonment in the dungeons of Volterra, others to short terms of internment, and others still to the payment of a fine. Machiavelli was able to breathe again, since he had only to find the money to buy back his freedom. I would not say that it was all due to the sonnets, but in fact he was later to acknowledge that he owed his freedom to Giuliano and Paolo Vettori,[19] who had perhaps commended the sonnets and the poet to Giuliano and thus spared him a worse imprisonment.

Meanwhile, on the 21st of February, Julius II had died, and on the 22nd, shortly before the heads of Capponi and Boscoli fell, Cardinal de' Medici went off to Rome. Going into the conclave on the 6th of March, he came out Pope on the 11th with the name of Leo X. The news, which by a prodigious feat reached Florence the same day, turned everyone into partisans of the Medici, each one thinking of the honour and profit which could be expected in public and private affairs from a Pope who was a fellow-citizen and lavish in spending and giving. Florence went mad. For five days in succession, in the squares, in the streets, in front of every house, bonfires burnt while there remained wood or faggots to burn; and when they were finished, they burnt floorboards, wooden roofs, barrels and furniture. It looked as though the whole city were ablaze. It was in Lent, but they built floats and triumphal wagons as though it were Carnival, and every evening one of them was burnt in front of the house of the Medici. The last was one representing peace, and this was not burnt, to signify that wars were at an end under the new Pope.[20] The prisons were opened, and those who had been sentenced for the conspiracy were freed, their fines and their prison sentences being entirely remitted. Shortly after, even the Soderini were pardoned.

Thus, 'amid the universal rejoicing of this city', Machiavelli came out of his stinking prison to breathe the pure Florentine air which already carried the scent of spring. He felt himself coming to life again as after a long and serious illness. He had escaped death, and felt a new appetite for life. After twenty-two days of manacles and shackles he could enjoy freedom all the more. He had plunged deep into that abyss, and now he had recovered from the fall, he wanted to try to climb up the slope again. To begin with he needed to win over those 'Medici princes', show them who he was, rise out of suspicion into their good graces. To this period—contrary to all the opinions of biographers and literary historians—we can ascribe his *Canto degli Spiriti beati* [Hymn of the blessed spirits],[21] which was almost certainly written for that triumph of peace we have mentioned above. And we should not be surprised that as soon as he came out of prison, he should have wanted to write poetry, for even in prison he had composed verses and satirical lines. It is the least carnival-like composition that can ever have gone under that title of *Canto carnascialesco*, and the most pious. In it he does nothing but weep over the long wars which had covered Christianity in blood during the reign of the late Vicar of Christ:

> e mostrare a chi erra
> si come al Signor nostro al tutto piace
> che si ponghin giù l'arme e stieno in pace

[and to show to those who err how it pleases Our Lord that we should lay down our arms and live at peace];

he speaks too of God's wrath and impatience,

> poichè vede il suo regno
> mancare a poco a poco, e la sua gregge,
> se pel nuovo pastor non si corregge

[because he sees his kingdom dwindle away, and his flock too, if it is not properly led by its new shepherd].

In order to commend himself to 'the new shepherd', he also tried other means. Writing on the 13th of March to Francesco Vettori to thank him for all that he had *not* done for him in his grave peril, he commended to him his brother Totto who wished to be inscribed in the roll of the Pope's familiars, and added: 'If you can, keep my name before His Holiness, so that either he or his family may think to use me; for I am sure I could do you honour, and profit myself.'[22] But Vettori, while explaining that he had had to wait for the Pope's election before seeking Machiavelli's release, and by that time he had already been freed, and so his assistance had come too late to be of any use, could only give him affectionate words in return, urging him 'to suffer that persecution cheerfully as he had suffered the others done to him', and have good hopes 'that he would not always be cast down'.[23]

Although of little substance, such kind words gave Machiavelli encouragement and revived his hopes. On the 18th of March he replies to his friend, and his mind and his pen go back over the things which had lately befallen him: 'And as for meeting fortune courageously, I want you to have this pleasure from my sufferings—to know that I bore them so well that I am pleased with myself and feel that I am a better man than I thought. And if our new masters think fit not to leave me where I am, I shall be pleased, and I believe that I will bear myself in such a way that they too will be pleased. If they do not think fit, I shall live as best I can, for I was born poor and I learned to know want before enjoyment.' The reader must like him the better for these words, as I do in transcribing them; and like him too for his very human attachment to life, 'dwelling on these universal pleasures, enoying this residue of life, which seems like a dream'.[24]

Passing from one dream to another, while he awaits the help his friend the ambassador might obtain from the Pope, he thinks to help himself by reminding Giuliano of his existence. It was perhaps at this time that he sent him a string of thrushes caught in his snares at Sant' Andrea (the last of the season!), accompanying them with another sonnet; and the sonnet was the cause of the gift, not as usually happens, the other way round:

> *Io vi mando, Giuliano, alquanti tordi*
> *non perchè questo don sia buono o bello*
> *ma perchè un po' del pover Machiavello*
> *Vostra Magnificenza si ricordi*

[I send you, Giuliano, a few thrushes, not because the gift is good or fine, but so that Your Magnificence may be reminded of poor Machiavelli].

And he went on to say that if among those around him there were some biting calumniator, he should give him these birds to bite on so that he might forget to sink his teeth in others. No matter if the birds are thin:

> *ch'io son maghero anch'io, come lor sanno*
> *e spiccon pur di me di buon bocconi*[25]

[for I am thin too, as they know, and yet they take some good bites out of me].

We have no real evidence whether he ever had kind words, if not favours, from Giuliano.[26] The fount of all favours, or rather the well, as Ariosto puts it in his 'satire', was in Rome, but it held no water for 'poor Machiavelli', even though he had at Rome one who professed friendship for him and seemed to be in the best position to tap this source. Who better than the Florentine ambassador to the Florentine Pope could have access to the pontifical ear and favour? And yet on the 30th of March Vettori wrote that he did not seem very popular with the Pope; he had not even been able to secure that favour for Totto, purely formal and nominal though it was.[27] Perhaps he really had made this and other approaches for Machiavelli and had an answer such that he was unwilling to report it to his friend. Perhaps, as was his nature, he had not even taken so much trouble when he saw or thought he saw that the Pope was ill-disposed.

This letter really left poor Niccolò without hope. He replied to Vettori that he had 'shaken him more than the strappado had done', the more so because of the reserves and precautions with which he had surrounded the bitter news. He told Vettori that he should not worry about him or about Totto and his roll. 'I do not think of it', he wrote, 'and if he cannot enrol, let him roll.' He adds: 'I tell you once and for all that you should not trouble yourself in any way for any of the things I ever asked you, because I shall not feel passionately if I do not get them.'[28] He was certainly the man not to feel passionately! How much greater than Vettori does Machiavelli appear in this exchange of letters!

However, if he were not to draw more substantial benefits from this correspondence with his friend which had begun with such hopes, there was one benefit he refused to give up—the pleasure of discussing the affairs of the world with him, even though, as he wrote, such discussions were becoming wearisome to him, since events were always turning out differently from what he had expected. He writes: 'I could not help but fill your head with illusions, for my fate is such that, since I cannot talk of the weaving of silk or the weaving of wool, or of profit and loss, I am forced to talk of politics; and I must either vow myself to silence or speak of this subject.' He signs his letter sadly: *Niccolò Machiavelli, quondam Secretarius.*[29]

When he does not talk about politics, he retails to Vettori the ribald jokes going round Florence, and gossips amusingly about their mutual friends. Then, suddenly he breaks into these humorous remarks with the lines of Petrarch:

Però se alcuna volta io rido o canto,
facciol perchè non ho se non quest'una
via da celare il mio angoscioso pianto[30]

[So if I sometimes laugh or sing, I do so because I have only this way of
hiding my anguished weeping]

and beneath the comic mask his tragic unhappy face reappears. It is
the idleness which wearies him, who was so well able to endure fatigue;
his spirit is humiliated, want is knocking at the door of his house where
there are a good many hungry mouths to feed, and there are the debts
incurred in better times for his transaction with Totto. Almost in
spite of himself his talk turns to his usual and only hopes. In past days
he had written: 'If I could get out of Florentine territory, I too would
come to see if the Pope is at home.' Cardinal Soderini, his former patron
and admirer, had returned to favour in Rome, and Machiavelli asked
Vettori if he should write to him for a recommendation to Leo, or if
it were better for Vettori to do this verbally, or if it were better still
to do neither.[31] Vettori advised him to adopt the latter course since the
favour enjoyed by the Cardinal was more a matter of words than
deeds; a recommendation from him would revive the memory of the
old relationship between the Soderini and the Secretary, making
matters worse rather than better.[32]

This was wise advice, but Machiavelli could not contain himself any
longer. On the 16th of April he writes to tell his friend that Giuliano is
coming to Rome and reminds him: 'You will of course find some way
to do me a favour . . .; I cannot believe that if my case were handled
with skill, I might not be used in some way, if not by Florence, at least
by Rome and the papacy where I should be less suspect . . .; I cannot
think that if His Holiness began to use me, I would not do well for
myself and be useful to all my friends. I do not write this because I
desire these things exceedingly, nor because I want you to go to any
trouble or expense on my account, but so that you may know my
mind.'[33]

But for the reasons already mentioned these insistent demands embarrassed Vettori, who in his reply changed the subject as quickly as
he could. It was better to please his poor friend by discussing with him
his political fantasies: they filled the pages, leaving little space for less
agreeable topics, and Machiavelli became so engrossed in them that
he was able to forget his troubles and his needs. Besides, the great con-

test between the Christian princes still went on, and at heart Vettori too enjoyed making forecasts about the outcome, and stimulating Machiavelli to express his acute judgements on these matters.

Events gave plenty of scope for 'castles in Spain'. The King of France, beaten beyond the Alps by the English and the Spaniards, ejected from Italy where only a few fortresses remained in his possession, with the Emperor, the Swiss and the Venetians for his enemies, was on the point of being crushed beneath the avalanche brought down on him by the anger of Julius II, when it became known that a truce had been signed by him with the King of Spain. It seemed a great and astonishing event to everyone. It virtually untied his hands so that he could strike in Italy. Not long after, a treaty was made between the Venetians and the French, who thereby prepared the way for an expedition into Italy to retake the Duchy of Milan, which had been placed by the confederates under the nominal rule of Massimiliano Sforza, though in fact the Swiss were masters of Milan and occupied it with their forces.

Vettori judged the King of Spain to be a fox and the truce an empty affair, believing that he could not have signed it without some good reason and that underneath there must be hidden some deep plot.[34] He thought and thought about this one morning, staying 'more than two hours longer than usual in bed', without managing to get his thoughts clear, and so he decided to seek his friend's opinion, 'having found him in these matters (he wrote) sounder than any other man he had ever talked to'.[35] To ask Machiavelli this was to offer him a treat; to acknowledge in him that excellence which others did not know or would not see in him, was to give him new life, and God knows he needed something to revive him! In those days, after he had dragged himself up the steps of the Palazzo to work afresh on those vile and odious accounts,[36] his heart chilled by his friend's coldness towards his Roman hopes, and no longer able to cope with the expense of city life or bear the idleness there, he had withdrawn to his humble villa at Sant' Andrea. He had made a resolution not to think any more about politics or to talk about them;[37] but these were sailor's vows, and the ambassador's letter was quite enough to make him feel that he was again the man he had once been. He confessed: 'While I was reading it, and I read it several times, I forgot my unhappy condition.'[38]

In a remarkably acute reply which he sent on the 29th of April, he discussed the reasons which had led the King of Spain to concede that truce and the consequences which might derive from it, very different

from those the acute Vettori had foreseen. Vettori enjoyed Machiavelli's reasoning very much, but perhaps thought it more clever than
realistic, as many people thought Machiavelli's ideas, and as indeed
they often were. But three months later, when the King of France
again came down into Italy and again rapidly took and lost the Duchy
of Milan, he looked for that letter, re-read it, and admired and praised[39]
the seer who could penetrate the thoughts and future actions of princes
even in the dark as he was, cut off from information and conversation,
'withdrawn in the country and far from any human face'.[40]

Chapter 14

THE 'IDLENESS' OF SANT 'ANDREA:
THE *DISCOURSES* AND THE *PRINCE*

◇◇

S ANT 'ANDREA in Percussina is a little village set on the old
Roman postal road,[1] seven miles from Florence and two from
San Casciano. A small parish church, a house used as an inn, and
close beside it a 'great house' as it was then called, but which would be
better described as a poor man's house; a bit of open tower with
various hovels built up against it, and others across the road used as
oil-press, bakehouse, cowshed and stable; a poor farmhouse inhabited
by peasants who work the farm: these houses, these hovels and this
farm, called *Borgo* or *Strada*, together with another farm called the
Poggio and the lands of Montepugliano and Fontalle, form the little
kingdom of the Florentine Secretary, now become a countryman and
his own farm bailiff. The 'great house' is called the *Albergaccio* after the
inn which stands beside it, and this name 'the wretched inn' tells us all
we need to know about the quality of both of them. To the west, on
the right-hand side of the road which leads to San Casciano, he owns
only a few pieces of land: all his property, vineyards, olive groves and
woodland, runs down the southern slope from the little village to the
stream called the Greve, which can be seen right at the bottom of the
valley with so little water in it in the summer that it shows a skeleton
of white stones.

Here Niccolò Machiavelli has come to shut himself away *post res
perditas*, 'resolved to think no more about politics or to discuss them'.
This is, after the dark prison, his green and sunny place of confinement.

145

It is the country of his childhood, the land dear to his forefathers, but at first he is somewhat unhappy and resentful to be there. It seems a suitable place to retire to quietly for the enjoyment of his last leisured days, in the evening, not the high noon of life, and the full vigour of his powers. Simple country things seem to him unworthy of his talents. Men find it difficult to realize that their great preoccupations are, in the face of nature, but small and ephemeral.

But he is also a poet, and the Tuscan countryside is really beautiful, sober and varied, at once gentle and harsh, hesitating like Machiavelli's own nature between laughter and tears. One who goes back to it as he was doing after a long absence, is helped to rediscover forgotten aspects of himself; it is not only the winds and the sun, the dawn and the sunset that have this effect, but the humblest things: a simple river shell, the scent of a flower, the aroma of wild herbs, the song of a bird, suffice to regenerate senses that are dulled and distorted. Physical contact with the earth, smelling of roots and herbs, has power to renew in every man the myth of Anteus.

Thus it is with Machiavelli. After so many trials and sufferings, he is soothed by that peace, his misfortune loses its sting and becomes an active ferment as does his continued idleness. His mind, full of things that no one has ever said before, germinates as the trees and grasses do around him after the long winter's rest. The letters of Vettori too had acted as a first stimulus, bringing his thoughts back to political affairs. After the famous letter of the 29th of April concerning the truce, which marked the lapse of his vow to silence after an interval lasting the whole of May and part of June, their exchange of letters begins again.[2]

On the 12th of July his friend the ambassador proposed a new theme, even though the subject was still the usual one: 'I would like to be with you and see if we could reorganize this world, and if not the world, at least this part of it; this seems to me very difficult to deal with in theory, so that if it were to be put into practice, I would regard it as impossible.' With this premiss and having discussed the conditions and intentions of the great powers, he ended by asking the former secretary to 'arrange a peace in writing' for him.[3] So the two friends exchanged letters throughout July and August, each devising a peace settlement in his own way. Machiavelli would have liked the Pope, who was still neutral more from doubt or cunning than from the goodness of heart which was ascribed to him, to take the part of the King of France and that the latter should have back the Duchy of Milan.[4]

On the 20th of August, Vettori, who thought otherwise, wrote a letter in which, after bringing the exile up to date on the events of the outside world, he marshalled his arguments which seemed to him to support his peace as opposed to Machiavelli's.[5] The latter replied humorously on the 26th that this letter had at first amazed him by the order and multiplicity of its arguments, but later when he had examined it more closely he had the same experience 'as the fox when he saw the lion; the first time he nearly died of fright, the second time he stopped to observe him from behind a bush, and the third time he spoke to him.' Speaking, therefore, with his friend he reproved him for the error of 'taking this King of France to be a nothing and this King of England to be a great thing'.[6] Once again Machiavelli judged right, even though by digressing into his favourite idea of a nation strong in its own arms and taking little account of what Aristotle wrote about republics, he went on to lose himself in pursuit of his prejudice about the Swiss menace, just as Vettori did about the Turks.

Whether he did not care for the fable of the fox, or whether he had nothing to say in reply, though the princes, continuing to play their wretched game at the people's expense, daily furnished new material for reflection, Vettori did not answer his letter, and for several months gave no sign of life. Machiavelli did not write to him either to stimulate and urge him on. He had other things to occupy his leisure and his thoughts: he had found his way at last, 'a way as yet untrodden by any',[7] and he moved swiftly along it.

For many years past, perhaps from the very time of his embassy to Caesar Borgia, he had employed his rare and brief *otia inter negotia* in writing down some of his memorable experiences of human actions and comparing them with those of the ancients. In this way, by practice and by intuition, his genius had led him to be the first to appreciate in history 'that flavour which it possesses',[8] and to draw from it the principles and general rules of a new science. This has as its basis the theory that human nature, with its desires and vices, its virtues and weaknesses, does not change with the passage of time[9]—a theory which certainly needs modifying as do nearly all those formulated through the centuries by innovators, but which contains a part of truth and opens the way to truth even where it errs.

It is probable, and I would say almost certain, that the first propositions of this doctrine were formulated as notes to the Decades of Livy, as, re-reading this history and comparing his 'continual reading' with his 'long experience', he discovered 'the flavour which it [history] possesses'. These notes were perhaps written in the margins of that same copy given by the printer Niccolò della Magna to messer Bernardo, which Niccolò had long gazed upon and savoured in his father's study.[10] When misfortune came, 'withdrawn into the country and far from any human face', idleness, unhappiness and necessity caused him to seek those pages again, and what was not yet written in them he sought within himself, for he was now full to overflowing with ideas. And so, in the form of discourses on the Decades of Livy he began to write a treatise on republics, even though the resulting book, originating as a commentary, was to retain basically the form of a commentary.

He was to work on this great book for many years, never entirely abandoning it; but it is evident that he completed a part of it in the first impetus given by the early days of his leisure. We see him working on it with the enthusiasm of a discoverer, his joy and fervour increasing when a fresh example ancient or modern comes to mind and confirms his theories, the truth he suspected. The greatness and the novelty of the enterprise excite him beyond measure, almost frighten him, as he foresees for himself the dangers, the unhappy destiny of one who 'seeks unknown lands and seas'.[11]

But while he is immersed in this book of his, whose only real unity is constituted by his new doctrines and the logic of his own thought, another book germinates from the same shapeless material he is working on. This one is entirely concrete, perfect in shape, straight and sharp as a sword. By virtue of his age, nation, family and class, he always inclined with all his heart to the popular state, and this inclination he long nourished on the deeds of republican Rome, the only Rome he loved. But, against this inclination, his farsighted intellect told him that Italy was moving into the age of princes; therefore, he must write of principalities. In those very days, as his *Discourses* on Livy reached the chapter where it is shown that 'a corrupt people attaining freedom has the greatest difficulty in maintaining its liberty', turning his eyes from ancient Rome to the Italian cities of his own times, he considered 'that all those members were corrupt'.[12] Now 'it is necessary to resort to extraordinary means such as violent action and force of arms, and above all to become prince of the state.'[13] Only a 'new prince' could revive those rotting limbs; only in such a prince would Lazarus in the end find 'his redeemer'. Ten years before, Borgia had nearly succeeded with the help of good fortune and a Pope; and after the disappearance of the Borgias, Julius II again showed what the Church might do in Italy. Now the Church was led by a Florentine, who united the power of the Florentine state with his ecclesiastical power; he had a young brother and a young nephew, both seeking to rule, and he himself was also marvellously 'favoured by heaven and by fortune'.

Thus did the book *de Principatibus*, the *Prince*, germinate in the mind of the exile of Sant 'Andrea, with the intention of dedicating it to one who seemed to possess all the qualities of the awaited 'new prince' except one: 'virtue'. For that reason, in his book he passes quickly over hereditary principalities and deals briefly with those acquired by virtue, to expatiate instead on those acquired by good fortune. This had been the case with Valentino and Pope Alexander, and it was repeating itself with Giuliano and Pope Leo. The fortunes of Italy may depend on these men, and Machiavelli's own certainly do. Italy! a name until then sacred only to poets. To turn it into a political concept it needed a politician who was also a poet.

The pattern of the prince which he wants to set before Giuliano, if he enjoys 'the flavour of history', is not that commonly approved by divine and human precepts, which 'everyone understands how praiseworthy it is',[14] but one which, given the state of the times, may lead to the desired results. He has taken on the task of guiding this redeemer to a difficult redemption, of doing battle with wickedness and with the wicked, of usurping the usurpers. As a captain only reasons in military terms and a man of science in scientific terms, he does not take into account moral considerations foreign to the development of his theories. He is guided only by an iron logic. As he theorizes about the triumph of the state, only the state counts for him, and he wants religion itself organized by and subordinated to the state. If his task were, like that of the Friar, to theorize about the triumph of religion in men's hearts, the same inexorable logic would lead him down the opposite road. The war is just which is necessary; the prince is merciful who in his cruelty saves a nation from much worse cruelties; deeds, whatever they may be, are holy, which lead to holy ends; the end will redeem the means, just as the famous final exhortation redeems his book from its impious and cruel maxims:

'One should not therefore allow this occasion to pass for Italy after so long a time to find her redeemer. Nor can I express with what affection he would be received in all those provinces which have suffered from the floods of these foreign invasions, with what thirst for revenge, what unshakeable fidelity, what piety, what tears. What gates would be shut against him? What peoples would refuse him obedience? What jealousy would oppose him? What Italian would deny him respect? This barbarian rule stinks in everyone's nostrils! Therefore let your illustrious House take up this task with that spirit and those hopes which attend just enterprises, so that under its banner this country may be ennobled, and under its auspices what Petrarch wrote may come true:

> Virtù contro a furore
> prenderà l'arme; e fia el combatter corto:
> chè l'antico valore
> nell 'italici cor non è ancor morto[15]

[Virtue will take up arms against fury, and the fight will be brief; for the ancient valour is not yet dead in Italian hearts].

In this work Machiavelli's new political theories, rewoven on the fabric of a dream, rise in the final lyrical exhortation, to the realms of poetry. No one would wish to insult him by supposing that he did not realize the differences there were between the Medici and the Borgias. But, whatever they were, those differences could not inhibit his great vision of the redemption of Italy, or that, as was only human, of his own redemption.

Under the impulse of that vision the work issued whole and complete in a very short time. I do not think any man in the depths of his misfortune was ever so happy as Machiavelli was during those evenings by lantern light as he chiselled out from the shapeless mass of his old annotations and his new doctrines the sharp outline of his *Prince*.

Immersed in his subject, he thought of nothing else. He went to Florence on business or to fetch books. He had not written again to Vettori, and it was his friend who finally on the 23rd of November broke the long silence and began their correspondence again. It was Machiavelli's fate to owe all his masterpieces to other men's malevolence, indifference and selfishness. He owed the *Prince*, the *Discourses*, and many other of his immortal pages to the Medici, who drove him out of office, interned him, and left him for a long time in poverty and neglect. It has been well said that 'just as with Dante one cannot imagine the *Comedy* without his exile, so with Machiavelli [these works] cannot be conceived ... without his exile from political affairs'.[16] Similarly he owes a great deal to Vettori who by failing to give him that assistance which he certainly might have done, left him to the inspiration of misfortune, and furthermore, by writing him these idle letters, evoked answers some of which between jest and earnest are extremely fine. Then, with that letter of his of the 23rd of November to which we have already referred, he gave Machiavelli not just the occasion but the very theme itself for the most famous letter in the whole of Italian literature.

With his usual indolent urbanity his friend the ambassador had described to him his comfortable but useless life in Rome.[17] Replying on the 10th of December, Machiavelli narrates in return his own life at Sant 'Andrea.[18] In recent months he has been snaring thrushes with his own hand; rising before dawn, he prepared his snares, and went off with a pile of cages on his back looking like 'Geta returning from the port with Amphitryon's books'. This went on throughout November (according to my amended reading of the text),[19] and then when the migration of the thrushes came to an end, and with it to his sorrow this pastime, 'although a strange and disagreeable one', his life had become what I would not dare to describe with words other than those of the great writer himself:

'I rise in the morning with the sun, and I go off to a wood of mine which I am having cut down, where I stop for two hours to see what was done the day before and to talk to the woodcutters who always have some trouble on hand either among themselves or with their neighbours ... Leaving the wood I go to a spring and thence to some bird-traps of mine. I have a book with me, Dante or Petrarch or one of the minor poets, Tibullus, Ovid or the like. I read about their amorous passions and their loves, I remember my own, and dwell enjoyably on these thoughts for a while. Then I go on to the road and into the tavern. I talk to the passers-by, I ask what news of their villages, I hear all sorts of things, and observe the various tastes and ideas of men. In the meanwhile it is time for dinner, and with my folk I eat what food this poor farm and miserable patrimony of mine provides. When I have eaten I go back to the tavern. Here I find the host, and usually a butcher, a miller, and a couple of kilnmen. With them I degrade myself playing all day at *cricca* and tric-trac, and this gives rise to a thousand arguments and endless vexations with insulting words, and most times there is a fight over a penny, and we can be heard shouting from as far away as San Casciano. And so, surrounded by these lice, I blow the cobwebs out of my brain and relieve the unkindness of my fate, content that she trample on me in this way to see if she is not ashamed to treat me thus.

'When evening comes I return home and go into my study, and at the door I take off my daytime dress covered in mud and dirt, and put on royal and curial robes; and then decently attired I enter the courts of the ancients, where affectionately greeted by them, I partake of that food which is mine alone and for which I was born; where I am not ashamed to talk with them and inquire the reasons of their actions; and they out of their human kindness answer me, and for four hours at a stretch I feel no worry of any kind; I forget all my troubles, I am not afraid of poverty or of death. I give myself up entirely to them. And because Dante says that understanding does not constitute knowledge unless it is retained in the memory, I have written down what I have learned from their conversation and composed a short work *de Principatibus*. . . .'

In such a mixture of happiness and unhappiness, of dream and reality, of base things and greatness, wholly resembling the man himself, the *Discourses* and the *Prince* had their origin. Machiavelli tells his friend about the *Prince* in this same letter of the 10th of December with words shot through with satisfaction, love and hopefulness. He tells him to ask Filippo Casavecchia about it, as he has read it, although he is still busy expanding and polishing it. Machiavelli did indeed expand and polish but not transform it entirely as those critics pretended who believed in the existence of two versions.[20] He also tells him that he proposes to address the book to Giuliano, and of his hesitation whether to present or not to present it to Giuliano. Against presenting it stood the eloquent doubt 'that it might not even be read by Giuliano'; against not presenting it was his own overwhelming need, the fear of becoming 'contemptible through poverty'. He writes further of '. . . the desire I have that these Medici princes should begin to employ me, even if at first it were only something menial; for if I then did not gain their favour, I should blame myself. And if they read this work of mine, they would see that the fifteen years I have spent in the study of politics, I have not wasted or gambled away; and anyone ought to be glad to use a man who has gained a great deal of experience at other people's expense. Of my fidelity there should be no doubt, for having always kept faith, I should not now learn to break it. A man who has been faithful and virtuous for forty-three years as I have, cannot change his nature; and my poverty is evidence of my fidelity and virtue'.

Vettori at first did not even reply to this remarkable letter, and to obtain an answer Machiavelli had to write again to remind him of it, at the same time commending to him the ambitious intrigues of his friend Donato.[21] He got his reply, written on the 24th of December, and it was full of the usual chatter, which certainly pleased Machiavelli, though rather less when fame and hunger were at stake. Of the things which most mattered to him, 'being without occupation and earnings', his friend the ambassador said only that he could see nothing suitable for him in Rome, unless certain vague ideas about a mission to France by Giulio de' Medici materialized. This was the bastard son of the old Giuliano, recently made a cardinal by the Pope. In France the old Secretary with his knowledge of the country and the language might be useful. On the subject of the *Prince* his cold reply was: 'when you have sent me that treatise, I will tell you if I think it is a good idea for you to come and present it.'[22]

Machiavelli did not lose heart. He went on polishing his work, but still dressed his noble ideas in a popular garb.[23] In the meantime he kept up his correspondence with his friend, idly answering his idle letters. Vettori had complained jokingly of his guests, Casavecchia and Brancacci, who had admonished him to reform his house and lead a more sober life; in reply Machiavelli advised him to keep them on lenten fare so that they might regret their lost carnival.[24] This advice had so prompt an effect that Vettori was obliged to congratulate the giver of it and recognize in him 'judgement in matters both great and small'.[25] Machiavelli, however, who gladly dealt in small things, but aspired to great ones, and had begun to make a fair copy of his book, hastened to send Vettori a few chapters as soon as he had copied them. Vettori's reply, full of the usual gossip and amorous anecdotes, gave them no more than a mention: 'I have seen the chapters of your work, and they please me beyond measure; but I do not want to offer an opinion, until I have seen the rest.'[26]

With that 'beyond measure' the quiet and cautious ambassador may have thought he had said a great deal. To Machiavelli, who was still in the first flush of enthusiasm, it must have seemed a cold as well as an indecisive judgement. But he did not worry about it. About that time he moved with his family back to the city,[27] perhaps to spend the rest of the winter in greater comfort, perhaps to help himself better than

Vettori was doing, by publishing his work among his friends. He had gone into the country empty-handed and almost in despair; he came back eight months later full of hope. He brought with him from his study at the Albergaccio certain notebooks containing nothing less than part of the *Discourses* and the *Prince*, as yet untouched by the ill-will or indifference of men.

Chapter 15

LOVE AND SUFFERING

◇◇◇

FLORENCE, however, was not for Machiavelli what it had once been, and city idleness seemed no better to him than idleness in the country. A merry companion and lover of conversation, he must have enjoyed seeing faces and hearing talk more urbane than those of the innkeeper, butcher and kilnmen of Sant 'Andrea. In the wine cellars where Florentine wit, mordacity and subtlety flourished, he was the sort of man to win the honours every day, and this too was a way of exercising his intellect. But combats of this kind were not enough for him without other employment. When evening came he found himself with that ephemeral harvest of useless jests, more alone than in the solitude of the Albergaccio which was peopled with immortal voices.

He frequented the shop of Donato del Corno, who was always on the look-out for handsome boys, and the house of Riccia, a 'respectable' but not too respectable courtesan. His reputation for wisdom won him a place at the fireside of the merchant, who aspired to rise above his plebeian origins, and a few kisses 'on the quiet' stolen from the handsome woman. Fireside and kisses he repaid with good advice. When this turned out badly (in life as in politics!), one called him a shop-pest, the other a house-pest.[1] Poor Machiavelli!

At this period too his correspondence with Vettori takes a really important place in his life, and not only in his biography for lack of other documents. Among his old friends Vettori was one of the few who was acceptable to the new régime, which had now kept him in

Rome as ambassador for two years; and it was from Rome that favours and jobs had to come. The arrival of each letter from Vettori was, therefore, an event awaited with impatience in Machiavelli's house, but more than ever during the last part of this winter. On the 23rd of November Vettori had invited him to share his restful life in Rome, where he promised him 'no other employment than walking about looking at things, and then returning home to joke and laugh'. A lover of his ease and freedom, Vettori did nót live like an ambassador; he saw few people, because there were few people who interested him, nor, among the great concourse of men who poured into Rome from every corner of Europe, had he found, he said, anyone to compare with Machiavelli.[2] A rare compliment indeed from a man so cold and hard to please.

But Machiavelli, though grateful for the invitation, hesitated to accept it. He was held back by the thought of the Soderini. After the relations he had had with them, he did not think it proper to stay in Rome without calling on them; and yet if he did so, he feared he would end up in the Bargello as soon as he returned home.[3] Despite Vettori's reassurances,[4] he did not go. However tempting the luxurious life that was offered him might be, he wanted to go to Rome with the *Prince* and there present it. He wanted to be sent for by those 'Medici princes', as he had written in his famous letter of the 10th of December; he wanted to come up from the country and say 'here I am'.

Instead time passed and every letter from Vettori was a fresh disappointment. He talked about frivolities, about his amorous affairs, about the boorishness of his critics, 'Casa' and Brancacci. Machiavelli, partly because he did not at all dislike such subjects, partly to keep the correspondence going, played up to him. He reminded his friend that the man who is thought wise by day cannot be thought a fool by night;[5] he urged him to love without restraint,[6] and related to him the jokes of the Florentine wine-cellars. On the 25th of February he gives an account of a dirty trick played by Brancacci on Casavecchia, who had come to Florence for the carnival. It would have required very little to make this letter, full of freshness and vitality, into one of the best short stories, for all its obscenity, in the whole of Italian literature.[7]

Suddenly Machiavelli changes the subject, and passes from facetious matters to political ones. 'After an interval of a thousand years'—as it seems to him—he returns to his old loves with a speculation on the

King of Spain, who had always been 'the prime mover of the disorders of Christendom'.[8] But he ends his letter by asking for a recommendation for the Ufficiali di Monte [loan-office], as he is threatened with a tax demand for forty florins, and his income is only ninety. Vettori replies to these caprices with others of his own, and wonder of wonders! recommends his friend, at the same time ingeniously contriving to recommend himself. He writes to the Ufficiali that Machiavelli 'is poor and worthy, no matter what anyone says to the contrary, and I can vouch for him . . . He has heavy tax to pay and little income; he has no money and many children'.[9]

Vettori was like that: a good companion, affectionate, helpful to his friends when all he had to do was to write a letter. But if it was a case of pressing a matter, coaxing someone unwilling to listen, swimming against the current, risking the loss of a scrap of good will on behalf of someone who had lost all favour—this was not a task for him. He had wit enough to be fond of Machiavelli and appreciate him, but not heart enough to help him if it were going to be inconvenient or require effort. So, having received and read the rest of the *Prince*, and perhaps having tried out the ground again and found it unpropitious, he said nothing more to his friend either about the book or about his coming to Rome, for he did not want to come without the book. He went on filling his letters with amusing chatter, pleased to find that the replies were in the same vein. At last Niccolò, who was the more embarrassed of the two, seeing how things were dragging on, had to ask him for a definite answer; and then the answer came at once, and although it was what he had been expecting,[10] it was a terrible blow.[11]

At first he was so angry that he did not even reply, though he did later say he had written and forgotten his letter in the country, where he had returned in the meantime with his family.[12] On the 10th of June he replied more briefly than usual and with considerable bitterness:

'So I shall stay here among my lice, without there being anyone who remembers my services or believes that I can be useful in any way. But it is impossible for me to go on like this for long, because I am rotting away in idleness, and I see that if God does not help me, I shall some day be forced to leave home and take a job as a tutor or as secretary to a governor if I cannot find anything else, or settle in some deserted spot to teach reading to children, and leave my family here to carry on as though I were dead; for they will get on much better without me, because I am an expense to them, being inclined to spend and unable to live without spending. I am not writing this to you because I want you to take trouble on my behalf, but simply to get it off my chest and not to write again about it, for it is as disagreeable a subject as may be.'

After this, the correspondence languished. Vettori did not reply to that cry of despair for more than six weeks, seeing his friend to be 'afflicted beyond measure', and being unable to offer him the consolation he would have liked.[13] When at last he wrote on the 27th of July, his letter was entirely given over to the venal ambitions of Donato del Corno. No more than a dozen words were spared for Machiavelli's noble ambitions and the bread he had begged with such dignified insistence. Help came to him, very different from what he had hoped, and from a quarter whence he could least expect it: from Love.

In a letter of the 3rd of August, which should have been an answer to Vettori's of the 27th of July but is not, he no longer speaks of Donato's affairs nor of his own unhappiness, but only of the happiness he derived from having fallen in love. This was no longer like his dalliance with Riccia; it was an affair into which Niccolò put all his passionate nature, almost, I would say, the same fervour with which shortly before he had written the *Prince*:

'While in the country I have met a creature so delicate, so noble by nature and by fortune, that I could never praise or love her as much as she deserves . . . Suffice it to say that, now nearing my fiftieth year, the heat of the sun does not offend me, nor rough roads weary me, nor the darkness of the night frighten me. Everything seems easy to me; and I bend myself to every whim, even to those which ought to seem different and contrary to my own. And although I feel myself now in great travail, yet I feel so great a sweetness in it, both because of the delight that rare and gentle aspect brings me, and because I have forgotten all my troubles, that for nothing in the world would I desire my freedom even could I have it. Therefore I have given up thinking of great and grave matters. I no longer delight in reading ancient histories nor in reasoning of modern events: all have been transformed into tender thoughts . . .'[14]

The object of this love was, then, one of his country neighbours, but not so close a neighbour that to enjoy her company he had not to face rough roads under a blazing sun or in the darkness of the night. His friends were well acquainted with the transports of his love-affairs and the passion they aroused in him[15]; and this one had taken hold of him late in life, and after many labours and sufferings. Farewell curial robes; farewell shades of famous men conversing in the study at the Albergaccio of an evening! At forty-five Machiavelli no longer writes of politics, nor of the 'flavour of history', but love poems: *Avea tentato il giovinetto arciere . . .*[16]

This is certainly not one of those usual literary loves that are all pretence. Machiavelli disliked literary invention in all things, and most of all, I imagine, in love. There is in fact no evidence of his writing any major work at this time, which partly confirms the sincerity of the letter we have quoted (if indeed further confirmation were needed other than what we know of his character). Not even among the datable additions to the *Discourses* do we find anything which can be attributed to this period. As for the *Prince*, it has been shown that he did not touch it again.[17] This amour, however, was not entirely a bad thing for him, because it delivered him out of utter despair, and though possibly bringing him fresh anxieties, made him forget his cruellest sufferings. A powerful love affair is always an enrichment of the spirit; and if this one of Machiavelli's was not, as such affairs often are, a stimulus to action, one cannot exclude the possibility that in time it did have an effect: as flood waters do, which, when they recede, leave on the fields a fertile deposit.

At this point too there is a gap in the correspondence with Vettori, and it is not simply that we have lost trace of the letters of that time.[18] In December, however, when Machiavelli was in the country tempering the rigours of winter with his amorous ardour, a letter from his friend the ambassador came to revive the languishing flame of politics. He had promised, when he wrote about his falling in love, never to discuss politics again, since he had 'never got anything but trouble' from them; but even this time he did not have any difficulty in breaking his vow. How could he resist? His friend put a problem to him and gave him clearly to understand that the Pope would read the answer. He added: 'I know that you are a man of such talent that, although it is two years since you gave up the business, I do not believe you have forgotten your skill.'[19]

The questions were these: supposing that the Pope wished to maintain the Church in that same spiritual and temporal dignity in which he had found it, and supposing that the King of France wanted to retake the state of Milan, having with him the Venetians and against him the Emperor, the King of Spain and the Swiss, what should the

Pope do? What dangers and advantages would derive from an alliance with France, or from one with Spain, or from neutrality? The stake, as Vettori put it, might be the Pope's favour. The desire to restore his fortunes had not been destroyed in Machiavelli by his amorous desires, for in a Latin letter to his friend written to recommend to him one Niccolò Tafani, which crossed with the one from Vettori, bringing these papal questions, he spoke again about his old worries.[20]

He therefore takes up the challenge, and on the 10th he replies in a long letter entirely consistent with his theories and faithful to his own inclinations. Excluding the possibility of neutrality, recognizing greater chances of victory on the side of the French, considering a victory of the King of France 'less to be feared and more easily borne' than the victory of his enemies, and a defeat suffered in his company less disastrous, he advises the Pope to join with France. Events were to show that the advice was sound.[21]

When this reply had been sent, suspense began again for Machiavelli, and his correspondence with Vettori at once revived. In the space of two days two letters went from Sant 'Andrea to Rome besides the one already mentioned to recommend Tafani or rather his sister who, abandoned by her husband, wanted to settle her affairs one way or the other. I personally am convinced that she was the object of the Secretary's passion. *Qua nihil est in hoc nostro rure suavius* are in fact the words used in his recommendation with reference to the Tafani family; but it is a kind of synecdoche, by which the whole stands for the part. Machiavelli must have found one member of that family particularly delightful. Of the two letters I have mentioned, sent in two days, one was to ask for some blue wool for a pair of stockings; and his friend did well to write and say that he did not want to know who it was for, because it evidently was not difficult to guess.

To revive Machiavelli's hopes there came on the 15th of December a letter from Vettori, who having read and approved the answer to his questions, now had no scruples about saying openly that the commission to propose them had been given to him by the all powerful Cardinal de' Medici.[22] The Secretary's impatience and hopes increased as the days went by. On the 20th of December, unable to bear it any longer, under colour of wanting to say more about the question of neutrality and of what the Pope had to fear from the victor, he sent a substantial addition to his very long letter of the 10th.[23] On the same day he also wrote yet another letter to his friend in reply to one of the

15th, showing himself more than ever hopeful of being employed by the Medici 'in Florentine affairs or elsewhere'.[24] This brought an answer to the effect that both letters had been seen by the Pope, by Cardinal de' Medici and by Bibbiena, 'and all have marvelled at their cleverness, and praised the judgement of their contents'. But Vettori adds at once and quite frankly that he has got no other response than kind words, 'because I am not a man who knows how to help his friends'.[25]

At last he had said it! He tried to compensate the poor Secretary with the blue wool for his lady, not wishing to fail him 'in a hundred years', as he wrote, at least in this small thing he had asked. I do not know how far this material can have softened the blow, but luckily Machiavelli had by now developed a thick skin. Soon afterwards he was again full of fresh hopes.

Paolo Vettori had been in Rome about that time and had often discussed Machiavelli and ways of helping him with his brother the ambassador.[26] He returned to Florence towards the end of December, and set to work to try to do something for him. Being less punctilious, less egotistical, and more of a courtier than his brother, he made far better progress in a short time. Amid the great variety of plans that were milling around at that time in Pope Leo's mind to appease the ambitions of members of his family, it now seemed more or less certain that Giuliano would become ruler of Parma, Piacenza, Modena and Reggio.[27] Paolo, for whom Giuliano had great affection and trust, would have a leading role in the new state, and Machiavelli would have his share too.

On the last day of January 1515 one of his letters to Francesco Vettori shows him back in his old form again, bold as a young cock. He sends the verses he has written for his beloved, tells of his love, his tears and his laughter. Then suddenly, with a brusque transition he writes:

'Anyone who saw our letters, my honourable friend, and saw the differences in them, would be very astonished, because he would think that sometimes we are serious men, entirely absorbed in great matters, and that no thought could enter our heads that had not in it decency and greatness. But then, turning the page, he would think those same men to be frivolous, inconstant and lewd, and quite absorbed in vanities. This behaviour, though to some it may seem blameworthy, seems to me laudable, for we imitate nature which is variable; and anyone who imitates nature cannot be reproved. And although we usually show this variety in different letters, this time I want to bring it into a single one, as you will see if you read the other side. Purge yourself.'

And so on the next page he discusses the advice given to Giuliano through Paolo on the manner of ruling the new state.[28]

The thing therefore seemed to be settled. But even in the smallest details, Florence proposed and Rome disposed. When these proposals became known, Piero Ardinghelli, papal secretary, wrote to Giuliano: 'Cardinal de' Medici questioned me yesterday very closely if I knew whether Your Excellency had taken into his service Niccolò Machiavelli, and as I replied that I knew nothing of it nor believed it, His Lordship said to me these words: "I do not believe it either, but as there has been word of it from Florence, I would remind him that it is not to his profit or to ours. This must be an invention of Paolo Vettori; . . . write to him on my behalf that I advise him not to have anything to do with Niccolò".'[29] If it were not clearly expressed in the unadorned eloquence of these documents, it would be difficult to believe in so implacable a hatred!

Perhaps Niccolò never knew even from Paolo of this formal Roman veto, which would have filled him with terror and utter despair, even though he was soon to feel its consequences. At this period we know little of him, nor can this lack of information be entirely due to the accidental loss of documents.[30] Any man would speak little and get himself little spoken of when, despairing henceforth of all assistance, he shuts himself within himself away in his country hermitage, forgotten and trying to forget. Still, this gap in our information well expresses symbolically the low ebb of Machiavelli's fortunes at this point in his life.

We have some letters to his nephew Giovanni Vernaccia who was trading in Turkey. Some of these letters, which are simple and straightforward and concern domestic affairs, have been neglected by the present biographer whilst he had on hand, like Machiavelli himself, more important matters. It will be enough to give a brief indication in our notes of what has been neglected up to now.[31] At this point, however, this correspondence suddenly becomes valuable because of the absence of other documents, and more so because the poor Secretary, hounded by ill luck, seems to take refuge in family ties. Furthermore, with men like Vettori whom he regarded as his equals in intellect though superior in rank and fortune, he would hide behind his usual mask, now jocular, now over-bold, now cynical, and occasionally don his curial robes; but with his nephew he always showed his miseries naked and shamelessly. He wrote to him on the 18th of August 1515: 'If I have not written to you earlier, I do not wish you to blame me or anyone else, but only the state of the times. These have been and are still such that they have made me forget myself.'[32] And again some months later, on the 19th of November: 'Fate has left me nothing but my family and my friends.'[33]

While he wrote these words, Florence was in turmoil for the great preparations being made to welcome the Pope. Great events had recently again disturbed the affairs of Italy. Not long after Machiavelli sent his valuable counsels to Rome, King Louis died and the young and belligerent Francis I mounted the French throne, resolved to regain Milan and restore the honour of French arms. When the moment for a decision arrived, Pope Leo grew ever more irresolute; as Machiavelli had acutely foreseen from the beginning, 'present need or present fear, or both together',[34] caused the Pope to avoid making the simple choice set before him by his great fellow-citizen. Then, setting aside the idea of neutrality, he chose the worse alternative and renewed his league with the King of Spain. When Francis I entered Italy and defeated the Swiss at Marignano, the Pope found himself on the losing side. However, owing to his own duplicity which was well supported by his nephew Lorenzo de' Medici, captain of the armies of the Church, and by Francesco Vettori, commissioner of the Florentines, the papal forces had not been involved in the fighting. Leo must have been convinced by that victory, though he had not wished to believe, as he might have done, to his greater honour and profit, in Machiavelli's forecast. Now he was passing through Florence on his way to Bologna to meet the victor.

The Florentine state was now ruled by Lorenzo de' Medici. Giuliano, who was older and more closely related to the Pope, but had much less ambition, had been removed from his side by a lack of aptitude for dealing with Florentine affairs, and by the illness from which he died eight months later, in March 1516. Lorenzo had himself elected captain general of the Florentines in May 1515, and having failed in his first enterprise to capture Piombino, now turned his ambitions towards Siena and Lucca. Leo had him march on Urbino which he took in the course of a few days during June 1516, and on the 8th of October he became Duke of Urbino by papal investiture.

Great things had been said for some time of this young prince, 'not quite as astute as Valentino but almost',[35] and even more enthusiastic things were said of him in the heat of that victory.

It is not surprising, therefore, if Machiavelli, who had painted a fine portrait of Lorenzo two years before,[36] saw in him, rather than in the unwarlike Giuliano, his new Prince. At Urbino he had followed in the footsteps of the usurping Borgia, and now yet further conquests were expected of him. It is to him, therefore, that Machiavelli addresses his new illusions, his book of the *Prince*, urging him to the conquest of Italy with his fine dedicatory letter. In it he again asks with his usual dignity for what he knows is his due, a position suited to his talents: 'And if Your Magnificence from the summit of your greatness will sometime turn your eyes upon these lowly places, you will see how undeservedly I suffer great and continuous ill fortune'.[37]

At this time Francesco Vettori is constantly with Lorenzo, almost more a friend than a counsellor, and although 'he is not a man who knows how to help his friends', one may suppose he could help Machiavelli to present a book to a man with whom he stood in such a relationship of daily contact and friendship. It has been doubted whether the presentation was ever made, but the alternative made no difference to Machiavelli. Either he was not able to present the book and his disappointment was extreme, or he did so and its reception was such that it disappointed him no less. If one wishes to believe an anecdote attributed to Machiavelli, he took the book to Lorenzo 'at a moment when he was being offered a pair of coursing dogs, and he spoke and looked more kindly on the man who gave him the dogs than on him (Machiavelli); so that he departed in anger'.[38]

Be that as it may. The dedication of the *Prince* to Lorenzo is not earlier than September 1515, nor later, whatever may have been said on the subject, than September 1516.[39] Between these two dates, on the 15th of February he had written to his nephew Vernaccia: 'I have become useless to myself and to my family and my friends, because my grievous fate has so willed it'.[40] In October of the same year 1516, in order to have something to do, he accepted some humble commission at Leghorn.[41] He reached there on the 10th and was still there on the 15th.[42] Then we know nothing more of him until the 8th of June 1517, when he wrote again to Vernaccia: 'As I am forced to stay in the country by the adversities I have suffered and suffer still, I am sometimes a month together forgetful of my true self'.[43]

Chapter 16

LITERARY DIVERSIONS
THE ASS; MANDRAGOLA; BELFAGOR

◇◇◇

EXCLUDED from politics after the sufferings of the last few years and the disillusion of the last few months, now that the final seal seems to have been set on his sentence by the Pope's ill-will and the Duke's fatuous indifference, Machiavelli seeks solace and outlet for his talents in other ways. His leisure and his writings take on a colour which we might call more literary, if we did not see them as inspired by his misfortune. We have learnt to measure Machiavelli's sufferings by his smiles no less than by his sighs; and now smiles and sighs suddenly fill his pages.

The pages I refer to are those of the *Ass* (*L'Asino*)—to which 'Golden' was added later in error.[1] This short poem in terza rima, where the imitation of Dante has at times the flavour of caricature, should not be overlooked in these pages, although it has been neglected and misinterpreted by most people. The idea of the author's disguise as a beast so that he can bite those who are beasts in another sense, is a happy one. Some passages are very successful, though many others are prosaic, as is often the case with the verse of this great prose writer. But the autobiographical content with which we are here more concerned, is extremely valuable. The poem gains more distinction from its author than the author from his poem.

His caustic tone appears from the first lines. Having protested that he will not trouble Phoebus to come to his aid,

> *sì perchè questa grazia non s'impetra*
> *in questi tempi, sì perch'io son certo*
> *che al suon di un raglio non bisogna cetra*

[Both because such favour is not asked these days and because I am sure that the sound of braying needs no lyre],

he at once declares that he does not seek (as he had sought with the *Prince*!) 'return, reward or recompense', nor does he mind if he is bitten (as had happened with the *Prince*!)² by 'an open or hidden detractor', adding:

> *morsi o mazzate io non istimo tanto*
> *quanto io soleva, sendo divenuto*
> *della natura di colui che canto*

[I do not mind bites or blows as much as I did, having come to resemble the one (i.e. the ass) I sing].

Like the ass he will dispense bites and a few kicks³: accustomed at one time to giving them, he has been for long 'quiet, kind and patient': he has long travelled the roads of the world observing mankind, and will not now refrain from passing judgement on it, giving as good as he has got:

> *e l'asin nostro, che per tante scale*
> *di questo nostro mondo ha mosso i passi*
> *per lo ingegno veder d'ogni mortale,*
> . . . .
> *non lo terrebbe il ciel che non ragghiassi*⁴

[And our ass, who has trodden so many of the stairs of this world to observe the mind of every mortal man. . , heaven itself could not prevent him from braying].

Unfortunately the promise of the first chapter is not kept, because the poem stops short at the best point before the metamorphosis, but not before Niccolò has had the opportunity to lament again his bitter destiny:

> *Tra la gente moderna e tra l'antica*
> *. . . alcun mai non sostenne*
> *più ingratitudin, nè maggior fatica*⁵

[Among all people ancient and modern . . . no man ever suffered greater ingratitude nor greater labours];

and not before he has philosophized and theorized about states and their decline just as in one of the chapters of his *Discourses*, but here with less elegance and forcefulness.⁶

Naturally a poem imitating Dante could not fail to have its Beatrice, even if it is only a Beatrice who is a keeper of wild animals, including the less proud and less noble beasts, a Beatrice who goes to bed unchastely with her poet. It is quite possible that he may have wished to depict in her the woman whom he loved at that time. It is she who finds him when he is lost in the dark vale of his misfortune, and comforts and revives him, even though she is unable to prevent his being turned into an ass for a short time and for his own good. There are too many things we do not know about this affair, and first of all how long it lasted; and so we do not know if it had any influence on his renewed activity as a writer. If the lady did have such an influence, she certainly brought about one metamorphosis!

Machiavelli left off his *Ass* in the middle after a few weak chapters which show that his heart was no longer in the poem. Perhaps he realized in time that it was not the sort of poem that would overcome the cruelty which kept him out of government employment, or console him with some personal satisfaction. But he enjoyed the beginning just as we do; and he liked the idea he had clearly worked out in his mind for the final dénouement, because he spoke about it and perhaps read some bits of it to his friends.[7]

At this time his friendships and his interests in reading also appear more literary. In a letter to the poet Luigi Alamanni at Rome on the 17th of December 1517, again written in support of Donato del Corno, who had still not achieved his ambition to sit among the Signori, and had not yet been repaid 500 florins lent to Giuliano de' Medici in 1512, Machiavelli suddenly comes out with these words: 'I have been reading Ariosto's *Orlando Furioso*; and truly the whole poem is very fine and in many places quite marvellous. If he is there with you, commend me to him and tell him that my only complaint is that in his mention of so many poets he has left me out, and that he has treated me in his *Orlando* in a way in which I will not treat him in my *Ass*.'[8]

It makes one smile to see these two so immensely different poems brought together in this way; and it is only slightly less odd to read Machiavelli's complaint that Ariosto had not mentioned him among the numerous band of mediocre poets. One elegant critic unkindly remarked that Machiavilli was there confusing the qualities he really possessed with those he would have liked to have.[9] I would say rather that he confused the poetry he really felt within himself and which he had poured forth in the prose of the *Prince*, with that meagre and inferior poetry he put into his verse. Of this, Ariosto could only have known the first *Decennale*, or at most a 'capitolo' or two which circulated in manuscript.

A literary Machiavelli, and an academic into the bargain—that really would be (without intending any unkindness towards literary men) an even more amazing transformation than that described in the *Ass*! And yet at this very period, a little earlier or a little later, he was an habitué of the learned gatherings in the Orti Oricellari, which have been described, I do not know with how much justification, as an academy, even as a continuation of the Platonic Academy.[10] There, around the couch of Cosimino Rucellai, whose infirmity of body sharpened the avid curiosity of his mind, the cleverest young Florentines used to meet, and with them whatever gifted men of letters, of arms and of law, happened to be passing through Florence. Among the most faithful were Luigi Alamanni, the two Jacopo da Diacceto and Diaccetino, Jacopo Nardi, Filippo de' Nerli, Battista della Palla, Antonfrancesco degli Albizi; and there was always Zanobi Buondelmonti in whose house as well as at the Roman Court at the beginning of the papacy of Julius II, the Florentine Secretary must have struck up that acquaintance with Ariosto referred to in Machiavelli's letter to Alamanni.[11]

In this same letter we find gathered together in friendly intercourse just as they were in the Orti, a good many of those habitués. It was not then the season for sitting in the cool shade of the great trees; and as the moving spirit of the place was in Rome with Alamanni and Nerli, Machiavelli begged them to remember those they had left behind, 'poor, unfortunate, and dying of cold'. However, he added that, 'to seem alive', he, Zanobi Buondelmonti and Battista della Palla sometimes met to discuss a trip to Flanders they were planning to make, and became so enthusiastic about their project that they dreamed they were already on the road, with the result that they had used up a good half of the pleasures they expected to enjoy on the way. They had also considered doing 'a short version' of this great journey, and going to Venice for carnival time, but they could not decide whether to set off and go via Rome first to collect their friends, or whether to await their return and with them 'go straight there'.

Perhaps these were merely fantasies. But Niccolò did make one journey in fact: he went to Genoa in Lent on a mission for some great Florentine merchants, who sent him to save as much as could be saved in a case of bankruptcy. On the 3rd of March 1518 he was on the eve of departing,[12] and on the 26th he wrote from Genoa to those who had sent him. On the 8th of April they gave him detailed instructions on what to do in this tiresome business, and nothing was then said about the date of his return.[13] To earn a few florins, perhaps only to pay his expenses, but most of all to move, 'to seem alive', the former Secretary has gone back to his travels—he has accepted and will accept again to go as ambassador, not of the republic to other republics and to princes, but from one merchant to another. And all he will now talk of is debts and credits, dye-stuff and cloth.

There was no hope now of winning over the affections and the favours of those Medici princes, least of all of the degenerate Lorenzo. Vettori was in France, and would return from France with Lorenzo, becoming more of a courtier as his master became less of a citizen. So Machiavelli is reconciled to the situation, even though his recent wound still smarts. Having lost all hope that princes will appreciate and favour him, he has taken refuge in the kindness and generosity of private citizens: Rucellai, Buondelmonti, and Lorenzo Strozzi. We do not know what form their liberality took, and conjectures are of little use when evidence is lacking, but we know that Machiavelli expressed himself grateful for their help, and that an habitué of the Orti spoke of 'some emolument' given to him.[14] Perhaps it was the discreet settlement of some small debt, perhaps small rewards for services rendered to Strozzi's literary ambitions, or to the commercial interests of others. This assistance was accompanied with kindness, esteem and appreciation which to him were probably worth more than money. Thus, 'greatly loved and also helped out of kindness' by his noble friends, he had at last found some who knew his worth and 'greatly valued all his works'.[15]

If these favours cheered him, the learned conversations of the Orti must also have nourished and stimulated his mind. There, he had probably begun some time before to read those *Discourses on the First Decade of Livy* which, as we saw, suddenly germinated from earlier roots in the first leisured days at Sant 'Andrea. Since then he had worked on the book, probably in the first half of 1514, certainly in 1516 after his first amorous passions had cooled, and again in 1517.[16] This turning back to an old project cannot be described as a return from literature to politics. One might add speciously that these republican discourses read during the triumph of the Medici princes to a literary gathering, had a flavour that was more literary than political. Politics other than theory were not yet a subject of conversation in the Orti, whose habitués during Leo's lifetime were all convinced Medici partisans, whatever may inaccurately have been said to the contrary. Machiavelli was perhaps the least medicean of them all.

He read the *Discourses* beneath the shade of those hospitable trees to that group of clever young men who prized them more than 'coursing dogs'. Then at their instance he put his work together in a volume, as Filippo de' Nerli one of their number tells us, and dedicated it to those who had done most for him: Cosimo Rucellai and Zanobi Buondelmonti.[17] The dedicatory letter he wrote is perhaps the most important document we have for his state of mind at this time, and it surprises me that other biographers have not understood it for what it is: a protest against the man who had so long despised his talent and held his book of the *Prince* to be of no account. One can almost read between the lines the name of Lorenzo himself where the author declares that he did not wish to dedicate this other book of his to any prince, but to private citizens 'who for their infinite good qualities would greatly deserve to be [princes]'; not to anyone who could endow him with rank, honour and wealth (and had not done so !), but to those who, if they could, would like to do so—to those who knew how a state should be governed, not to one who governed without knowing how.[18] After reading this dedication the story about the coursing dogs preferred to the book, appears more likely.

This would be one of the most obscure periods of his life *post res perditas* if it were not studded with his masterpieces. New considerations which have escaped the notice of biographers and literary historians, enable us to place in this period with absolute certainty, that is in 1518,[19] the comedy entitled *Messer Nicia* or *Commedia di Callimaco e di Lucrezia*, and then better known as *Mandragola*.[20] This is a document which can console even the biographer for the lack of documents in archives, and which tells us no less than they would.

The very fine prologue to the comedy[21] is written with the same bitterness as the dedication of the *Discourses*:

> *E se questa materia non è degna,*
> *per esser più leggieri,*
> *d'un uom che voglia parer saggio e grave,*
> *scusatelo con questo, che s'ingegna*
> *con questi van pensieri*

> *fare el suo tristo tempo più suave,*
> *perch'altrove non have*
> *dove voltare el viso;*
> *chè gli è stato interciso*
> *mostrar con altre imprese altra virtue,*
> *non sendo premio alle fatiche sue*[22]

[And if this subject for being lighter, is not worthy of a man who wishes to appear wise and grave, pray excuse him because he is trying with these vain thoughts to relieve his misfortune, as he has nowhere else to turn; for he has been prevented from showing other virtue with different works, his labours having received no reward].

In the *Ass* he had sung not long before

> *de le fatiche sue senza ristoro*[23]

[of his labours without reward];

and here he returns again to his inconsolable sorrow. In the *Ass* he had threatened to revive his old art of 'biting' others, now in the *Mandragola* he repeats the same thing, throwing in the teeth of princes and those who think they are superior to him in rank, nobility and riches, his proud words of contempt:

> *Pur se credessi alcun, dicendo male,*
> *tenerlo pe' capegli*
> *e sbigottirlo o ritirarlo in parte,*
> *io lo ammunisco, e dico a questo tale*
> *che sa dir male anch'egli,*
> *e come questa fu la sua prim'arte;*
> *e come in ogni parte*
> *del mondo ove el sì suona,*
> *non istima persona,*
> *ancor che facci el sergieri a colui*
> *che può portar miglior mantel di lui*

[If any man should think by calumnies to hold him by the hair or frighten him or make him change his mind, I warn that man and tell him that he too can speak ill, and this was his first art; and that in every part of the world where Italian is spoken, he esteems no man, though he may play the servant to him who can wear a finer garb than he].

If the prologue in which one can already sense the certainty of a masterpiece, is a major biographical, i.e. autobiographical document, one can also say that all Machiavelli is to be found in all the comedy, laughing at the defects of his country and of religion and at his own misfortunes. As a great modern poet writes in prose, the power of laughter is a terrible thing,[24] and it is Machiavelli's favourite weapon. He uses laughter to defend himself, to save himself from the shame of tears as he had already written in the *Ass*:

> *Ma perchè il pianto a l'uom fu sempre brutto,*
> *si debbe al volto della sua fortuna*
> *voltare il viso di lacrime asciutto*[25]

[But because weeping was always unseemly for a man, one must to the countenance of one's fortune turn a face dry of tears].

I would dare to say, knowing Machiavelli, that the bitterness and long struggles he had suffered, crowned with his cruel disappointment over the *Prince*, could not end otherwise than with a *Mandragola*—with a smile full of suppressed anguish. We are reminded of those brief lines in which Machiavelli put all of himself:

> *Io rido e il rider mio non passa drento,*
> *Io ardo e l'arsion mia non par di fore.*

[I laugh and my laughter does not touch my soul; I burn and no one sees my passion].

In this marvellous comedy some have been able to discern some moral and social purposes; others have denied that it had any other purpose than to make people laugh:

> *pure, se non ridete,*
> *io son contento di pagarvi el vino*[26]

[moreover, if you do not laugh, I promise to pay for your wine].

I believe that Machiavelli wrote this play without thinking of farce or satire, and merely followed the irrepressible poetic spirit which inspired him sometimes to laughter and sometimes to tears. If, however, there were a purpose behind it, one could hardly say that this was to make people laugh when the comedy has far more the effect of making people think. It is easier to recognize in it, both for its thought and its poetic and human insight, the writer of the *Prince* than the author of the *Discourses*, even if Fra Timoteo with his cynical arguments and his 'face of a great rogue' may seem the artistic representation of the concepts theorized over in chapter 12 of book I of the *Discourses*: 'On the importance of respect for religion, and how Italy has come to ruin because that respect has failed on account of the Roman Church.'

There is a glimmer of tragedy, though far off, which chills the laughter of the comic farce until a smile or a grin comes to chase the sighs away again, just as in certain letters of Machiavelli, just as in his everyday life. And then there are those amusing sallies placed in the mouth of the foolish messer Nicia, and those sayings that have almost an autobiographical flavour: 'People like us who haven't got power in this city won't find even a dog to bark at us'.[27] The biographer does not wish to venture beyond his limits which here become somewhat blurred; but Machiavelli has put too much of himself into the *Mandragola*, even when it does not rise to the surface in some phrase like this last one, for us not to be compelled to notice it.

Nor does the biographer go beyond his duty in observing that the author's joy in composing the comedy shines through every part of it. This seems to me to be vouched for also by the fact that it was one of his favourite works. It is the elation which goes with the creation of masterpieces, the same which one feels in the pages of the *Prince*. This explains everything about the work: the novelty of the form almost entirely independent of ancient models, the modernity and humanity of the characters, the most Plautine of which, the parasite Ligurio, is just like a Florentine of the Mercato—all these new things from a man who is in so many ways linked to an earlier age. Genius and poetry have broken all these bonds and alone produced this novel work.

It is possible that *Mandragola* was read in the Orti before it was acted.[28] One might be tempted to conjecture that a performance was given during the great celebrations which took place on the return of Lorenzo with his French bride (7 September 1518), provided it were admitted that at that date the play was already finished and the actors had learnt their parts. If this condition were fulfilled, not even the mistrust and indignation that Machiavelli felt against the Medici would render the conjecture improbable.[28a] During the carnival and the Spring of 1519 there were few celebrations in Florence, at least openly, because of the Duke's grave illness and his death which occurred on the 4th of May in his twenty-seventh year. He had become unpopular in the city because of his behaviour, and he disliked the city because he could not rule it as he pleased. In the last years he trusted only in Filippo Strozzi and Francesco Vettori, who although in such favour never did anything for Machiavelli. Lorenzo was also fond of a certain citizen of small account, a great eater and a great chatterer, 'so that for his eating and chattering the Pope had given him an income of 200 scudi a year'.[29] To Machiavelli, who knew how to do other things besides eating and chattering, neither the Pope nor his nephew had ever given anything.

When Lorenzo died having disappointed everyone's hopes, Niccolò certainly did not go into mourning. But another death in the same year was a terrible blow: that of Cosimo Rucellai.[30] The meetings still went on in the Orti, which had been left to his paternal uncles Palla and Giovanni, the first a literary man in name, the second in fact. But the loss was great for the gatherings and for Niccolò, since they had lost the man who was their life and soul, and Machiavelli a patron generous in more than encouragement and praise, though this was the assistance he most needed.

Besides Machiavelli's literary works already mentioned here because of their chronology, we should also refer, because of their subject, to others whose date of composition is uncertain, but which probably belong to about this same period. I do not mean his poems such as the long and beautiful *Serenata* which Foscolo boasted he knew entirely by heart, and which chronologically would not be out of place here at the time of his love-affair.[31] I mean his *Dialogo intorno alla nostra lingua* [Dialogue concerning our language] and the story originally called *Il demonio che prese moglie* [The devil who took a wife] and now known as *Novella di Belfagor* [Tale of Belfagor]. A biography of Machiavelli cannot fail to mention them even though their date is uncertain.

There is no tangible evidence that the *Dialogo* is Machiavelli's, although critics and literary historians are today unanimous in attributing it to him. I too am more in favour of giving it to him than of taking it away, in spite of certain discrepancies of thought and style, which are, however, balanced by many features that are undoubtedly his.[32] Only Machiavelli could at that period say things so new about an old dispute. Only he could have said, for instance, of the neologisms required by every language 'whenever new thought or new trades come into a city': 'That language is said to be a national one, which adapts the words it has taken from others to its own use, and is so potent that the words it has borrowed do not alter it, rather it re-shapes them.'[33]

With an originality and acuteness rare in other writers on language, he closely argues a subject much debated at that period particularly since the re-discovery of the *De vulgari eloquentia*, that is, the question of the illustrious vernacular and the Florentine language. In his *Dialogo* he debates with no less a person than Dante himself, and as he has the advantage of being both plaintiff and judge, he is able to award himself the victory without difficulty. In quarrels, as one knows, 'blows are dealt regardless', and I do not think that certain contemptuous words about Dante should be seen as arguments against the attribution of the *Dialogo* to Machiavelli; although Dante was the poet whose work he carried with him in the woods at Sant 'Andrea, and imitated in the *Decennali* and the *Asino*, and whom he quoted, more than any of his contemporaries did, often from memory in his private letters.

The *Novella di Belfagor* is the only one Machiavelli put on paper of the many stories he invented and told at suppers or in wine-shops.[34] It is enough, however, to show us, with some of his letters, how far he might have excelled in this literary genre which seemed made for him. If *Mandragola* seemed to one critic a dramatized novella,[35] yet another felt that *Belfagor* was written up from a dramatic scenario.[36] Perhaps both are right, and the matter would merit further consideration, were it not outside the scope of these pages.

One thing, however, we must point out. There have been few Italian authors, even among the greatest, able to reach the heights in more than one literary genre. Machiavelli was supreme or left a profound mark on almost all those which his genius explored. An incomparable political and historical writer, he wrote only one novella, but that of outstanding merit. He wrote only one play arising spontaneously from his own inspiration, not from the importunity of friends or worked up for an occasion on the basis of Latin models; and with it he produced the best comedy in the whole of the Italian theatre, where even Ariosto had had only moderate success—the best play any modern author had written up to them, and perhaps the best Italian play of all time.

Chapter 17

THE *LIFE OF CASTRUCCIO* AND THE *ART OF WAR*. HISTORIES FOR FLORINS

◇◇◇

THE death of Lorenzo de' Medici did the Medici cause in Florence as much good as the death of his father Piero had done. The fresh infusion of Orsini blood, the newly created dukedom, the recent connection by marriage with the royal house of France, his mother's bad influence, and the bad advice of his courtiers, had stripped the last legitimate descendant of the great Lorenzo of that Florentine urbanity which the Florentines loved better than their liberty, for they sometimes might seem to have given up the latter willingly, the former never. In the last years of his life he lived surrounded by a few trusted advisers like a prince, and would have liked to make himself absolute master, held in check only by Pope Leo, who like a true son of the Magnificent deeply disliked Lorenzo's behaviour. Needless to say how he also displeased citizens like Jacopo Salviati, Lanfredini and others who were at once partisans of the Medici and of the Republic. Even his uncle, Cardinal Giulio, had been at loggerheads with him.

Lorenzo was not yet buried before the Cardinal came in all haste to Florence to take the city in hand, and at once reconquered the goodwill of the people. He restored authority or at least dignity to the magistrates; he lent an ear or pretended to do so, to the supporters of more liberal government; he showed himself humane in his actions and very patient in giving audiences; he handed out offices in proportion to the merit not the importunity of those who sought them. As careful of public money as of his own, the Florentines, always most sensitive on this point, were grateful to him for that first quality if not for the second. Unlike Pope Leo he hated gossips, gamblers and buffoons; 'a curious investigator of the quality of men . . . , he willingly conversed in his leisure time with men learned in any profession'.[1]

In these renewed conditions of the Florentine state, and with a man of this kind ruling it in the Pope's name, a talent like Machiavelli's could not remain forgotten and downcast as in the time of the empty-headed Lorenzo. We have already said that more than his friendship with Soderini, more than the services he had rendered to the free Republic, Leo could not forgive the Secretary's lack of cordiality towards himself and his brother Giuliano when they had met at the courts of France and Rome—a coldness in fact dictated by duty. But Giulio, a bastard, who had lived in the shade while the Medici family tree was full of green young shoots, had not been present on those occasions. While he was in Rome, therefore, his attitude reflected Leo's resentment, at whose express wish he opposed Machiavelli's employment by Giuliano, as we have already seen. But when he came to Florence, he had freedom to do as he liked at least in small things. Lorenzo Strozzi, more helpful than Vettori, and some other friends from the Orti brought Machiavelli to meet Giulio about the 10th of March 1520, and he was received with kindness. When he heard of that visit, Filippo Strozzi wrote to his brother: 'I am very glad you took Machiavelli to see the Medici, for if he can get the masters' confidence, he is a man who must rise.'[2]

Of his ability no intelligent man had any doubts, and these words of Strozzi's are further confirmation of it. What had prevented him from rising was the hostility of the ruling family, together with certain aspects of his character which might have diminished his reputation: lack of gravity, a certain extravagance in his opinions, and the curse of poetry. Now at last the ice was broken, and perhaps they would give him something to do. We know nothing of what passed between him and the Cardinal, but judging by slightly later documents and by later developments we may conjecture that the Cardinal asked him about the works that 'were still under construction in his workshop', and how he could help him. Perhaps the way was found that very day, and was suggested by those thoughts of writing histories which he had nourished since the days of the first *Decennale*.[3]

The work Machiavelli was engaged on at the moment, dedicated in gratitude for his recent kindness to Lorenzo Strozzi, was the *Art of War*[4] in seven books, which, following his habit of giving Latin titles to his vernacular works, he called from the beginning, *De re militari*. Military science was for him only an aspect of political science, and he was convinced that the beginning of Italy's troubles lay in having separated military from civil life. In consequence this new book is nothing less than the necessary complement to the *Prince* and the *Discourses*, and shows a remarkable coherence of thought and feeling. It is written in dialogue form, supposedly spoken in the Orti by Fabrizio Colonna in 1516 in conversation with Luigi Alamanni, Zanobi Buondelmonti, Battista della Palla, and first and foremost Cosimo Rucellai, who is mourned in these pages with deep affection.

What is most relevant to our purpose in the pages of the *Art of War* is first that here too Machiavelli combines the 'constant reading' of ancient authors[5] with his 'long experience' of modern affairs. During the Pisan war, the legations to Valentino and to Julius II, to France, Switzerland and Germany, he had observed carefully and concentrated his insatiable curiosity on military affairs, towards which he always had a marked inclination. The observations he had made there had helped him in instituting the Militia, which in turn had enriched his experience of military matters. The writer, undertaking to teach men of war their own art, is not afraid to assert that 'he did not think it wrong to assume with words a role which many with greater presumption have assumed with actions'[6]—and there were a good many princes who must have deserved this criticism.

Machiavelli's genius was such that in whatever direction he might turn his thoughts, he was capable of marvellous innovations and intuitions, even though he may also have been led into errors by passion and prejudice. The brilliant reflection of ancient times occasionally dazzled more than it illuminated his thought, and this may have prevented him from foreseeing the terrible future of firearms. At the time the book was written he could not possibly have seen their effects except in the quite recent battle of Marignano, of which he may not have had detailed reports. This has not prevented the book being recognized even in our own day as 'a portent not only for its own age, but also considered absolutely',[7] in so far as it concerns the unchanging aspects of military science. Villari's masterly judgement is still valid, that Machiavelli was the first to lay the foundations of modern tactics, 'and did so with an intellectual boldness no less than that with which he embarked on the founding of political science'.[8]

Where these pages are most closely connected with the *Discourses* and the *Prince* and with his efforts of past years, where the biographer most finds enthusiasm as well as sharpness of insight, is in the fundamental concept that the state must be strong with its own arms, that the soldiers must be decent, 'God fearing' men, good citizens willing to die for their country, not mercenaries dealing in violence, plunder and fraud.[9] So we hear the author through the mouth of Fabrizio Colonna (who probably thought just the opposite!) singing the praises of the Florentine militia, his own militia, and defending it against attack. To the objection that 'many wise men have always criticized it' on account of the 'poor results it has always given', he answers: 'Mark well that the fault may be in you, not in the system.' These words are spoken almost at the beginning of the first book and repeated almost unchanged in the last pages of the work. These final pages do not seem unworthy in passion and efficacy to be compared with the closing pages of the *Prince*; where old Colonna exhorts the young listeners to revive ancient valour in Italian breasts, 'for this province seems born to revive dead things, as we have seen in poetry, painting and sculpture'.[10]

While he is working on this book, his prospects improve for Medici favour. On the 26th of April his friend and close companion at the Orti, Battista della Palla, who is on very good terms at court because of his long record of allegiance and a gift he has made of extremely valuable sables, sends him from Rome a whole budget of good news. He has told the Pope, who is very fond of such things, about their meetings in the Orti, and how much they all value Machiavelli's intellect. He has spoken warmly of the *Mandragola* which was ready to be acted in His Holiness's presence. Leo was the sort of man who might more easily be won by a coarse comedy than by a *Prince*: he would have enjoyed the jokes and rejected what was bitter. Having thus first got him in a good mood, the clever courtier induced the Pope to give him a message for Cardinal de' Medici telling him to give effect to his goodwill towards Machiavelli with a 'commission to write, or something similar'. This was not all: Machiavelli had some time before sent to Cardinal Bibbiena the compliments of messer Nicia for his Calandro, and now receives 'most courteous messages' in return; Cardinal Salviati sends him kind words too; and finally, to add substance to fine words, Donato del Corno is to have his famous 500 ducats back, and some of them will be for the friend who had done so much to secure their return.[11]

Of course, more than the 'salary for writing' that any literary man might have desired beyond all else, as it would leave him free to go on quietly with his studies or even to live in idleness, the Florentine Secretary would have liked to have the office and all the worries he had had before, but for the Medici who did not really trust him, it was a convenient way out. The allusion in the letter of Battista della Palla would seem to confirm that it had already been spoken of, as I have suggested, at that first visit to the Cardinal. Certainly it had been discussed among the 'friends of the cool shade', as the habitués of the Orti used to describe themselves.[12]

In the meantime the poor man had to live somehow, and while he was waiting for his salary, which was appropriately to mature in the autumn, he was sent to Lucca to busy himself with the great bankruptcy of Michele Guinigi, in which some Florentine merchants, including the Salviati who were related to the Pope, had suffered losses. He was to represent these creditors, and make sure that business debts should take precedence over gambling ones, inquire into the bankrupt's assets and so forth.[13] He had had the earlier experience at Genoa, and they used him for a lawyer or an accountant.

He set off on the 9th of July. He was being sent by private interests and private citizens, but the size of the debt and the importance of the creditors were such that the Republic could not fail to take an interest in the affair. The Cardinal himself decided on the commission and supported it with letters of recommendation for the Elders of Lucca. On the 7th a letter had been sent ahead by the Signoria.[14] While the Secretary was working on this matter, other things arose concerning Lucca: first, a question regarding the Mint, and then a problem of some troublesome Pisan students who had taken refuge there. Over these small and tiresome affairs there were endless manœuvres and correspondence. We have a letter from the Cardinal to Machiavelli on the subject of the students, with kind expressions which are clearly mere formulae and not sincere.[15] We also have one from the Signoria to the Elders of Lucca which begins: 'Our citizens and merchants . . . sent to you two months ago one Niccolò Machiavelli . . .'.[16] The Signoria is not very considerate with its former secretary, who used to be described as 'noble and honourable', now that he is reduced to dealing with those Elders of St. Zita in the affairs of a bankrupt merchant!

But he, with his resilient nature, adapted himself patiently to everything, and found an opportunity everywhere to do something worthy of his talents. Being on the spot, a theoretician of politics and an observer like himself could not fail to take advantage of the fact, to study the government of that republic and write an account of it. It was the least he could do, and he did it.[17] But months passed in negotiating and waiting, and during that long interval of idleness at Lucca he also wrote the *Life of Castruccio Castracani*[18]—a great scandal for the pedants of posterity who were determined to regard it as a historical work, picking out all the historical errors, or rather the inventions in what was a political or even more a literary work! Even more perspicacious modern critics, who finally recognized its true nature, did not really understand how it came into being.

For it is clear that now Machiavelli was being considered for the task of historian of the Florentine Republic, this fine and powerful prose was to be a sample for his patrons, and for himself an essay in historical style. These are not imaginings of mine; it is a document which speaks. He sent it to his friends as a 'model for a history', and they judged it as such.[19] The attempt was a great success, the essay achieved its purpose. Between one colloquy and the next ('*colloqui*' were in Lucca what '*pratiche*' were in Florence), he read either in the 15th century edition[20] or in a manuscript the *Castrucci Antelminelli vita* by Niccolò Tegrimi, and drew from it this fantasy, giving it an antique flavour on the model of Diodorus Siculus and Diogenes Laertius.[21] That is all. But he would not have been Machiavelli if within these classical forms he had not given some room to his favourite political and military ideas, idealizing once more his new prince. Also in this superimposing of politics and poetry on history this short work will be the 'little model' for the longer histories.

The *Life of Castruccio* was finished before the end of August. On the 29th he sent it to Zanobi Buondelmonti and Luigi Alamanni, to both of whom it was dedicated. On the 6th of September Zanobi sent Machiavelli his opinion of the book and that of the other 'friends of the cool shade'. He, Luigi, Diaccetino, Guidetti and Anton Francesco degli Albizi had read and discussed the book together and judged it 'a good and well written work', and they had picked out certain minor details, 'which, although they are all right, might nevertheless be improved', such as the apophthegms at the end which seemed too numerous; they would like to see removed some of those borrowed from other sources (even they had noticed!). Their other remarks largely concerned small details of language and style; and the same applies to the observations of Jacopo Nardi, Battista della Palla and others who had also read the work which everyone liked and praised.[22]

Machiavelli's success with this 'model for a history', as Zanobi in fact describes it in the same letter, had increased among his friends the desire to see him go on to the major work. Zanobi wrote: 'We all feel that you should set out with the greatest diligence to write this history, and I desire it most of all. . . .' He therefore urged him to return, because in the first place they all wanted to see him, and in particular they wanted to talk to him 'about that plan of ours that you know of'[23]— and this was to have him commissioned to write the history of Florence.

The matter was as good as settled, having the support of all those citizens who were in constant contact with the Cardinal, and he being already favourably disposed. To be ready to receive these favours, Machiavelli returned to Florence some time between the 8th and the 10th of September, leaving his business in Lucca not quite finished, but well on the way to a satisfactory conclusion.[24] On his arrival he may have found the decision already taken to have him employed by the Florentine Studio, of which Cardinal de' Medici was head and Machiavelli's brother-in-law, Francesco del Nero, administrator. The exact conditions were yet to be determined, and the future historian himself drafted them in his own hand to del Nero:

'The substance of the commission should be as follows: that he be employed for . . . . years, at an annual salary of . . . ., his duties to be to write the annals or the history of the things that have been done by the state and city of Florence from the date that seems most appropriate to him, and either in Latin or Tuscan whichever he pleases.'[25]

But the terms of his employment were in fact established as follows: by decision of the Officials of the University on the 8th of November, Niccolò Machiavelli was commissioned to serve their institution for two years beginning on the 1st of November, one year definitely and the second subject to re-election, in whatever they should think necessary, *et inter alia ad componendum annalia et cronacas florentinas, et alia faciendum,*[26] with a salary of 100 *fiorini di studio*. This was a conventional currency, 'not palpable', worth only four lire, while the current large gold florin then had a value of about seven lire. The so-called 'studio' florin, typical of the generosity which governments have always shown towards study and men of learning, was devalued currency like the *fiorino di suggello*.[27] Thus the salary he was to receive was really about 57 florins, little more than half what he had earned in his prosperous days as secretary to the Signoria. But it had its uses. At last he had 'somewhere to turn'.

The honour was the best part of it. In the past the historians of the Florentine Republic had included Leonardo Aretino, Poggio and Scala, all great men, all first chancellors of the Signoria; and he felt almost as though he too had become chancellor again, or had found the way back to office. At last a loophole was opened for him, and through it something was visible. A commission from the Cardinal himself seemed to make the loophole wider. Beginning to employ him *ad alia faciendum*, as the terms ran, the Cardinal had asked him to write a *Discourse on Florentine affairs after the death of Lorenzo*,[28] to be presented to the Pope who was seeking advice on the way to organize the State of Florence now controlled by two ecclesiastics, himself and the Cardinal, without legitimate heirs.

Machiavelli cannot have had a very pleasant memory of the last time Pope Leo had asked his advice through the medium of the Cardinal and Vettori; but this time he had been asked directly as an employee of the Republic, and furthermore this was about the government of Florence which was a subject he was longing to write about again. Because Florence was in question, he sought in his discourse the nation's good far more than the Pope's approval. As usual his proposals were too different from public opinion: for instance, with the exception of the Gonfalonier, who was to be elected for life or for a long term, he would alter the entire ancient system of government. This extravagance probably made his sensible proposals appear bad and unreal. Then, in this discourse there were things that were better or worse according to how you looked at them, because he advised the Pope to give Florence back her liberty after his lifetime and that of the Cardinal. This was a magnanimous piece of advice which might not have displeased Leo, who, as his house had no legitimate descendants, was in the best position possible to give way to generous impulses. On the other hand it must have been extremely displeasing to his relations and their most compromised partisans, who could already see themselves despoiled of all honour and profit, exposed to the revenge of a popular state.

One learned literary historian has written that such noble concepts 'raise the author of the *Prince* a good deal in our estimation'.[29] I would say rather that they keep him at the same ideal eminence. Not only the elevated concepts but the poetic solemnity of the *Prince* are heard again in the following words with which the *Discourse* draws to its close:

'I believe that the greatest honour men can receive is that which is bestowed spontaneously upon them by their native land; I believe that the greatest good one may do and the most pleasing to God is the good one does to one's native land. Beyond this, no man is exalted in any of his actions as much as those who have reformed kingdoms and republics with laws and institutions; after those who have been gods, these men are the most praised. . . . Therefore Heaven gives no greater gift to a man, nor can show him a more glorious path than this; and among so much good fortune that God has bestowed on your house and on Your Holiness, this is the greatest to give you power and occasion to make yourself immortal and to surpass the glory both of your father and your grandfather . . .'[30]

The *Discourse* was sent to Rome during the Cardinal's absence; he had left Florence on the 6th of November of that year 1520, while Leo's complex plans for Italy were maturing. The Empire had fallen vacant by the death of Maximilian and passed to Charles of Spain, and this had disturbed the balance of power. In the meantime Machiavelli's reputation had been increased, if not by this *Discourse*, by his recent works and the promise of his future history, and he seemed still more 'a person who must rise'. From Rome another future historian, his friend Filippo de' Nerli, abandoned his usual acid pleasantries and wrote respectfully on the 17th of November protesting that he eagerly awaited the *Life of Castruccio* and the *De re militari*. The latter was also desired by Cardinal de' Medici, and Nerli became impatient with Zanobi Buondelmonti who had promised it to him: 'He will make the reverend Monsignor think I am a liar, if he does not send it; so between you, don't let me down.'[31]

As if this were not enough, Lucrezia Salviati had been given a *Life* of Alexander composed by one of the writers at court, and she did not care for it after the one by Quintus Rufus which Nerli had been reading to her,[32] so she conceived the idea of having it improved by Machiavelli. What a muddle! Of course Machiavelli did nothing of the sort with the complicity of Nerli who took all the blame. Since Contessina Ridolfi had died in '15 and Maddalena Cybo in '19, madonna Lucrezia was the Pope's last surviving sister amid the destruction which the course of four years had wrought in that family, which had been so happy and full of high hopes at the time of Leo's election to the papacy.

Machiavelli, therefore, was content with what he had, and hoped for better in the future. Even his letters to his nephew Vernaccia at last became more cheerful.[33] I do not think that the letter written to him on the 13th of April by Piero Soderini could have disturbed his newly found peace of mind. Some time before, Soderini had offered him the job of secretary to the small Adriatic republic of Ragusa, which Machiavelli declined.[34] He now returned to the charge with another plan. Prospero Colonna was looking for a secretary, and the ex-Gonfalonier had suggested the ex-Secretary of the Florentine Republic for the post. This great Roman prince and condottiere, knowing by reputation the man who had honoured his cousin Fabrizio in the *Art of War*, was eager to accept the proposal and left it to Soderini to clinch the bargain. The salary was magnificent: two hundred gold ducats and expenses. If it suited him, the Gonfalonier advised him to confide in no one, but to mount his horse at once and go to join Colonna before anyone in Florence knew of his departure. He urged him to accept this great opportunity, considering it 'much better than staying there writing history for *fiorini di suggello*'.[35]

Two hundred gold ducats and expenses! Marcello Virgilio, first secretary of the Republic, did not earn half that. Machiavelli, for his post as historian, earned a quarter or a fifth of it. Yet we may be sure that he did not spare it a thought. To accept would have meant leaving an honourable public office to serve at the court of a foreign master. He would have more pleasure from a florin enjoyed in liberty in Florence than from five received as a courtier. He would have been breaking his agreement with the University and with his dear friends in the Orti, betraying the faith they had placed in him, bidding farewell to his native Florence, to his Albergaccio which he both loved and hated, burning his boats with those 'Medici princes' just when he was at last about to rise, just when that '*ad alia faciendum*' of his contract allowed him to hope for some crumb from the Republic, a commission, perhaps an embassy! Colonna's offer was a rich one, but he would not have accepted it even in leaner times.

Chapter 18

THE LEGATION TO THE FRANCISCANS

◇◇◇

ONE May day of the year 1521 Machiavelli, leaving the ridge of the Appenines behind him, was riding down the road into Bologna. In his saddle-bag he had a commission from the Otto di Pratica (the Eight), the body which had superseded the republican Ten, written in the very office where he had served so many years, and signed by the man who had taken his place there, Niccolò Michelozzi.[1] Still, he was at last again being sent on a mission beyond the borders of the Republic, outside Tuscany, and with a pocketful of government credentials. Could it be that his country had remembered him, remembered the acute observer, the far-sighted politician? Was he off again to the King of France, or the Emperor?

Poor Machiavelli! He was merely going to the Chapter General of the Minor Friars which was being held at Carpi. There he was to ask on behalf of the Signoria and of Cardinal de' Medici, the real master of Florence, that the minorite convents in Florentine territory should be separated from those in the rest of Tuscany. In other words, the Cardinal with the consent of the Pope, who had strengthened his hand with the appropriate Briefs, wished to do for the Franciscans of the Florentine convents what Savonarola had done for the Dominicans, thereby providing Alexander VI with a pretext for his destruction. A strange errand for a politician, and strangest of all for a Machiavelli. The greatness, the genius, the character of the man, the views of the author of the *Mandragola*, all make his being chosen for this task seem more comic.

186

It had never occurred to him to refuse. He had asked those Medici princes to begin to employ him, even in something quite small, and now they had given him something small to do. Once more he was content to let his fate trample on him in this way to see if it were not ashamed to treat him thus; and at the moment, this way led him to a chapter of Minor Friars. The mission, in any case, was more to the discredit of those who had given it to him; and he, like the last time he had been oppressed by injustice, covered his bitterness with jokes and laughter, and thought the better of himself for his fortitude.

So Machiavelli was on his way down the road that wound among the last foothills of the Appennines, and the rich plain unrolled itself at his feet. He knew the road well, for he had travelled it many times before with very different hopes. He recognized some of the places, and remembered the cares of those earlier days and of those more ambitious journeys. Here was a peasant's house where he had stopped for a while on his way to Germany to see the Emperor. Here was the stream rushing down from the hillside, that he had sought when going to the Court of France for the third time in the hot summer of 1510. But now he is on his way to Carpi to negotiate with the friars, and in his bags he has instructions and credentials for the 'republic of clogs'.

Carpi, the ancient city of the Pio family, is twelve miles from Modena, and at Modena, through which Machiavelli was to pass, the governor was another Florentine, Francesco Guicciardini. The two great politicians had had some acquaintance before. In 1509 Niccolò, writing from Verona to Luigi Guicciardini, charged him with some friendly office to his brother Francesco. They certainly had relations while Machiavelli was Secretary and Francesco was ambassador in Spain; in fact the latter had complained that Machiavelli had given him a one-sided account of the battle of Ravenna.[2] Returning from his legation at the end of 1513, Guicciardini had at once been employed in honourable and lucrative positions as governor in the states of the Church, while Machiavelli, shut up in the country, was sunk in that idleness which was to bring him so much unhappiness and such great fame. In consequence, up to this moment they had had no opportunity for a closer acquaintance.

I would say, too, that real friendship and congeniality between these two were not possible until the storms of Italy found them both in the same boat. Guicciardini was aristocratic, coldly selfish, solemn and respectable; Machiavelli was a man of the people, warm-hearted and generous, frivolous and pleasure-loving. One was inclined to theory and idealism, the other was a practical man and a realist. Both kept hidden within them their true greatness, but Guicciardini imprisoned his within the rock of a haughty reserve, while Machiavelli disguised his genius without shame and decorum beneath those everyday garments covered with mud and dirt. No wonder, therefore, if he lacked in his lifetime the reputation and authority which the other enjoyed in plenty. It was this which, in addition to the curse which falls on poets and innovators, dug a pit between himself and his contemporaries, while Guicciardini alienated everyone, even posterity, with his cold grandeur.

Between the good fortune of one and the misfortune of the other there was so great a distance during their lifetime, that there could be no rivalry between them. Rivalry began after their deaths. At the time we have now reached in this chapter Machiavelli had composed and published in print or in manuscript all his most famous works during his painful period of idleness, and was now writing his *Histories*. Guicciardini, busy with government and other affairs, had written very little and published nothing. He fully appreciated Machiavelli's thought, but he did not follow it. He felt the fascination of his mind, so that in their correspondence something of Machiavelli's warmth seems to have communicated itself to him, and the letters he wrote to Machiavelli are among the best and most human that he wrote; but he never took pleasure in poets, and in politics they seemed to him dangerous. Certain words written by him to his friend during this mission to Carpi reveal the full extent of the gulf separating Machiavelli from all his contemporaries: he wrote that Machiavelli 'had always been *ut plurimum* a promoter of extravagant opinions and an inventor of new things'. There is perhaps a hint of irony in these words, which nevertheless redounds to the honour of the man who is its target.

Machiavelli for his part was sincerely fond of Guicciardini, and was one day to say so impetuously in one of his letters. When Guicciardini could not follow him in his 'extravagances' as a poet and innovator, he was sorry but in no way resentful. He admired Guiccardini's virtues and even more his good fortune; he honoured the man whom the 'Medici princes' employed in such great affairs, the Florentine who did such credit to his native city. He loved the politician with whom he could talk as an equal on matters of state, the man who for him would come out of his hard cold shell.

He must have stopped, therefore, at Modena on the way to Carpi, and then again on his return. Together they would have talked at length of Florence and the latest events in Italy, and made broad jokes about this absurd mission to the friars. They were probably the best moments of his trip, and for these alone it was worth having left the backwater of San Casciano and travelled so many miles on horseback, an exercise he was beginning to find too strenuous. Leaving Florence on the 11th or 12th of May, he stopped one night at Modena and rather less than one day. On the 16th he was at Carpi as the Eight intended, and before the friars rang for vespers, as a certain fra Ilarione had enjoined him to do,[3] for now he took orders from everybody. From there he continued his exchange of ideas and jokes with his friend.

A further commission, even stranger than this one, gave them still more to talk about. The Consuls of the Wool Guild had written to him on the 14th of May asking him to persuade the friars to send a noted preacher, one fra Giovanni Gualberto da Firenze, known as 'il Rovaio', to preach in the Duomo for the coming Lent. This message left Florence two or three days after Machiavelli, and travelling faster by post, reached Carpi almost at the same time as he did.[4] Guicciardini, informed of this perhaps by a letter from his friend, was able to crack further jokes at his expense. He wrote to Machiavelli on the 17th that to have given him the task of finding a preacher was a really clever notion, as though Pacchierotto, a famous glutton and pederast in Florence,[5] 'had been charged to find a beautiful and gallant wife for a friend'. He added: 'I believe that you will serve them as is expected of you and according to your honour, which would be blemished if you turned religious at your age, because as you have so far lived with quite opposite ideas, it would be attributed to infantilism rather than to virtue'. He concluded with the advice to make haste with his business so that the friars should not accuse him of hypocrisy, and lest the air of Carpi, according to its ancient influence, turn him into a liar. And if by mischance he should be lodged in the house of some native of Carpi, his infection would be incurable.[6]

Machiavelli was in fact lodged in the house of a certain Gismondo Santi, chancellor of Alberto Pio, lord of the city. Soon he had the idea of playing a trick on his host and on the friars by getting Guicciardini to send him frequent special messengers, so that they might think him a man of great importance and therefore respect and dine him the better: 'I must tell you that when that archer arrived with his letter and said with a deep bow that he had been sent specially in all haste, everyone stood up with signs of great respect and much noise so that all was thrown into confusion, and I was asked for news by several people. In order to increase my reputation, I said that the Emperor was expected at Trent and the Swiss had summoned fresh assemblies, and that the King of France wanted to go and meet that King, but his counsellors were against it; so that they all stood amazed and cap in hand, and while I write they are still standing around me in a circle, and seeing me write at length they marvel and gaze at me as though I were possessed; and I, to astonish them still more, sometimes stop writing and look stern, so that they positively dribble; if they knew what I was writing, they would be even more surprised.' [7]

In the same letter of the 17th of May he had first joked at length about choosing the preacher; as for the business of the separation of the convents, everything was held up until the friars' elections were concluded, and this gave him material for further jokes: 'I have nothing to do here because I cannot carry out my mission until the General and the definitors are elected, and I am ruminating some way in which I might sow such scandal among them that here or elsewhere they will get busy with their clogs, and if I do not lose my head, I think I shall be successful and that your help and advice would be very useful'. As for the influence of the air of Carpi, he replied shamelessly that he had nothing left to learn, being by now a doctor of lies, 'because for some time now I never say what I believe, nor ever believe what I say, and if by chance I sometimes tell the truth, I hide it behind so many lies that it is hard to find'. Once again he was boasting of vices he did not have. [8]

Guicciardini, spurred on by his friend's pleasantries, kept up the game, and on the 18th sent him two letters in one day [9] : 'As I have not, my dear Machiavelli, either time or wit to advise you, and though I do not usually give such services without payment, I do not wish to fail you altogether, so that at least in appearance you may be able to carry out your arduous enterprises. So I send you this archer riding post, [10] and I have ordered him to travel with all speed as it is a most important matter, so he comes without his shirt touching his bottom; and I doubt not that, what with his galloping and what he will tell the bystanders, everyone will think you a most important person and your business much more vital than anything to do with friars. And so that the nature of my plump letter may convince your host, I have put in certain messages which have come from Zurich which you may make use of either by showing them or holding them in your hand, whichever you judge more expedient.' On receiving this, Machiavelli replied: 'I can tell you that the smoke rose high in the sky, for between the breathlessness of the messenger and the size of your package of letters, there is no one in this house or in this neighbourhood who is not filled with wonder; and so as not to appear ungrateful to messer Gismondo, I showed him those agreements between the Swiss and the King. He thought it was very important. I told him of the Emperor's illness and the states he wanted to buy in France, and he was agape with wonder. But I really think that in spite of all this he wonders whether he has not been had, because he feels doubtful and cannot understand why such immense letters have to be sent to these Arabian deserts where there is nothing but friars; and I do not think I appear to him as quite the extraordinary man that you have written to him about, because I stay at home and sleep and read and keep quiet; so that I fear he realizes that you are making game of me and of him. All the same he keeps on sounding me, and I reply with a few ill chosen words, and I talk about the deluge that is to come or about the Turk who is bound to invade, or whether it would be a good idea to have a Crusade these days, and similar wine-shop gossip; so that I think he is longing to speak to you personally to find out what it is all about, as it is you who have landed him in this situation, for I am a nuisance in his house and keep him busy here. And yet I believe that he feels the game will not last long, and so he goes on being pleasant and providing splendid meals, and I eat like six dogs and three wolves, and I say at dinner-time: this morning I am saving two *giulios*; and at supper: tonight I am saving four.'[11] And so the two Florentines continued to enjoy their joke, and Machiavelli his lavish hospitality as well.

Guicciardini was the first to return to serious matters and to revive, in his second letter of the 18th, the almost tragic sadness of this farce where a man like Machiavelli had to go as ambassador to some friars on account of a preacher: 'When I read your titles as orator of the Republic and the friars,[12] and I think with how many kings, dukes and princes you have negotiated in former times, I remember Lysander who after so many victories and trophies was given the job of distributing rations to those same soldiers whom he had led with so much glory, and I say: See how only the faces of men and the outer appearances of things change, the events all recur, nor do we witness any occurrence which has not been seen before; but this changing of names and faces of things means that only the wise recognize them, and so history is good and useful because it places before you and makes you see and recognize what you had never known or seen. From this follows a monkish syllogism, that those who have commissioned you to write histories are greatly to be commended, and that you must be urged to accomplish with diligence the task you have been given. For this purpose I do not think that this legation will have been completely useless to you, because during these three days' rest you will have sucked all the goodness out of the Friars' Republic, and you will use this example for some purpose, comparing or contrasting it with some one of those models of yours'.[13] There are times when it seems almost as if he were here referring to the *Prince* and the *Discourses*.

Immediately after, he goes back to his usual humour: 'I did not think it to your advantage to waste time or leave hold of fortune while it shows itself favourable; so I followed the practice of sending the messenger, which if it serves no other purpose, should earn you an extra cake to nibble tomorrow evening.' But the joke was by now running out, and the mission too, as we see in the letter Machiavelli wrote on the 19th to tell his friend the governor about the suspicious attitude of his host, and to put an end to the joke:

'*Cazzus!* We have to be sharp with this fellow, for he is as clever as thirty thousand devils. I think he has realized that you are having him on, because when the messenger came, he said: Here, there must be something going on; messengers are coming thick and fast. Then, when he had read your letter, he said: I think the governor is making game of me and you. . . . So I am scared stiff, for I am afraid he will make a clean sweep and send me off to the inn. I beg you then to take a holiday tomorrow, so that this joke does not go too far, and the good it has done me is not spoilt: splendid meals, glorious beds and the like, in which I have delighted these three days.

This morning I made a start with the affair of the separation, and I shall be busy with it all day; tomorrow I hope to finish it . . .

As for histories and the Friars' Republic, I do not think I have lost anything by coming here, because I have found out about many of their constitutions and orders which have good things in them, and so I think I may make use of them some time . . .'[14]

·   ·   ·   ·   ·

This last passage about the things observed in the customs and constitutions of the friars is pure Machiavelli—the Machiavelli who exercised his insatiable curiosity on everybody and everything. But apart
from that, apart from the splendid meals and glorious beds, I believe
that he derived little profit from this mission. As for the preacher, he
had in fact also made use of ancient history to soften the hardness of
that blessed Rovaio, and to give the Florentines the consolation of the
sermons of so worthy and saintly a man; for, as Machiavelli wrote,
abandoning his irreverent humour for a moment, 'when one sees . . .
how much credit some wretch receives who hides under the cloak of
religion, one can readily imagine how much a good man might have,
who in truth and not in pretence trod in the steps of St. Francis'.[15]
But Rovaio made difficulties, and that extraordinary ambassador reported: 'He says he does not get the right respect in Florence,
and that when he preached there before, he made a rule that the whores
should go about wearing a yellow veil, and he has letters from his
sister that they are wearing what they like and are more debauched
than ever, and he complained bitterly of this fact. However, I tried to
console him, by telling him that he should not be surprised for it was
usual in big cities not to stick to anything for long and to do one thing
today and to undo it tomorrow; and I reminded him of Rome and
Athens, so that he was quite comforted, and he almost gave me his
word'.[16] But the next day he started to waver again, and his superiors
came and said that he was promised elsewhere; so that I do not know
how it all ended, nor do I think it matters much to history to know it.

In the affair of the separation too, which as we have seen was begun
on the 19th and finished on the 20th, it seems that the arts of Machiavelli were lost among the intricacies of the friars' cavillations. When
he talked to the assessors separately 'he used stronger and sharper terms
than he had done with them all together'. He bared the claws of his
diplomacy, which were strengthened by papal intentions, and finally
gave them to understand, when they told him that it was as serious a
matter as had been discussed by the Order in two hundred years, that
'the wisdom of men lies in knowing when to give up what cannot be
held or sold'.[17]

Sapienti pauca. Having said that, Machiavelli could only wait for the
wretched friars to digest his words; and possibly their ruminations
were assisted by further letters from the Cardinal and the Eight. When
fra Ilarione wrote advising him to get on his horse and hurry to Florence

to collect these letters,[18] Machiavelli, who had had enough of Carpi, thought it was a good opportunity to get away and make game of those who had sent him. For, when he was at Modena, instead of going on to reach Florence on the 22nd as fra Ilarione intended, he wrote a long account to the Cardinal, adding that he could not ride fast 'because of some indisposition'[19]; and he got out of it by sending one of those hard-riding messengers of the governor, and himself remained in Modena enjoying a few days of Guicciardini's company, in spite of the Eight, the Cardinal and the Minor Friars.

Such was his mission to Carpi, which seems to me to symbolize the whole of Machiavelli's life. He benefited from it not only in splendid meals and beds, for although his efforts brought him no credit with those who foolishly had sent him, he gained esteem with posterity for having, as always, put on a cheerful countenance and won honour with his brilliant letters even in times of adversity.[20]

Chapter 19

NICCOLÒ MACHIAVELLI, HISTORIAN

◇◇◇

MACHIAVELLI is in the country writing his *Histories*. Between himself and the life he longs for, there stand once more those woods and olive groves and the indifferent forgetfulness of men. By day he leads his usual life as he had described it to Vettori. If there are no thrushes to snare, there are beccafichi to catch with a net, there are the woods and the tavern. So he sinks again into that stagnant atmosphere, full of nostalgia for the fine discussions he had had in Modena with Guicciardini and the pleasing odour of public affairs he had been able to savour for a few days in the shadow of his friend the governor. Then, when evening comes, his solitude is again peopled with the shades of great men, and he converses with them. But these are now men of modern times, Florentines, and no longer those ancient Romans who had greater things to tell him and to whom he listened with greater reverence. Now that he has become the historian of the Republic by order of a Medici Cardinal, he no longer feels as free as he used to be when he followed his own inspiration; and besides, being a political writer and philosopher of history rather than a historian, he was more at home extracting principles of political science from history than writing it, even though writing history was for him simply to reduce it to principles of political science.

Doubts and difficulties crept in from the very beginning. The problem of which language to choose, Latin or the vernacular, did not trouble him long; and perhaps when he asked that in his contract he should be given *carte blanche* for the choice of language, he had already decided within himself which he would use. A history written by him could not be a dead thing wrapped in old forms, but alive, in the live language of the people he was writing about. Then there were the doubts about the date from which his history should run. He had originally thought to begin from the year 1434, when with Cosimo's return the Medici family attained supremacy in Florence.[1] Leonardo Bruni had broken off his history not long before that date, and Poggio had continued his only a little beyond it. He was encouraged in this idea by the thought that he would thereby be doing something more agreeable to those in power and more useful to himself; and there were other reasons too: the proximity of the period, making investigation easier, the convenience of having those extracts he had made for the annals he had been planning ever since the happy days at the Chancery, and the desirability of not going over ground already covered by his predecessors. On the other hand he was deterred by the fear that he might be accused of flattery, by the consideration that the other historians had paid little or no attention to the internal affairs of the city, and finally by the conviction that his work, which was to be so original and different, could not continue the histories of his predecessors and thus depend upon them, for this would rob it of its importance. He decides therefore to go back to the origins of the city and summarize the internal events up to 1434, setting before it in the first book, by way of introduction, an outline of Italian history which from the dissolution of the Roman Empire would come almost to join up with the date he had first thought of. In this way his account would be fuller and more complete.

So he sets to work. From the first words of the foreword we see him smirking at the famous volumes of Leonardo and Poggio, 'two most excellent historians'. He gives fresh forms, a new unity and dignity to history; he turns off on a new road leaving behind him the fashions and traditions of the humanist school, the compilations of the annalists, the popular chronicles, and lays the foundations of modern historical writing. As in the *Prince* and the *Discourses* he takes a road as yet untrodden by others.

But he writes history as a politician rather than as a historian, to serve the purposes of political science. He is not interested in that minute and diligent search for facts which will for quite different qualities make Guicciardini's truer histories famous. He wants to derive from the facts lessons, principles, doctrines, and on occasions he will, have no scruples about fitting the facts to his theories. It is better so; one must look in his pages for something quite different. Florence and Italy had already had diligent annalists, and were later to have genuine historians, patient distillers of the truth from sources and documents more contradictory than the clocks of Charles V. They had not yet had a Machiavelli and were never to have another like him.

He knows where he wants to go and flies straight to his target. He does not bother to compare his sources, Biondo, Villani, and Bruni for the first part, and Poggio, Marchionne di Coppo Stefani and Cavalcanti later, to select his material, collating them one with the other. This would not suit his purpose. He is content to follow them one at a time, and following in others' footsteps he transforms everything he touches, co-ordinating their confused and accumulated material, finding the connection between the various events, illuminating them with sudden revealing flashes, enlivening everything with the force and brilliance of his style. When people and events leave him indifferent as a man and as a politician, his narrative dozes off or moves by fits and starts, and even his style descends to the level of the source he is following: but style and thought revive miraculously whenever he divines beneath the garb of a Theodoric or even of a Walter de Brienne his myth of a new prince.[2]

With this method of composing histories he had not far to go to find his material: he had all the sources to hand in his study at the Albergaccio. We know there was a Biondo in the Machiavelli household in 1485; Bruni and Poggio (in the translations of Acciaioli and Jacopo Bracciolini) were in print in recent editions which enjoyed great popularity, and could not fail to have been among the books left by his father. If among these there were no manuscript of Villani, it would not have been difficult to buy or borrow one at that time in Florence. Even in those days, however, manuscripts of Stefani and Cavalcanti must have been less easy to find. Although he made little use of other sources, he did make some effort to find them. He certainly borrowed, read and annotated in his own hand a manuscript of the *Cronica fiorentina* of Piero Minerbetti, on the fly-leaf of which the witty owner wrote the usual tercet of warning, very common at that time, but adapting it to the occasion and the borrower:

> *O Machiavel, che meco ti trastulli,*
> *guarda co' la lucerna non m'azzuffi,*
> *rendimi presto e guarda da' fanciulli*[3]

[O Machiavelli, who amuse yourself with me, be careful not to touch me with the lamp; give me back soon, and keep me away from children].

Thus the need for books or the desire for women and more cultivated conversation brought him into the city from time to time. Other visits, perhaps a short stay, he must have made in August 1521 when his *Art of War* was being printed by Giunta and was nearly ready. The proofs were lovingly corrected by the author as the *errata* shows.[4] It was the first of his major works to be printed, and he cannot have failed to give himself the pleasure of reviewing and handling the freshly printed pages, and showing them to his friends at the Orti.

Although Cosimino Rucellai was dead, these friends had not dispersed, and in those brilliant gatherings Machiavelli forgot the trivial arguments of San Casciano and felt himself alive again. There were old friends who wanted to hear about the *Histories*; there was a young man of plebeian family, but polished and very clever: Donato Giannotti. Up to that time little had been seen of his work; among other things, a few Latin distichs printed in the *Lauretum* in honour of Lorenzo de' Medici Duke of Urbino, in which he urged the 'new prince' to the pursuit of military virtue.[5] However, he gave great attention to the study of Greek and Latin authors, and had gained such a reputation in these studies that he had recently been made lecturer in Greek language and literature in the University of Pisa. For his modesty, his kind and companionable nature, Machiavelli had taken a fancy to him and held him in extraordinary affection; it was almost as though he foresaw that this young man would soon occupy his own old place in the secretariat of the Ten, and take up and develop his dream of a citizen militia, and furthermore, that he would have the third place of honour after himself and Guicciardini among the political writers of his time.[6]

Meanwhile Machiavelli confided in Giannotti (though perhaps not in him alone). He read him some parts of the *Histories* as he composed them; he unburdened himself to him. And their conversation always came back to the sore point of sincerity with regard to the Medici who had commissioned him to write them. What he said to him in substance was this: 'Donato, I cannot write this history from the time when Cosimo took power to the death of Lorenzo as I would write it if I were free from all obligations. The facts will be accurate and I will not leave anything out; I will simply avoid discussing the general causes of events. Thus I will describe the events which occurred when Cosimo seized power, but I will not say how and with what means a man may attain such heights. Anyone who also wishes to know this, should note well what I make his adversaries say, because that which I do not wish to say as coming from myself, I shall put in the mouths of his adversaries.'[7]

These words or something very like them, which Giannotti states he heard from Machiavelli more than once, were evidently spoken before the composition of the *Histories* had reached the fatal year 1434, except perhaps for some of those fragments with which the author used to try it out in advance. But it is difficult, and in the end not very rewarding, to attempt to establish the stages of the book's composition. I may be mistaken, but I believe that Machiavelli, who wrote his first drafts rapidly and afterwards polished them with loving care, pro-- gressed more slowly in the composition of this work than with others. Perhaps he was hindered by the necessary research, though, as we have seen, he did not take much trouble over this; perhaps he was less driven by inspiration. The composition of his major works occupied the 'leisures' of the last quarter of his strangely symmetrical life, in which he set down the things he had learned from his 'continual reading' (first half, 29 years) and his 'long experience' (third quarter, $14\frac{1}{2}$ years). He spent seven years of the last eighth of his life almost entirely in writing his *Histories*, whereas in the preceding seven he had composed no less than the *Prince*, the *Mandragola*, the *Life of Castruccio*, the *Discourses*, and the *Art of War*.

One might even observe that, looking back on it from our times and through the few documents which remain, the years which Machiavelli spent on the *Histories*, particularly these first ones, seem more meditative and withdrawn, as though he were entirely absorbed in his work. In fact a curious gap appears in his biography and his correspondence at this point, a gap which, symbolically at least, represents the meditation and solitude of the author, completely occupied with the greatness and difficulty of his task; although the biographer is aware that it is not permissible to spin fantasies where there is no information, which may simply be the result of an accidental lack of documents.

Immersed as he is in the solitude of the country and that of his studies, Machiavelli does not lose the thread of the events which unravel themselves beneath his eager eyes from the tangled skein of Italian politics. He, who used to open the ambassadors' letters in the Palazzo, now gleans news in the wine-shops and in the Orti when he is in town (and we know he was there for Christmas 1521)[8]; and when he is in the country, he picks it up sitting outside the tavern by the road to Rome, along which so much of the life of Europe passes, and his friends also send him word, perhaps even Guicciardini sometimes, who is fortunate enough to be in the midst of all these events not as a spectator but as an actor.

At that time Pope Leo, a great gambler in politics as well as in life, was chancing the greatest gamble of all. He had remained without apparent family ambitions to satisfy after fate, as Vettori writes, had made his nephew die, and it is not clear whether he meant simply to enlarge the state of the Church or whether he had some grander national scheme in mind. It was even said that he wanted to carve out a state for his cousin Giulio, who would then cease to be a cardinal. It is a fact that after having conducted for the last few years a most subtle double game with King Francis of France and King Charles of Spain, made treaties with one without the other's knowledge, then supported Francis for the succession to the Empire, finally, when the imperial crown was won by Charles, suddenly and against everyone's advice he changed over to Charles' side.

Having made an alliance with Charles on the 8th of May 1521, ratified on the 29th (Machiavelli was then back from Carpi), hostilities began. The legate with the highly successful papal and imperial armies was Cardinal de' Medici, and Guicciardini was commissioner general. Again fortune smiled on Leo. The French were routed by the Spaniards at Vauri on the Adda, where Giovanni de' Medici, the young son of Caterina Sforza, distinguished himself; and soon afterwards they lost Milan. Leo was able to enjoy the first rapture of such a victory, but not the later fruits, for these were denied him by his sudden demise on the 1st of December. This was the last stroke that fortune held in store for him after having favoured him exceedingly.

The League was broken up by the Pope's death, and since the war was being carried on with his money, or rather the money of the Church, the imperial armies dispersed. The city of Parma, newly acquired with Piacenza by the Church, was however well defended by Guicciardini against the renewed onslaught of the French. Cardinal de' Medici who had been left without anything to do in Lombardy, went to Rome for the conclave. There, though unable to secure his own election, he managed to prevent that of Cardinal Soderini who was openly ambitious for the papacy, thereby adding fresh grounds for resentment to the old. Adrian VI was elected on the 9th of January 1522, a pious stiff Fleming who offered the most extraordinary contrast with his predecessor and the Roman Court. While the astonished city was emptying of its people, Cardinal de' Medici went back to govern the Republic and the Archbishopric of Florence.

Machiavelli must have felt that he had sustained a loss with the death of Leo, although he might have said of him with truth what Berni was to say of Cardinal Bibbiena:

che non gli fece mai nè ben nè male[9]

[that he never did him either good or ill]

or rather more ill than good. But perhaps Pope Leo, the benefactor of so many mediocre poets and literary men, without knowing it himself and without anyone else then noticing it, had really benefited the great Florentine Secretary: firstly by arousing his illusions and his great imagination with his changing ambitions, and secondly by leaving him to despairing and fruitful idleness. So literature which owes so much to the Medici family for its assistance, owes a good deal more to Leo because he did not assist Machiavelli.

However, Machiavelli like every other Florentine undoubtedly lost something by the death of Leo. If nothing else, he lost the hope that some day something good might come his way from Rome. If Soderini had been victorious in the conclave, Machiavelli's hopes would have become certainties. The ex-Gonfalonier would certainly have remembered Machiavelli's former services rather than his recent forced coldness. Instead of which, these Soderini, including Piero, were now in violent opposition to the Medici state, and their former protégé must have been on tenterhooks because of the Medici protection he enjoyed. The ambitious cardinal in collusion with the King of France was collecting in the Siena area an army under the command of Renzo da Ceri with the object of changing the Florentine government by more rapid means and in quite another form than that which Giulio de' Medici showed signs of wishing to adopt.

In fact at that period, as he remained sole master of the city which he governed very reasonably, outwardly favouring the company of former *piagnoni* and supporters of liberty, Giulio was again seeking opinions about the reform of the state. It was a clever way of investigating people's thoughts and discovering what ambitions were fermenting in certain Florentine minds. Perhaps, as that branch of his family was now broken without any legitimate descendants, his intention was at first sincere. Then, ill advised by his own sympathies or by the ambitions of his followers, or irritated by the hatred of his adversaries, he turned his plans to the aggrandisement of two Medici bastards: Ippolito, the son of Giuliano, and Alessandro, who was thought to be the Cardinal's own child, although at that time he passed as the son of Lorenzo Duke of Urbino.

In the meantime, with those flattering inquiries the Cardinal had inflamed desires and unleashed imaginations which would henceforth not be easy to hold back. Many projects of government were presented to him, and caught in his own game, he went on asking everyone's opinion. He asked Machiavelli for his, and he revived with only a few changes the plan he had drawn up for Leo X, giving it the form of a decree or proclamation, since it seemed things were now coming to a head.[10]. Alessandro de' Pazzi also presented one in which Machiavelli's proposal was described as 'unheard of and extravagant'[11]; but Machiavelli must have been used to this sort of thing by now. Indeed his scheme did seem somewhat artificial and impracticable in its details, but the substance was anything but extravagant, since it involved, to put it briefly, a return to the popular state, to be governed by the Medici during the Cardinal's lifetime, and thereafter to be free.

This was also the basis of the decree which we read that the Cardinal had already had drawn up ready for publication on the 1st of May;[12] but I am not sure that things had gone so far. Certainly nothing was heard of it on that day. On the 11th Alessandro de' Pazzi put out an appropriate Latin oration in which he praised the Cardinal for the restoration of the city's liberty. When the author tried to present it to him, he was received instead by the faithful Schomberg who told him: 'Your oration pleases me greatly, but not its subject.'[13] Reasons or pretexts for putting off thoughts of reform were found first in the expedition of Renzo da Ceri, and then when that proved abortive due to the preparations of the Florentine government and the improvidence of its author, out came the details of a conspiracy connected with it. On the day of Corpus Christi (19th June) Cardinal de' Medici was to be assassinated; and this too was to be one of the expeditious ways of reforming the state.

At the head of that conspiracy were Machiavelli's two greatest friends, Zanobi Buondelmonti and the poet Luigi Alamanni; and also taking part in it were another Luigi Alamanni, Diaccetino and Brucioli, all of them belonging to the literary group of the Orti. It was a gloomy prospect for poor Niccolò, who was one of their friends and a reputed former conspirator against the Medici. Worse still, Buondelmonti was supposed to have mentioned his name to one of the accomplices, among those of several citizens whom it was suggested should be invited to join the plot. I do not know whether he was in fact approached, nor could the accomplice say when interrogated, but he did say that he had advised Zanobi against it, telling him that as Machiavelli was a poor man and known not to be a great friend of the Medici, he would not have been able to do the things they wanted without arousing suspicion.[14]

Luckily in the first trials nothing was said of Buondelmonti's intention, since he, being warned in time, fled, and with him Luigi Alamanni the poet. Only the other Luigi Alamanni and Diaccetino were taken. They were tried and confessed, and beheaded on the 6th of June. When the accomplice I mentioned, a certain Niccolò Martelli, who escaped like Brucioli, Battista della Palla and other conspirators, fell into the hands of the Medici government in 1524 and eventually confessed those secret thoughts of Buondelmonti, they were already entering the year 1526 and a lot of water had flowed under the Arno bridges in the meantime.

A lot of water had flowed under the Tiber bridges too. Cardinal Soderini, after having been much favoured by Pope Adrian to the disgust of Cardinal de' Medici, had finally been imprisoned in the Castel Sant 'Angelo on account of information about his intrigues diligently supplied by his rival. His brother Piero had died on the 13th of June 1522 a few days after the discovery of the plot. The memory of that devoted citizen was publicly condemned by a pronouncement of the Medici government. The tomb built for him in the church of the Carmine by Benedetto da Rovezzano remained empty, and his true epitaph for posterity was the one composed by Machiavelli:

> *La notte che morì Pier Soderini*
> *l'alma n'andò de l'Inferno a la bocca;*
> *e Pluto le gridò: Anima sciocca,*
> *che Inferno? va' nel Limbo tra' bambini*[15]

[The night Pier Soderini died, his soul went to the mouth of Hell, and Pluto cried: 'Silly soul, why come to Hell? Go to Limbo with the infants'].

Too many pages have been written about these four lines. Other foolish souls took offence at them out of fellow feeling, and there were even some who, to relieve Machiavelli of the responsibility, denied against all the evidence that they could be his work.[16] But although some people might not like to see the former Secretary jeering at the Gonfalonier who had always shown him kindness and favour, this does not seem a good reason to distort the truth and Machiavelli's true nature, always ready for a joke, and certainly not compassionate towards fallen heroes, especially if they were wicked like Valentino or somewhat weak and soft like Soderini. This famous epigram is really only one of those spicy jokes which no Florentine has ever been able to resist making at anyone's expense or under any circumstances. And jokes do not have to show pity or generosity; they have to be sharp. It is an entirely verbal joke, an end in itself, and as Machiavelli used to say about his own laughter, 'it does not touch the soul'. Nearer the truth than those moderns who have insisted on taking the joke seriously, is the sixteenth-century comment of Giuliano de' Ricci, when he remarks that his uncle wrote this epitaph for fun and as a joke, 'as a poet'.[17]

What Machiavelli's feelings may have been during the trials and after the sentences which followed the conspiracy, the documents do not tell us, but it is easy to imagine it more clearly than any document could show it. At that very time he also suffered the grievous loss of his brother Totto, a good and pious priest who was universally loved. Niccolò had come to Florence to be with him.[18] Unable to go abroad as the city's ambassador, he is content to give advice at this time to others who do. [19] Even his trips to Florence, once so happy, now seem tiresome and empty. The gatherings in the Orti—one of the few good things left to him in life—are no more. Grieving for his friends who were dead or in flight, afraid for himself, he withdraws more than ever into his rural home, once a place of exile and now a refuge. It is also a refuge from the plague which had just begun to appear and spread terror in Florence. On the 27th of November 1522 he makes his second and final will.[20]

At that time it became known in the city that Buondelmonti and Alamanni had been captured while re-entering Italy from France.[21] The affair was not dangerous for the two exiles, who were eventually released, but everything which reminded Machiavelli of the Orti renewed his grief and his fears.[22] Vivid memories return of the torture and imprisonment he had suffered when he was accused of conspiring against another cardinal de' Medici. He looks back gloomily on those last years, that period 'caught between two conspiracies', just like the beginning of the 8th book of the *Histories* to which he must have been getting near at the end of that year or at the beginning of 1523. To fill his cup with bitterness, there came at this moment the publication of the famous and infamous plagiarism of Agostino Nifo: a deformed version of the *Prince*.[23]

Meanwhile the plague, which was to last till the beginning of August, was increasing in violence. The people were leaving Florence and scattering into the country.[24] But history did not stand still for all that. The war in Lombardy between the Spanish and the French still went on. The French, after losing Milan, returned with fresh troops and renewed energy under the leadership of admiral Bonnivet, and were met by the two Charles in the service of Charles V—Lannoy, Viceroy of Naples, and Bourbon who had rebelled against and betrayed the King of France. At this time (14th September 1523) Pope Adrian died amid the rejoicings of the Romans who gave thanks to his doctor with wreaths and writings hailing him as saviour of the city. The long conclave, where the bitter contest between the old and new cardinals, the former led by Giulio de' Medici and the latter by Pompeo Colonna, reminded literary men of the ancient contests between another Julius and another Pompey, ended with the victory of Giulio who took the name of Clement VII (18th November). Conspiracies tended to bring Medici cardinals good luck.

Now that his fright was over, this election was to revive Machiavelli's hopes, inclined as he was to such bursts of enthusiasm. His first thought was to present the pontiff with the work he had been commissioned to write when the Pope was a cardinal, and to receive his reward. The book he had been working at slowly and which had been rather dragging on until then, suddenly became most precious to him. I believe that he had by then got to a point in the eighth book where he had to discuss the actions of Lorenzo, uncle of the Pope and true founder of the Medici state; and by virtue of the nearness and importance of these events, they needed careful handling.

On the 30th of August 1524 in reply to Guicciardini who had given him some errand to perform for his property at Poppiano, he first complained that there were no beccafichi that year (another pastime gone and fewer delicacies for the table!), and then, with one of those sudden changes of tone of his, he wrote: 'I have been spending my time in the country writing my *History*, and I would give ten soldi—I won't say more—to have you at my side so that I could show you where I have got to, because I am coming to certain details and need to have your opinion whether I offend either by exaggerating or under-stating the facts. Still, I will take counsel with myself, and arrange things so that, while I tell the truth, no one can complain.'[25]

The death of Lorenzo came at the right point for him to close this eighth book and conclude that part of the work which he now wished to present to the Pope. He finished it rapidly and then began to polish it. All his changes were to make the style clearer and barer, not, as was then the fashion, to make it more ornamental. His object was to make it more forceful, not more decorative.[26] He worked with the rapid enthusiasm of his greatest hours when he was riding an illusion. Then, raising his head from the pages he had written, he could ponder on the news heard from his friends or while sitting outside the tavern. He followed the varying fortunes of the war between the two great rivals, in the plain of Lombardy and in Provence. He held his breath over the dangerous game played by Pope Clement, who was now going over from the Emperor's side to the French, as though he wanted to carry on the manœuvres of Leo X without his ability or his luck. As he thought of these things, Machiavelli's pen often paused. And to console him for the beccafichi the first thrushes were already whistling among the dark holm-oaks of his snaring grounds in the cold Autumn dawns.

Chapter 20

NICCOLÒ MACHIAVELLI, HISTORIAN AND COMEDIAN

<><><><><><><><><><><><><><><><><><><><><><><><><><><><><><><><><>

Now something new arises, something which gives him new life, stimulates his illusions and his intelligence, and draws him out of that stagnant country atmosphere. It is something quite different from thrushes. He has taken on a new lease of life, goes into the city oftener and stays there more willingly. The Orti are closed for ever, but another garden is open to him: that of Jacopo Fornaciaio outside the Porta a San Frediano.[1] It is not frequented by literary men or philosophers, nor are learned discussions heard there; instead they banquet, and the food is real, not philosophical. Fornaciaio is a rich plebeian, but his house is not despised by the nobility, for particularly in Florence prejudices are easily swallowed with good food. This in itself, in spite of the jokes at Carpi, would be an attraction for the gourmand Machiavelli.[2] Then too, there is Barbera.

She is a young singer, full of charm. Machiavelli seeks her company, as his friends have noticed for some time. The first indication is found in a letter that Vettori, who had gone with a large embassy to greet the new Pope, wrote to Francesco del Nero on the 5th of February 1524: 'Remember me to Niccolò Machiavelli and tell him I think it is much better to sup occasionally with Barbera at the expense of Fornaciaio than to be here standing by a door around supper-time, which even after a long wait has still not opened up.'[3]

In fact Machiavelli had fallen in love with her more than he or his friends realized. Barbera's charms were perhaps not difficult to conquer, but to him, like a poor unsuccessful 'new prince', they gave for an hour or two the illusion of conquest and power: he was a poet and knew how to create illusions, and in his unhappiness he had learned the art of prolonging them and feeding upon them. It was a light love affair, at times animating at others painful, as such a thing can be at fifty-six; a small fire that sometimes burned brightly, and sometimes smouldered, according to his changing moods and the character of the woman. She, although her middle-aged lover was rich only in intelligence, showed affection for him, even if she sometimes affectionately made fun of him. She liked his wit, she was flattered by his brilliance. Greatness may sometimes drive people away, sometimes even in small things it shines through and attracts. Something out of the common run of things must have existed between them if in 1544, no less than seventeen years after Machiavelli's death, she could ask Lorenzo Ridolfi, 'for the love he bore to the memory of Niccolò Machiavelli', to help her in certain law suits.[4]

The human heart is a strange mixture, but not, however, very hard to understand. Niccolò loved his good Marietta, the affectionate wife, the good housekeeper, the mother of his beloved children. But these things, which were not always enough for a cloth-merchant in the Calimala, could hardly suffice for a Machiavelli. His country house, his woods, his bird-catching were very dear to him, but they were not enough. And his dear Marietta too was like that house, those woods and that bird-catching.

He attended as often as he could those suppers at Fornaciaio's, and Barbera was there too. At those suppers and in that company the *Clizia* had its origin. The Compagnia della Cazzuola had recently acted *Mandragola* in the house of Bernardino di Giordano at Monteloro, where Andrea del Sarto and Aristotele da San Gallo had painted the scenery.[5] Fornaciaio had the notion of emulating that magnificence at a party to be given on the 13th of January to celebrate the revocation of his exile[6]; but when there was talk of putting on *Mandragola* again, Machiavelli, either to please his generous host or to please Barbera, offered a new comedy instead.

He set to work at once, for the day of the party was not far off and time pressed. Having made the offer before he had written a word and without any idea of what he was going to write, there was nothing else for it this time but to tap the sources of ancient comedy. He therefore took as his model the *Casina* of Plautus, and I do not think the choice was a mere coincidence. He was accustomed to make fun of everything and everybody, himself included, and he took pleasure in this new comedy in making game of his own amours.[7] For, if he were not as old as Stalino, transformed by him into the Florentine Nicomaco (where the first two syllables are those of his own name), certain of his letters and poems addressed to Barbera show that he liked to play, not without a touch of melancholy, on this tardy love affair of his:

> Nè doler mi poss'io
> di voi ma di me stesso,
> Poich'i' veggo e confesso
> come tanta beltade
> ama più verde etade[8]

[I cannot complain of you, but rather of myself, because I see and confess that such beauty must love more tender years].

These lines are echoed in a different metre, but almost in the same words, in a 'canzone' in the comedy:

> Sì che, o vecchi amorosi, el meglio fora
> lasciar l'impresa a' giovanetti ardenti[9]

[So, old men in love, it would be better to leave the task to ardent young men].

These origins of the work which have not been considered before by biographers and literary historians, easily explain the great difference in artistic value that exists between *Mandragola* and *Clizia*, which till now seemed inexplicable. One sprang from pure inspiration, the other was composed deliberately and perhaps in a race against time for the party which Fornaciaio wished to give. The theory of a diptych designed for particular moral ends consequently lacks all foundation.[10]

This then was how *Clizia* came into being. He dashed it off (one can imagine him doing it) in a short time, now translating directly from Plautus, now imitating him more freely according to the spirit of the times, now inventing and renewing. But what is new and fresh in it, is the style, the Florentine witticisms, which are often better than those of Plautus, although they do not bear comparison with those of *Mandragola*; and this is confirmation of its hasty composition, in which inspiration plays little part. Perhaps Machiavelli put his *Histories* on one side for a few weeks; perhaps he worked on both at the same time, writing the comedy when he was bored with the history and wanted some relaxation.

The evening of the play came. Fornaciaio had ordered a splendid banquet, 'to which all the leading citizens came and the most distinguished men of the government then in power',[11] beginning with the young Ippolito de' Medici whom the Pope had sent a few months before to take his place at the head of the Republic. But after these major figures, middle-class citizens were invited and the populace too. The comedy was then acted, 'its fame having aroused in everyone the desire to see it'.[12] The backcloth and scenery were painted by Bastiano da San Gallo and, according to Vasari, 'pleased everyone very much'.[13]

The party made a great impression, and so did the comedy because of the sumptuousness of the feast. Its fame spread outside Florence, even though we may not take literally the facetious exaggerations of Filippo de' Nerli, who wrote to Machiavelli from Modena where he was governor, on the 22nd of February 1525: 'The fame of your comedy has spread everywhere; and do not think I have had this from friends' letters, I have had it from travellers who all along the roads go proclaiming the glorious displays and fine games[14] of Porta a San Frediano. I am sure that as the greatness of such magnificence has not been content to remain within the bounds of Tuscany, but has also come as far as here, it will cross the mountains too . . . . . .'.[15] There were some who out of prudishness or hypocrisy or jealousy were scandalized by the *Clizia* and its author, among them Nerli himself, who a few days after writing those humorous congratulations, bitterly complained to Francesco del Nero about 'Machia's' behaviour, accusing him of 'running after' Barbera and of having written 'a comedy with some fine things in it'. He ended his attack by urging del Nero to do something about it, without however 'mentioning his name'. As del Nero was Niccolò's brother-in-law, this was a fine hypocritical way of making trouble for him.[16]

In the meantime Machiavelli had finished revising his *Histories*, and as he wished to go and present the work in person, he asked his friend Vettori, who was returning to Rome shortly after the production of *Clizia*, to find out how the land lay. However, the Pope, who must have had other things on his mind at that time, immediately asked Vettori the moment he saw him, how Machiavelli was and if he had finished his book. Vettori replied that the work had been completed up to the death of Lorenzo, and that he had read some of it and thought it was a success. When he added that the author would have come to present it himself if he had not dissuaded him because of the uncertainty of the times, the Pope answered with these words: 'He should have come! I think his books will please and be read gladly.'[17]

Vettori, however, either out of coldness or jealousy, as in the days of Pope Leo, again hastened to temper Machiavelli's hopes. Writing to him on the 8th of March to tell him what the Pope had said, he watered down the text with the gloss that he did not know whether to advise him to come with the book or not, 'because the times are unpropitious for presentation and reading'. He added: ' I would not like you to be encouraged to come and then find yourself empty-handed, which is what might happen with the Pope in his present mood'. He also wrote the same thing to Francesco del Nero.[18]

It was quite true that the times were unfavourable for presentations and reading. A few days before, on the 24th of February, the imperial army had routed the King of France at Pavia. The Pope had concluded certain agreements with the latter, which the Emperor felt amounted to an alliance. The King himself had been taken prisoner. Italy was threatened by Spanish domination. Clement was without money or troops, and at the mercy of the conqueror. Still pursuing the vacillating policy which in Leo meant cleverness and in him implied timidity and irresolution, he then hastened to make an alliance with the Emperor which was concluded on the 1st of April. In virtue of this agreement the Pope and the Emperor were mutually bound to defend the Duchy of Milan held by Francesco Sforza 'under Caesar's shadow'. The Emperor undertook to defend the territories of the Church (including Reggio which he promised to have restored to the Church by the Duke of Ferrara), the Florentine state and the Medici pre-eminence in it. Still according to the treaty, the Florentines were as usual to pay for all this by giving Caesar a hundred thousand ducats, not only for his protection of the Papal States but for his support of the Medici rule. In these circumstances it is not surprising if festivities for this confederation were held with little joy in Florence.

The Pope's joy did not last long either for an agreement which would have brought him security at the expense of the peace of Italy. Caesar had ratified the treaty made in his name by the Viceroy, but the ratification of the extra clauses, including the one about Reggio, was delayed. Signs of the ill disposition of the Emperor were continually appearing. In such a situation the Pope decided to send as legate to the court of Madrid, which was now the hub of European politics, his nephew Cardinal Salviati. It was then that there was some talk of sending Niccolò Machiavelli with him.

Machiavelli had in the past professed some devotion to the Cardinal who had been the first in Rome to receive the printed edition of the *Art of War*[19]; and the Cardinal had shown him that he appreciated his talent more than others did at that time. However, the person who had most influence with the Cardinal was his father Jacopo, a fine old man and a great citizen. The purple cloth was sometimes no protection for him against his father's chiding. Thus it was Jacopo who put forward Machiavelli's name in a letter to his son on the 3rd of May[20]; and on the 13th he returned to the subject: 'As a secretary, and as a man with whom you might take counsel, Niccolò Machiavelli would please me better than anyone. I have spoken about it to His Holiness, and he is undecided; I shall see if I cannot get him to make up his mind.'[21]

That fine old man had the right idea. Furthermore, he was extremely strict about manners and morals, and a blunt critic of his son's court;[22] which shows that Machiavelli's reputation in this respect cannot have been as bad as some would have us believe, or that Jacopo was inclined to pay more attention to facts than to gossip. However, the Pope decided to decline his proposal. We do not know whether this decision was due to his political ideas, or his morals, or the intention of using him in some other way. We only know that on the 17th of May Jacopo wrote to his son: 'We shall have to give up Niccolò Machiavelli, because I see that the Pope is reluctant'[23]; and on the 24th: 'So we shall say no more of Niccolò Machiavelli.'[24] What a pity! With such a secretary the embassy would have taken on far greater importance; and who can say what would have come out of Machiavelli after that new experience?

Giving up these Iberian ideas, of which he may only have known when it was all over, Machiavelli finally decided to go to Rome to present his *Histories* to the Pope. He went during the last days of the month of May.[25] There is no record of the Pope's reception of him, but that it was kind and friendly is shown by a gift of 120 gold ducats which Clement caused him to be paid on the 9th of June from his private treasury.[26] It is true that he took to Rome not only the book, but also an idea, with which and with his usual enthusiasm, he managed for a short time to rouse the Pope's cold nature.[27] Clement was asking everyone for cures for the ills of his policies; full of irresolution himself, he was at the mercy of a most resolute conqueror; he lacked soldiers because he would not pay for them, and was without money because he could not make up his mind to sell offices and benefices as Leo had done. In other words, he could not make up his mind to be a good temporal prince for fear of being a bad pope.

Machiavelli had the answer ready: the national militia. It was his great idea, his old war-cry! The Pope and his advisers, Salviati, Sadoleto, even the phlegmatic Schomberg, were persuaded and overcome. Arm the people of Romagna! To the President of Romagna, therefore, to his old friend Francesco Guicciardini then resident in Faenza, Machiavelli was sent with an urgent papal brief composed by Sadoleto. Extraordinary diseases call for extraordinary remedies was the substance of the brief: the President should therefore listen attentively to what Machiavelli would tell him and at once send his opinion. *Res magna est*, it went on, 'the matter is of great importance and on it depends the safety of the Papal States as well as that of the whole of Italy, and practically of the whole of Christendom'.[28] It remained to be seen whether this enthusiasm and that of the bearer would dissipate the President's coldness or be chilled by it.

Guicciardini was warned in advance of Machiavelli's arrival and the reason for it by his agent at the court of Rome, Cesare Colombo. Replying to him on the 16th of June he at once put the question which first suggested itself to his lucid and practical mind: 'Ask on my behalf to what end the Pope plans this, for if he intends it as a remedy for present dangers, it is a provision which cannot come in time.'[29] Machiavelli took a long view, Guicciardini a short one, and the Pope, as usual, could not decide whether to look to the present or the future.

Machiavelli reached Faenza shortly after the advance notice of his arrival. He had left Rome, full of fresh enthusiasm, on the 10th or 11th of June without waiting for the results of his efforts to obtain an increase in his salary for the *Histories*.[30] On the 21st Guicciardini wrote to his agent that the papal envoy had come and had explained his commission. In this first letter he was not able to deny the grandeur and nobility of the idea, 'which if it could be brought to the desired fruition, there is no doubt that it would be one of the most useful and praiseworthy things which His Holiness could do'. But coming to the practical effects, he hastened to dampen with his cold and cautious realism his friend's generous idealism. Leaving on one side the good that would be achieved, 'for this is evident', and conceding that he himself 'would see no difficulty or fear of scandal in arming the population', if the people were

P

of a different character, he went on to enumerate the reasons against it: the inveterate private and political hatreds dividing the province; the lack of loyalty of the subjects towards the Church, whereas Machiavelli's plan depended on the people's patriotism; the expense involved, which could not, as the Pope supposed, be drawn from the financially exhausted communes. He protested that he did not put forward these difficulties to dissuade His Holiness, but so that he might consider them, and when he had considered them, either withdraw or face them 'with all that support an enterprise deserves which His Holiness expects one day may bring him fame and glory'.[31]

The same reasons in similar words were written by Guicciardini to his agent on the 23rd of June in a letter to be shown to the Pope. In a note of instructions sent separately he added: 'Observe particularly as far as you can his gestures and his words and let me know everything.'[32] He was to do the same with Salviati and Schomberg. Another letter (no longer extant) was written by Machiavelli to Sadoleto the following day, which was also to be shown to the Pontiff.[33] This one rang quite a different bell.

After that the usual irresolution and tergiversation of Clement began, which Berni satirized in a famous sonnet.[34] In Faenza Guicciardini's and Machiavelli's anxious wait began, anxious for opposite reasons. We do not know to what extent Machiavelli had been persuaded by his friend's practical arguments, but he must have seen their force in this particular case; and they were strong enough at all events to make him lose the game with that timid Pope. Meanwhile he, who was hardened to misunderstandings and disappointments, had some consolation from the discussions, the excellent meals and splendid beds of his friend the President.

On the 8th of July, since nothing had been heard of the Pope's deliberations, Guicciardini reminded his agent that they were awaiting a decision.[35] Again on the 12th he wrote asking for 'a decision for Machiavelli; as he has heard nothing up to now, you will speak to Sadoleto, because he does not know what to do here'.[36] But Sadoleto had already written to Machiavelli on the 6th that he had passed on his letter and Guicciardini's to the Pope; and his reply had been that 'he wanted to think it over a bit more'. He had asked him again another day, and had received the same answer that he wished to think it over further, and in the meantime Machiavelli should remain in Faenza.[37]

He stayed there in fact until the 26th, and then, feeling he had waited long enough, he went back to Florence 'on certain affairs of his': so wrote Guicciardini to Colombo, instructing him to tell the Pope and to add that it did not matter where Machiavelli was, 'for he will go at once wherever His Holiness orders him to go'.[38] In fact Machiavelli had understood the Pope's resolution, or rather his irresolution, before the Pope himself.

All the biographers speak of his great bitterness at this fresh disappointment.[39] It may be that he felt such bitterness within him, but there is not one word of evidence to that effect. As I have said, we do not even know if he had accepted some of the objections put to him by the practical-minded Guicciardini, who did not deny the excellence of the idea—and this must have been some comfort to Machiavelli—but only the advisability of applying it at that moment to the subjects of the Papal States, especially in that province.

Even if he were disappointed, he knew how to console himself. I do not mean the kind and cordial hospitality afforded him by Guicciardini who was not at all cold with him as the biographers affirm. Indeed, after that long stay in Faenza, perhaps under the same roof,[40] the relations between the two men became much warmer and closer, so much so that the reserved President objected in one letter to the title of 'illustrious' given him by his friend, threatening to repay him in the same coin.[41] I refer instead to another kind of favour shown him by a certain 'respectable courtesan'. On the 2nd of July Guicciardini wrote to him jokingly: 'After your departure Maliscotta spoke most honourably of you and praised very much your manners and conversation. I am delighted with this, for I desire your every pleasure'.[42] On this subject and in the same tone Machiavelli replied in a letter of the 3rd of August: 'I received your letter, in which you tell me how much I am favoured by Maliscotta; and I am prouder of this than of anything I have in this world.'[43]

Now the letters between the two great politicians come oftener. During his stay in Faenza Machiavelli had promised his friend to inspect a property he had bought, unseen, by proxy, and another he proposed buying, and to report on them. He inspected and reported on the 3rd of August, showing that he had profited from his rustic experience at San Casciano: '*Rem omnem a Finochieto ordiar*. And the first thing I have to tell you is that for three miles around you can see nothing that pleases: Arabia Petrœa is not otherwise. The house cannot be called bad, but I would never call it good, because it lacks the necessary commodities: the rooms are small, the windows are high: it is just like the bottom of a tower. There is a little meadow of a kind in front; all the approaches are steep except for one which is flat for perhaps a hundred yards; and withal it is so buried in the hills that the best view is only half a mile . . .' He advises him to sell, but in the meantime, whether he wishes to sell or to keep it, to have fertilizers spread: 'These fertilizers will be useful for either of two things: first if you want to sell, anyone who came to see it would see something to his liking, and that may bring him to discuss a sale; because, in its present state . . . I do not think you would ever sell it except to someone who had not seen it like yourself. If you want to keep it, those fertilizers will enable you to get from the land more wine, which is good here, and not to die of grief when you go to see it . . .'[44]

There is a humour in this description which roused, and perhaps stung, the more serious Guicciardini, who replied with a burlesque moralizing tale in which he makes the villa of Finocchieto speak in the first person. This, or rather its rustic nymph, attributed Machiavelli's unfavourable judgement to his habit of consorting with women of easy virtue who sought to please everyone: he could not appreciate the blunt honesty of one who sought only to please her own master. He should not have stopped at appearances but should rather have sought the inner substance: 'and this,' he continued, 'your Barbera should have shown you, for although her name stands for cruelty and violence, she has within her, by your own account, so much gentleness and kindness that it would season a whole city'.[45]

Barbera: here was a way to forget the forgetfulness of men, the indecision of the Pope, the poverty and disgrace which continued to be his lot. Barbera and his bitter-sweet love for her were more than ever Machiavelli's pastime in the city. It was proverbial among his friends; so much so that when in August the Accoppiatori [magistrates charged with forming a government] restored his eligibility for government offices (would he then be seen again in the Palazzo, no longer as a secretary but as a prior or gonfalonier?), Filippo de' Nerli wrote to him maliciously that this was the result of favours which came to him 'from Barbary'.[46]

In any case, fortune seemed no longer unkind to him. Meanwhile the seed he had sown during his Roman expedition for an increase in his salary for the *Histories* had germinated and was soon to bear fruit. At the end of the previous July Francesco del Nero wrote to him that Filippo Strozzi had heard encouraging news from the Pope.[47] Soon after the officials of the university were to receive the order that 'Machiavelli should be paid a hundred gold ducats instead of a hundred "studio" florins'[48]—that is, a hundred genuine florins, not academic ones. It was doubling his salary.[49]

Then, on the 19th of August the Provveditori del Levante sent him to Venice for some 'Turkish frauds' committed against certain Florentine merchants by a Venetian.[50] It was a small commission, but anything was welcome if it exercised his mind and let him see and hear 'diverse generations of men'. It was also a good opportunity to stop on the way with his friend the President, to see his friends again (as he wrote to Guicciardini), and to talk with him about the Italian political situation which daily grew more desperate. In the meantime he sent him the recipe for certain famous digestive and purgative pills which had 'resuscitated' him, or at least helped him to digest so many bitter experiences.[51]

Machiavelli went to Venice and negotiated; and he discussed politics also with the Papal Nuncio in Venice, the bishop Ludovico Canossa, to whom he had been sent by his friend Vettori.[52] I do not know what else he did; it was said that he won a lottery, but he certainly did not win the two or three thousand ducats which, with his usual sarcasm, Filippo de' Nerli mentioned in a letter. He started back on the 16th of September;[53] if he stayed a few days with the President, he was not in Florence again until the end of the month. After his return he kept up a frequent correspondence with Guicciardini.

In this correspondence the *Mandragola* is now to the fore. In a letter of the 12th of August now lost, Guicciardini, to whom his friend had given or sent a printed copy of the comedy, had praised it enthusiastically, proposing to have it performed in Faenza. To this Machiavelli replied: 'I am glad that you like messer Nicia, and if you have it acted during Carnival we will come and help you.'[54] Perhaps on the 13th of October, Guicciardini again wrote to get the author to explain to him, a Florentine, certain Florentine jokes and proverbial expressions in the comedy! To this Machiavelli replied with another letter which is really brilliant: 'I have delved into many books like fra Timoteo to discover the origin of this harrow business; and at last I have found in Burchiello a text which is just right for me, where he says in one of his sonnets:

217

Temendo che lo Imperio non passasse
si mandò imbasciator un paiol d'accia . . .
Ma l'erpice di Fiesole vi trasse . . . .

[Fearing the Emperor would invade, they sent as ambassador a spool of thread . . . But the harrow of Fiesole came along. . . .].

This sonnet seems very mysterious to me, and I think, if one looks at it closely, it is a satire on our times. There is just this difference, that if then they sent a spool of thread, it has now turned into maccheroni, so that it seems to me that history repeats itself and men go on being the same throughout the ages. . . . Burchiello mentions the Fiesolan harrow because it is the oldest in Tuscany, for the Fiesolans, as Livy says in the second Decade, were the first to invent this tool. And one day as a peasant was raking the ground, a toad who had never seen such cultivation before was sitting there in astonishment and peering out to see what it was, when the harrow caught her and scraped her back planting its teeth in her several times, so that when the harrow passed over her and she felt it scratching her hard, she shouted: Don't come back again! This cry gave rise to the proverb which says, when you don't want someone to come back, "as the toad said to the harrow".'[55]

   This is remarkable for its burlesque erudition (even the *second* Decade of Livy!), the comic effect of pretentiousness, the irony on the subject of papal policies in relation to the Emperor. The maccheroni stand for Cardinal Salviati who had not been allowed to have this fine secretary in his embassy, in which, as Guicciardini's *History* observes, 'he was no more vigorous or steadfast than his master',[56] i.e. Pope Clement. Machiavelli's correspondence is all, as has recently been said, a masterpiece,[57] but in these last letters to Guicciardini, to use a phrase of his own messer Nicia, '*ci raffinisce tra le mani*'—it gets more and more brilliant. In a letter which he wrote shortly after the 20th of October, he discusses at length the way to find a fatter dowry for his daughters at the Pope's expense, and then suddenly breaks into these words: 'Morone was taken prisoner and the Duchy of Milan is lost: and as he has been put out of action, all the other princes will be too, and there is nothing to be done about it. *Sic datum desuper.*

Veggio d'Alagna tornar lo fiordaliso
E nel Vicario suo, etc. . . . .
[I see the fleur-de-lys return from Alagna and in his Vicar . . .].

Nosti versus, caetera per te ipsum lege. Let us have a merry carnival for once; arrange for Barbera a room with those friars, and if they do not go crazy about her, I won't take the money; commend me to Maliscotta and let me know where the comedy has got to, and when you intend to put it on. I had that increase to a hundred ducats for the *History*. I am now starting to write again and I vent my feelings by accusing the princes who have all done their best to bring us to this pass.'[58]

Sic datum desuper. The tragedy was now at its fifth act, and Italy was its subject. All its tragic force is contained in this brief prose of Machiavelli, with its sudden passage from the 'particular' to the apocalyptic universal judgement on the ruinous policies of princes, and from the illuminating prophecy expressed with miraculous foresight in a line of Dante

> *nel Vicario suo Cristo esser catto,*

[Christ in his Vicar made prisoner],

to the carefree carnival spirit. Here is all Machiavelli, and here he is more than ever the symbol of his times and of Italy. Appropriately he signs this letter, half seriously and half in jest: 'Niccolò Machiavelli, *istorico, comico e tragico.*'

Chapter 21

NICCOLÒ MACHIAVELLI, 'HISTORIAN, COMIC AND TRAGIC AUTHOR'

◇◇

ACHIAVELLI never wrote any tragedies or ever contemplated doing so other than the tragedy he now described as he took up his history again. Nevertheless he had tragic thoughts enough in his mind to give a dramatic air to his denunciation of the princes who had not been willing to heed the exhortation which ends the *Prince*. He had already drawn with bold strokes an outline of the story which, starting with the 'foreign invasions' following the death of Lorenzo, and proceeding through a maze of mistakes and deceptions, led towards the fatal *dénouement* prophesied in his recent letter.

'Morone was taken prisoner and the Duchy of Milan is lost.' This event which seemed to him one of the last scenes of the last act of the tragedy he was sketching, in fact concluded and set the seal on the wretched political game resumed by Italian rulers after the battle of Pavia. Pope Clement, seeing himself falling into the hands of the Emperor, had again decided to join a league to drive the Spaniards out of Italy and first of all out of the state of Milan, where Francesco Sforza by virtue of ruling 'under the shadow of Caesar' according to agreement, had become the shadow of a duke. To make the enterprise easier the Pope had, according to the political habits of the time, taken the longest and most devious route, that of enlisting on his side and giving the command of the joint armies to the Marchese of Pescara, Italian by birth, Spanish by origin and enemy of the name of Italy, captain

220

of those very Spanish forces against which the Pope intended him to fight. The inventor of this intrigue was that master of weathercocks, Girolamo Morone, secretary of the Duke of Milan.

Pescara had listened without protest to the overtures made to him and at once informed the Emperor: this was a clever way of assuring his own position leaving him free to betray whichever side he wanted. He was not the only one to adopt this course. He did it with Morone and the Emperor; Sforza did it with the Emperor and the King, and the Pope with both the great rivals. Clement, while attempting to seduce the Emperor's captain, was writing to the Emperor warning him against his captains. They were all playing a double game. For some time it had been said that Pescara and Morone were traitors (the latter betraying his friends, the former the faith sworn to his enemies), and now Morone had been taken prisoner and the Spaniards, seizing the opportunity to take complete possession of the duchy, had Italy more than ever at their mercy. Then Clement, who was in a weaker position than before and more suspect to the Emperor, would have liked all the more to ally himself with France, but he knew he could not find firm support there until the King was freed from captivity; and this was encountering serious difficulties because of the impossible demands being made by Charles V. He was therefore almost in despair when some consolation came in the form of the death of the Marchese di Pescara. He felt he had gained a considerable advantage by the loss of the principal enemy captain. He consoled himself with these false hopes: a dramatic figure in his perpetual uncertainty, more worthy of a tragic muse than of the impassioned insults of Berni:[1]

> Può far il Ciel però, papa Chimenti,
> cioè papa castron, papa balordo,
> che tu sia diventato cieco e sordo
> et abbi persi tutti i sentimenti?

[Pope Clement, impotent, stupid pope, can Heaven have made you blind and deaf and made you take leave of your senses?]

There is also Machiavelli's gloss on the Pope's extraordinary folly: 'Thinking he has time, he gives time to the enemy'. Then, turning to consider the spirit and attitude of his fellow Florentines in those decisive days, he was forced to conclude that neither they nor the other powers in Italy would ever do 'anything honourable and bold worth living or dying for'.[2] He wrote this to Guicciardini on the 19th of December

1525 in a letter otherwise entirely devoted to personal affairs, urging him once more, as he had already done after his stay in Faenza, to give his daughters a good dowry at the Pope's expense. Dante came to his assistance here again, when he quoted to his friend the example of Romeo:

Quattro figlie ebbe e ciascuna regina . . . [3]
[He had four daughters and each one a queen . . .].

Guicciardini who was not a poet and unlike Machiavelli had little familiarity with poets, replied to this letter on the 26th and confessed that he 'had looked everywhere in Romagna for a Dante to find the fable or tale of Romeo', and in the end could only find a text without the commentary. He ended with a mixture of admiration and diffidence towards his facetious friend: 'I think it must be one of those things you always have an endless store of'. Romeo, and who might he be? Even *de rebus publicis* the President did not know what to say, having lost his bearings and seeing everyone opposed to taking that bold course which, though he did not like it, seemed the only one possible: 'I never heard of anyone who when he saw a storm coming did not attempt to take cover, except ourselves who prefer to wait for it in the middle of the road without any protection. So . . . we shall not be able to say that government has been taken from us, but that *turpiter elapsa sit de manibus*'.[4]

In the circumstances it was better to think about the performance of *Mandragola*, which Guicciardini in fact put before anything else in his letter, 'because at least it is something which is within our power, so that one is not wasting one's time thinking about it, and entertainment is more than ever necessary in these turbulent times'. The actors were all ready, but they did not care for the fine prologue, clever and bitter as it is, and so they had re-written it in their own way.[5] Guicciardini proposed that his friend should write another one suited to the mediocrity of the listeners, in which he might portray them rather than himself. He wanted to have this performance given in the last days of carnival which ended that year on the 13th of February, and the author must at all costs be present. So he invited him to come towards the end of January and stay until Lent. By then the 'lodgings for their lordships' would be ready, that is, for Barbera too, who was to sing the songs at the beginning of the acts.[6] Guicciardini ended his letter by asking his friend to tell him what he had decided, but 'seriously, for these are matters not to be neglected'.[7] That he himself was serious about it, is shown by the fine little edition of the comedy which everything leads one to suppose he had made by his printer Girolamo Soncino.[8] He was used to publishing for the grave President texts of a much less entertaining nature, such as proclamations and the like, and he must have been amazed at this commission.

A strange mixture of comedy and tragedy lends an extraordinary fascination to their correspondence and is present too in Machiavelli's answer written on the 3rd of January. As for the comedy he could not say for certain that Barbera would come, 'because she has certain lovers who might make it difficult; but one might contrive to keep them quiet'. Poor Niccolò! All the same, both he and his mistress really intended to come, and the proof was to be seen in five new songs composed and set to music especially for this occasion to be sung between the acts. His letter gave their texts.[9] As for the tragedy, he thought that if the Emperor intended to make himself politically supreme, he would never free the King; for while he held him prisoner, he could tempt now France and now the Pope with the hope of an agreement without ever either breaking off negotiations or bringing them to a conclusion, 'and when he sees that the Italians are about to join with France, he takes up the negotiations with France again so that they do not reach agreement, and he wins the game'.[10]

A few days earlier news had come of an Italian league, that is, the Pope and the Venetians with the French, and it seemed the bargain was a very good one. But at the last moment fresh news arrived: the King and the Emperor had reached an agreement, whereby the former handed over in exchange for his freedom: Burgundy, a large sum of money, all his claims in Italy and elsewhere, and two sons as hostages. All he received in return—if it were any return—was the sister of his conqueror as a wife. Machiavelli judged that Charles had entered into this agreement so that France should break off the league with the Pope, and that when this was done, he would then break his word with France.[11]

These discordant rumours of the alliance with the Pope and the agreement with the Emperor became actual fact a few weeks later. Guicciardini, who had more direct information of the league, must certainly have smiled when he read his friend's wine-shop gossip on the subject. Perhaps, as he thought of a secret of his own, that smile may not have been unlike the smirk which he often saw disquietingly

appear on Machiavelli's face. The secret was this. In mid November
the Pope had hinted to him how glad he would be to employ him in
Rome for some matter of great importance. He finally accepted this
proposal after cautious researches and not a few negotiations about the
emoluments involved. Until the 4th of December he was not told
what the Pope wanted to use his services for, and even then it was
merely conjecture. Then having heard of the league that Clement
wanted to form with France and having guessed that the intention was
to give him the job of first negotiating and then conducting the war,
his usually cold nature suddenly burned with generous impulses. We
hear him regret, now that he is sufficiently sure of the matter, that he
negotiated at such length over the emoluments, 'for the greatest satisfaction I can have from my service is to see that Your Holiness does
not intend to wait to be conquered'.[12]

He kept the secret as he was obliged to do. But when he wrote to
Machiavelli about the comedy to be acted at carnival time, and invited
him and his Barbera, it was not entirely disingenuous. He not only did
not know when he would be sent for, but several times because of the
vacillating policies of the Emperor and the indecision of the Pope it
seemed doubtful whether the plan would come to anything. On the
3rd of January everything was still unsettled, and Guicciardini thought
it was all off.[13] But then, receiving the order to move on the 6th, he
set off on the 20th for Florence where he stopped for four days. There,
since he had to keep the reason for his journey secret, he must have
hidden it also from his friend. One thing, however, was clear: that
production of *Mandragola* at Faenza would never take place, or if it
did, it would be without the presence of Guicciardini and hence also
of Machiavelli.

Machiavelli had some consolation nevertheless from the unprecedented triumphs the comedy was enjoying at carnival time in Venice.
It had been put on there at the instance of the Florentine community,
and on the same evening a company of Venetian gentlemen put on a
rival production of Plautus's *Menaechmi* in translation. Although this
play had excellent actors and lavish scenery and costumes, 'nevertheless
it was regarded as dead' compared with the Florentine comedy. In
consequence those same Venetian gentlemen and actors, when they
heard of the much greater success of *Mandragola*, earnestly desired the
Florentines to act it again in the same house where they had put on
their own play; and this was done to the great satisfaction of the

spectators and with enthusiastic praise of the author and the actors.[14] This was not the first time that the comedy had triumphed in Venice, for as Sanuto tells us, it had been acted during carnival in 1523 when they had not been able to finish the play because of the great crush of spectators.[15] However, it was this comparison with the ancient author in an age when the ancients were axiomatically the best, that marked the greatest triumph of Machiavelli's comic muse.

At this time, however, the historian, comic and tragic author, is not concerned with writing comedies but histories. He had begun writing them again not without some thought of tragedy, as we have already seen from his correspondence with Guicciardini, 'and he was very enthusiastic about them'.[16] He is now busy summarizing and digesting the extracts of letters compiled in his office when, *ante res perditas*, he was planning to continue the historiographical tradition of the Florentine chancellors.[17] In those papers which were now twenty years old there is already in part the outline of the drama. Some characters are rapidly sketched. Here is Alexander VI: 'Wicked Pope, his head full of his own designs, preyed on Milan and Florence: the times serve him well'. Here is the Moor: 'Ludovico Sforza, as a shallow man, hopes, then fears, and anchors now to one thing now to another'.[18]

From the policies of men such as these, feeble and clumsy from trying to be too astute and subtle, stem all the ills from which Italy suffers while Machiavelli is writing; so that whether he is listening to the news of the present world or picking up the threads of those distant beginnings, it is all the same. The agreement between the Emperor and the King had been reached just then, and as soon as it became known in Italy on the 20th of February, arguments broke out whether the Emperor would keep his side of it and free the King, or if the King once he was free would maintain his sworn faith.

Writing at length to his friend on the subject, 'with his head full of fancies', Machiavelli felt that all the reasons which might be used to justify him 'could not prevent the Emperor from being made to look a fool if the King decided to be a sensible man', by simply not observing such outrageous conditions. But, in spite of his celebrated pessimism, he thinks the King might observe them for the sake of his sons given in hostage, his desire for peace after such a hard time, his hatred for the Italians because of the faithless policies of the Pope and the Venetians. One thing seems certain to him amid so much uncertainty: whatever else might happen, there would be war again and soon, on the bloody lands of Italy. Therefore, nothing remains for the Italians to do but provide themselves with good arms and courageous thoughts. Machiavelli writes: 'I tell you one thing which will seem to you absurd, I'll put forward a plan that you will think rash or ridiculous: nonetheless these times of ours demand bold, unusual and strange decisions. . . . A few days ago it was being said in Florence that Giovanni de' Medici was raising his standard at venture in order to fight wherever seemed best. This rumour led me to consider whether the people were not saying what in fact ought to be done. I believe everyone is agreed that among Italians there is no leader whom the soldiers more willingly follow or whom the Spaniards fear more or are more cautious of. Everyone feels that Signor Giovanni is brave, impetuous, with great ambitions and capable of bold decisions. One could therefore get him to raise this standard, secretly increasing his forces and putting under his command as many soldiers and horsemen as possible.' It would not matter if the Spaniards believed this was being done on purpose, because they would think it was the Pope's doing or the King's, and perhaps they might thereby be induced to break their agreement with him. This is pure Machiavelli. Not less characteristic is the crude transition from such great thoughts to the words which follow: 'Barbera is there in Rome; if you can serve her in any way, I commend her to you, for she gives me more concern than the Emperor.'[19]

When these letters reached Rome, whoever received them, either Guicciardini, Filippo Strozzi or others, at once communicated them to their friends and read them to the Pope. This was the case with a letter written to Strozzi on the 10th still on the subject of the agreement between the Emperor and the King and his doubts whether the pact would be observed.[20] The Pontiff 'heard it most attentively, praised its points, it seeming to him that the letter had dealt with everything that anyone could do, who was discussing such matters without inside information, and he was very pleased with it.'[21] But when Guicciardini showed his letter of the 15th of March[22] with the plan to have Giovanni de' Medici raise a standard, with him providing the colours and the Pope the money, it did not meet with approval. It was objected that the Spaniards would realize without any difficulty who was behind that banner—which Machiavelli would not have minded at all; but what weighed with Clement must have been his jealousy of Giovanni, or merely the boldness of a plan greater than he was.

Finally to silence conjecture and make all clear came the news that the King had been liberated; and soon it also became clear that he would not keep his side of the bargain. Then Machiavelli, seeing that the Emperor's only remedy against seeming a fool was that expressed in his letter of the 15th of March, 'that all the Emperor's bad decisions do him no harm, and all the King's good ones do him no good', sums up his feelings in an epigram in which he makes a figure of Argos say that he took all his eyes from the princes of Christendom,

> e quivi avvien che il matto
> Carlo, re dei Romani, e il Vicerè,
> per non vedere hanno lasciato il Re.[23]

[and that is why the foolish Charles, King of the Romans, and the Viceroy, have let the King go because they could not see].

War was inevitable, and it was not enough to sneer: it was necessary to think of defence and attack. As for defence, the first thing the Florentine Pope and his Florentine minister thought of was Florence, which was so vulnerable on the Oltrarno side. Count Pietro Navarra, a famous military engineer, had been sent there to see to the defences, but it was decided to set beside this Spanish refugee, Machiavelli, a theoretician of the art of war and a Florentine. Machiavelli was always prompt and ready, and when Guicciardini had written to him by order of the Pope on the 4th of April, he consulted the same evening with the Cardinal of Cortona and the next day he was up on the walls discussing with Navarra a bold design.[24] This was sent to Rome with a report written by Machiavelli, which has been praised in recent times by historians of military art.[25]

First it must have been praised by Clement VII and his counsellors, as its author was at once called to Rome where he succeeded in firing the Pope's enthusiasm and even Guicciardini's.[26] He left again on the 26th or 27th of April with the order for the provisions to be made and his head 'full of ramparts'.[27] During that time the new magistrature of the Curators of the Walls (Procuratori delle mura) was formed at the instigation of Machiavelli during his discussions in Rome; and he was elected secretary and quartermaster with his son Bernardo as assistant.[28]

So here he is again in the Palazzo, a secretary again, writing letters in nomine publico. We do not even know if he had a salary or if his pay for the Histories had to do for everything.[29] But he had been dreaming for so many years of having a post in the Republic, any position at all, and if it were one of small importance he would have

227

made it important with his activities, his writings, and if necessary with his imagination. This new magistrature was a small affair, but its purpose was very great—the defence of Florence. It was another job to be done, and he at once set about doing it in such a way as to make it a bulwark against the enemy. From the very beginning he had had to do and write a great deal to Pope Clement to dissuade him from his fancy for enclosing the hill of San Miniato in the walls of Florence, and on this subject he was to write three letters in one day to Guicciardini on the 2nd of June.[30] Finally he got his own way.

But even with his head full of ramparts, his thoughts and his pen turned to the affairs of Italy. At this time he wrote to Guicciardini who was working at the heart of all these matters: 'I can imagine the Emperor when the King fails him, making great offers to the Pope; such offers should fall on deaf ears . . . You know how many opportunities have been lost; do not lose this one or trust in having it again!' From the heart which had dictated the closing chapter of the *Prince* there came in that same letter the fateful invocation: *Liberate diuturna cura Italiam!*[31]

Whilst he was writing this exhortation, the league between the King of France, the Pope, the Florentines and the Venetians had been signed on the same day, the 17th of May. They at once declared war to take the Spaniards unawares, and without waiting for the help the King had undertaken to send. Indeed his assistance was both tardy and meagre. The Venetians sent off their troops under the command of the Duke of Urbino, and the Pope his under the command of Guido Rangoni and Giovanni de' Medici. Vitello Vitelli was the captain of the Florentine contingent; and lieutenant-general 'with full and almost absolute powers' was Francesco Guicciardini. At the end of June this great army arrived before Lodi which at once capitulated. Then they camped before Milan with great hopes of gaining the city since it was in a bad way. But after they had been there a day and a night, the Duke of Urbino withdrew his forces without warning the Lieutenant, who later exchanged some harsh words with him on this account. That over prudent move of the Duke's and that quarrel were to be the first of a lamentable series.

While the days most propitious for a rapid victory were being wasted in this way, one might suppose (and indeed biographers have done) that Machiavelli was in Florence designing bastions and writing the letters of his Curators. Instead, foremost as always in the breach, he was, from the first troop movements, in the camp of the 'most fortunate' armies of the League—for so it was obligatory to call them, although they were in fact most unfortunate. As we possess no instructions or letters patent issued to him by the Eight (Otto di Pratica), it is not known whether he was sent out by the Cardinal of Cortona or whether his friend the Lieutenant had him under his orders. Guicciardini in fact frequently employed him and sent him on errands to various places for the purposes of the war with his own instructions. We know why he had been sent from one of Guicciardini's letters: 'Machiavelli is here. He came to reorganize the militia, but seeing what a poor state it is in, he does not think they will do him credit. He will just laugh at men's weaknesses, since he cannot remedy them'.[32] We do not know exactly when he arrived in Lombardy, but the fact is that the register of the Curators of the Walls which Machiavelli kept, breaks off on the 8th of June; and a fragment of a letter written by him, and hitherto unnoticed, bears the date 13th July 'in the field',[33] where, as the context shows, he had been for some time.

The camp was then at Marignano, and a few days later, on the 22nd of July, it was moved to the Badia a Casaretto near Milan. In that long idleness while a great army stood watching, without taking any action, the fine towers of the Lombard capital, Machiavelli either wandered about the camp listening to everything that was said and jotting down military ideas, or he divided his time between Guicciardini and Giovanni de' Medici, 'who is all the strength and bravery there is in this camp, feared by friends and enemies alike'. He was a rough soldier, but he liked the conversation of clever and witty men like Aretino, and he must have liked Machiavelli too, who was hardly less daring and facetious and in addition was the author of a famous book on the art of war, the only art for Giovanni. If their talk was merely of pleasant matters, it was Machiavelli who led the dance; and when it turned on military affairs, he could still hold his own with Giovanni; on this topic he certainly knew what he was talking about.

One day, however, the great captain challenged him to drill three thousand soldiers after the fashion he had so well described in his *Art of War*. The biter was bit. For two hours he shouted orders and counter orders, got heated and swore, without ever managing to get them in order. Those poor infantrymen sweated under the hot sun, and Machiavelli sweated with anxiety. At last Giovanni said with a grin: 'I will get us all out of our difficulty and we will go and have dinner.' In the twinkling of an eye, assisted by the drummers he drilled his men in various forms and orders. It was a splendid and cruel revenge of the practical man over the theoretician. Then during dinner Niccolò took his revenge, narrating as he alone could, a delightful and indecent story. Matteo Bandello, who was also a guest of Giovanni, was there listening, and he was a connoisseur of food as well as of indecent tales. A Dominican and nephew of a famous Dominican general, he has preserved for us that obscene narrative but not unfortunately the wit and the style of the teller.[34]

Meanwhile the war was at a standstill in the sun-drenched plain of Lombardy. Machiavelli in those 'Arabian deserts' must have longed for the gentle Florentine hills and the merry bands of his friends. He also thought about Barbera, was distressed because she did not write to him, and wrote to Fornaciaio for news of her. Then the helpful Fornaciaio ran to Barbera to tell her a 'heap of insults', to receive her excuses, for she had evidently been out of Florence, to hear her protests of affection for her distant friend, her promises to write every week, her hopes of seeing him back in Florence soon, because when he was there 'she felt as though she slept with his eyes'.[35]

Then there was the correspondence with his friends which kept him busy and carried him back to Florence in spirit. Vettori wrote him some of his long letters, full of facts and vigour like his *Sommario della storia d'Italia*; in these he recounts the excessive favours recently meted out by fortune to the Emperor, or discusses the misfortunes of Italy and the Pope. The latter had recently attempted to change the government of Siena by force, and had seen his troops comprising five thousand foot and several hundred horse driven off by four hundred Sienese.[36] Reading these letters full of interesting considerations, and replying to them in kind, was one of the occupations which most pleased Machiavelli in these long periods of idleness in the field. His replies were eagerly awaited in Florence for their abundance of information about the quality of the armies and the captains, the acuteness of his judgements on military and political affairs, and the wit of his style. As soon as Vettori received one (and he had one written on 31st July, and no fewer than three others between then and 24th August, none of which survive), he gave them to Ippolito de' Medici to read or sent them to Filippo Strozzi in Rome for him to read them to the Pope, 'thinking they might assist the campaign'; and they were all read, re-read, pondered and praised.[37] Only one proposal, to carry the war into the Kingdom of Naples, did not please the timid Pope Clement. Nor did these old and important friends make Niccolò forget his younger acquaintances, among whom we now find Bartolomeo Cavalcanti,[38] who was soon to win honours in both the republics he served; that of Florence and that of letters.

At that time part of the allied armies were surrounding Cremona; but the siege was so long drawn out that on the 10th of September Guicciardini sent Machiavelli there, 'a man of great competence',[39] with credentials and instructions. He was to see what stage things had reached and what hopes there were. If he thought there was little prospect of an early victory, he was to make every effort to persuade the Venetian adjutant Pesaro to quit the siege and attack Genoa.[40] He went, he saw, he discussed not only with Pesaro but also with the Duke of Urbino, who was as lively and arrogant in this argument as he was timid and tardy with the enemy. Machiavelli reported to the Lieutenant in frequent letters. In other words, he did his work as only he could.[41] He returned to the camp under the walls of Milan in the evening of the 14th of September, able to report the captains' confidence and his own in an early victory.

In fact the city capitulated on the 23rd, the actual handing over being deferred until the end of the month. But while this good news was being celebrated in the camp of the League, another terrible misfortune reported from Rome changed rejoicing into bitterness and mourning. Pope Clement had as usual allowed himself to be deceived by a false truce offered him by the Colonna faction in league with don Ugo da Moncada, the Imperial captain and agent, who boasted he was a disciple of Caesar Borgia; and he had been induced to dismiss the few troops he kept around him. He was attacked by Colonna forces during the night of the 19th of September and had barely time to flee and shut himself up in Castel Sant 'Angelo, while the Borghi, the apostolic palace and the very church of St. Peter were cruelly put to sack. Machiavelli's prophecy, when he saw 'Christ in his Vicar made prisoner', had therefore been marvellously accomplished. Yet this, with all its dramatic force, was only the first rehearsal of the last scene of the tragedy.

Chapter 22

'SIXTY YEARS'

◇◇

*A*VE, *rex Iudeorum! et dabant ei alapas;* so Clement VII said with a bitter smile to the devilish don Ugo and the Spanish captains who kneeling respectfully and implacably before him sought absolution for their sacrilegious outrage. But apart from this typically Florentine quip, the Medici Pope had no other means of revenging himself on his enemies. He was therefore obliged to accept a truce for four months, under which he was to withdraw his forces from Lombardy, forgive the Colonna party, and hand over Filippo Strozzi as hostage for his good intentions. Strozzi was a man who besides being a relation of the Pope was said to be worth a million ducats. With the signing of this pact, and as long as he observed its conditions, the war was over as far as he was concerned; and so too was Machiavelli's military life.

Guicciardini's heart was ready to break at so great a disaster brought about by sheer folly, but although he protested that there was no obligation to observe a pact which had been extorted rather than negotiated, and although he temporized for a while in various ways, he was at last forced to withdraw his troops to Piacenza, and followed them there himself on the 9th of October. Machiavelli went with him; but before he did so, about the 7th he wrote a long letter to his young friend Bartolomeo Cavalcanti, which was designed in part to clarify the situation in his own mind, and written in such a way that Villari took it for an office memorandum. In this letter he discusses with marvellous lucidity the errors committed in the campaign by the captains

232

and by the Pope up to the final blunder of 'living in Rome in such a way
as to let himself be captured like a child'.[1] So, 'to the limbo of infants'
with Pope Clement too! In his heart Machiavelli must have sent him
there long ago.

There was nothing for Machiavelli to do in Piacenza during the
truce. The Florentine forces under Vitelli had in the meantime gone to
Rome, first with the idea of belatedly protecting the Pope's person,
and then, as Clement was determined to punish the Colonnas in spite
of the treaty, to put the lands of that family to fire and the sword, after
Pompeo Colonna, who had been largely responsible for that sacrilegious insult, had been deprived of his cardinalate. On the point of
returning to Florence, Machiavelli wrote to Jacopo Salviati that he
would gladly have gone with the troops,[2] evidently as papal commissioner; and this encourages us to believe that he had held the same
position with those forces when they were before Milan. When Cesare
Colombo, to whom Guicciardini had written recommending his
friend, discussed it with the Pope, he replied: 'Write to him to come,
for it would give me pleasure,' and he said the same thing to Salviati.[3]

However, Machiavelli did not come straight to Florence where the
Pope's assent was awaiting him. He had on hand some errand of
Guicciardini's sending him 'on tour' in the Pope's service,[4] and he
stopped first at Borgo a San Donnino, where he may have gone on
account of the Spanish troops who were leaving Cremona under the
truce, and then at Modena. Here he remained for two days and did
his best to stick up for the Lieutenant with two men who had felt his
wrath. One was Count Guido Rangoni, who had also returned from
the field not many days earlier. The other was the governor Filippo
de' Nerli, who had been severely reproached. When Nerli said: 'Is it
possible that I have never done anything right?', Machiavelli swiftly
replied, grinning with humorous compunction: 'My Lord Governor, do
not be surprised, for it is not your fault but the fault of this year, when
there is no one who has done anything right. The Emperor could not
have behaved worse, since in all this time he has sent no help whatever to
his people when he could easily have done so; the Spaniards could have
beaten us several times, and they have not contrived to do so; we could
have been victorious, and we have not known how; the Pope believed
in a stroke of the pen more than in a thousand soldiers who could have
kept him safe; only the Sienese have done well, and it is not surprising
if in a mad age the mad show up best. And so, my Lord Governor, it

would be a worse sign to have done something right than to have made a mistake.'[5] With the tragedy turned in this way into comedy Nerli could not help but laugh at it. At that point Rangoni came in and said: 'Is the Lieutenant still angry?' To which Machiavelli replied promptly: 'No, because he no longer has anyone beside him to make him angry.' And so all their irritation ended in laughter.

Machiavelli may not have felt so cheerful when, having reached Florence at last, he found that old letter from Salviati with the Pope's agreement to his new appointment. While he was getting ready to leave he received another letter cancelling his move. As he had delayed too long and Vitelli was in a hurry, it had been necessary to choose someone else in his place. He had only the consolation at once suggested to him by Guicciardini—that he had not lost much, for there was little satisfaction to be had from staying 'in those shacks of the Colonnas'.[6]

Besides, as the ice was broken and he was now in moderate favour with the Pope and those who ruled Florence for him, Machiavelli would now have plenty of those modest employments involving a lot of inconvenience and little gain in the way of money or honour. He needed both, yet he went on being satisfied with what he was given. He will never again return to the tragedy of the *Histories*, being entirely absorbed by the real life tragedy now nearing its climax. In this he went on playing minor parts, and was sent on the 30th of November by the Eight to Guicciardini who was then in Modena.

Meanwhile Frundsberg's German pikemen, of whom there had been much talk for some time, had not been stopped by the Venetians at the mountain passes and had reached the crossings of the Po where the Duke of Urbino did not seem likely to do any better. All hopes rested on the few troops and the courage of Giovanni de' Medici, when, on the 25th of November, while fighting as was his habit, more as a soldier than as a captain, he was wounded in the thigh by a cannon-ball. Guicciardini at once judged this a mortal blow, and not only for Giovanni. The last defence had fallen, and while that brave soldier now fought only with the pain of his wound and the doctors, the Germans crossed the Po, their pikes aiming at the very heart of Italy. They crossed on the 28th of November, and on the 30th Giovanni de' Medici died.

Machiavelli therefore set off the same day with instructions that said little and which stated that they were merely given *pro forma* to an envoy of 'such worth'[7]; but between the lines one could read clearly enough that the Florentine government did not know which way to turn. Niccolò was to go and tell the Lieutenant the state and mind the city was in—which Guicciardini already knew better than he did. He was to tell him that the Florentine people would prefer to sign an agreement than to make generous offers, but 'would leave His Lordship to negotiate as he thinks best', and 'as the times may indicate'. What a curious commission!

Riding day and night across the wind-swept Appenines in the cold season, in spite of the fact that hard riding was now painful and harmful to him, he reached Modena in the early morning of the 2nd of December.[8] He at once conferred with the Lieutenant and reported the news and views he had collected in a letter to the Eight on that same day. In this letter I feel that he is deliberately using the words spoken by Guicciardini without adding anything of his own by way of comment or opinion. This is something very unusual and strange for him. The conclusion was, in brief, that the Florentines could not expect any other help, if the enemy came to attack them, than six or seven thousand foot-soldiers of the Church; and as for an agreement, this would have to be discussed not in the field but in Rome or in Florence. At the end of this weary letter we find this postscript: 'Your Worships will have heard of the death of Signor Giovanni, which has filled everyone with sorrow'. The news was already well known, but a thought which fills the mind is hard to keep silent.

He sent another letter to the Eight on the following day, in which he added little that was new: the Duke of Ferrara was giving clearer signs than ever that he was coming out on the Emperor's side: the pike-men seemed to be moving towards Piacenza; the Lieutenant, seeing the war moving in that direction, had gone to Parma; and Machiavelli too was getting ready to travel home the next day. He wrote this on the 3rd, but he lingered until the 5th, then came riding slowly by daily stages 'so as not to get needlessly tired'.[9] He was no longer his old self.

Yet on the 3rd of February at the height of winter which that year was wet and snowy, he was riding again, once more sent by the Eight to Guicciardini. The Spanish had come out of Milan and crossed the Po following the German pikemen who had crossed to the other side of the Trebbia, and it was now clear that the Imperial hordes were advancing to the sack of Florence, to sack and take revenge on Rome.

All the hopes of the Florentines were placed in the few Papal foot-soldiers and the Pope's Florentine Lieutenant, and Machiavelli was to explain to the latter the views and wishes of the city. He was aged and weary in body, perhaps in mind as well; but he went. As he had done before going to the camp before Milan, he closed, this time for ever, the book in which he wrote the few letters of his office.[10] He had not re-opened the books of his *Histories*.

On this occasion he rode more slowly, and excused himself with the Eight on the grounds of the 'obstacles raised by the enemy'.[11] He reached Parma only on the 7th, and there Guicciardini, who had been informed by the Cardinal of Cortona several days before that the government was thinking of sending him, was longing to see him[12]; he even sent him a message to make haste.[13] The Lieutenant was not so eager to receive his information on the wishes of the city with which he was perfectly acquainted, nor to inform Machiavelli of the help he might expect from the League; he wanted the support of the envoy of the Republic 'in telling the Duke (of Urbino) and the Marchese (of Saluzzo) what was needed', to urge them to give greater assistance. The same day he went to see the Duke with Machiavelli, who explained to the best of his ability 'the need for prompt and vigorous support'. Temporizing as usual and quite determined what he would do, the Duke pointed out that Saluzzo was to enter Tuscany with the vanguard while he remained in the enemy's rear with the bulk of the army; but it was agreed to meet the next day and 'arrange everything pen in hand'.[14]

Machiavelli reported this to the Eight that same day. The conclusion of the meeting in black and white was this: if the enemy made for Tuscany by way of Pontremoli, all the French forces with the Venetians and the armies of the Church would go ahead of them; but if they turned towards Bologna, then only the Marchese di Saluzzo would enter Tuscany and the Duke would bring up the rear. It was not possible to budge him from this position.[15] On the 11th of February Machiavelli reported the uncertainty of the enemy's movements to the Eight, and added: 'I have not left yet, because I wanted to see which way the water was going to flow; so that, if it was coming your way, I could return fully informed of the nature of the remedies: so I shall stay another three or four days . . .'[16]

Instead he stayed nearly three months; which is not surprising, since that 'water' lay stagnant for a long time in the plain of Emilia. Following the papal camps facing those of the enemy from Parma (whence he wrote on the 14th to the Eight)[17], he reached Bologna by way of Scandiano and Sassuolo. There he arrived on the 27th, and stayed for more than a month while the pikemen and the Spanish, held up first by lack of provisions and money and then by the inclement weather, were at a standstill in the great plain covered with flood-water and snow. Like Guicciardini Machiavelli did not find anything else to write about in his letters than the struggles of the enemy with hunger and bad weather, as the Duke of Urbino, who might easily have overcome them in the midst of all their tribulations, did not dare to fight.

At Bologna, even with the snow 'a yard deep in every part of this city', Machiavelli had quite a good time. The Legate there was the Pope's cousin Cardinal Innocenzo Cibo, who lived in splendid style and not without some intercourse with men of letters, since in him his descent from the Magnificent was more active an influence than his Ligurian see.[18] The Cardinal at once took a liking to Machiavelli, and the warmth of this favour revived him far better than his famous pills could do. Poor Niccolò! We know what his trouble is. Knowing himself, he cannot understand his long neglect by men and by fortune. Crushed and forgotten, he measures his own ability against the mediocrity of those who grudge him their esteem. He feels himself worthy of greater things and sees himself perpetually reduced to the humblest tasks. Not even his books, showing a path as yet untrodden, have been able to break the cruelty which excludes him from the just esteem of men. He had hoped much of them, now he despairs. In this infirmity which has been gnawing at him for some time, the extraordinary kindness shown him by the Cardinal is a unique medicine which he grasps at with the eagerness of a sick man. This medicine and the Cardinal's bounteous meals restore him in rich Bologna.

If I am not mistaken, his Bologna letters bear the signs of this short-lived improvement. They are livelier; the acute judgements and the brilliant style of former times reappear, while there is more hope of human and heavenly assistance: 'If the Duke of Ferrara had a bit of sense in his head and this weather lasted another two days, he could finish off this war with his eyes shut.'[19] The weather held, but the Duke did not come to his senses; an Italian, he drew ever closer to the Emperor at the expense of Italy. Worse still, even the Pope showed no more sense. At that very time he perpetrated one of his usual follies, concluding with the enemy a fresh truce which delayed and distracted him in various ways, while the tumultuous Imperial army now under the command of Bourbon, after the death of Frundsberg, was on the move again.

On the last day of March, as the forces of the Church were about to set out from Bologna to get ahead of the enemy, Machiavelli went to Imola to arrange the billets.[20] From there he wrote to the Eight that they should not allow themselves to be blackmailed by Bourbon who was demanding enormous sums of money to stop his army: 'What agreement can you hope for with the sort of enemy who, when the Alps are still between you, and your forces are still in the field, asks for a hundred thousand florins within three days and a hundred and fifty thousand within ten days? When they come down there, the first thing they will ask for will be your entire wealth, for without any doubt (and would it were not so!) their advance is prompted only by the prospect of your booty, and there is no other remedy against this evil than to disabuse them; and if you have to do this, it is better to do it at the Alps than at your very walls.'[21]

It was no longer a question of saving Italy, of some political design with the air of a dream about it. This was a more fleshly love that was roused in him, for his own land, Florence, which was under the growing threat of the cruel Spaniards and the barbarous pikemen. Beyond the mountains were those sacred walls, within the walls his family and his children. There was Bernardo, the eldest, and the younger ones, the dearer ones, who not being old enough yet to disappoint him still allowed him some illusions: Guido, Piero, Baccina, and Totto the baby still at the breast.[22]

He had placed Bernardo in the office of the Curators of the Walls, but with small hopes that he might follow in his own footsteps, for he had neither intelligence nor learning nor any liking for it. Bernardo should at least have looked after the country property now he was a man, and so have relieved his father of those responsibilities while he was away and had other things to think about besides wood-cutting; but recently he had written to him twice and had no reply. He had had trouble with Ludovico, the second child, because of his violent nature, which was evident even in his letters to his father, and because of which he had come to the notice of the Otto di Guardia. Now for the second time he was in the Levant, where he was engaged in trade.[23] Guido and Piero were still young boys and studying[24]; but it was Guido perhaps whom Niccolò loved best, delicate in health with

238

a quiet, studious nature; perhaps he of all those children might one day have understood what kind of man his father was. Machiavelli's old unhappy heart softened at the thought.

It was to the young Guido that he wrote an affectionate letter on the 2nd of April after he had written to the Eight about the Alps and the walls.[25] 'If God grants you and me long life, I think I may make you a man of substance, if you are willing to do your share.' That grown-up child tells his son about his new friendship with Cardinal Cibo, 'so great that I myself am astonished'. Thus the honour so recently shown him by the Cardinal gives him the opportunity to urge on his favourite son with affectionate seriousness: 'As you no longer have the excuse of illness, take pains to learn letters and music, for you see how much honour comes to me from that little ability I have. Thus, my son, if you want to please me and bring profit and honour to yourself, do well and learn, for if you help yourself, everyone will help you'.

But also with this beloved son, after the serious arguments must come the flights of fancy. Their subject is provided by the vagaries of a little mule of which the boy was very fond. 'The little mule, as he is wild, must be treated in the opposite way to other lunatics; for they are tied up, and I want you to let him loose. Give him to Vangelo and tell him to take him to Montepugliano and then take off his headstall and bridle and let him go where he likes to earn his living and get over his wildness. The country is vast, and the beast is small. . . .' Here it seems Machiavelli wants to rouse his boy's fancy by imagining his little colt wandering adventurously in the vast woods of Montepugliano; and one is led to think that with his children too Niccolò must have been an incomparable storyteller. Then his thoughts turn to present dangers, and he is impatient to get home: 'Greet monna Marietta for me and tell her I have been expecting to leave any day and still do so, and I have never longed so much to return to Florence as I do now, but I cannot help the delay. Just tell her that whatever she hears, she should be of good cheer as I shall be back before any danger comes. Kiss Baccina, Piero and Totto if he is there; I should have been glad to hear whether his eyes are better. Live cheerfully and spend as little as you can . . . Christ preserve you all.' Thus the man, who has been reputed wicked, cynical and an atheist, wrote to his son.

The promise that he would be home before any danger came was no empty one. The Lieutenant, that other great Florentine, had long ago discussed with him and decided during their long vigils that they should assist the lands of Romagna while 'they can be defended at sixteen soldi to the lira', but then 'with those Italian troops that can be collected and with what money is left come . . . and save Florence at all costs'. To this end, so Machiavelli wrote to Vettori on the 5th of April,[26] it was essential to go ahead of the enemy into Tuscany, while the dilatory Duke could draw up the rear as he pleased.

The most essential thing was to combat the irresolution of the Pope, which was a good deal more dangerous than the enemy's resolution or the Venetians' small and doubtful courage. Without money to pursue the war and still unwilling to use the remedy of simony, reserved for later on when he would have the blame without the benefit, Clement became daily more involved in his puerile hopes of a truce. His recent experience had taught him nothing. The Spanish Viceroy who had negotiated the truce pledging Caesar's name to it, wrote to Bourbon, the Imperial captain, telling him to halt; and the Pope trusted him. Bourbon continued to advance as though he had heard nothing, and the Viceroy sent him envoys, then went to meet him himself to stop him; and Clement felt secure in these hopes. Meanwhile, however, Bourbon still came on, and the allies, seeing that the Pope was about to fail them, more and more abandoned him.

In vain Guicciardini wrote to Rome and to Florence about the dangers inherent in that agreement if the imperial forces did not honour it, as everything led one to fear. In vain Machiavelli sent the same warning to the Eight and to Vettori who had so great a share in the Florentine government. The letter of the 5th of April, from which I have just quoted a few words, was written from Forlì where he had gone with Guicciardini and the few papal troops which remained under their command.[27] They had stationed the others here and there on the way as garrisons for the cities they left behind them. 'We began . . . to divide the army at Parma and we have been reducing it bit by bit right up to Forlì,' he wrote on the 11th of April to the Eight in a letter which ends with these words: 'Things are at such a pass that we must either reconstruct the war or conclude peace.'[28]

Peace, and a decisive peace (he wrote two days later to Vettori), not an agreement that is 'uncertain and false like this one, made in Rome and not observed in Lombardy'. From Florence they observed that the agreement was nearly settled; but, in God's name, it was necessary to have greater certainty, because if there was to be war, the sixty thousand ducats to be paid to Bourbon as the first instalment would be better spent on paying the soldiers. 'Otherwise, if we enter into a false agreement which means we have to pay both for it and for war, neither the one nor the other will be provided for, and this will be to our loss and the enemy's profit; they are thinking only of war as they advance upon you, and they are letting you become confused between war and agreements.'[29]

The same things, almost at times with the same words, were being written in those days by Francesco Guicciardini to Rome and to Florence. Camp life together for all those months, and common feelings, had bridged the gap which separated the two politicians. The differences between the aristocrat and the plebeian, between the practical man and the theorist, between prose and poetry, had all disappeared: Guicciardini appreciates Machiavelli more,[30] and Machiavelli loves Guicciardini the better. On the 16th, the pact was still being discussed, and the Spanish Viceroy had come to Florence to halt Bourbon and make him observe the treaty; but he continued to advance along the Galeata road. Guicciardini wrote to the Eight: 'Never was there a more complicated and dangerous affair than this. . . . In these difficulties, I feel that the most perilous aspect of all is the fact that we have the enemy in Tuscany and are without armed forces, and so I have taken the decision on my own initiative, as I have no assistance from Rome, to send towards Florence all the forces at my disposal . . .'[31]

It was the decision that Machiavelli wanted and perhaps helped him to make. Writing to Vettori on the same day and in the same tone as Guicciardini, Machiavelli suddenly bursts out with these words: 'I love messer Francesco Guicciardini, I love my country more than my own soul; and I tell you by the experience I have gained in sixty years that I do not believe there was ever a more difficult situation than this, where peace is necessary and war cannot be avoided, and having on our hands a prince who is hard put to it to do what is needed either for peace or for war alone.'[32] The prince, of course, was that poor Clement who had not yet decided, with his usual lack of resolution, whether to be prince or pope.

'Sixty years.' He was not yet as old as that, and the reason why he added years to his age was probably not merely to increase the authority of his words or to round out the number: he felt the weight of those years, and on top of them, all the labours he had endured, all the disappointments he had suffered, all the small miseries which depress unspeakably, great men and poets.

Chapter 23

THE END

<><><><><><><><><><><><><><><><><><><><><><><><><><><><><><><><><><><><><>

A MAN getting on for sixty, his head bent, his face marked with the labours of the mind and the spirit, the poor face of a tired and unhappy man, is what is shown us by that Florentine bust of painted terracotta which is said to represent Niccolò Machiavelli.[1] Beneath the weariness and the bitterness on that face the pathetic remains of a clever and subtle smile is what is most characteristic of him. If that portrait is his, no page of writing can better tell the story of Machiavelli's tragedy. If it is not Machiavelli, it is exactly as I imagine him at this stage of his life and of this present biography.

We cannot read his last letters without comparing in our mind's eye this melancholy image with that other portrait which shows him in the full vigour of life and of his illusions. The man who in his prison bonds, his limbs wasted with torture, joked and smiled, the man who with the same smile suffered all his life the unjust neglect of princes and the indifference of his fellow citizens, this man has suddenly stopped smiling, he has stopped putting up a fight. There is not even another word about Barbera. His *Esortazione alla penitenza*[2] may or may not be of this period which followed his return from the camp before Milan, but in his face and in his letters we seem to read the supreme knowledge contained in the Petrarchan lines with which it closes:

cognoscer chiaramente
che quanto piace al mondo è breve sogno
[to know clearly that what pleases the world is but a brief dream].

242

Meanwhile one thing only mattered: that cursed war. The enemy was still advancing, and the allied forces too. Driven on by the Lieutenant the armies of the League were already massing to defend Florence. First came the troops of Count Guido Rangoni, then the foot-soldiers which had belonged to Giovanni de' Medici, then the infantry and cavalry of the Conte di Caiazzo. Finally even the tardy Duke of Urbino, spurred on by the restitution of San Leo by the Florentines, moved up by forced marches. On the 18th Machiavelli went to Brisighella with Guicciardini and the French troops of the Marchese di Saluzzo. From there he wrote again to Vettori,[3] and there he must have received a short letter sent him on the 17th at Forlì by his little son Guido telling him of his progress in his studies and promising that on his return he would recite by heart the whole of the first book of Ovid's *Metamorphoses*.[4]

From the letters we know of (and certainly many of them are lost without trace), we see that Niccolò was writing to his family with unusual frequency during those anxious days. Besides the two letters to Bernardo mentioned in his letter to Guido, there is reference and a partial reply in Guido's letter of the 17th to another letter sent to Marietta. As the armies drew near, so did the hour of the great adventure. Affections grew stronger, and there were a thousand different things to be done to make safe family, possessions and crops. The scattered farms and defenceless villages were at all times the first prey of troops, and the Albergaccio was on the main road. It was therefore necessary to bring part of the crops into the city where they would be useful in case of siege, not to mention the fact that by virtue of certain government proclamations they would thereby gain on the taxes.[5] All the best furniture would have to be brought in too, and the rest stored in the nearby walled town of San Casciano.[6]

Niccolò had taken these and other simple precautions like a good master of his household, giving his family instructions in his letters. They were now more reassured, and Guido wrote to him: 'We don't think about the Landsknechte any more, because you promised to be here with us.'[7] In fact he was in Florence on the 22nd, the day before Guicciardini arrived.[8]

He found the city in a bad mood, almost in insurrection; the general hatred for the Medici had increased, and even their friends were discontented. The inept and unlucky government of the Cardinal of Cortona, hard enough to put up with in easy, quiet times, had become unbearable to a people skinned alive to pay for the war. Guicciardini at once made this forecast: 'If the city does defend itself, the government will not be able to'.[9] And a little later he added: 'This great bloated Cortona . . . wants to do everything and knows how to do nothing . . .'[10] Recently Clement had sent him his cousin Cardinal Ridolfi, Archbishop of Florence, to back him up; but as he was linked in friendship or family relationship with the great citizens who were hostile to the government, his arrival had the opposite effect to the one the Pope intended.[11] Lately Cardinal Cibo had arrived too, and he as a foreigner enjoyed neither authority nor favour with the people. For the Medici therefore things were going from bad to worse. The first warning sign came four days after Machiavelli's return. The surroundings of the city were overflowing with soldiers; they were supposedly friendly troops, but they were worse than enemies, stealing, burning, and raping women. The idea of bringing such defenders into the city did not appeal to the Florentines, and the more courageous of the young men were demanding arms. Cortona was not sure about this, fearing to see them turned against himself; but, as Ridolfi and the principal citizens were willing, he finally ordered that arms should be distributed on the 26th of April.

That day the Piazza dei Signori was full of impatient young men, when the arrogance of some soldier caused a minor disturbance. Meanwhile the cardinals Cortona, Ridolfi and Cibo, with the young Ippolito, had mounted their horses to go to meet the Duke of Urbino, and the cry was raised that the Medici were fleeing. Immediately from all directions the young men came running, and in a moment the Palazzo was full of them. More important and older citizens came up too, and even many supporters of the Medici; they wanted that government but not in those hands. Even the gonfalonier Luigi Guicciardini, Francesco's brother, came to the door and called some of the more eminent citizens by name, inviting them to come in, showing that he agreed with them, or had not understood what they wanted. But within, the young people, now quite out of hand, forced the Signoria with threats and blows to ban the Medici as rebels, to restore the government of the city as it was in Soderini's day, and ring the great bell to call an uprising of the people.

While these things were being debated and settled in the Palazzo, the cardinals, informed of what had happened, returned in all haste to Florence, and into the Piazza with them rode the captains of the League and a good number of soldiers. Those within defended themselves with stones; those outside had artillery. If the Palazzo were taken by force, the flower of the citizens of Florence would be massacred and the city might be sacked. Then Cardinal Ridolfi and Francesco Guicciardini, out of love for their native city, begged Federigo da Bozzolo to go into the Palazzo to negotiate a truce.[12] As he did not succeed at the first attempt, he went back in with the Lieutenant, and an agreement was concluded with a general pardon. This agreement was then signed by the cardinals and the Duke of Urbino.

It is not known where Machiavelli may have been during this short-lived revolution which Florentine historians called 'the Friday tumult'. We know, however, that he was now doubly linked with Guicciardini, by friendship as well as by the functions, whatever they might have been, which he fulfilled during these last lays with the Lieutenant and the papal armies.[13] Guicciardini had gone early that morning to meet the Duke of Urbino ahead of the cardinals, and I think it is certain that Machiavelli went with him. In that case, having returned to Florence with his friend messer Francesco, he would have been in the piazza among the assailants, but in spirit inside the Palazzo with the defenders. Within were all his friends, beginning with Francesco Vettori and Bartolomeo Cavalcanti; within was the free Florentine republic.

Meanwhile Bourbon had drawn near the city, moving down the Arno valley. Realizing, however, that Florence was too hard a nut to crack for him, being powerfully fortified and well-manned, he suddenly turned off at Montevarchi and took the road to Rome, even leaving behind his light artillery in order to move faster.

After some delay the dilatory Duke of Urbino set off after him. The papal troops were a day ahead of him. Francesco Guicciardini left Florence with them on the 2nd of May, and it appears that with him went his now inseparable companion, Machiavelli. They went 'in good order and with reasonable speed as soldiers do when on the way to rescue someone who can wait'. No one imagined that Rome could not defend herself two or three days, which was all Bourbon's advantage, against a rabble of men without good captains, without discipline or artillery. Only Count Rangoni, 'taking a band of 5,000 foot and 1,000 light horse set off rapidly towards Rome'.

Bourbon, hurrying desperately on, got there before him on the evening of the 4th of May. He found the city empty of defenders, collected his men the following day, and on the morning of the 6th attacked between the gate of the Borgo and that of Santo Spirito. Bourbon was killed at the first assault by a shot from an arquebuss which Benvenuto Cellini claimed to have fired, and after his treachery had thus paid the price at the very moment of victory, his savage hordes now led only by their greed for pillage and rape fought ferociously for two hours. Being without siege artillery, they tore down the weak defences with their bare hands, and finally overwhelmed the few defenders gathered there. The Pope hastened to take refuge in the Castle while Catholic Spaniards and Lutheran pikemen, meeting no further opposition, vied with one another in profaning the city which had ruled under the Emperors and still ruled under Christ. The violation of people and sacred objects, the atrocities, insults, plunder and rape which were then committed, are recalled here only so as not to leave unfinished the apocalyptic end of the tragedy foreseen by Machiavelli. For the second time in a few months 'Christ in His Vicar was taken prisoner'; this time with more cruel and prolonged impiety.

The ruin of Rome and the Medici Pope inevitably brought with it the fall of the Medici government in Florence. The news, terrible to every Christian and Italian heart, reached Florence only on the 11th; and, though horrified, the Florentines at once thought of profiting by it. A Pratica (Council) met on the 16th at the Palazzo and decided that the Grand Council of the Savonarolan constitution should be re-established and that the two young Medici should remain as private citizens. This appeared to settle matters. But the Florentines did not feel safe with the young falcons in the nest. Suspicion and jealousy, rumours and gossip, at once broke out, until the Medici, advised to leave for their own safety and the peace of the city, set off on the 17th into exile, passing through a crowd which showed itself neither obsequious nor openly hostile. They thereby signified their submission to the will of the people; and when he learnt of it in the wretchedness into which he had fallen, the Pope too showed that he freely consented. In consequence Machiavelli was to mock him in his last days saying that he had given away what was no longer his to give. Clement VII, who had benefited him less than Soderini and had allowed himself to be duped with even greater simplicity, could not expect Machiavelli to treat him with less irony.

But in the meantime Machiavelli was on the move labouring to improve the Pope's situation. He had reached Orvieto with Guicciardini, and from there I believe the Lieutenant, 'when they heard the dreadful news from Rome', sent him to Civitavecchia, where it was said the Pope had taken refuge, and where, if that information were not correct, there was Andrea Doria with his ships, now of the greatest importance. At Civitavecchia, whence he wrote on the 22nd to inform Guicciardini of his discussions with Doria,[14] he must have learnt of the change in the government of Florence. Republican to the core and yet an envoy of the Medici government, now that his city was again a free republic, he found himself once more on the losing side. At once he prepared to return.[15]

While with a few companions and many preoccupations he was nearing Florence through the rejoicing villages and countryside, he was several times heard to sigh.[16] He regretted that his associations with the Pope and those 'Medici princes', whom he had never loved, might now spoil his chance, unless fate were especially kind to him, of serving the state with all his heart under a free government which corresponded to his true desires.

He was also worried by the thought of his own and his family's fortune, appalled by the prospect of idleness, of becoming 'contemptible through poverty''. Perhaps he repeated to himself those words which he had put into the mouth of messer Nicia: 'People like us who haven't got power in this city won't find even a dog to bark at us.'[17] The change of 1512 had caught him still young in the full vigour of his powers and hopes. This change in 1527 found him old, tired and disillusioned. Then, if they would only employ him, his courage would have been equal to any task; now he could have done nothing. Perhaps he was no longer even tempted by the memory of his study at the Albergaccio, peopled with the shades of the great. He felt that he had produced all the immortal pages he was capable of. There was no longer anyone to whom he could say 'here I am'—no redeemer to call on in the ruin of Italy.

Indeed he can have had little hope that now the Medici had been removed, he would be given back what the Medici had taken away from him: his beloved office in the second Chancery. He knew the mind of the city all too well and that the new government was entirely piagnone, to which a Machiavelli could not be acceptable. However, helped by his friends, especially by Zanobi Buondelmonti and Luigi Alamanni,[18] according to a contemporary Florentine whose word it would hardly be reasonable to doubt in this case, he did try to gain employment. One thing was left to the old poet: sometimes he could still dream.

And so, as was only human, he again felt an almost mortal blow when on the 10th of June Francesco Tarugi, who had been first secretary of the now defunct Eight (Otto di Pratica) for two years, was confirmed in his place.[19] The Medici government had not been willing to keep him in the office given him by the republican government; and now the republican government, instead of reinstating its former secretary, confirmed in office one chosen by the Medici government. The first had preferred a Niccolò Michelozzi to Machiavelli, the second preferred a Francesco Tarugi.

While amid the rejoicing for their regained liberty one could see the citizens embracing in the streets and the city full of such happiness 'that there was no one who did not feel . . . he had almost been given new life',[20] this great citizen, the greatest with Michelangelo after Dante, was shunned by almost everyone and despised. He might easily have been forgiven for having accepted some humble office from the Medici, but he could not be forgiven for his greatness which made him different from others in his ways, bold in his words, frank in his vices. 'Everyone hated him because of the *Prince*': the rich thought that his *Prince* was a document written to teach the Duke 'how to take away all their property, from the poor all their liberty, the Piagnoni regarded him as a heretic, the good thought him sinful, the wicked thought him more wicked or more capable than themselves, so that all hated him.'[21] So Busini wrote—a malicious and hostile commentator, but at least in these words a faithful mirror of the malice and hostility of his fellow-citizens.

Machiavelli sighed; then he remembered who he was and he mingled with his sighs some weary jibes at the Pope's ineptitude.[22] But for him it was the end. The strain of the last few months, when old in years and in disillusionment he rode under the lash of the sun, the rain and the snow, from Lombardy to Florence, from Romagna to Rome, with the last of his own and Italy's illusions, had now worn out his strength. After his recent bitter disappointment, his mental condition aggravated his physical condition, as commonly happens. Nor did his passionate nature beneath his satirical smile and devil-may-care outward air promise him anything better.

He fell ill shortly after Tarugi's appointment. On the 20th he took his usual medicine, those famous pills to which he would turn in all his illnesses. They had no greater power to cure than those remedies he had recommended to the princes and commanders of his age. Indeed, they were of no benefit to him, and he was shortly assailed with violent colic pains and rapidly got worse, so that his case was feared to be hopeless.[23] Around him were those few good friends that remained to him: Francesco del Nero, kind Zanobi Buondelmonti, the poet Luigi Alamanni, Jacopo Nardi, a good man of letters and even better citizen, and Filippo Strozzi, to whom the part he had recently played in the liberation of his country, brought fresh favour and envy to add to those he already had for his wealth and nobility.

The sick man lay prostrated by painful reflections and the agony which tore at his vitals, interrupted at intervals by strangely happy thoughts. He thought of his children, of his country, of messer Francesco Guicciardini who would again know the joy of dealing with affairs of state even if they were ill-fated ones. He thought about the study at the Albergaccio and the office in the Palazzo where others were now writing the letters of the Republic, so insipid and flaccid compared with his own. He thought of the woods at San Casciano and his bird snaring there, where the thrushes would return in the sweet Autumn mists. Perhaps he thought of all these things, great and small, and of women and life which were now rejecting him. Occasionally the thought of death seemed unbearable, sometimes it was a refuge and a respite. Yet, ill and unhappy as he was, he was still 'Machia'. He wanted to show his friends that he was not changed, and laugh with them at his ill fortune, rebel against his pain, perhaps against his own emotions. Then, overcoming his misery, he began to laugh and joke, almost emulating in his intrepid death-bed defiance his last hero, Giovanni de' Medici.

He told a story as he used to in his best days, a funny story about a dream he had had; but it was all imaginary. He told how he had seen a sparse crowd of poor people, ragged and emaciated; and when he asked who they were, he received the answer that they were the blessed souls of Paradise, of whom we read in Scripture: *Beati pauperes quoniam ipsorum est regnum caelorum.* When they had disappeared, he saw a large crowd of people of noble appearance in royal and courtly robes, who were gravely discussing affairs of state, and among them he recognized Plato, Plutarch, Tacitus and other famous men of antiquity. Having asked who these newcomers were, he was told they were condemned to Hell, because it is written: *Sapientia huius saeculi inimica est Dei.* When they too had vanished, he was asked which lot he would like to be with. He replied that he would rather go to Hell with noble minds to discuss politics than to be in Paradise with that first beggarly contingent. It was the last tale of that great and almost entirely unpublished story-teller. It is not true, however, that when he told 'this celebrated dream of his', Machiavelli 'died unreconciled and jeering'.[24] When his friends had gone, he remained alone with his family, and quietly preparing himself for death, 'he allowed fra Matteo to hear him confess his sins', and the latter stayed with him until his last breath.[25] He died on the 21st of June, and on the 22nd he was buried in Santa Croce.[26]

In death, therefore, he was just as he had been in life. In the brave bearing of his last hours and in that final composing of himself for death is all Machiavelli:

> *Io rido e il rider mio non passa drento,*
> *Io ardo e l'arsion mia non par di fore.*

The man who, when evening came, used to take off his day clothes covered in mud, and dress himself in worthy fashion, must, when death came, again don his courtly robes; just as in his famous letters to Guicciardini after the frivolous and merry words he turned to serious matters, just as he had done at the end of the *Prince*, so at the end of his life he must at last invoke 'his redeemer'.

Chapter 24

THE UNARMED PROPHET

D EATH, which in the end usually brings men peace and the reputation they deserve, at first brought Machiavelli only violent attacks and ill fame. Misfortune, after having ravaged so great a part of his life, now burst into flames over his ashes like a funeral pyre. The background of the times had rapidly changed, while the quality of men remained the same, and the Florentine Secretary was 'made a symbol of wickedness, because he was a great man and because he was unfortunate'[1]; the immortal pages, printed with the grace and privilege of one pope, were condemned and forbidden by another.[2]

Machiavellianism, which is both parent and offspring of anti-machiavellianism, was born, grew up and was baptized in France,[3] out of hatred for the man who had once said that the French knew nothing about statecraft. Thus that name, of which it had been said that no praise could be too great, became a term of insult and reproach. Nouns, adjectives and verbs were coined from it; around it was built up a legend that has the air of a myth.

Rarely can an unjust legend have weighed so long on any man. Even when his day finally came and Machiavelli revived with the resurgence of the nation as a passionate and generous man, where before he had been a great but coldly inhuman writer, even then the old prejudices were only overcome by new ones. Even his first great biographer Pasquale Villari could not entirely overlook that old dark shadow of sin, and always felt uneasy with him. Pistelli remarked acutely that Villari 'admires his protagonist but has no affection for him, even if he always does his best to make excuses for him'.[4] I on the other hand am really fond of him, and I do not feel the need to make excuses, but rather to understand him, to draw close to him as a man in the reverses he suffered.

One would find no one today to say, as Capponi did, that he had 'an evil mind'.[5] Certainly, that 'crudeness of his desperate aphorisms' must have had too sharp a taste in that great house in Via San Sebastiano, where I too spent my early years and breathed that same air. May the candid Gino forgive his dissenting nephew for these words! In that age, in that house, it was perhaps impossible to judge otherwise. Today we have a better idea of what to think, though not even today have the philosophers reached agreement about Machiavelli's philosophy; and in fact, as some of them have at last admitted, he was certainly not a philosopher.

He was and remains a politician, an artist, a poet, who besides his scientific reasoning power felt the sudden and varied impulses of artists and poets; and if one cannot cast doubt on the fundamental coherence and logic of his thought, in order to understand what has been and still is called the enigma of Machiavelli,[6] we must take account of those impulses and of his nature full of contrast and variety.[7] After having tried to describe his character in my own words in the early pages of this book, I cannot do better here than sum it up with the words he himself used about another great Florentine: 'In him there were two different people joined together in an almost impossible union.'[8]

Those 'desperate aphorisms' we have learnt to consider as hard pure scientific propositions, painfully removed from any outside consideration, dictated by a cast iron necessity,[9] the intrinsic necessity of the state. We know, however, that Machiavelli often wrote *stato* [state] when he meant *patria* [native land]; and we know furthermore that while many pages of the *Discourses* and the *Prince* might seem to justify the conclusion that 'the *patria* is the limit and the basis of Machiavelli's moral thought',[10] we must acknowledge that Machiavelli possessed a concept of morality which goes beyond that limit,[11] and recognize in his works 'visible signs of austerity and painful moral conscience'.[12]

His ethics have been described as 'belonging to the heights',[13] and this image which is expressive rather than beautiful might be applied to his religion.[14] To me today it seems logical that, theorizing about the state, he wished to adapt religion to the state, making it almost an *instrumentum regni.* As has been written : 'every form of human activity, in the process of its execution, draws strength from all the others'.[15] But it was difficult, in the rigid and inflammatory years of the Counter-reformation, for anyone who considered individually certain maxims detached from the main structure of Machiavelli's thought, not to link them with his famous sarcastic comments on the corruption of the Roman Church which had ruined Italy and religion, 'disarmed the Heavens', not to mention the all too frequent jokes about the Secretary's indifference towards the practices of religion *et similia,*[16] exaggerated by one who 'calumnied even himself'.[17]

A great mountain was made out of all this, which went to swell the already vast heap of misunderstanding and scandals aroused by the bold ethics of Machiavelli. Thus through the centuries there was built up layer by layer a mass of prejudices under which the religious and Christian conscience of the Florentine Secretary was deeply buried. Prejudice is so weighty and potent, particularly when petrified by time, that even the sad and pious pages of his *Esortazione alla penitenza,* rightly described as the climax of the author's Christian thought, have yet been adjudged by some otherwise most clear-sighted scholars, who had upheld his moral and religious qualities, as a frivolous joke ![18]

The reverent words written by Machiavelli in later life 'of such a great man' (Savonarola) were never able to dispel the memory of the irreverent humour he had once directed against the Friar's party.[19] In the same way, neither his love for those peoples who had preserved the original purity of the Christian religion, nor his admiration for those who followed 'the example of the life of Christ', for the friars who 'trod in the footsteps of St. Francis', for soldiers 'full of the fear of God',[20] sufficed for a long time to remove those hardened prejudices.

They did not suffice, because there was no one who understood them, who appreciated his 'essential Christianity',[21] the intimate religious foundation of his conscience which breathes from all his works. It was no good his having written: 'As where there is religion one presupposes every kind of goodness, so where there is no religion one presupposes the opposite',[22] and other like statements, of which there are so many in his works that in the last century someone actually compiled for the edification of the faithful a collection of *Massime religiose estratte fedelmente dalle opere di Niccolò Machiavelli* [Religious maxims faithfully extracted from the works of N.M.].[23] This strange selection, just like some pages of certain modern apologists, reminds one of the horseman who, leaping too energetically into the saddle, falls on the other side. Apologists do no less harm than the bitterest accusers.

It is not inappropriate to remember Machiavelli's foreboding that he might get lost by taking the road 'as yet untrodden by any man', and those words of the good Filippo da Casavecchia, written half in jest and half in earnest, when he discovered in the Secretary 'the greatest prophet that the Jews or any other generation ever had'.[24] A prophet, but an unarmed prophet like Savonarola, he too had to submit to the fate to which he had condemned his fellows, even if it were only his effigy and his books that went on the pyre. It was inevitable that he should rise again from the pyre *post fata* and take his revenge with those weapons which equip unarmed prophets and make them invincible.

BIBLIOGRAPHICAL NOTE

◇◇◇

As a general rule I make no mention in the footnotes of works which I regard as having been absorbed by others which are cited. A full Machiavelli bibliography, containing 2143 items between the years 1740 and 1935, is to be found in A. NORSA, *Il principio della forza nel pensiero politico del M. Seguito da un Contributo bibliografico*. Milan, Hoepli, 1936.

Abbreviation of principal works cited in the footnotes

ALDERISIO = FELICE ALDERISIO, *Machiavelli. L'Arte dello Stato nell' azione e negli scritti*, 2nd ed., Bologna, C. Zuffi, 1950.

A.S.I. = *Archivio Storico Italiano*, Florence, 1842 ff.

GERBER = ADOLF GERBER, *Niccolò Machiavelli, Die Handschriften, Ausgaben und Uebersetzungen seiner Werke, etc.*, Gotha, Perthes, 1912–13 (the facsimiles, Munich, Riffarth & Co., 1914). 3 parts and a fascicule of facsimiles.

G.S.A.T. = *Giornale Storico degli Archivi Toscani*, Florence, 1857–63.

G.S.L.I. = *Giornale Storico della Letteratura Italiana*, Turin, 1883 ff.

GUICCIARDINI, *Opere inedite* = FRANCESCO GUICCIARDINI, *Opere Inedite*, edited by Counts Piero and Luigi Guicciardini with a commentary by Giuseppe Canestrini, Florence, 1857–67. 10 vols. (This old and by no means perfect edition is quoted only for the correspondence after 1521. The more recent and reliable editions of other works of Guicciardini are cited where appropriate in the notes.)

Istorie fiorentine = MACHIAVELLI, *Istorie fiorentine*. Critical text with introduction and notes by P. Carli, Florence, Sansoni, 1927. 2 vols.

Lett. fam. = NICCOLÒ MACHIAVELLI, *Lettere familiari*, ed. Edoardo Alvisi, Florence, Sansoni, 1883.

Lett. L. = MACHIAVELLI, *Lettere* (ed. Giuseppe Lesca), Florence, Rinascimento del Libro, 1929. (This ed. is slightly more correct, but omits almost all the letters addressed to Machiavelli as well as those of Machiavelli which had come to light since the ed. of Alvisi cit.

sup. It also lacks, for reasons of moral scruple, the famous letter of 25 February 1514.)★

Opp. MC. = NICCOLÒ MACHIAVELLI, *Tutte le opere storiche e letterarie,* ed. Guido Mazzoni and Mario Casella, Florence, G. Barbera, 1929.

Opp. P. = NICCOLÒ MACHIAVELLI, *Le Opere,* ed. P. Fanfani and L. Passerini (from vol. II onwards, ed. L. Passerini and G. Milanesi), Florence, Tip. Cenniniana, 1873–7. 6 vols. (incomplete).

Opp. U. = NICCOLÒ MACHIAVELLI, *Opere complete, novamente collazionate sulle migliori edizioni e sui manoscritti originali e arricchite di annotazioni da un compilatore dell' Archivio Storico Italiano.* In 1 vol., Florence, Usigli, 1857.

RIDOLFI, *Opuscoli* = ROBERTO RIDOFLI, *Opuscoli di storia letteraria e di erudizione: Savonarola, Machiavelli, Guicciardini, Giannotti,* Florence, Bibliopolis (L. S. Olschki), 1942.

RIDOLFI, *Guicciardini* = ROBERTO RIDOLFI, *Vita di Francesco Guicciardini,* Rome, Belardetti, 1960.

RUSSO = LUIGI RUSSO, *Machiavelli,* 3rd enlarged edition, Bari, Laterza, 1949. (A 4th ed., which hardly contains anything new apart from a long note on this biography of mine on pp. 202–203, was published in 1957.)

Scritti inediti = NICCOLÒ MACHIAVELLI, *Scritti inediti riguardanti la storia e la milizia,* ed. Giuseppe Canestrini, Florence, Barbera, Bianchi & Co., 1857.

TOFFANIN = GIUSEPPE TOFFANIN, *Il Cinquecento* (in 'Storia letteraria d'Italia'), Milan, Vallardi, 1929.

TOMMASINI = ORESTE TOMMASINI, *La vita e gli scritti di Niccolò Machiavelli,* Rome, Loescher, 1883–1911. 2 vols. (the second in two parts).

VILLARI¹ = PASQUALE VILLARI, *Niccolò Machiavelli e i suoi tempi illustrati con nuovi documenti,* Florence, Le Monnier, 1877–82. 3 vols.

VILLARI² = PASQUALE VILLARI, 2nd ed. revised and corrected by the author, Milan, Hoepli, 1895–7. 3 vols.

VILLARI⁴ = PASQUALE VILLARI, 4th ed. posthumous, ed. Michele Scherillo, Milan, Hoepli, 1927. 2 vols.

A.S.F. = Archivio di Stato, Florence.

A.S.R. = Archivio di Stato, Rome.

B.L.F. = Biblioteca Mediceo-Laurenziana, Florence.

B.M. = British Museum, London.

B.N.F. = Biblioteca Nazionale, Florence.

B.R.F. = Biblioteca Riccardiana, Florence.

★ When this translation was already in an advanced stage of preparation, a new edition of M's *Lettere* appeared, edited by F. GAETA, Milan, Feltrinelli Ed., 1961; on which see R. RIDOLFI, *Schede per l'epistolario del M.*(II): *Le lettere di F. Vettori del 7 e del 24 agosto 1526,* in *G.S.L.I.,* cxxxviii, 1961, pp. 552–556.

NOTES

CHAPTER 1

[1] R. RIDOLFI, *Vita di Girolamo Savonarola*, Rome, Belardetti, 1952, vol. I, p. 374 ff., vol. II, p. 28 (English trans. *The Life of G. S.*, London, Routledge & Kegan Paul, 1959, pp. 250 ff. and p. 289).

[2] B. AGNOLETTI, *Alessandro Braccesi*, etc., Florence, Seeber, 1901; cf. R. RIDOLFI, op. cit., vol. I, pp. 280, 299 ff., vol II, p. 181. The *Carmina* of Bracci were recently published in an excellent edition by A. Perosa, Florence, Bibliopolis (L. S. Olschki), 1944.

[3] P. LITTA, *Famiglie celebri italiane*, Famiglia Machiavelli; VILLARI, vol. I⁴, p. 277 ff.

[4] Tommasini, on the basis of certain attacks made on Machiavelli by his political enemies, maintained that Bernardo was illegitimate; but my belief is that these attacks were probably made because his father was on the 'specchio' (debtors' list). It is true that Cerretani writes in his *Ricordi*: 'Niccolò Machiavelli, chancellor, son of a bastard of the Machiavellis' (cf. TOMMASINI, II, 959); but it must be added that these words are spoken in malice out of hatred for Soderini and his 'mannerino' [tool], and that in the Italian text ('figlio d'uno bastardo') the *uno* is crossed out, and the phrase could be interpreted simply as a sneer at that decayed and, according to him, degenerate branch of the family. The matter is very obscure, because there is evidence to prove Bernardo's legitimacy (TOMMASINI, I, 482). I mention all this out of scruple as a historian, not to purge Machiavelli of the shame—which is no shame at all—of a spurious father.

[5] G. BALDELLI, *Elogio di N.M.*, London (Florence), 1784; it is a fact in any case that Bernardo was a doctor of laws, as is proved by the title of *messere* given him in official documents—a title at that time strictly applied. That he exercised his profession very seldom and that his earnings were small, as I say above, is apparent from his *Libro di Ricordi*, cit. infra. It is of course pure conjecture, but it is possible that the words Niccolò put in the mouth of messer Nicia, who was also a doctor of laws, in Act II, sc. iii of *Mandragola*, are ones he often heard his father speak in jest.

[6] *Libro di Ricordi di Bernardo Machiavelli*, ed. C. OLSCHKI, Florence, Le Monnier, 1954. The memoirs run from 30 Sept. 1471 to 19 Aug. 1487. Up to now biographers have had no information on the early studies and the family of Niccolò; and I myself had been able to find nothing but a few details my forerunners had missed in the *Extracts from the Tax Registers* (Catasto). We are therefore greatly indebted to Cesare Olschki for having discovered and edited with impeccable diligence Bernardo's precious notebook. Much greater is the debt I personally owe him for his extraordinary kindness in allowing me to use his work while still in proof.

[7] We find among the books which he bought or already owned: Livy, Macrobius, Priscian, Donato Acciaioli on the *Ethics* of Aristotle, the *Deche* of Biondo; and among those he borrowed: the *Philippics*, *De officiis*, *De oratore*, the *Ethics* of Aristotle,

the *Cosmography* of Ptolemy, a Pliny in translation, Justin, Biondo's *Italia Illustrata*, and the Bible. Could it be that there was no Bible among all those books in the Machiavelli household?

[8] *Libro di Ricordi*, cit., pp. 14, 222, 223; the binding of the Livy did not turn out as he had agreed with the binder ('with boards overlapping the pages, in half leather with two clasps'), and the meticulous messer Bernardo notes the fact with irritation.

[9] For some unknown reason Litta (but the section on the Machiavelli family was done by the genealogist L. Passerini) re-christens the daughters of Bernardo, Primerana and Ginevra, and this is followed by VILLARI, I[4], p. 280, TOMMASINI, I, p. 195, and by all the others. The real names are found not only in the *Libro di Ricordi*, but also in A. S. F., *Catasto*, Gonfalone Nicchio, 1470, where the name of Niccolò also appears. No biographer, strangely enough, ever bothered to consult this source, or the *catasto* of 1480 where there is a piece of biographical information of some importance on Niccolò (especially so before the discovery of the *Libro di Ricordi*). In the register for 1470, f. 80, in fact, among the dependants we read:

Bernardo	age 38
Bartolomea, wife	„ 29
Primavera, daughter	„ 5
Margherita, „	„ 2
Niccolò, son	„ 4 months

To these, in the register for 1480, f. 128, is added Totto, 'age 5'. From this information we can tell the age of each member of the family, unknown up to now. Totto, to whom G. AMICO, *La vita di N.M.: Commentari storico-critici*, Florence, 1875, attributed the age of Methuselah, was until now believed to be the eldest child. VILLARI (I[1], 280) states that he was born in 1463; and even more recently G. LESCA, *Lettere machiavelliane inedite*, in *Rivista Storica degli Archivi Toscani*, vol. III (1931), p. 1 ff., said he was 'six years older than Niccolò.' As we see, he was in fact six years younger, being born in 1475.

[10] Archives of S. Maria del Fiore, *Libri dei battesimi*: 'On the 4th of the said month (May 1469): Niccolò Piero Michele son of messer Bernardo Machiavelli, p. di S. Trinita, born on the 3rd at 4 o'clock, baptized on the 4th.'

[11] *Discorsi di Architettura del Senatore* GIOVAN BATTISTA NELLI, con la vita del medesimo (composed by G. B. C. NELLI), Florence, 1753, p. 8. The *laudi* (religious poems) of Bartolomea Nelli were at that time preserved in the family library, and were actually dedicated to her son Niccolò.

[12] *Libro di Ricordi*, cit., pp. 31, 70.

[13] *Libro di Ricordi*, cit., p. 103.

[14] A. S. F., *Catasto*, register, of 1480.

[15] *Libro di Ricordi*, cit., p. 138. A short passage translated from the *Historia persecutionis vandalicae* of Victor Uticensis was at first placed, not among these childhood exercises, but among M's youthful writings, and published in an appendix by VILLARI, I[4], p. 543 ff. Gerber, however, (I, p. 8) dates it, and I think rightly so, at about 1516.

[16] The question was debated at length by Triantafillis who claimed that M. did know Greek, and Villari (I[4], p. 284 ff.) who denied it. For some bibliography cf. Villari, loc. cit.

[17] Lorenzo the Magnificent, for instance, studied Justin at the age of 12: see G. PIERACCINI, *La stirpe dei Medici di Cafaggiolo*, Florence, Vallecchi, 1924-25, vol. I, p. 95.

[18] *Libro di Ricordi*, cit., p. 222 ff.

[19] MACHIAVELLI, *Discorsi*, bk. III, ch. 46; *Opp. MC.*, p. 259 ff.

[20] VESPASIANO DA BISTICCI, *Vita di messer Lorenzo Ridolfi*, in *A.S.I.*, vol .I⁴, pt. I, p. 315 ff.

[21] *Istorie fiorentine*, vol. II, p. 184.

[22] *Istorie fiorentine*, vol. I, p. 198 ff.

[23] MACHIAVELLI, *Principe*, I, 17.

[24] MACHIAVELLI, *Principe*, I, 18.

[25] MACHIAVELLI, *Istorie fiorentine*, vol. II, p. 156.

[26] F. ERCOLE, *Da Carlo VIII a Carlo V*, Florence, Vallecchi, 1932, p. 136, states that M. 'was never either Piagnone or Arrabbiato'; but as far as the second part of this statement goes, I would not be prepared to put my hand in the fire—or even in boiling water.

[27] *Lett. fam.*, p. 4 ff.; *Lett. L.*, p. 3, also with the name of the addressee wrong (on whom see R. RIDOLFI, op. cit., vol. II, p. 201).

[28] RIDOLFI, *Vita di G. Savonarola*, cit., vol II, p. 27.

[29] U. SPIRITO, *Machiavelli e Guicciardini*, 2nd ed., Rome, Ed. Leonardo, 1945, p. 57.

[30] B. CROCE, *Etica e politica*, Bari, Laterza, 1945, p. 250 ff.

[31] G. CAPPONI, *Storia della repubblica di Firenze*, 2nd ed. revised by the author, Florence, Barbera, 1876, vol. III, p. 190 ff.

[32] No one, as far as I know, ever suspected M. of having given way to the vice of that age and place, 'the Florentine vice'. Some doubt on this score might be aroused by his poem 'Se avessi l'arco e l'ale giovinetto giulio'; by certain words in a letter to Francesco Vettori (where, facetiously pretending to be frightened by one of the famous sermons of frate Francesco da Montepulciano, he writes: 'I was supposed to go and see Riccia this morning and I didn't go, but if I had been going to see Riccio, I am not sure that I should have been put off'), and finally by a general statement of the gossiping Busini (*Lettere a B. Varchi*, etc., Florence, Le Monnier, 1860, p. 84) that M. was 'very depraved in his old age'. On the other hand, in his works we find that sodomy is deplored. Many documents show him as being entirely absorbed by women, and others bear witness that Jacopo Salviati, a bitter adversary of that vice (cf. BUSINI, op. cit., p. 89 ff.), was extremely anxious that Niccolò should become secretary to his son the cardinal, whom at that very time (May 1525) he bitterly reproached with allowing at his court those who took pleasure in talking about sodomy, if nothing worse. I shall return to this episode at the appropriate time. We must conclude (without of course excluding the possibility of some isolated instance of curiosity or experience) that M. was almost alone among his friends (Donato del Corno and perhaps Giuliano Brancacci also were guilty of excesses in this respect) in being free from this vice. Furthermore, if one considers closely Busini's statement, which includes to some extent also the vice of gluttony, it may well refer to his mature affair with Barbera, for which he was censured in those years by other contemporaries. The *canzonetta* may have been written at the request of a friend (perhaps Donato del Corno who helped him financially), as he did on other occasions: 'at the request of Barbera', he even wrote verses in the character of a woman to

amuse and flatter a young man in love! Those words in the letter to Vettori, which appear the most serious indication, obviously cannot suffice by themselves to accuse a man whom we so often find in the act of boasting to his friends of vices which he obviously did not have. In this instance too, he cannot have failed to take pleasure in declaring himself tarred with the same brush as so many others around him, all the more so as it offered the temptation of a play on words which he probably could not resist.

³³ *Opp. MC.*, p. 868.

³⁴ On M. and humanism, an unavoidable and inexhaustible subject, see *Umanesimo e scienza politica*, Atti del Congresso Internazionale di Studi Umanistici (1949), Rome, Marzorati, 1951, passim. (Most of this is of small substance).

³⁵ F. ROSSI, *I ritratti di Machiavelli*, in *Illustrazione Toscana*, V (1927), fasc. 4, p. 17 ff.; cf. A. LENSI, *La donazione Loeser in Palazzo Vecchio*, Florence, 1934, p. 41; M. MANSFIELD, *Di un ritratto inedito di N.M.*, in *Rivista d'Arte*, vol. XI, p. 129, p. 361 ff. The fame of M. encouraged posterity to recognize as his, portraits which are definitely not his, like the fine marble bust by Pollaiolo in the Bargello dated 1495, of which a painted plaster copy exists in the Berlin Museum dated 1490. In this year (1490) M. would have been twenty-one, while the bust shows a man of about thirty. Besides, certain features are too unlike those which can be deduced from other iconographical sources. A similar, perhaps even greater, discordance of this kind appears in the portrait published by Mansfield, *op. cit.*; the tradition that this is M.'s portrait rests on no other authority than that it was so described in an inventory probably made in the 19th century, and what is more no scholar has ever set eyes on this inventory! To find the true effigy of M. one must start from the cast which is supposed to have been made from the death mask. The objection has been raised that, as M.'s fame was not great when he died, it is not likely that anyone would have thought of making a death mask (cf. H. E. KINCK, *Machiavelli, seine Geschichte und seine Zeit* [Transl. from the Norwegian], Basle, Benno Schwabe & Co. Verlag, 1938; the great Norwegian artist often makes up for his shortcomings as a scholar with poetic intuition and literary talent: I am not sure, however, whether we can believe him when he guesses that M. had blue eyes!). But we know from Busini that there were present at M.'s death-bed men of talent who were his great admirers, men like Buondelmonti and Alamanni, and it is not improbable that they may have wished to preserve for themselves and posterity the features of their friend, in order to make from the mask—as we know from Vasari was common practice in Florence at that time—posthumous portraits. The well-known bust in painted terracotta from the Loeser collection now in the Palazzo Vecchio (plate I) seems probably to have been derived from that mask, as also, via the Loeser bust, the portrait painted by Santi di Tito, also in the Palazzo Vecchio (pl. II), besides the two attributed to Bronzino. This bust, as Rossi rightly remarks, 'we must regard as the best effigy of M. which has come down to us'. There is also another bust in painted terracotta, seemingly representing M. in the last years of his life, of inferior workmanship (pl. III); it was preserved in the Accademia Colombaria in Florence until it was destroyed when the building was blown up by German mines in 1944. There is a copy in London in private hands. The bust will be described at the beginning of the next to the last chap. of this book. I do not agree with Rossi as regards the engraving of the so-called 'Testina'; the date printed on

the frontispiece (1550) is, as bibliographers know, false and antedated by more than half a century (cf. Gerber, II, 92); and it would in any event be better to cite the edition from which the engraving was copied (*Principe*, Venice, 1540). I also disagree with the doubts expressed about the identity of the portrait in the Galleria Doria, which is a most faithful copy from the Loeser bust—and Rossi himself acknowledges the supreme value of this bust. His doubts can be explained by the fact that up to now no profile of this bust had been published, and so I have put it side by side with the Doria portrait for comparison in plate IV. The authenticity of this and other portraits which are presumed to have derived from the death mask, may safely be conjectured on the strength of an unbroken family tradition among M.'s descendants; and this is also confirmed by bishop SCIPIONE DE' RICCI, *Memorie*, ed. A. Gelli, Florence, Le Monnier, 1865, vol. II, p. 134 ff. He speaks of the 'bust derived from the mask', which had come down to him 'by inheritance', together with 'painted portraits'.

On the fortunes of some of these portraits and in general on the iconography of M., TOMMASINI (vol. I, pp. 64–70, II, 958) gives copious but as usual inconclusive information. The historian of machiavellianism also embarks on an interesting digression on iconographical anti-machiavellianism. He points out how G. B. PORTA, in his famous book *De humana phisiognomia*, Vico Equense, 1586, p. 96 (Tommasini cites the Ital. translation in the Naples edition, 1610) puts side by side for comparison with the head of a monkey and the head of a cat, two human heads, of which the first in particular bears some resemblance, in the cheeks and mouth, to the portrait done by Santi di Tito. The text which accompanies the head compares it 'to cats and monkeys . . . full of wiles and hidden deceits . . . clever and malicious'. But even if one were to accept all this, it is difficult to accept the 'physiognomical syllogism' in the best Tommasinian style which then follows, viz. that the identification of M. in the portrait by Santi di Tito is owed to its likeness to the Porta figure, and to the anti-machiavellian correspondence with the qualities of M. of the features described in the text below the figure. If at all, it is the opposite of Tommasini's reasoning which would appear more plausible, viz that Porta, in an age of machiavellianism, put some features of M.'s portrait into his figure.

CHAPTER 2

[1] Letter from Bartolomeo da Dicomano, 29 May 1498, in D. MARZI, *La cancelleria della repubblica fiorentina*, Rocca S. Casciano, Cappelli, 1910, p. 288.

[2] On him see D. MARZI, op. cit., p. 265 ff.

[3] R. RIDOLFI, op. cit., vol. I, p. 376 ff.

[4] The decisions regarding the election of M. were published in *Opp. P.*, vol. I, p. LXIX; but cf. VILLARI, vol. I⁴, p. 288 n. Other documents, some of which add new information on this subject, have been published since the 2nd Italian ed. of this book, in the important article of N. RUBINSTEIN, *The beginning of Niccolò Machiavelli's career in the Florentine chancery*, in *Italian Studies*, XI (1956), pp. 72–91.

[5] The new ruling gave permission to the newly elected officers to write and draw up documents as public notaries, even though not so qualified. Cf. MARZI, op. cit., p. 280 ff.

⁶ All were attributed by most people to his youth, on the assumption that carnival songs must necessarily have been composed in the age and around the figure of Lorenzo de' Medici. We shall see farther on, those which are to be attributed to a much later date.

⁷ MACHIAVELLI, *Lett. fam.*, p. 1 ff. The Latin fragment published after this letter dated 1 December (1497?) may not refer to the same matter, even if it is really by Machiavelli. It is certainly not sent to the same addressee Cardinal Lopez, as was first stated by Giuliano de' Ricci (TOMMASINI, vol. II, p. 618) and repeated by Villari (vol. I⁴, p. 281 ff.). In fact the tone of the letter is different; and the style and manner are not those which M. would have used to a cardinal. The most important biographical detail to be drawn from this Latin fragment is that M. had recently recovered from an illness.

⁸ F. NITTI, *Machiavelli nella vita e nelle opere*, Naples, 1876, vol. I, p. 39.

⁹ E. REPETTI, *Dizionario geograficio-fisico-storico della Toscana*, Florence, 1835.

¹⁰ Cf. D. MARZI, op. cit., p. 287.

¹¹ Passerini states that M. entered the chancery 'round about '94 under the direction of Marcello Virgilio Adriani in the second chancery', but puts his election as chancellor in '98: *Opp. P.*, pp. XII, XLIX.

¹² D. MARZI, op. cit., p. 287, quotes the unequivocal but undocumented statements of Rüdiger, Reumont and Passerini, and acting on the respectful, but, alas, unreliable assumption that 'such men cannot simply have invented the information', takes a deal of trouble to find the document on which these noted scholars, according to him, must have based their assertions. He thought he had found it in a well-known letter from ser Agostino Vespucci to M. dated 20 Oct. 1500, in which the assistant in the chancery, after relating the proposals of Caesar Borgia to restore Piero de' Medici in Florence, concludes: 'Avertat Dominus a nobis mala, quorum quinquennium pars magna fuimus'—in which, as even a child would understand, that first person plural refers to all the Florentines who by their mistakes had brought the city to such a pass. Not so, however, Marzi: he thought that Agostino Vespucci and Machiavelli, as employees of the chancery—not in the lowly office of assistants because we know the names of the assistants at that time, but in some more humble employment— were in great part the cause of the ills which threatened Florence! Ergo, M. had been employed in the chancery for five years. I say no more. But the best of it is that VILLARI (I⁴, 288 n) repeats this fine argument without turning a hair.

¹³ Letter to Francesco Vettori, 10 Dec. 1513, *Opp. MC.*, p. 884: 'fifteen years that I have been studying the art of statecraft'.

¹⁴ D. MARZI, op. cit., p. 289.

¹⁵ RIDOLFI, *Opuscoli*, pp. 69 ff., 78-82.

¹⁶ He is usually known and referred to by this name, although he was really called Marcello Virgilio di Adriano Berti. For information about him see VILLARI, vol. I⁴, p. 289 ff.; MARZI, op. cit., p. 281 ff.; W. RÜDIGER, *M. V. Adriani*, etc., Halle a Saale, 1897.

¹⁷ *Elogia clarorum virorum*, Venice, Tramezzino, 1546, f. 55v: 'Constat eum, sicuti ipse nobis fatebatur, a Marcello Virgilio, cuius et notarius et assecla publici muneris fuit, graecae atque latinae linguae flores accepisse quos scriptis suis insereret.' Of course it is difficult to reject the main part of this information, viz. that Adriani taught M.,

but as for the details not a little must be attributed to the far from kindly invention of Giovio.

[18] There is perhaps one doubt: that the statement may derive from an erroneous interpretation on Giovio's part, rather than from inaccurate information. To put it more precisely, it is possible that Giovio, hearing that M. was under Adriani in the chancery, may have been led to form wrong conclusions from this fact. As for his having had it from M. himself—anyone who feels like it can believe that!

[19] VILLARI, vol I⁴, p. 289.

[20] RUBINSTEIN, op. cit., pp. 79, 89.

[21] The Otto di Pratica (council of Eight), which had the functions of the Ten during the periods of Medici domination, also had an internal and an external chancery. On this subject see the decree of 22 Jan. 1488, in MARZI, op. cit., p. 610 ff. I believe that the distinction between the chancery of the Signoria and that of the Ten was not as important as that between foreign and domestic affairs, in which offices the secretaries served either branch of the administration according to need, although nominally dependent on one or the other. Besides, it was the importance of the correspondents and the content of the letters which determined the sharing of business between Signoria and Ten.

[22] G. F. PAGNINI, *Della decima*, . . . Lucca, 1765–66, vol. I, p. 121 ff. and plate I; cf. R. RIDOLFI, *Opuscoli*, p. 167 ff. The value of the 'fiorino di suggello' (or little florin), which was constantly decreasing in relation to that of the gold florin, was at that time calculated at 4 lire, as against 6 lire for the gold florin.

[23] For this material I have summarized and in part corrected the muddled account given by MARZI, op. cit., pp. 278–306 and passim. The subject is in itself a confused one, and Marzi is not only unable to clarify it, but to make himself clear. I have made no attempt to deal singly with his inaccuracies. Others working in the secretariat of the Ten were Antonio della Valle, Agostino Vespucci, Luca Fecini (TOMMASINI, II, 667).

[24] In one register of 1502 is the note: 'dictante . . . seu iubente Nicolao Maclavello, a secretis in secunda cancellaria primario'.

CHAPTER 3

[1] GUICCIARDINI, *Storia d'Italia*, ed. A. Gherardi, Florence, Sansoni, 1919, vol I, p. 246.

[2] A list of the registers containing letters of M. was published by TOMMASINI, vol I, p. 671 ff. Much information and comment, which is however not very useful, on M.'s official correspondence can be found in Canestrini's preface to the *Scritti inediti*.

[3] *Opp. P.*, vol VI, p. 284 ff. The work can be dated with precision because of certain references in the text. Reference is made to the 'recent' abandoning of the Pisans by the Venetians (April 1498), and to the coolness shown them by the Duke of Milan, which was not spoken of after August that year. Further, the *Discorso* is addressed to the officials of the Ten, and this magistrature was vacant after 31 May, as it had not been possible to re-elect the new Ten who should have held office for the second half of the year. This allows us to date the work with certainty in May 1498.

⁴ Numerous errors have been repeated about the legations, or rather commissions of the secretaries of the republic: most people called them embassies, although they were not, and M. thereby has been incorrectly honoured with the title of ambassador. On the other hand, it is not quite accurate either to say as does TOFFANIN, p. 379: 'He had an extremely modest career, and never managed to be promoted ambassador'; and elsewhere (p. 386): 'The republic never promoted him to be ambassador.' In the ordinary way, he could never be an ambassador, because he was a secretary. The statement of F. ERCOLE, op. cit., p. 140: 'Abroad he was always the secretary, never the ambassador', is therefore accurate if not highly original.

⁵ Opp. P., vol II, p. 127. The instructions for this commission, which was *infra dominium* because Appiano was then encamped at Pontedera, were published in Opp. P., vol. III, p. 2 ff.

⁶ Instructions and credentials in Opp. P., vol III, p. 8 ff.

⁷ Letter of 16 July, in Opp. P., vol. III, p. 12 ff.

⁸ Letter of 17 July, in Opp P., vol. III, p. 15 ff.

⁹ Letter of 24 July, in Opp. P., vol. III, p. 30 ff.

¹⁰ Letter of 19 July, in Lett. fam., p. 21 ff, full of items of information about the second chancery; and from which it would appear there was someone trying to oust M. from his office during his absence.

¹¹ Letter of 24 July, cit.

¹² Letter of Buonaccorsi to M., cit., and a further letter of B. to M. of 27 July, published in Lett. fam., p. 23 ff.

¹³ Letter of the Ten to Paolo Vitelli, dated 20 Aug. 1499, published by VILLARI, vol. I², p. 558 ff. A large group of letters of this period, almost all in M.'s hand and relating to the Pisan war, were published by Canestrini in Scritti inediti, pp. 63–132.

¹⁴ CAMBI, Istorie, in Delizie degli eruditi toscani, vol. XXI, p. 148.

¹⁵ Opp. MC., p. 787 ff. The autograph minute is preserved in B.N.F. CarteMachiavelli, I, 49. VILLARI, who at first (vol. I¹, p. 338) had denied that it was autograph, later (vol. I⁴, p. 311 n.) gave in on this point, but clung to the view that it was not M.'s work on grounds of style, without considering that the style was adapted to the nature of the communication. Cf. TOMMASINI, vol. I, p. 157 ff. It is likely that the letter of the Lucchese secretary, addressed to a certain Jacopo Corbino, a Pisan canon, was found among the papers of messer Francesco da Lucca, who died round about the date when Vitelli was beheaded, and whose possessions Machiavelli ordered, in a letter of 4 October, to be collected and handed over to the heirs. I believe, therefore, that M.'s letter (in which MARZI, op. cit., p. 291, insisted on seeing a continuation of the tradition of chancery 'invectives') can reasonably be dated about 5 October.

¹⁶ GUICCIARDINI, Storia d'Italia, ed. cit., vol. I, p. 313.

¹⁷ The Countess, who had been accepted into the protection of Florence soon after M.'s commission (cf. Opp. P., vol. III, p. 33), wrote a letter to the Florentines on 16 Oct. 1499 (Scritti inediti, p. 250 ff.) begging them to include her as their ally in the League of the King of France.

¹⁸ The letters and credentials were published in Opp. P., vol. III, pp. 33–36. In the margin of the credentials dated 5 February there is a note in the register: *vacat*.

¹⁹ GUICCIARDINI, Storia d'Italia, ed. cit., vol. I, p. 321.

²⁰ Opp. MC., p. 805.

[21] His letter *ex Palatio* is published by R. RIDOLFI, *Gli archivi delle famiglie fiorentine,* Florence, Olschki, 1934, vol. I, p. 23 ff.

[22] TOMMASINI, vol. I, p. 204.

[23] Beaumont was similarly regarded by the French themselves; DESJARDINS, *Négociations,* . . . Paris, 1859, vol. II, p. 36. Cf. TOMMASINI, vol. I, p. 201.

[24] Besides the letters that Albizzi wrote to the Signoria, which are published in *Opp. P.,* p. 51 ff., one should see those he wrote to other Florentine envoys, particularly those to G. B. Bartolini, listed and some of them published in their entirety by R. RIDOLFI, *Gli archivi,* cit., p. 16 ff.

[25] For the history of this ill-fated enterprise, see especially the contemporary first-hand account written in the secretariat of the Ten and now preserved in incomplete form in B. N. F. *Carte Machiavelli* I, 83, 1, and published in *Opp. P.,* vol. III, p. 42 ff. It is believed to have been made by Buonaccorsi for use in the office, judging by a famous note which M. wrote at one point in the margin: *Mentiris, Blasi.* Also by Buonaccorsi is the fuller account dedicated to Albizzi's son at a later date, with the title *Impresa fatta dai Signori Fiorentini l'anno* 1500 . . ., which was published in *A.S.I.,* vol. IV, pt. II (1853), p. 401 ff. See also the other contemporary account given in the *Diario* of Buonaccorsi, and the one by the contemporary NARDI in his later *Istorie.*

[26] In the *Discorsi sopra la prima Deca di Tito Livio,* I, 28, M. criticized the rejection of these Pisan offers.

[27] *Decennali,* in *Opp. MC.,* p. 805.

[28] Buonaccorsi, *Impresa* . . . cit., says that Albizzi gave this commission to one of his followers, but that that person was M. himself is shown by the letter he wrote at that very moment to Florence (quoted in the next note) and by the letter to the commissioner Bartolini.

[29] Published in *Opp. P.,* vol. III, p. 54.

CHAPTER 4

[1] A.S.F., *Grascia,* 5, f. 288v. Villari and Tommasini both have 19 May, which is a mistake. According to the above mentioned register M.'s mother was buried on 12 Oct. 1496.

[2] The sonnet, 'A messer Bernardo suo padre, in villa a S. Casciano', is in *Opp. MC.,* p. 870, where lines 15–17 should more correctly read:

> Dite a quel mio fratello
> che venga a trionfar con esso noi
> l'oca che avemmo giovedì da voi.

[3] *Priorista di Giuliano de' Ricci,* quoted by TOMMASINI, p. 900 n.

[4] Memoirs of sister Brigida del Paradiso, in MS Riccardiano (BRF) 2397, f. 13: 'Bernardo Machiavelli gave to us out of piety an unfinished painted altar piece, which we received after his death. As there was no record of this donation, his son Niccolò gave it to us officially this 21st day of April, in order that we should not have any trouble over the gift. Ser Chimenti Bernardi drew up the documents. For which gift a mass shall be said for his soul and for him who painted it.'

[5] The arrangements for his payment were published in *Opp. P.*, vol. I, p. LX. The date must, however, be corrected to 28 Aug. 1501.

[6] Published in *Opp. P.*, vol. III, p. 90.

[7] VILLARI, vol. 1⁴, p. 325; and even worse TOMMASINI, vol. I, p. 208, 'without . . . a salary higher than that of chancellor, and attached to Casa, the envoy'. This is a gross error, for he has taken the *secretarium suum*, which appears in the instruction, to refer to Casa and not, as it should, to the Republic. The amount of the initial salary is indicated in the decision quoted in the preceding note.

[8] The instruction and patent bear the date 17 July, and so were drawn up before the formal appointment. They are published in *Opp. P.*, vol. III, p. 91 ff.

[9] Letters from Casa and Machiavelli from Lyons, 28 and 29 July, in *Opp. P.*, vol. III, p. 106 ff.

[10] Letter from Lenzi to the Signoria from Lyons, 26 July, in *Opp. P.*, vol. III, p. 102 ff.

[11] Lenzi's orders are published in *Opp. P.*, vol. III, p. 96 ff.

[12] Letter from Lenzi, cit. sup.

[13] *Opp. P.*, vol. III, p. 124 ff.

[14] *Opp. P.*, vol. III, p. 125 ff.

[15] Letter of 7 August in *Opp. P.*, vol. III, pp. 134–40.

[16] Letter of 27 August in *Opp. P.*, vol. III, p. 160 ff. I say that M. wrote these letters, because, although in this and all the earlier ones Casa signed first, they are in his hand and style. The words quoted are sufficient evidence of this.

[17] Letter of 27 August, cit.

[18] Letter from M. at Montargis, 14 August, in *Opp. P.*, vol. III, p. 143 ff.

[19] Letter from Totto Machiavelli, 27 August, published in *Lett. fam.*, p. 35 ff. Biagio Buonaccorsi had already informed M. of the steps taken to obtain this increase in stipend in a letter of 23 August, published in *Lett. fam.*, p. 31 ff. The increase took effect from 28 August; cf. the relative document published by TOMMASINI, vol. I, p. 208 n.

[20] Letter from Biagio Buonaccorsi, 23 August, cit.

[21] Ibidem.

[22] *Lett. fam.*, p. 34.

[23] Letter from Luca degli Albizzi to M., 24 Sept., in *Lett. fam.*, p. 37 ff.

[24] Letter of 23 Sept., in *Opp. P.*, vol. III, p. 167 ff.

[25] Letter, cit.

[26] Letter from the Signoria, 20 Sept., in *Opp P.*, vol. III, p. 181 ff.

[27] *Opp. P.,* vol. III, p. 195.

[28] Letter of 2 Oct., in *Opp. P.,* vol. III, p. 193 ff.

[29] Blois, 11 Oct.; *Opp. P.,* vol. III, p. 201.

[30] This reply is reported by M. in the *Principe*, chap. III. Villari supposed that these words between the cardinal of Rouen and M. occurred in the conversation they had at Tours on 21 November, described by M. in a letter to the Ten the same day. But in the *Principe*, it says that it was 'at Nantes with Rouen, when Valentino . . . was occupying Romagna'. There can be no doubt that M., writing these words a dozen years later, must have had a visual recollection of the place where the exchange occurred. Further, in a letter from Nantes of 4 November M.

describes two conversations he had there with the Cardinal, the second of them on 2nd November, which were both entirely concerned with Borgia's campaigns.

[31] Letter from Nantes, 25 Oct., in *Opp. P.*, vol. III, p. 216 ff.

[32] Letter from Agostino Vespucci to M., 20 Oct., in *Lett. fam.*, p. 38 ff.

[33] Writing from Melun on 26 August (in *Opp. P.*, vol. III, p. 154 ff) à propos of the Lucchese ambassador, who was favoured at court, he observed that 'it all comes of being able to acquire *amicos de mammona iniquitatis* and of Your Excellencies believing that reason alone will help you.'

[34] *Opp. P.*, vol. III, p. 246.

[35] See the financial provision quoted above in note 19.

[36] In the letter of 4 Nov. from Nantes he quotes a *rien* with which the cardinal of Rouen had answered him (*Opp. P.*, III, 219). At other times he gives Italian endings to French words, as in the letter of 27 Aug. from Melun, when he says that in reply to the proposal that the King himself should undertake the Pisan war, 'His Majesty says that it is a *mocheria*' (i.e. moquerie); cf. *Opp. P.*, III, 160.

[37] GERBER, I, p. 21, puts the short *De natura Gallorum* 'during or immediately after the mission to France', but in fact he has not noticed that some words refer to an event of 1503 ('. . . sent to Siena to demand Montepulciano, and not been obeyed').

CHAPTER 5

[1] GUICCIARDINI, *Storia d'Italia*, ed. cit., vol. II, p. 8.

[2] Of this mission nothing remains but the letters patent issued to him by the Signoria, published in *Opp. P.*, vol. III, p. 249 ff, and the provision of two florins made him for this expedition, in *Opp. P.*, vol. I, p. LX.

[3] Many documents (too many perhaps to be included among the *Opere* of M.) regarding the affairs of Pistoia are published in *Opp. P.*, vol. III, pp. 250–351, i.e. letters from the Signori and the Ten to the commissioners, most of them written in M.'s own hand, and letters from the commissioners to the Signoria and the Ten.

[4] Letter from the Signoria to the commissioners in Pistoia, 16 May 1501, in *Opp. P.*, vol. III, p. 313 ff.

[5] We have the credentials of this commission dated 14 July and a letter from the Signoria of the following day, in *Opp. P.*, vol. III, p. 330 ff. We also have the allocation of 'five gold florins, which are given him for having gone to Cascina, Pistoia and Siena by their lordships orders, and been away ten days on this expedition' (*Opp. P.*, vol. I, p. LXI).

[6] The credentials to Pandolfo Petrucci are published in *Opp. P.*, vol. III, p. 358; for the allowance for this commission, see the preceding note. The approximate date of the trip to Cascina can be deduced partly from the order in which it is quoted in the above-mentioned allocation of funds, partly from the date when Vitellozzo went to Pisa, which seems the most likely reason for M.'s commission, on account of the suspicions Vitellozzo's move aroused in the city. Cf. BUONACCORSI, *Diario*, cit., p. 44.

[7] As can be gathered from the allowance of 10 florins made him on 30 Oct., published in *Opp. P.*, vol. I, p. LXI, M. went to Pistoia twice in October 'first riding

post, and then on the 18th of this month with Niccolò Valori, and stayed a week'. Letters from Valori's commission were published in *Opp. P.*, vol. III, p. 332 ff. M. returned to Florence on the morning of the 26th, as may be gathered from the letter from the Signoria to Valori, ibid., p. 345 ff. After M.'s return to Florence Valori wrote him a very friendly letter, published in *Lett. Fam.*, p. 50 ff.

[8] *Mandragola*, Act V, scene 5.

[9] L. PASSERINI, *Genealogia e storia della famiglia Corsini*, Florence, 1858, p. 24.

[10] The first certain allusion to the marriage is found in a letter from Agostino Vespucci to M. dated 13 Oct. 1502 (*Lett. fam.*, p. 54 ff.): *Uxor tua*, etc. . . . But in a letter of the same Vespucci on 25 Aug. 1501 (*Lett. fam.*, p. 45 ff.) we read the following burlesque passage which might lead one to suppose that M. had already taken or was about to take a wife: 'And when His Beatitude the Pope comes here, you and any others who want a dispensation either to take or leave a wife, shall have it willingly . . .' In fact, we shall see that early in December 1503 when his first son was born, Marietta already had a daughter, unknown to M.'s previous biographers, who must have been born in 1502. M.'s marriage must, therefore, be situated about the Autumn of 1501, just as Vespucci's letter suggests along with the other biographical considerations cited in the text. See below, Chap. VII, note 40.

[11] Letter of 25 Aug. 1501, published in *Lett. fam.*, p. 45 ff.

[12] LANDUCCI, *Diario fiorentino dal 1450 al 1516* . . ., published by I. Del Badia, Florence, Sansoni, 1883, p. 245.

[13] The decision and the credentials relating to this legation of Soderini, in which there is no mention at all of M., were published in *Opp. P.*, vol. IV, p. 3 ff.

[14] *Opp. P.*, vol. IV, p. 4 ff.

[15] Letter of 26 June 1502, *ante lucem*, to the Ten (not to the Signoria as stated in the edition), signed by Soderini, but entirely in M.'s hand, in *Opp. P.*, vol. IV, pp. 8–15.

[16] Letter of 26 June, cit.

[17] Letter of 26 June, cit. In the letter of the same day written at a later hour by Soderini himself (*Opp. P.*, vol. IV, p. 17) we read: 'This morning Niccolò has set off back so that your lordships may understand by letter and word of mouth exactly what we have learned, and may the better resolve what to do, having heard Niccolò who has been present throughout.' We need say nothing here of the impression Borgia made on M. The impression he made on Soderini is expressed in his later letters of this mission, published in *Opp. P.*, vol. IV, pp. 17–63. In M.'s *Del modo di trattare* . . . quoted below he talks of 'the praise as a great man' which Soderini gave to the Duke.

[18] GUICCIARDINI, *Storia d'Italia*, ed. cit., vol. II, p. 36.

[19] Letter from Vespucci to M., 13 Oct. 1502, in *Lett. fam.*, p. 54 ff.

[20] Among those he wrote was one to the commissioner Piero Soderini in Arezzo on 8 September; in fact there are two letters to him of the same date, both written by M. and in very similar terms, one for the Signoria, cit. by VILLARI, vol. I^2, p. 383, and the other for the Ten, published in *Scritti inediti*, p. 28 ff. In the one written on behalf of the Signoria M. ordered Soderini to arrest in Arezzo and send to Florence all those men 'whom you think either by intelligence or courage or wickedness or wealth are capable of acquiring a following; and you should err on the side of sending

twenty more (*thirty*, he writes in the letter of the Ten) rather than one less, without concern for the total number or for the possibility that the city may be so emptied of its men'.

[21] The few letters and replies regarding these Aretine commissions of M. are published in *Opp. P.*, vol. III, pp. 360–4. Many of the letters written in the Chancery in M.'s hand to the commissioners Antonio Giacomini, Piero Soderini, Giovanni Ridolfi, to the French captains and others, were published in *Scritti inediti*, pp. 3–57.

[22] This may be gathered from the letters of the Ten to the commissioner Andrea de' Pazzi, of 13 and 17 Sept., in *Opp. P.*, vol. III, p. 363.

[23] Passerini declares categorically that M. 'was responsible for those severe measures, perhaps indeed too severe, though the only ones capable of restoring peace for some time' in the city of Pistoia; *Opp. P.*, vol. III, p. 248. Tommasini is no less categorical in similar affirmations on this subject (vol. I, p. 214 ff., 216). For the Arezzo rebellion see VILLARI, vol. I,[2] p. 287.

[24] This report was published for the first time in *Opp. P.*, vol. III, pp. 352–5. It is merely a brief account of the disturbances in Pistoia from August 1500, and of the steps taken to remedy the situation up to 17 March 1502. It was written between 17 and 25 April 1502, probably on the instruction of the newly elected Ten. This report on past events was to be completed, in relation to future provisions, by the addition of a *Sommario della città* (Summary account of the city) and a *Sommario del contado* (Summary account of the country district), published in *Opp. P.*, vol. III, p. 355 ff.

[25] Published in *Opp. P.*, vol. III, p. 365 ff. The date of this work, which Passerini assigned to 1502, is certainly between 1 June and 18 Aug. 1503. The year is indicated by the author himself with the phrase: 'in Arezzo last year'; the *terminus post quem* by the title of cardinal given to Francesco Soderini, the news of whose elevation reached Florence on 1st June; and the *terminus ante quem* by the death of Alexander VI, who is spoken of in the work as still alive. The subject of this work was treated again by M. in his *Discorsi sopra la prima Deca di Tito Livio*, Bk. II, ch. 23. According to TOFFANIN, p. 379, this notable work was 'sent to the Ten'; but it is more likely that in using the plural M. was addressing the Signoria, or even the Florentines as a whole; or again it may be that the *Voi* (like Dante's '*voi* che prima Roma sofferie': *Paradiso*, XVI, 10) was addressed to one man, to the Gonfalonier Piero Soderini, whose brother is mentioned in the text. I would add that the late Prof. F. Chabod, in a course of lectures at the University of Rome in 1953, arrived quite independently of me at the same conclusions about the dating of this work and basing himself on the same arguments. These lectures were later published in a cyclostyled edition (F. CHABOD, *Niccolò Machiavelli*, Rome, Edizioni dell'Ateneo, 1953) when the first edition of this book was being printed, and not knowing of their existence, I was unable to refer to them at the time. In this present edition there is no need to comment further on those lectures, which agree substantially with what I have said, at least those points which are of most direct concern to my argument.

[26] TOMMASINI, vol. I, p. 235; FLAMINI, *Il Cinquecento*, in the series 'Storia Letteraria d'Italia', Milan, Vallardi, 1902, p. 11; cf. VILLARI, vol. I,[2] p. 384 ff.

[27] TOFFANIN aptly qualifies it as 'dimly but not unworthily foreshadowing the *Prince*'.

CHAPTER 6

[1] GUICCIARDINI, *Storie fiorentine*, ed. R. Palmarocchi, Bari, Laterza, 1931 ('Scrittori d'Italia', *Opere di F. G.*, vol. VI), p. 251.

[2] Villari (I⁴, p. 359) also says that M. was able 'to win those with whom he came in direct contact', and he is right; but the trouble is that he says this with the object of paraphrasing and commenting on Cerretani's view of M., which is not favourable: 'a man suited to serve the interest of a few'—which means something quite different.

[3] Letter from Francesco Soderini to M., 29 Sept. 1502, in *Lett. fam.*, p. 52.

[4] The nomination, instructions and credentials relative to this mission were published in *Opp. P.*, vol. IV, pp. 64 ff.: the document regarding his salary, which on this occasion was also two 'little' florins a day, is in *Opp. P.*, vol. I, p. LXI. Villari (I⁴, p. 359) says of this legation that M. 'seems to have accepted it with great regret and to have gone much against his will', and he mentions this discontent of M. also elsewhere: I myself have been unable to find any confirmation of his assertions. Perhaps he was basing himself on the assumption, which I have shown to be erroneous, that M. had only recently been married.

[5] VILLARI, vol. I⁴, p. 362: 'si mise in vettura' (!), and evidently intending *vettura* as 'carriage' and not with the meaning it had in M.'s day of hiring horses.

[6] Letter from M. to the Ten dated 7 October, sent on the 8th, published in *Opp. P.*, vol. IV, p. 67.

[7] Letter, cit.

[8] Letter of 9 October, in *Opp. P.*, vol. IV, p. 72. M. sent a detailed account of all the Duke's forces, with the names of the various companies, in his letter of 13 November, *Opp. P.*, vol. IV, pp. 174 ff.

[9] Letter from Niccolò Valori of 11 Oct. 1502, published without date in *Lett. fam.*, p. 53. The date, however, is on the original in B.N.F., *Carte Machiavelli*, III, 12. In his letter of 31 Oct. (*Lett. fam.*, p. 77) he told M. that, as he had none of his own, he wished him to be his brother, adding 'take this letter in lieu of a bond'.

[10] Letter of 23 Oct., in *Lett. fam.*, p. 71.

[11] Letter from Niccolò Valori of 31 October, cit.

[12] Letter from Biagio Buonaccorsi to M., 17 October, in *Lett. fam.*, p. 58.

[13] Letter from Buonaccorsi to M., 28 October, in *Lett. fam.*, p. 73.

[14] Letter of 28 October, cit.

[15] *Opp. P.*, vol. IV, p. 132 ff.

[16] Letter from M. to the Ten, 20 October, in *Opp. P.*, vol. IV, p. 107 ff. This was not the only lesson M. made bold to teach the Signoria. Notable for their foresight are the words he used at that time about the example set by Vitellozzo's peasant militia when it defeated at Fossombrone the highly paid mercenaries of Valentino: 'I have written freely of this matter to Your Lordships so that you may see that . . . the man who is well armed with his own arms achieves the same results wherever he may turn.'

[17] A. GIUSTINIAN, *Dispacci*, ed. P. Villari, Florence, Le Monnier, 1876, vol. II, p. 94.

[18] Letter from Buonaccorsi to M., 21 October, published in *Lett. fam.*, p. 65: 'We have made a search for Plutarch's *Lives*, but there are no copies for sale in

Florence. I am sorry: we shall have to write to Venice.' He would get one immediately there, because the *Lives* (which had few editions in the 15th century in the
Latin translations of Guarino and others, and none printed in Florence) had been
printed in Venice in 1496 by Bartolomeo Zanni. An earlier edition had appeared
three years before that in Brescia printed by Jacopo Britannico.

[19] M. repeats in several letters during this legation the fact that Borgia did not
concede audiences easily, especially if they only brought him words as did Machiavelli. On Valentino see the recent full study by G. SACERDOTE, *Cesare Borgia*, Milan,
Rizzoli, 1950.

[20] Letter from M. to the Ten, 8 November, in *Opp. P.*, vol. IV, p. 157. [The
phrase quoted means literally: 'to lead rather than to be led', with a pun on the verb
'condurre' meaning also 'to commission', 'to employ as a hired captain'].

[21] M. to the Ten, 20 November, in *Opp. P.*, vol. IV, p. 188.

[22] Letter of 15 November, in *Lett. fam.*, p. 88 ff.

[23] Letter from M. to the Ten, 18 November, in *Opp. P.*, vol. IV, p. 233 ff.

[24] Letter from Buonaccorsi to M., 18 November, in *Lett. fam.*, p. 58 ff.

[25] Buonaccorsi to M., 21 December, *Lett. fam.*, p. 96 ff.

[26] Letter from Alamanno Salviati to M., 24 December, in VILLARI, vol. I², p. 608 n.
Cf. the letter from Buonaccorsi to M., 4 November, in *Lett. fam.*, p. 82 ff.: 'The
time for reappointment is drawing near . . .'

[27] Letter from Marcello Virgilio to M., 7 November, in *Lett. fam.*, p. 84 ff.

[28] Letter from Buonaccorsi to M., 21 December, cit. In his letter of 3 November
(*Lett. fam.*, p. 80 ff.), where he tells of the changes which have taken place in the
Palazzo since Soderini took office, he writes: 'Our chancery will for the present
serve the Ten and the hall will accommodate us.' I believe that the 'hall' refers, at
least in part, to the offices of the second chancery.

[29] Letter, *ex cancelleria, die XIII octobris* 1502, *raptim et cum strepitu*, in *Lett. fam.*,
p. 54 ff.

[30] Letter from Bartolomeo Ruffini 'in chancery' to M., 21 October, in *Lett. fam.*,
p. 69 ff.

[31] *Opp. P.*, vol. IV, p. 195 ff.

[32] *Opp. P.*, vol. IV, p. 214 ff.

[33] Letter from M. to the Ten, 13 November, in *Opp. P.*, vol. IV, p. 177 ff.

[34] M. to the Ten, 20 November, in *Opp. P.*, vol. IV, p. 188 ff.

[35] The word is M.'s in his letter of 20 November, cit.

[36] Letter of M. to the Ten, 20 November, cit.

[37] M. to the Ten, 28 November, in *Opp. P.*, vol. IV, p. 201 ff.

[38] Letter from the Gonfalonier Soderini to M., 21 December, in *Lett. fam.*, p. 96.

[39] M. to the Ten, 14 December, *Opp. P.*, vol. IV, p. 229 ff.

[40] A. GIUSTINIAN, *Dispacci*, ed. cit., vol. I., p. 283 ff.: letter of 23 Dec. 1502.

[41] Letter from M. to the Ten, 26 December, in *Opp. P.*, vol. IV, p. 249 ff; cf.
Principe, ch. VII. The autograph letter of 20 Dec. 1503, published in *Opp. P.*, vol.
IV, p. 241 ff., is preserved in British Museum, Egerton MS. 23.

[42] Valentino, speaking to M. immediately after the capture of the *condottieri*,
reminded him that he had 'spoken of this the day before, but not told him all'. This
is reported in M.'s letter to the Ten of 1 Jan. 1503, in *Opp. P.*, vol. IV, p. 258 ff.

[43] Letter from M. to the Ten, 31 Dec. 1502, in *Opp. P.*, vol. IV, p. 253 ff.

[44] Letter of 1 January, cit. The last words here quoted were spoken that day, but not reported formally until M.'s letter of 8 January, in *Opp. P.*, vol. IV, p. 271 ff.

[45] Of the letters which M. wrote to the Ten in those memorable days with great trouble and no little expense because of the difficulty of finding messengers amid all the disturbances, some were lost and others arrived with considerable delay; so much so that in Florence they feared for his safety. See the letter from the Ten of 9 January, in *Opp. P.*, vol. IV, p. 273 ff., and the one from Buonaccorsi of 8 January, in *Lett. fam.*, p. 99 ff.

[46] *Decennali*, in *Opp. MC.*, p. 808.

[47] The letters written by M. from Perugia and Siena are published in *Opp. P.*, vol. IV, pp. 271–286.

[48] This information comes from the note written at the foot of Machiavelli's appointment published in *Opp. P.*, vol. IV, p. 64.

[49] *Opp. MC.*, p. 743.

[50] This was asserted by Villari and has been repeated in some form or another by all biographers, on the basis of certain differences found in the incomplete letter published in *Opp. P.*, vol. IV, p. 254 ff. and other documents. I regard it as unnecessary for me to go into these differences here, as they were examined, though not altogether satisfactorily, by A. MEDIN, *Il duca Valentino nella mente di N.M.*, in *Rivista Europea-Rivista internazionale*, vol. XXXII (1883), fasc. V; though it may be said that almost all the differences regard topics that were the subject of similar controversy among contemporary historians. Some of Villari's remarks are the result of ignorance, as e.g. the first one about the 'calumnies' levelled by the Florentines at Borgia (*Descrizione*, loc. cit.), where it is quite clear that the word (*calunnie*) is used with the sense it commonly had in M.'s times of 'criticisms'. GERBER, I, p. 38, basing himself on his researches into the handwriting of M., would assign the *Descrizione* to a dozen years after the events themselves (putting it even later than the *Principe*!)—a wild assertion that needs proving by different methods. Even if it were possible to prove that the autograph examined by Gerber was written when he affirms it was, no one could prove that it was not transcribed from an earlier copy—an argument that could be used in other instances against the method followed by the learned German scholar.

CHAPTER 7

[1] *Parole da dirle sopra la provvisione del danaio, fatto un poco di proemio e di scusa* (Words to be spoken on the provision of money, with a short preface and apology), in *Opp. MC.*, p. 788 ff. Tommasini (I, 269), who rarely gets things right, maintains that the speech was made by M. himself; he quotes, misunderstanding its meaning, a passage from Giannotti to show that a secretary (though it cannot possibly have been M., and if I am not mistaken, it would be the chancellor of the *Riformagioni* [New Laws]) used to present and read the laws—read and present, not speak formally in favour. Villari, more correctly, rules out the possibility that M. made the speech and believes that it was prepared for the Gonfalonier, or that it was merely a literary exercise of

the kind frequently composed by Guicciardini. He is right for Guicciardini, but not for Machiavelli. Several reasons, first among them the title of the speech, make me disinclined to regard it as a literary exercise; because, if he had had time and inclination to exercise himself in this way, he would have done so in that 'short preface and apology'. I would hesitate to regard it as written for Soderini; because the terms used in it with reference to Soderini's election would have been inappropriate if spoken by him. The autograph of the *Parole* is in B.N.F., *Carte Machiavelli*, I, 77.

[2] The deliberation of the Ten and the instructions to M. for this commission are published in *Opp. P.*, vol. IV, p. 295 ff.

[3] GUICCIARDINI, *Storia d'Italia*, ed. cit., vol. II, p. 79.

[4] MACHIAVELLI, *Il Principe*, chap. VII: 'And hee told mee on that day that Julius the second was created Pope, that hee had forethought on all that which could happen, in case his father chanc'd to dye, and for every thing provided its remedy; this only excepted, that hee foresaw not that hee himselfe should at the same time be brought unto deaths dore also' (trans. by Edw. Dacres).

[5] Credentials from the Ten to cardinal Soderini, in *Opp. P.*, vol. IV, p. 302. The decision of the Ten, in *Opp. P.*, vol. I, p. LXII (where there is a mistake in the date: XI October instead of XXI October. Cf. vol. IV. p. 299) reads, however, 'apud summum pontificem quando fuerit creatus'.

[6] The financial provision for this journey is published in *Opp. P.*, vol. I, p. LXI ff. For the Ten's decision to send M. to Rome after the death of Alexander VI, see *Opp. P.*, vol. IV, p. 298. A gross misunderstanding by Passerini (*Opp. P.*, vol. IV, p. 297 ff.) led him to believe in a non-existent mission of M. to Rome in May 1503. Cf. VILLARI, I², 449.

[7] His instructions, dated 23 October, are published in *Opp. P.*, vol. IV, p. 299 ff. Among the credentials he carried was also one for cardinal Della Rovere, who was later elected. In the first letter from the Ten to M., dated 24 October, they write: 'This morning immediately after your departure . . .'

[8] M. wrote his first letter on the 27th just after his arrival, but it has since been lost and we know of it only through a letter written on the 28th, *Opp. P.*, vol. IV, p. 306 ff.

[9] Letter of 28 October, cit.

[10] Letter to the Ten, 30 October, in *Opp. P.*, vol. IV, p. 312.

[11] M. to the Ten, *hora octava noctis inter ultimum diem octobris et primum novembris*, in *Opp. P.*, vol. IV, p. 316 ff.

[12] *Opp. P.*, vol. IV, p. 318.

[13] Letter from M. to the Ten, cit. sup., note 11: 'This and many other things which occur from day to day deserve to be despatched by post-rider, but I have no orders to this effect from Your Lordships, and, without your orders, I shall not enter into such expense'. The Ten, as on other occasions, pretended not to hear.

[14] Letter of 1 November, *Opp. P.*, vol. IV, p. 319 ff.

[15] Letter of 4 November, *Opp. P.*, vol. IV, p. 326 ff.

[16] Letter of 4 November, cit.

[17] M. to the Ten [6 November], *Opp. P.*, vol. IV, p. 333 ff. The letter bears no date, but this may be deduced from the letters of 7 and 10 November.

[18] Letter of 6 November, cit.

[19] See above, note 4.

[20] Letter from M. to the Ten, 18 November, *Opp. P.*, vol. IV, p. 373 ff; cf. the letter of 29 November, loc. cit., p. 422.

[21] Letter of 18 November, cit.

[22] Letter from Buonaccorsi to M., 15 November, in *Lett. fam.*, p. 104 ff.

[23] M. to the Ten, 30 November, in *Opp. P.*, vol. IV, p. 424 ff.

[24] Letter from M. to the Ten, 1 December, *Opp. P.*, vol. IV, p. 428 ff.

[25] Extract from a letter from Rome, 5 [December], inserted in one of 23 December 1503, published by F. UGOLINI, *Storia dei Conti e Duchi di Urbino*, Florence, 1859, vol. II, p. 523 ff.

[26] Letter from M. to the Ten, 26 November, *Opp. P.*, vol. IV, p. 411 ff.

[27] Letter from M. to the Ten, 28 November, *Opp. P.*, vol. IV, p. 416 ff.

[28] M. to the Ten, 3 December, in *Opp. P.*, vol. IV, p. 437 ff.

[29] MACHIAVELLI, *Discorsi sopra la prima Deca di Tito Livio*, III, 47.

[30] *Opp. MC.*, p. 809.

[31] Letters of 11 and 20 November, *Opp. P.*, vol. IV, pp. 346 ff., 383 ff.

[32] Letter of 24 November, *Opp. P.*, vol. IV, p. 404 ff.

[33] Letter of 22 November, *Opp. P.*, vol. IV, p. 398.

[34] The letter (*Lett. fam.*, p. 112 ff.) is undated and lacks the name of the addressee, but there is no doubt this was a certain Angiolo Tucci, a stationer, who was one of the Priors in November and December. Cf. the letter of Buonaccorsi, 4 December, in *Lett. fam.*, p. 109 ff. In this edition the letter is cautiously headed 'To one of the Signori', so that it is surprising to find that Lesca (*Lett. L.*, pp. 14 ff., 250), following Villari, reprinted it under the heading: 'To Piero Soderini'.

[35] Letter of 25 November, *Opp. P.*, vol. IV, p. 408.

[36] Letter from M. to the Ten, 12 November, *Opp. P.*, vol. IV, p. 453 ff. The indisposition complained of was a cough and catarrh, though evidently without fever.

[37] The first news reached M. from Battista Machiavelli in a letter of 9 November published in *Lett. fam.*, p. 103 ff. Buonaccorsi wrote about it on 12 November in a letter published in *Lett. fam.*, p. 106 ff. (where for some inexplicable reason it is put after another letter of Buonaccorsi dated 15 November and one from Soderini dated 17 November).

[38] Letter of 2 November, in *Lett. fam.*, p. 101 ff.

[39] Letter of 15 November, in *Lett. fam.*, p. 104 ff.

[40] This letter is written in a hand that is no better and perhaps even a little worse than that found among women of Marietta's class at that time. It was published in *Lett. fam.*, p. 114 ff., and by Villari, vol. III^2, p. 399 ff., and in *Lett. L.*, p. 224 ff. In the autograph in the B.L.F., Codice Tempi, II, f. 165, the month and year are missing from the date, and Amico and others who published it assigned the letter to 1524, deducing this from the indication on the original: 'a dì 24' (i.e. on the 24th day). Villari (II^4, 273) cannot date it, but thinks it belongs to 1506. Tommasini (II, 1315) states that the date 'may be conjectured with certainty', and assigns it to 24 December 1503, and this is the date given in *Lett. fam.* and *Lett. L.* This is completely unjustified because on the 24th of December M. had been back in Florence three days! I remarked above that Tommasini rarely got things right. The date which 'may be conjectured with certainty' is 24 November 1503, i.e. 16 days after the birth of M.'s son: in fact Marietta says that she has been unable to write before because of her

confinement, and she could not have said this on 24 December. This dating disturbs the chronology of the birth of M.'s children. Up to now it was believed (though without any firm proof) that Bernardo was the first-born; whereas it is now evident from this letter that there was a female child before him (in the letter it says: 'la bambina sta male'), probably Primerana, whose name would in fact suggest she was the first child. Further, the date established by me, which is supported by other circumstances such as the plague then rife in Rome and a source of grave concern to Marietta, agrees with the conjecture put forward above in note 10, chap. V, viz. that the date of M's marriage should be put a year earlier than other biographers have done: they based themselves on the date of birth of this son, who now turns out to be the second not the first child.

[41] This appears from the Cardinal's letter to M., 29 May 1504, published in *Lett. fam.*, p. 115.

[42] Letter from cardinal Soderini to the Ten, Rome 18 December 1503, *Opp. P.*, vol. IV, p. 464. In fact, M. uses the Cardinal's name in his letter of 12 December, *Opp. P.*, vol. IV, p. 453 ff. Tommasini (I, 300) thinks, and he is certainly wrong, that M. put off his return to Florence because he was afraid of being sent to Germany after Buonaccorsi had told him in a letter that the Gonfalonier had thought of this possibility. He was more probably held up by the discussions he was having with the Cardinal about the bold plan which, as we shall show in the next chapter, he launched during the time of this legation. The last letter from Rome is dated 16 December, published in *Opp. P.*, vol. IV, p. 464: the autograph original is in the British Museum, Egerton MS. 23.

[43] Letter from Soderini, 18 December, cit. M. arrived in Florence on 21 December, as we learn from the note appended to the document regarding his nomination, *Opp. P.*, vol. IV, p. 299. From the financial provision for this mission (*Opp. P.*, vol. I, p. LXII) it appears that his salary was paid up to and including the 22nd.

CHAPTER 8

[1] The letters patent for M. for this commission to Firenzuola are published in *Opp. P.*, vol. I, p. LXII ff. Cf. TOMMASINI, vol. I, p. 301.

[2] *Opp. P.*, vol. V., p. 20.

[3] *Opp. P.*, vol. V, p. 3 ff.; ibid., p. 2, the credentials to the King, the cardinal of Rouen, etc. On his departure M. received an advance of 80 gold florins: the relative document is in *Opp. P.*, vol. I, p. LXIII.

[4] Letter of 22 Jan. 1504, in *Opp. P.*, vol. V, p. 8 ff. The autograph has *Non de rien dotté*.

[5] Letter from Niccolò Valori to the Ten, 27 January, in *Opp. P.*, vol. V. p. 11.

[6] *Lett. fam.*, p. 77 ff.

[7] Letter from M. to the Ten, 30 Jan. 1503/4, in *Opp. P.*, vol. V, p. 20. The letters from Valori to the Ten and from the Ten to him are published in and among these few from M. in *Opp. P.*, vol. V, pp. 10–91: ibid., p. 7, is the letter from the Ten to Valori accrediting M. to him and justifying his mission.

[8] Letter from Valori, 27 January, cit.

[9] Letter, cit.

[10] Valori to the Ten, 2 February, *Opp. P.* vol. V, p. 28 ff.

[11] Letter from M. to the Ten, 25 Feb., in *Opp. P.*, V, p. 79: 'Next Friday I shall leave without fail.' In an earlier letter from Valori to the Ten, 11 February: 'Niccolò Machiavelli will return to Italy in short stages'.

[12] His instructions are published in *Opp. P.*, vol. V, p. 92 ff.; ibid. also the decision to send him, and the credentials. He was paid 10 florins for this commission; see the allocation in *Opp. P.*, vol. I, p. LXIII.

[13] *Riforma santa e preziosa per conservazione della città di Firenze*, Florence, Francesco di Dino, 24 Feb. 1496. The work was never reprinted, and this too is an indication of the little favour it enjoyed. The *Avvertenze* published by G. CANESTRINI, *Documenti per servire alla storia della milizia italiana*, etc., in *A.S.I.*, ser. i, vol. XV, p. 258 ff., have nothing whatever to do with the militia and cannot be attributed to Machiavelli.

[14] Letter from cardinal Soderini to M., 29 May 1504, published in *Lett. fam.*, p. 115. M.'s letter to the Cardinal has been lost. My account of the first approaches made by M. to have the Militia instituted is somewhat different from that of other biographers, who have placed them later, at the end of 1505, when in fact they had already borne solid fruit.

[15] M. wrote an endless series of letters in his own hand regarding the organization of this hydraulic operation. Cf. VILLARI, vol. I[4], p. 433.

[16] Dedicatory letter to Alamanno Salviati, 8 Nov. 1504, *Opp. MC.*, p. 799 (I take the date from the Italian text: the Latin has *V idus Novembris*, i.e. 9 November).

[17] Ed. and loc. cit. Ibid., p. 798, brief information on the MS tradition of the text. For the early editions see later in this book.

[18] M. BARBI, *Delle fortune di Dante nel sec. XVI*, Pisa, Nistri, 1890, p. 297.

[19] This child was probably Lodovico. He must have been born early in October because cardinal Soderini speaks of him in his letter of 26 October published in *Lett. fam.*, p. 119 ff.

[20] In the letter from cardinal Soderini of 26 October, cit. there is the following passage so far overlooked or misunderstood by biographers: 'We suspect that the person you say has cooled off, has done so in order to give no cause to those who would speak and act ill and interpret what is done for public good as done for private interest'. Yet these words are quite clear when read in conjunction with those we have quoted in the text from Soderini's letter of 29 May.

[21] Some of the official letters written by M. at this time are published by Canestrini, *Scritti inediti*, pp. 165–93.

[22] Letter from Totto Machiavelli, 15 March 1504/5, in *Lett. fam.*, p. 122 ff. ibid., p. 123, there is another letter from cardinal Soderini of 23 March 1505, which is rather obscure but probably concerns ecclesiastical benefices. An unpublished letter from Totto Machiavelli from Rome, 26 Sept. 1504, unknown to earlier editors, was published by G. LESCA, in *Rivista Storica degli Archivi Toscani*, vol. III, p. 3 ff.

[23] Letter from Niccolò Valori to M., 12 Jan. 1504/5, in *Lett. fam.*, p. 121.

[24] The instructions are dated 9 April 1505 and published in *Opp. P.*, vol. V, p. 94 ff. This mission to Baglioni is also mentioned by Buonaccorsi, *Diario*, cit., p. 101, though he does not name Machiavelli: 'The Signoria sent a man . . . In his short stay in Perugia (*sic*) he discovered that there was an agreement between him and the Orsini, Pandolfo Petrucci, Consalvo Ferrando, Bartolomeo d'Alviano and all the rest of

that group', etc. For this mission M. was paid 10 florins: see the allocation in *Opp. P.*, vol. I, p. LXIII.

[25] Letter to the Ten, 11 April, in *Opp. P.*, vol. V, pp. 96–103.

[26] The commission, dated 4 May, is published in *Opp. P.*, vol. V, p. 104. The relative financial provision of 20 florins is in *Opp. P.*, vol. I, p. LXIII.

[27] GUICCIARDINI, *Storie fiorentine*, ed. cit., p. 277. Roberto (not Donato, as Tommasini says!) Acciaiuoli was sent to Naples, 'this decision having been arrived at with great difficulty because the Gonfalonier opposed it and wanted, in order to have one of his own people there, to send Niccolò Machiavelli in whom he had great trust'. Tommasini (I, 316) published some of the opinions favourable to sending M. advanced in the debate held on the subject of this legation.

[28] The brief instructions issued to M. for this mission to Siena are dated 16 July, in *Opp. P.*, vol. V, p. 110.

[29] These are published together with the letters from the Ten to him, in *Opp. P.*, vol. V, pp. 111–39.

[30] Letter from Buonaccorsi to M., 24 July, in *Lett. fam.*, p. 124 ff.

[31] M. was in the field about 20 August (I. PITTI, *Vita di Antonio Giacomini Tebalducci*, cit., pp. 225, 227). After the failure to take Pisa the commissioner Giacomini, hearing the calumnies voiced by the malcontents, asked leave to return (PITTI, op. cit., p. 237) and threatened to do so without leave if it was not granted. It was then that M. wrote to him privately a letter published by F. NOVATI, *Una letterina inedita e sconosciuta di N.M.*, in *Il libro e la stampa*, VI (1912), p. 183, in which he tries to dissuade him 'so as not to give further pretext to these malicious traitors, who are many, and I would not wish them to have cause to raise their voices again'. It is strange that the learned Novati should have found the name of Giacomini so obscure as to refer to him as 'a certain Antonio Tebalducci'. As a historian of literature it should have meant something to him at least through the two well known biographies of Nardi and Pitti!

[32] GUICCIARDINI, *Storie fiorentine*, ed. cit., p. 282 ff.

[33] GUICCIARDINI, op. cit., p. 281. G. writes that these leading citizens feared that Soderini would employ don Michele not only to make himself a tyrant, but 'to remove the citizens who were his enemies'.

[34] *Opp. P.*, vol V, p. 142 ff. Here, together with other letters from M. to the Ten, and from the Ten to him, and letters patent, etc., is published also, from an autograph draft by M., the text of the proclamation of enlistment. There is also (p. 147) a letter from Marcello Virgilio written to him on 6 Feb. 1505/6 on the instruction of the Gonfalonier.

[35] On 27 Jan. 1506 an allocation of money was made for expenses incurred by M. 'for certain journeys made in Mugello'; *Opp. P.*, vol. I, p. LXIII.

[36] LANDUCCI, *Diario*, cit., p. 273.

[37] GUICCIARDINI, *Storie fiorentine*, ed. cit., p. 282 ff.

[38] LANDUCCI, op. et loc. cit.

CHAPTER 9

[1] Published in *Lett. fam.*, p. 127 ff., and more correctly by Tommasini, vol. I, p. 675. The only contemporary edition which has come down to us, and the autograph MS.

of Vespucci in B.N.F., *Magl.* XXV, 604, both read, above the dedicatory letter: *Augustinus Mattei N. V. viris florentinis*, etc.; and Tommasini explains that this refers to the 'Cinque conservatori del contado' [Five curators of the country district]. This is, of course, one of Tommasini's usual inventions. There is no evident reason why Vespucci should dedicate the *Decennale* to the 'Conservatori del contado' (which was the usual way of referring to them, not the 'Cinque'), and less still why he should say that M. was repaying a debt to them with this minor work and with a more important one he was still working on. He might perhaps have dedicated it to the Ten, to whom M. was secretary and Vespucci assistant, and who had more concern with Florentine history than the 'Conservatori del contado'! Besides, the text itself shows that the work was directed to the Florentines, whom M. continually addresses in direct speech, as he does in the extracts and fragments quoted in the following note.

[2] Many extracts from public correspondence and summaries from other sources were published from autograph MSS. of M. or of other Chancery officials by the editors of M.'s works, and more fully in *Opp. P.*, vol. II, pp. 129-281. But some groups of these extracts were compiled for office use, not for writing the histories, even though M. collected and kept them together with other material he did intend to use for that purpose; such, for example, were for the most part the extracts from letters sent by the government (not replies, like those in other excerpts), compiled by the assistants Agostino da Terranova and Biagio Buonaccorsi (ed. cit., pp. 166-88). Of the historical extracts there are two main groups: I) Extracts from letters to the Ten, from 1497 to 1499, *Opp. P.*, vol. II, pp. 129-56, missing from the Ricci apograph and first published in the Cambiagi edition without any indication of their source, with the result that the editors of *Opp. P.* and Tommasini expressed some doubt as to their authenticity; until P. CARLI, *Un autografo poco noto del M.*, in *G.S.L.I.*, vol. L (1907), pp. 354-68, found and commented on the original in MS. Riccardiano 3627, which also contains part of the second group. In this article Carli recorded the most important variants between the autograph and the printed text. Later, GERBER, I, p. 10 ff., showed that the extracts in this first group are not in M.'s hand, but in that of Adriani. I would not, therefore, concern myself with these if it were not for the fact that, like the other summaries drawn up by other officials of the Chancery and published by the editors of M.'s works, they were obviously used by M. for his early historical works. We should also consider the possibility, however unlikely, that Adriani copied a MS. by M. or put into shape the summaries drawn up by the assistants. I realize that this kind of collaboration between the first and second chancellor is very improbable; so that, in view of the additional fact that Adriani has interleaved with these extracts some brief notes to be developed later (*Opp. P.*, vol. II, pp. 140, 152, 153), we must conclude (and the deduction is of considerable biographical importance) that Adriani too was preparing to write a history in the very same years as M., and that when he discovered the latter's intentions, he gave up the enterprise in his favour together with the material he had already collected. In any case, the fact that these extracts were written in Adriani's hand proves that they were not compiled for the *Istorie fiorentine*, as has hitherto been believed, but were collected by M. for his early historical works. II) Extracts from 1464 to 1501 (in *Opp. P.*, vol. II, pp. 217-81), conciser than those of the preceding group but often witty and pithy in their extreme brevity; preserved complete in a

copy of the Ricci apograph and in part in a fragment in M.'s hand in MS. Riccardiano 3627 (cf. P. CARLI, op. cit.). In these the compiler generally addresses the Florentines in direct speech as in the *Decennali*, and this feature would also incline me to attribute this group to a date not far distant from that work and from the other greater historical work which was then 'being made in his workshop'; and this is confirmed by GERBER's researches into M.'s handwriting (I, p. 16 ff.). Here too we find notes made by the compiler for future development ('Tell here of the negotiations with France' [ed. cit., p. 268]; 'Remember to say that the question of Pisa was put forward . . .' [p. 273], etc.). This second group, according to Fiorini in his edition of the *Istorie*, and others who have followed him, does not contain summaries from letters but from 'a Latin chronicle'; this conjecture, which CARLI, op. cit., p. 355, says 'needs proving', seems to me to rest simply on the presence of a few short titles and a word or phrase here and there in the text in Latin—as if this were not a habit with M. especially in his unelaborated works (cf. CHIAPPELLI, *op. cit.*, p. 8 ff.). At any rate, these summaries are by M. and written in his own hand during those years in the Chancery (the barbs he launched even at that time against mercenary soldiers are worthy of note: *Nulla fides apud mercenarios milites . . .*). Finally, in addition to lesser groups of extracts (among which are two in M.'s hand belonging to Nov.-Dec. 1494 and June-Dec. 1495: ed. cit., pp. 156–66), there are the so-called *Frammenti storici* from 1494 to 1498 (*Opp. P.*, vol. II, pp. 77–127) which belong to a more advanced stage of development of the text. The most authoritative Machiavelli scholars, among them VILLARI, vol. II⁴, p. 489 ff, have agreed in regarding them as portions of the *Istorie fiorentine*, or, as I would put it more precisely, a first draft of parts of the 9th book (there is a noteworthy reference on p. 116 to 'a notebook in my boxes'). It would, therefore, be premature and out of place to discuss these 'fragments' here; and I would not have mentioned them if the conclusions at which I have arrived regarding the early historical thoughts and works of M. did not justify the belief (in part corroborated by the feature of addressing the Florentines in direct speech as in the *Decennali*, already observed in the extracts of group II) that these fragments belong, like the Extracts, to this same period. This hypothesis was anticipated by GERBER, I, p. 13 ff., who was the first to see the importance of certain allusions in Vespucci's dedicatory letter. But, as if frightened by such a novel idea and afraid to go too far in his conclusions if he affirmed that M. was preparing himself even at that early date to write a history of the Republic, Gerber spoke of 'a fuller Decennale which of course would be in prose'. He did not realize that this was more arbitrary than a broader hypothesis which supposed the intention on M.'s part to continue the historiographical tradition of the Chancery, and he did not take into consideration the extracts *post mortem Cosimi* (group II) which range over three decades more than the limits of a *Decennale*. In any event this cautious and tentative reference by Gerber does not seem to have convinced those who wrote on M. after him, including Villari, who could have seen this contribution by the German scholar, published several years before the appearance of the penultimate edition of his own book.

³ *Lett. fam.*, p. 128 ff.

⁴ Letter from M. to the Ten, 3 March 1505/6, in *Opp. P.*, vol, V, p. 148 ff.

⁵ Letter from Vespucci to M., 13 March 1505/6, *Lett. fam.*, p. 130. The original edition of this first *Decennale* (in-4⁰, pp. 12) was described, though not entirely

satisfactorily, by G. TORRE, in *Il Bibliofilo*, vol. II (1881), p. 76 ff. The copy owned by Torre has since disappeared, and no others are known. One copy only is known of the second edition printed by Tubini which is the subject of Vespucci's letter: this is in the British Museum and was described with great care by GERBER, II, p. 69 (facsimile 103). It is in 8⁰, pp. 12. Gerber's doubts that this B.M. edition might not be the same as the counterfeit edition described by Vespucci can be completely ruled out, because the type is the 86R used by Antonio Tubini from the last two years of the 15th century onwards. On this pirated edition and especially for the 'note' of the 'most substantial errors' found in it by Vespucci and reported on by him in his letter, cit. sup., see R. RIDOLFI, *Spigolature machiavelliane: la 'contraffazione' del Decennale*, in *La Bibliofilia*, LVII (1955), pp. 196–202. This 'note', which was seen but not recognized for what it was by Villari, was found and recognized by me after the publication of the 2nd Italian edition of this biography. Thanks to this rediscovery we now know that there was a settlement between M. and Tubini, who agreed to reprint the pages containing the 'most substantial errors'. In effect, these errors do not figure at all in the copy in the B.M. or in another copy recently found in Italy and acquired by me.

[6] Letter, cit.

[7] Letter of 5 March 1505/6, in *Opp. P.*, vol. V, p. 150. The last letter we have of this mission in Casentino is one from the Ten to M. dated 14 March 1506, in which there is no reference as yet to his return: *Opp. P.*, vol. V, p. 152.

[8] GUICCIARDINI, *Storia d'Italia*, ed. cit., vol. II, p. 141.

[9] *Lett. fam.*, p. 135 ff. Another letter from M. to Giovanni Ridolfi dated 1 June 1504 is in *Lett. fam.*, p. 116 ff., the original autograph of which is in the hands of the Historical Association of Philadelphia.

[10] GUICCIARDINI, *Storie fiorentine*, ed. cit., p. 290.

[11] Instructions from the Signoria to M., 25 Aug. 1506, in *Opp. P.*, vol. V, p. 154 ff.; ibid., the credentials, etc.

[12] From the record in the *Libro delle partenze e tornate degli oratori*, in *Opp. P.*, vol. I, p. LXVI: ibid., various allocations and decisions regarding the salary paid to M. for this legation.

[13] Reported verbatim by M. in his letter to the Ten the same day, *Opp. P.*, vol. V, p. 157 ff.

[14] Letter, cit.

[15] The correspondence during this legation is published in *Opp. P.*, vol. V, pp. 155–240. As VILLARI, vol. I², p. 513 ff., remarked, this correspondence is not among the most important of M.'s legations. In a letter of 6 Sept. 1506 (*Lett. fam.*, p. 143 ff.) Buonaccorsi wrote to tell M. that certain monies would be paid to him through Michelangiolo who had left Florence to brave the wrath of Julius II; then, later, on 11 September (*Lett. fam.*, p. 147 ff.) he wrote to say that Michelangiolo 'had come back. for a good reason'. Cf. G. PAPINI, *Vita di Michelangiolo*, Milan, Garzanti, 1949, p. 144.

[16] Letter of 13 Sept. in *Opp. P.*, vol. V, p. 184 ff. Cf. MACHIAVELLI, *Discorsi*, I, 27, where M. denies that 'a pious reverence' for the Pope and the cardinals had restrained the parricide Giampaolo, and denies also that reverence was due 'to those who live and rule like them': only a base mediocrity of mind prevented Baglioni from being 'honourably wicked or perfectly good'.

[17] GUICCIARDINI, *Storia d'Italia*, ed. cit., vol. II, p. 149. This is not the only place in which G. almost cites word for word what Machiavelli wrote in letters during his legations; where it is possible to find far more cogent and persuasive instances than those *sui generis* quoted by Tommasini, vol. I, p. 187 ff. But Tommasini, misled as usual by his poor judgement, pursues strange conjectures, quoting unnecessarily the late *Peplus Italiae* of Giovan Matteo Toscano in support of his theory that Machiavelli left his extracts and summaries to Guicciardini when he died, or even gave them to him while still alive, when Guicciardini had not even begun to write his *Storia*. The truth of the matter is that all the correspondence of the Ten, and consequently M's. letters included, came into the hands of Guicciardini, as we know from a letter of the last secretary to that body, Donato Giannotti. See R. RIDOLFI, *Gli archivi delle famiglie fiorentine*, Florence, Olschki, 1934, vol. I, p. 157. Guicciardini, therefore, followed and also copied M. not from his historical notes but from his original letters in the archives of the Ten.

[18] Letter to the Ten, 13 September, *Opp. P.*, vol. V, p. 181 ff.

[19] Letter from M. to the Ten, 3 October, in *Opp. P.*, vol. V, p. 210 ff.

[20] Letter of 5 October in *Opp. P.*, vol. V, p. 215 ff. The autograph original of M.'s letter to the Ten from Urbino on 25 Sept. 1506, published in *Opp. P.*, vol. V, p. 199 ff., is now in the British Museum, Egerton MS 23.

[21] Letter of 11 October, in *Lett. fam.*, p. 158 ff.

[22] As in his letters of 8 September (*Lett. fam.*, p. 145 ff.) and 21 September (*Lett. fam.*, p. 148 ff.). The decision in favour of the Ordinance referred to in the letter of 11 October, cit., was that made on 2 October and published by Canestrini, *Scritti inediti*, p. 300. The Bernardo who spoke in favour was Bernardo Nasi who had recently been elected to the Ten in place of Piero Guicciardini.

[23] Letter from Buonaccorsi to M., 30 September, *Lett. fam.*, p. 150 ff.

[24] Buonaccorsi to M., 6 October, in *Lett. fam.*, p. 153 ff. Republished more fully by Villari, vol. I², p. 652 ff.

[25] Letter from M. to the Ten, 12 October, in *Opp. P.*, vol. V, p. 223 ff.

[26] M. to the Ten, 16 October, in *Opp. P.*, vol. V, p. 228 ff.

[27] Letter from M. to the Ten, 19 October, in *Opp. P.*, vol. V, p. 232 ff.

[28] Letter from M. to the Ten, 21 October, in *Opp. P.*, vol. V, p. 233 ff.

[29] *Libro delle partenze e delle tornate*, cit. sup., note 12.

[30] Letter from Carlo degli Abizzi to M., 24 November, *Lett. fam.*, p. 160 ff. M. had asked Albizzi to stand godparent. A baby of his a few months old died on 14 June 1506 (B.N.F., *Necrologio Cirri*, vol. XI, p. 434).

[31] Published in *Opp. P.*, vol. VI, p. 339; G. CANESTRINI, *Documenti . . .*, cit., p. 379. In *Lett. fam.*, p. 173 there is a letter from Roberto Acciaiuoli to M., for which see later, chap. X, n. 7.

[32] Published in *Opp. P.* vol. VI, p. 330 ff.; VILLARI, vol. I², p. 655 ff., and elsewhere. This speech was certainly written when the committee of the Nine had been planned but not yet set up; in effect it is a preamble to the law ('The first thing necessary is to pass a law governing them and to create a magistrate to administer it; and in this law provision should be made . . .') The other *Discorso sopra l'ordinanza e milizia fiorentina*, published on *Opp. P.* vol. VI, p. 335 ff., and almost entirely concerned with the number of men to be enlisted, is in my opinion earlier; and earlier still (not later as

Tommasini says, mistaking the sense of an 'I told you') are the *Ghiribizzi d'ordinanza*, published by Tommasini, vol. I, p. 682.

[33] Decision of 12 Jan. 1506/7, published in part by Tommasini, vol. I, p. 367 n.

[34] Letter from cardinal Soderini to M., 15 Dec. 1506, *Lett. fam.*, p. 161 ff.

[35] Letter from Vespucci to M., 28 Dec. 1506, *Lett. fam.*, p. 162 ff. Instead of Vespucci they elected ser Francesco di ser Tommè da San Gimignano as chancellor of the Nine; cf. G. CANESTRINI, *Documenti*, cit., p. CIX.

[36] For this journey he got an allocation of 17 florins (*Opp. P.*, vol. I, p. LXVIII ff.). For this and other similar commissions in connection with the militia M. received no extra salary above his normal stipend, but he got all his expenses.

[37] On this trip of Machiavelli's to San Gimignano see the few documents (surrounded with inaccuracies, ingenuous observations and rhetorical verbiage) published by U. NOMI PESCIOLINI, *N.M. a San Gimignano*, in *La Bibliofilia*, vol. X (1908), p. 49 ff.; cf. L. PECORI, *Storia della terra di San Gimignano*, Florence, 1853, p. 261.

[38] Letter from cardinal Soderini to M., 4 March 1506/7, *Lett. fam.*, p. 165 ff. The same day the Cardinal wrote to the Gonfalonier to congratulate him and recommend the observance of 'justice', i.e. discipline, in the new militia. VILLARI, vol. I², p. 524 ff.

CHAPTER 10

[1] GUICCIARDINI, *Storie fiorentine*, ed. cit., p. 273.

[2] CERRETANI, *Istoria fiorentina*; cf. VILLARI, vol. II², p. 66.

[3] GUICCIARDINI, *Storie fiorentine*, ed. cit., p. 297.

[4] The letters from Casavecchia and Nasi are published in *Lett. fam.*, pp. 166 and 169 respectively: ibid., p. 170 ff., another pair of letters from them to M., dated 22 Sept. and 19 Nov. 1507. With Casavecchia's letter of 22 Sept. there is a poem published by Tommasini, I, 356 ff., which begins: 'Machiavel mio, le tue buone vivande', and goes on to praise the 'divino ingegno' of his friend who had sent him a letter which is now unfortunately lost.

[5] Letter of 12 August to the Ten, *Opp. P.*, vol. V, p. 243, where the other documents relating to this commission may be found. The 'Stinche' were the Florentine prisons.

[6] GUICCIARDINI, *Storie fiorentine*, ed. cit., p. 302. It was in connection with this commission that Cerretani, who belonged to the faction opposed to Soderini, referred to M. as his 'mannerino', stating that the Gonfalonier sent him not only to keep an eye on Vettori but to get him to write back what suited his ends. The falseness of these suggestions is demonstrated by the part M. played in this legation.

[7] Letter from Roberto Acciaiuoli to M., Rome, 4 Dec. 1507, in *Lett. fam.*, p. 173 ff. Cf. TOMMASINI, vol. I, p. 353 ff., who is mistaken in thinking the reference here is to don Michele, whose commission was passed on 27 Feb. 1506/7. Machiavelli had asked Acciaiuoli, ambassador in Rome, to find him a successor to don Michele, but Acciaiuoli replied quite rightly that it would be difficult to find one among the condottieri, because 'the name of Bargello is hated among active soldiers, and they all detest it' (i.e. the condottieri, not the Florentines, as Tommasini thought!). He also asked what were the conditions of service, etc. All of which was not

understood by Tommasini (or by others), who on the basis of this letter even ventured to correct no less a person than Guicciardini.

[8] Letter from Vettori to the Ten (written by M.), 17 Jan. 1507/8, in *Opp. P.*, vol. V, p. 258.

[9] Letter from M. to the Ten, 25 Dec. 1507, in *Opp. P.*, vol. V, p. 253. Another letter written on the 22nd from Gabella has not come down to us and must have been lost on the way because the Ten never acknowledged it. It may have contained an account of the examination of M. carried out in Lombardy.

[10] This and other documents relating to the German legation (nomination, salary allocation, etc.) are in *Opp. P.*, vol. I, p. LXIX ff.

[11] Letter from M. to the Ten, Bolzano, 17 Jan. 1507/8, in *Opp. P.*, vol. V, p. 253.

[12] Letter from Vettori to the Ten, 17 January, cit.

[13] On Vettori see L. PASSY, *Un ami de Machiavel: François Vettori, sa vie et ses Oeuvres*, Paris, Plon, 1914; B. CROCE, *Poeti e scrittori del pieno e del tardo Rinascimento*, Bari, Laterza, 1945–52, vol. I, p. 69 ff. Of particular interest in the latter work are some acute observations on the materialism of Vettori, which 'led him to an entirely utilitarian, economic and materialistic view of life', far removed from the spirit and outlook of Machiavelli. I always feel there is something discordant in the correspondence between the two friends, also because Vettori was 'tutto di sé' (wrapped up in himself)—to use an expression elegantly applied by Guicciardini to cardinal Soderini—and this egoism makes this association of the unlike appear all the more curious and sterile as far as M. is concerned. Vettori gave an account of this legation in his *Viaggio in Alemagna*, Paris, Molini, 1837; but unfortunately this account, which is interspersed with tales and stories that do not help to make it more attractive and are often out of key, breaks off shortly before the arrival of Machiavelli, and there is nothing in it of interest for M. except a conversation between Vettori and an inn-keeper at Firenzuola (op. cit., p. 2 ff.) about the Militia.

[14] Letter of 8 February, in *Opp. P.*, vol. V, p. 282 ff.

[15] *Opp. P.*, vol. V, p. 334.

[16] For an analysis of M.'s writings on Germany and some bibliographical indications see VILLARI, vol. I[4], p. 540 ff.; to which add H. RÖSEMEIER, *N. Machiavelli's erste Legation zum Kaiser Maximilian und seine drei Schriften über Deutschland*, Bückeburg, 1894.

[17] The *Rapporto*, 'written this 17th day of June 1508', is in *Opp. P.*, vol. V, pp. 313–22.

[18] The *Ritratto* (*Opp. P.*, vol. V, pp. 324–30; *Opp. MC.*, pp. 740–3), which is a literary elaboration of the report written for the office, must be attributed to the middle of 1512, because, after speaking of the battle of Ravenna (11 April 1512), he refers to the war 'recently' begun by the Spaniards in Guyenne. Between the *Rapporto* and the *Ritratto* comes a *Discorso sopra le cose della Magna e sopra lo Imperatore*, which however deals only with the Emperor; it was written for the office in 1509 (the *Rapporto* is referred to in these words: 'Having written of these things on my arrival here . . .'), evidently at the time when Giovanvittorio Soderini and Piero Guicciardini were sent to Germany.

[19] Letter from Cesare Mauro to M., Cologne, June 1508, *Lett. fam.*, p. 174 ff.

[20] Letter of 23 Feb., *Opp. P.*, vol. V, p. 289 ff.

[21] GUICCIARDINI, *Storia d'Italia*, ed. cit., vol. II, p. 195.

[22] Letter of 22 March, in *Opp. P.*, vol. V, p. 305 ff.

[23] See above, note 13.

[24] Letter of 8 Feb. 1507/8, in *Opp. P.*, vol. V, p. 282. It is an autograph addition by Vettori at the foot of a letter written by Machiavelli.

[25] *Opp. P.*, vol. V, p. 324.

[26] Letters of 30 May and 8 June, in *Opp. P.*, vol. V, pp. 324, 332.

[27] Letter from M. to the Ten, Bologna, 14 June, *Opp. P.*, vol. V, p. 336; vol. I, p. LXIX.

[28] See the documents published in *Opp. P.*, vol. I, p. LXX ff., vol. V, pp. 338–42.

[29] *Opp. P.*, vol. I, p. LXXI; vol. V., p. 343.

[30] The correspondence of M. with the Ten and the commissioners, from 1 Feb. to 11 March 1508/9, in *Opp. P.*, vol. V, pp. 344–83. Some allocations of funds to M. for the pay of the soldiers, in *Opp. P.*, vol. I, p. LXXII.

[31] Letter from Buonaccorsi to M., 21 Feb. 1508/9, in *Lett. fam.*, p. 179 ff., in which B. also recommends M. to write to the Nine. In a letter of the previous day (*Lett. fam.*, p. 177) he says that Niccolò Capponi was complaining because M. did not write to him. And later on, in fact, he made trouble about this with the Ten.

[32] JACOPO PITTI, *Vita di Ant. Giacomini Tebalducci*, in *A.S.I.*, ser. i, vol. IV, pt. 2, p. 247.

[33] Letter of 15 Feb. 1508/9, in *Opp. P.*, vol V, p. 347 ff.

[34] GUICCIARDINI, *Storie fiorentine*, ed. cit., p. 333. At Cascina there was, in fact, the commissioner general Niccolò Capponi, but he only concerned himself with supplies. Machiavelli was very busy and did not bother with him much. When he complained to the Ten, they had to give him some satisfaction, unwillingly and simply for the sake of form. See the letter from Buonaccorsi, 20 February, cit. sup., note 31.

[35] Letter from the Ten to M., 6 March 1508/9, in *Opp. P.*, vol. V, p. 273.

[36] Letter from M. to the Ten, Piombino, 15 March 1509, in *Opp. P.*, vol. V, p. 387. Ibidem, p. 384, his commission.

[37] *Opp. P.*, vol. V, p. 398.

[38] Letter from Alamanno Salviati to M., 29 April, in *Opp. P.*, vol. V, p. 409. The correspondence of M. with the Ten and the commissioners, from 30 March to 29 April, op. cit., pp. 392–410.

[39] *Opp. P.*, vol. V, p. 411 ff.

[40] *Opp. P.*, vol. V, pp. 413–32.

[41] Published by Tommasini, vol. I, p. 685.

[42] Letter from Agostino Vespucci to M., 8 June, *Lett. fam.*, p. 182 ff. M.'s namesake, Niccolò di Alessandro Machiavelli, wrote him a short letter of recommendation the following day, which contains no mention of the acquisition of Pisa: G. LESCA, *Lettere machiavelliane*, cit., p. 6.

[43] Letter from Filippo Casavecchia to M., 17 June 1509, *Lett. fam.*, p. 183 ff.

CHAPTER 11

[1] His instructions in *Opp. P.*, vol. V, p. 433 ff.; the nomination and provision of money for this commission are in *Opp. P.*, vol. I, p. LXXIII. There was talk of sending

M. on this mission many days before. On 3 November Francesco Guicciardini wrote to his brother Luigi, who was in Mantua visiting Jacopo Guicciardini who was ill: 'Here it has not yet been decided who will go to the Emperor, and though there are some who would like to send an ambassador, I think in the end they will choose a chancellor, probably Machiavelli'; GUICCIARDINI, *Carteggi*, ed. Roberto Palmarocchi (in I.S.I., *Fonti per la storia d'Italia*), vol. I, Bologna, Zanichelli, 1938, p. 21.

[2] 'To observe, during his journey and stay there, the situation in that province and the state of the Emperor's plans': thus the decision of the Ten, loc. cit.

[3] The correspondence during this mission is published in *Opp. P.*, vol. V, pp. 437–65. For the sake of brevity, only the letters from which extracts are given in the text, are quoted in these notes.

[4] This description, written by M. in his letter of 12 December after his return to Mantua, was imitated by GUICCIARDINI, *Storia d'Italia*, ed. cit., vol. II, p. 271; and it is one more proof of the fact that G. used the legations of M. in the composition of his history (see supra chap. IX, note 17). It is worth noting that not only has Guicciardini copied parts of his description directly from M.'s letter, but he has also inserted it at the very point in his text where he used the papers of the legation, even though he speaks about the city of Verona in many other places in his *Storia*.

[5] Letter from Buonaccorsi to M., 20 Nov. 1509, in *Lett. fam.*, p. 188; reprinted as though unpublished by VILLARI, vol. II², p. 531 ff., together with another from Buonaccorsi and one from Francesco del Nero, 22 November.

[6] Letter from M. to the Ten, 29 November, in *Opp. P.*, vol. V, p. 448 ff.

[7] M. to the Ten, 1 December, in *Opp. P.*, vol. V, p. 452 ff.

[8] Letter to Luigi Guicciardini, 29 November, in *Lett. fam.*, p. 190 ff.; *Lett. L.*, p. 24 ff. Both editions have the incorrect date, 20 November. The autograph original is preserved in A.S.F., *Carte Strozziane*, ser. I, 137, f. 215.

[9] Letter to Luigi Guicciardini, 8 December, in *Lett. fam.*, p. 193 ff., but incomplete; more complete in *Lett. L.*, p. 25 ff., and in *Opp. MC.*, p. 877 ff. The autograph original is preserved in A.S.F., *Carte Strozziane*, ser. i, 137, f. 216.

[10] 'As for composing something, I am thinking about it'; letter of 29 November to Luigi Guicciardini, cit. This letter is the first, among those which have come down to us, in which M. refers to Francesco Guicciardini: 'If you write to your messer Francesco, tell him to commend me to the gang'. Francesco was at that time in Florence. For the reason which had brought Luigi to Mantua, see above note 1. It might be thought that the 'frivolous tale', or one of them, was the *Capitolo dell' Ambizione*, which was dedicated to Luigi Guicciardini—all the more so because there is reference to events of the time in words that seem taken from the letters he wrote to the Ten during those days. On 8 December he wrote from Verona: '. . . they are having a St. Mark painted with a sword in his hand instead of a book'; and in the *capitolo* to Luigi Guicciardini: 'San Marco alle sue spese, e forse invano/Tardi conosce come li bisogna/Tener la spada e non il libro in mano' (St. Mark to his cost and perhaps in vain is learning late that he must hold a sword and not a book in his hand). But a reference to 'this affair which has happened in Siena' suggests that the poem must be assigned to the beginning of the year 1516.

[11] *Opp. MC.*, p. 811 ff. (on p. 798, a brief indication of the MS. sources). Villari was the first to attribute this fragment to 1509 when he observed that it ended with the

rebellion of Vicenza against the Emperor which happened whilst M. was in Mantua. This view was followed down to TOFFANIN, p. 381. I do not find Toffanin's idea very plausible that M. began to write in 1509 because it was the 10th anniversary of his employment in the Chancery; I find more plausible his explanation of M.'s reference to himself as 'lost in grief' as a general allusion to the ills of Italy common in the tradition of popular ballads; but I still find it difficult to imagine a Florentine, especially a Machiavelli, saying this of himself immediately after the defeat of the Venetians and the taking of Pisa! The hypothesis that he began to write it in 1514 and that the interruption of the account in 1509 is merely accidental, must be seriously considered for the reasons stated in the text.

[12] PITTI, *Vita di Ant. Giacomini Tebalducci*, cit., p. 107. According to NARDI, *Vita di Ant. Giacomini Tebalducci*, Florence, 1597, Giacomini would have been 56 in 1509; but this does not alter matters much.

[13] MACHIAVELLI, *Decennale secondo*, line 9; *Opp. MC.*, p. 811.

[14] Letter of 8 December to L. Guicciardini, cit.

[15] *Opp. P.*, vol. V, p. 453.

[16] Ibidem, p. 462.

[17] This date appears from the order concerning his salary, *Opp. P.*, vol. I, p. LXXIII.

[18] Letter from Buonaccorsi to M., 27 December, *Lett. fam.*, p. 196 ff.

[19] D. MARZI, *La cancelleria della Repubblica fiorentina*, cit., p. 304.

[20] The son of a father who was on the debtors' list could not even practice as a notary, and the chancellors and their assistants were by right notaries. The irony of the situation is that the rubric of the Statutes governing this exclusion is quoted by Tommasini himself, vol. I, p. 481 n. See supra, chap. I, n. 4.

[21] Buonaccorsi admits this himself in this same letter, cit., when he writes: 'Don't go and suppose that I am just imagining sinister things, as you usually say'.

[22] The letter from Francesco del Nero to M., Florence, 22 Nov. 1509, *Lett. fam.*, p. 190 ff., is entirely concerned with this suit. For the importance which M. gave to it, see his letter to Luigi Guicciardini of 20 November, cit., 'Today I have received your letter of the 25th which has displeased me more than if I had lost the suit. . . .'

[23] See the document quoted by Tommasini, vol. I, p. 476.

[24] The agreement dated 21 June 1508, was drawn up by ser Niccolò di ser Francesco Cardi. See the corollary published in *Opp. P.*, vol. I, p. LVIII.

[25] *Opp. P.*, vol. I, p. LXXV; vol. VI, p. 1.

[26] *Opp. P.*, vol. I, p. LXXV.

[27] The instructions of the Ten have not come down to us; those of Soderini are published in *Opp. P.*, vol. VI, p. 2 ff., where, however, the date given, 2 June, should be corrected to 20 June, which is the date in the credentials (p. 4) and in the nomination by the Ten (in *Opp. P.*, vol. I, p. LXXVI; see ibid. the financial provisions).

[28] Letter from cardinal Soderini to M., 28 June 1510, in *Lett. fam.*, p. 199.

[29] Letter from M. to the Ten, Lyons, 7 July, in *Opp. P.*, vol. VI, p. 8 ff.

[30] Letter from M. to the Ten, Blois, 18 July, in *Opp. P.*, vol. VI, p. 15 ff.

[31] Letter of 21 July, in *Opp. P.*, vol. VI, p. 19 ff.

[32] Letter, cit. This papal nuncio had already been praised to M. by cardinal Soderini in his letter, cit. sup.

[33] M. to the Ten, 3 August, *Opp. P.*, vol. VI, p. 42.   Cf. letter of cardinal Soderini, cit.

[34] M. to the Ten, 9 August, *Opp. P.*, vol. VI, p. 55 ff.

[35] Letter of 13 August, *Opp. P.*, vol. VI, p. 66 ff.

[36] Letter to the Ten, 18 August, *Opp. P.*, vol. VI, p. 69 ff.

[37] Letter to the Ten, 24 August, *Opp. P.*, vol. VI, p. 79 ff. For information on the *coqueluche*, see Tommasini, vol. I, p. 508 ff.

[38] Letter of 18 August, cit.

[39] Roberto Acciaiuoli wrote to him about this after taking up his post at the French court, in his letter of 7 Oct. 1510, *Lett. fam.*, p. 208 ff.

[40] Letter from Vettori to M., 3 Aug. 1510, in *Lett. fam.*, p. 200 ff. Other letters to M.: from Buonaccorsi, 22 August, ibid., p. 203; from Giuliano della Valle, 25 August, ibid., p. 204 ff.

[41] B.N.F., *Necrologia Cirri*, vol. XI, p. 434.

[42] Letter from Buonaccorsi to M., 29 August, *Lett. fam.*, p. 206.

[43] Letter from M. to the Ten, 27 August, *Opp. P.*, vol. VI, p. 85 ff.

[44] Letter of 30–31 August to the Ten, *Opp. P.*, vol. VI, p. 100 ff.

[45] Letter from Antonio della Valle to M., 30 August, *Opp. P.*, vol. VI, p. 97 ff.

[46] Letter from the Ten to M., 2 September, *Opp. P.*, vol. VI, p. 107 ff.

[47] VILLARI, vol. I[4], p. 457 ff. RUSSO, p. 256 (cf. p. 119) writes: 'The esteem of M. is for bold and combative popes, for Alexander VI and Julius II.' I know what he means to say, but taking these words literally and reflecting on what the Florentine Secretary wrote about these two popes in his works, one could hardly agree that he held them in esteem.

[48] GUICCIARDINI, *Storia d'Italia*, ed. cit., vol. I, p. 54.

[49] Letter from M. to the Ten, 2 September, *Opp. P.*, vol. VI, p. 104 ff.

[50] See the financial provisions, cit. sup. Soon after this third French legation he wrote his *Ritratti delle cose della Francia* (*Opp. MC.*, p. 731 ff.), on which see TOMMASINI, vol. I, p. 509 ff.; GERBER, I, 81; V. OSIMO, *Per . . . la cronologia dei Ritratti delle cose della Francia,* in *G.S.L.I.*, vol. LII (1908), p. 270 ff.

CHAPTER 12

[1] The resolution of the Ten is published in *Opp. P.*, vol. I, p. LXXVII.

[2] See the relative financial provisions in *Opp. P.*, vol. I, p. LXXVII; the letters patent for Siena, ibidem, vol. VI, p. 124 ff. Cf. TOMMASINI, vol. I, p. 526 n.

[3] The resolutions of the Ten, letters patent and financial provisions from which the dates of these missions are taken, are published in *Opp. P.*, vol. I, p. LXXVII ff. For the mission to Pisa with Giuliano da San Gallo, cf. TOMMASINI, vol. I, p. 526 ff.

[4] GUICCIARDINI, *Storie fiorentine*, ed. cit., p. 323.

[5] *Vite degli uomini illustri della casa Strozzi* (composed by Lorenzo Strozzi), Florence, tip. Landi, 1892, p. 96. Lorenzo Strozzi was the brother of Filippo, and this adds authority to his account. All the Florentine historians write fully on this incident, but no one other than Strozzi reports the rumour that the accusation was drafted by M. Tommasini (I, 528) states that, whether it was true or not, this rumour caused the

nobles to hate the Secretary. I should hardly think so, if Filippo Strozzi remained his friend until the end.

[6] All the documents, financial provisions, instructions, etc., connected with this mission are in *Opp. P.*, vol. I, p. LXXIX; vol. VI, p. 125 ff. G. ROSSI, *Il diritto di porto della città di Monaco e N.M.*, in *A.S.I.*, ser. 5, vol. IV (1889), p. 190 ff., published, together with other useful information, the treaty signed in Monaco on 27 May 1511, 'domino Nicolao de Magiavellis, ambasiatore dicte communitatis (Florentie) pro eadem presente et stipulante'. Cf. N. ORENGO, *Monaco, il diritto di porto e la missione del M.*, in *Rivista d'Italia*, XXIX (1926), pt. II, p. 341 ff.

[7] VILLARI, vol. I[4], p. 597.

[8] The resolution of the Ten is in *Opp. P.*, vol. I, p. LXXIX ff.

[9] Resolution and financial provisions connected with this legation are in *Opp. P.*, vol. I, p. LXXX; his instructions, also his credentials, ibid., vol. VI, pp. 132–38

[10] Letter from M. to the Ten, Borgo San Donnino, 12 September, in *Opp. P.*, vol. VI., p. 140 ff. For the Pisan Council and the part played in it by M. both on missions and through the Chancery, see the documents collected by A. RENAUDET, *Le concile gallican de Pise-Milan: documents florentins* (1510–12), ('Bibliothèque de l'Institut français de Florence'), Paris, Champion, 1922.

[11] Letter from M. to the Ten, Milan, 15 September, in *Opp. P.*, vol. VI, p. 155 ff.

[12] Letter from Roberto Acciaiuoli to the Ten, Blois, 24 September, in *Opp. P.*, vol. VI, p. 164.

[13] From Blois, 24 September, in *Opp. P.*, vol. VI, p. 169.

[14] Letter from the Ten to M., [4 October], in *Opp. P.*, vol. VI, p. 175; the editor incorrectly gives it as addressed to Acciaiuoli.

[15] The credentials, dated 2 November, are published with other documents in *Opp. P.*, vol. VI, p. 176 ff.; the financial provisions for this mission, ibidem, vol. I., p. LXXXI ff.

[16] Letter from the Ten to M., in *Opp. P.*, vol. VI., p. 177.

[17] Letter from M. to the Ten, Pisa, 6 November, in *Opp. P.*, vol. VI, p. 177 ff. ibidem, in note, the report of the commissioners Rosso Ridolfi and Antonio Portinari on the session of the concilium; for further information they referred to the wisdom of M., more experienced in these matters than themselves.

[18] MACHIAVELLI, *Discorsi*, I, 56. Landucci, Cambi and others speak of this thunderbolt. Guicciardini, *Storia d'Italia*, ed. cit., vol. II, p. 23 ff., writes that the thunderbolt which fell on the Palazzo did not strike anything but a large silver urn in the Gonfalonier's room, and that another which fell on the Porta a Prato smashed the golden lilies of France.

[19] Drawn up by Francesco Ottaviani, 22 Nov. 1511; published several times, originally in *Lettere di N.M.* etc., Cosmopoli, 1769, p. 427 ff. In Soderini's will there was a bequest of 15 florins to M.; cf. Tommasini, vol. I, p. 568.

[20] GUICCIARDINI, *Storia d'Italia*, ed. cit., vol. II, p. 402.

[21] LANDUCCI, *Diario*, cit., p. 313.

[22] *Opp. P.*, vol. VI, p. 352 ff. Some of the letters written by M. for the office, in *Scritti inediti*, cit., pp. 377–93.

[23] Letter from M. to the Ten, Poggibonsi, 5 June, in *Opp. P.*, vol. IV, p. 193 ff. Ibid., in note, an extract from the *Historiae senenses* (in MS.) of Tizio, in which there is reference to this mission of M.

²⁴ The documents relative to these various military missions of M. are in *Opp. P.*, vol. VI, pp. 188–93, 194.

²⁵ The documents for this mission are in *Opp. P.*, vol. I, p. LXXXII; vol. VI, pp. 195–201.

²⁶ *Opp. P.*, vol. VI, pp. 201–203.

²⁷ Letters sent, replies, and other documents, in *Opp. P.*, vol. VI, pp. 204–10.

²⁸ *Lett. fam.*, p. 212.

²⁹ Letter 'a una Madonna' [later than 16 Sept. 1511], in *Lett. fam.*, pp. 212–19. This letter, of which we have a draft in M.'s hand, was there published by Alvisi as addressed to Alfonsina Orsini de' Medici. Others have conjectured that it was addressed to Contessina Medici Ridolfi or to Clarice Strozzi, but certain expressions in the text indicate that it was certainly not written to a Medici or to a Florentine lady. It could not have been Caterina Sforza, as some have suggested, as she was already dead at that time.

³⁰ Machiavelli himself, in the letter 'a una Madonna', cit., wrote, doubtless with a heavy heart, of the 'cowardice seen in our soldiers at Prato'; and all the historians attribute the weak defence of the town to Machiavelli's battalions, starting from Guicciardini (*Storia d'Italia*, ed. cit., vol. III, pp. 17–19, 21), who was very much against the militia. But, to be accurate, only 1000 of the 3000 (some put it at 4000) defenders of Prato were from those battalions; see CAMBI, *Istorie*, cit., p. 323.

³¹ Letter 'a una Madonna', cit.

³² F. VETTORI, *Sommario della storia d'Italia dal 1511 al 1527*, in *A.S.I.*, ser. 1. vol. VI (1848), p. 292.

³³ PITTI, *Istorie fiorentine*, cit., p. 103.

³⁴ Op. cit., p. 104 ff.; NARDI, *Istorie di Firenze*, Florence, Le Monnier, 1858, vol. II, p. 2 ff.

³⁵ VETTORI, op. cit., p. 293.

³⁶ Letter 'a una Madonna', cit. In the histories, chronicles and documents of the period we find no record of any task assigned to M. during the office of Ridolfi as Gonfalonier. There are no letters of his after August in the registers of the Signoria and the Ten. Nardi, however, refers to a small commission entrusted to Buonaccorsi at this time.

³⁷ Letter 'a una Madonna', cit.

³⁸ *Opp. P.*, vol VI, p. 379; *Opp. MC.*, p. 791 ff. This work is probably later than 1 November, which is the date on which the anger of Julius II against the Medici became known in Florence. Before that it would have been unthinkable that 'the old order might arise again with Piero Soderini'.

³⁹ *Opp. U.*, p. 1146. The autograph draft of these remarks addressed to Cardinal de' Medici, which was lost sight of by biographers and editors of Machiavelli, is preserved (without title), in A.S.F., *Carte Strozziane*, 2nd series, 86, f. 35.

⁴⁰ The resolution is published in *Opp. P.*, vol. I, p. LXXXIII ff.

CHAPTER 13

¹ These words are written in M.'s hand on the autograph copy of the discourse *Dello ordinare lo stato di Firenze alle armi* (B.N.F., *Carte Machiavelli*, I, 78), quoted

above (ch. 9, n. 32), in a note made when he was going over his papers during the time of his misfortune.

² The decision of the Signoria is published in *Opp. P.*, vol. I, p. LXXXIV. The caution, as is clear from this document, was 1000 florins, not 1000 lire as stated by Villari, vol. I⁴, p. 641, and on his authority repeated by Toffanin, op. cit., p. 382.

³ The decision is in *Opp. P.*, vol. I, p. LXXXIV.

⁴ The relevant decisions in *Opp. P.*, vol. I, p. LXXXIV ff.

⁵ 'Fantasies written to Soderini in Raugia' is what M. probably wrote on the draft, of which we now possess only the Ricci apograph. The best edition and the only complete one is that given in *Opp. MC.*, p. 878 ff. Villari, after having completely overlooked this most important letter in the course of his biographical account, deals with it very briefly in a footnote (III¹, p. 122; II⁴, p. 346), saying that it is written 'in a kind of almost unintelligible jargon'. Tommasini (I, 631 ff., II, 66 ff.) seems at first to have doubted its authenticity, and devotes an inadequate and erroneous commentary to it. Soderini's letter to M. has not come down to us.

⁶ That is, it gave M. occasion to write to Soderini, although he had advised him in his letter not to do so.

⁷ *Opp. MC.* puts a comma after *veggendo* in the Italian text, which in my opinion gives it an unintentional irony.

⁸ NARDI, *Istorie di Firenze*, ed. cit., vol. II, p. 14.

⁹ GUICCIARDINI, *Storia d'Italia*, ed. cit., vol. III, p. 39.

¹⁰ NARDI, op. cit., vol. II, p. 19 ff.

¹¹ See the famous *Recitazione del caso di Pietro Paolo Boscoli*, written by Luca della Robbia, in *A.S.I.*, ser. i, vol. I (1842), pp. 283–309.

¹² An extract from this proclamation was published by VILLARI, vol. I⁴, p. 648.

¹³ Of his friendship with Valori we have spoken fully in chaps. VI and VIII. M. dedicated to Folchi his poem *Dell 'Ingratitudine*, in *Opp. MC.*, p. 841 ff.

¹⁴ M. seems to be alluding to this sort of thing, and not to anything else, in his letter to Vettori written on 13 March after his release from prison, in *Lett. fam.*, p. 224: 'I hope not to incur such misfortune again, for in future I shall be more cautious. . .' And in fact, as he was acknowledged to have had no part in the plot, it is difficult to see how he could have been incautious except in speaking ill of the Medici.

¹⁵ Letter from Francesco Vettori to M., 15 March 1513, in *Lett. fam.*, p. 225.

¹⁶ *Recitazione*, cit. The hour of the execution was shortly after 10 according to the old Florentine way of reckoning, which corresponded at that time to about half past three in the morning. The avemaria at dawn was at about a quarter to five, so that M.'s indication 'near dawn' is correct.

¹⁷ I have not attempted, and there was no need here, to establish a critical text; I have given a composite one based on Vatican MS. 5225 (used by VILLARI, III², 429; cf. TOMMASINI, II, 967 ff.) with some corrections from the later copy in B.N.F., *Carte Machiavelli*, VI, 85, in. 5 (*Opp. MC.*, p. 871 ff.). I do not consider it my duty to spend words on exculpating M. (even if he needed exculpating, it is outside my scope) for the closing lines of this sonnet (another reading of line 8 is 'in mal'ora') which was judged to be cynical and wicked, and made certain historians of the moralizing and tyrannicidal Risorgimento raise their hands in horror. Villari at first wished to place its authenticity in doubt, and was unwillingly persuaded to accept it (I⁴, 650–654) only

by the evidence of a person who had seen the autograph and by the observations of Tommasini: but he did not agree that M. sent it with other sonnets to Giuliano. According to Villari, 'he wrote them down in a moment of bad humour . . . and then forgot them, not thinking that several centuries later they would be found and he would be called upon to explain words . . .' I do not believe it. Certainly those closing lines will seem odious to someone who has just finished reading the account of Boscoli's last moments; but one must put oneself in the place of M., who, innocent and unaware of the plot, was in prison, had been tortured and was in danger of losing his life on a charge of attempted assassination—a grave crime in his own eyes!—on account of the wild ideas of those two rash conspirators. E. PISTELLI (*Eroi, Uomini e Ragazzi*, Florence, Sansoni, 1927, p. 157) makes game, respectfully, of Villari for his shocked embarrassment before the cynicism of M., 'who was capable of laughing while the blond head of Pier Paolo Boscoli fell beneath the axe' (though it is less poetic, I fear it was not blond, but whitish, with red eyes), and speaks of Villari as at first 'so mortified that he seems to be wishing to beg your pardon for having written three volumes on a scoundrel of this ilk. Later he picks up courage and finds excuses', even to the point of saying that the crudest words were 'perhaps necessitated more than anything else by the dictates of rhyme'.

[18] *Opp. MC.*, p. 871.

[19] Letter from M. to Vettori, 18 March 1512/13, in *Lett. fam.*, p. 226 ff., and more fully in *Opp. MC.*, p. 888 ff. In the *Ricordi* of Cerretani cited by TOMMASINI, vol. II, p. 468 n., it says that 'after Niccolò Machiavelli had been tortured and kept up a few days, they confined him for life in the Stinche'. If this were true, one would readily understand M.'s gratitude to Giuliano for his release; but if he were recognized along with others as being completely innocent, he did not do him much of a favour. Cerretani's statement is, however, contradicted by Giuliano himself in a letter to Bibbiena on 7 March 1513, published by G. L. MONCALLERO, *Il Cardinale Bernardo Dovizi da Bibbiena*, Florence, Olschki, 1953, p. 333, in which after referring to Valori and Folchi who were to be imprisoned in the Tower of Volterra, he names some others 'confined for several years to the country district'; as M.'s name does not figure among these, he must be considered to have been among 'the others who were not guilty . . . who were released on payment of a caution'. Besides, M. always protested his innocence: he wrote, for instance, to his nephew Vernaccia on 26 June 1513 (*Lett. fam.*, p. 245 ff.): 'My job was taken from me and I almost lost my life, which God and my innocence have preserved.'

[20] LANDUCCI, *Diario*, cit., p. 337.

[21] *Opp. MC.*, p. 855 ff: the edition is based on MS. Riccardiano 2731, from which the original Torrentini edition, edited by il Lasca, *Tutti i trionfi . . .* , Florence, 1559, was also taken, though with far less care. The preconception which would see all carnival songs of this type as belonging to the age of Lorenzo de' Medici, has led to the general belief that all those written by M. belong to his early years. Tommasini, however, distinguishing more judiciously, attributed this *Canto degli Spiriti beati* to 1524 on the supposition that the 'new shepherd' must be Clement VII. But we know that for this new pontiff's election, unlike that of Leo X, 'festivities were held with little gaiety', and triumphal waggons were not made out of season; besides, the carnival of 1525 was too far off the time of Clement's election. The reason which most

persuades me to attribute this poem to the festivities after the election of Leo is the allusion to peace, taken together with the reference in Landucci's *Diario*, cit. sup.; and also the evident desire on M.'s part to obtain the pardon and the confidence of the Medici makes his participation in the 'universal rejoicing of the city' in this way very likely.

²² Letter, cit. sup. note 14.

²³ Letter from Vettori to M., 15 March, cit. sup., note 15.

²⁴ Letter, cit sup., note 19.

²⁵ *Opp. MC.*, p. 871 ff. Villari (cf. note 17 above) writes: 'No one will believe that Machiavelli really sent a gift of thrushes to Giuliano de' Medici'. I, for one, believe he did; and anyone who does not, shows his ignorance of Florentine customs at that time.

²⁶ Some indication that he did is possibly to be seen in M.'s insistence in sending him sonnets and in his proposal to dedicate the *Prince* to him. Cf. note 19 above.

²⁷ This letter from Vettori, which is lacking in *Lett. fam.*, was published by Tommasini, vol. II, p. 969 ff. M.'s reply (9 April 1513, in *Lett. fam.*, p. 228 ff.; *Opp. MC.*, p. 881 ff.) begins: '*Magnifice domine orator, Et io che del color mi fui accorto/Dissi: "Come verrò se tu paventi/che suoli al mio dubbiare esser conforto?"*' [DANTE, *Inferno*, IV, 17–19]. On the correspondence with Vettori, I would refer for purely bibliographical reasons (which is contrary to my habits and intentions) to the small volume by A. MORETTI, *Corrispondenza di N.M. con F. V. dal 1513 al 1515*, Florence, Le Monnier, 1948, although I have found nothing in it of any value for my purposes.

²⁸ Letter of 9 April, cit. in note 27.

²⁹ Ibidem.

³⁰ Letter from M. to Vettori, 16 April, in *Lett. fam.*, p. 232 ff., and more complete in *Opp. MC.*, p. 882 ff. In the quotation from Petrarch's sonnet 'Cesare poi che il traditor d'Egitto', made as usual from memory, M. has 'Via da *sfogare* il mio *acerbo* pianto'.

³¹ Letters of 9 and 16 April, cit. sup.

³² Letter from Vettori to M., 19 April, in *Lett. fam.*, p. 230 ff.

³³ Letter of 16 April, cit.

³⁴ Letter of 19 April, cit.

³⁵ Letter from Vettori to M., 21 April, in *Lett. fam.*, p. 235 ff.

³⁶ A decision of the Signoria, published in *Opp. P.*, vol. I, p. LXXXV, gives M. permission to enter the Palazzo *pro nonnullis Communi Florentie et sibi necessariis* from 21 March to 21 April inclusive. He also had to return there in July, when in the end it was recognized that an error of 79 florins had been made against him (*Opp. P.*, vol. I, p. 83).

³⁷ Letter of 29 April 1513, published in *Lett. fam.*, p. 255 ff., without date and lacking the end of the letter, which was published by Tommasini, vol. II, p. 86 n. The letter bears the indication 'Florence' as the place from where it was written; M. must have gone there on a visit, as in the text he says twice that he had 'gone into the country'. This occurred certainly after his letter of 16 April, in which he spoke at length of life in the city. It was perhaps after his friend's discouraging reply of the 19th, which reached Florence on the 22nd or the 23rd, that he resigned himself to the situation and decided to retire into the country.

[38] Letter of 9 April, cit.

[39] Letter from Vettori to M., 27 June 1513, in *Lett. fam.*, p. 246 ff. This letter was provoked by another sent by M. on 20 June, in *Lett. fam.*, p. 241 ff.

[40] Letter from M. to Vettori of 29 April, cit., in the part omitted in *Lett. fam.*, and published by Tommasini, loc. cit.

CHAPTER 14

[1] E. REPETTI, *Dizionario geografico fisico storico della Toscana*, Florence, 1841, vol. IV, p. 98 ff. There is no need here to go into the strange and idle discussions that have taken place about the identity of M.'s villa. The property registers for the year 1498, in which the possessions of Bernardo Machiavelli are described in detail, were published in *Opp. P.*, vol. I, p. LV ff., together with an addition of 1511 in which the entry is cancelled and put under the name of his son Niccolò. It should be noted that, although the lands are the same, in the will made by Niccolò on 27 Nov. 1522 there figure two farms, Montepugliano and Fontalle, which do not appear in the register for 1498. One may suppose that these lands were turned into farms at some period by Niccolò. The property of the Albergaccio with its lands and appurtenances came by the female line to the Ricci family, and from them to the Serristori. To Senator Umberto Serristori we owe the fact that the house of the Florentine Secretary, which had fallen into sad neglect, has been properly restored and made fit to house books and objects of interest to students of Machiavelli. Her father's work is at present being continued with loving care by Contessa Sofia Serristori, whom I should like to thank for the great kindness she has shown me.

[2] Letter from M. to Vettori, 20 June 1513, in *Lett. fam.*, p. 241ff. This asks for an answer to his letter of 29 April, and was sent from Florence where M. had gone on a visit. Vettori replied on 27 June (*Lett. fam.*, p. 246 ff.).

[3] Letter from Vettori to M., 12 July, in *Lett. fam.*, p. 250 ff. M.'s reply to this letter has been lost, but its contents can partly be deduced from another letter from Vettori of 5 August, in *Lett. fam.*, p. 267 ff.

[4] Letter from M. to Vettori, 10 August, replying to Vettori's of the 5th quoted in note 3, and published in *Lett. fam.*, p. 271 ff.

[5] Letter from Vettori to M., 20 August 1513, in *Lett. fam.*, p. 280 ff.

[6] Letter from M. to Vettori, 26 August 1513, in *Lett. fam.*, p. 292 ff. The day before, he had sent another letter recommending Donato del Corno, who was so anxious to have a seat among the Signori for two months that he was willing to pay 100 ducats for it. In the letter of 26 August there is this notable passage: 'We are governed by such princes, who have the following qualities either from nature or from fortune: We have a wise Pope, who is therefore grave and full of respect; an instable and variable Emperor; a proud and fearful King of France; a mean and miserly King of Spain; a King of England rich, fierce and avid for glory; the Swiss bestial, victorious and insolent; and we Italians, poor, ambitious, cowardly. I do not know the other kings. So, weighing these qualities with the present state of things, I believe in the Friar who said *Pax, pax et non erit pax*.'

[7] *Discorsi sopra la prima Deca di Tito Livio*, Introduction to bk. I. In my quotation

I have partly followed the reading of the Barberini MS. The first autograph draft has *trita* in place of *pesta* (una via non ancora da alcuno pesta). The whole of the first line of the Introduction is missing in the *editio princeps* published by Blado.

[8] *Discorsi*, Rome, Blado, 1531, f. 1ᵛ; *Opp. MC.*, p. 56. It should be noted that the famous principle that 'the world has always been inhabited by men who have always had the same passions' is already to be found in the discourse *Del modo di trattare . . .*, written in 1503. See ch. 5 of this book.

[9] L. OLSCHKI, *Machiavelli, the Scientist*, Berkeley, Cal., Gillick Press, 1945. See the end of ch. 5 of this book.

[10] See ch. I. The fact that M. had begun and made substantial progress with the *Discourses* before writing the *Prince* is borne out by the well-known phrase: 'I will not speak of republics because I dealt with them at length on another occasion' (*Prince*, ch. II). On the other hand, the references to the *Prince* in the *Discourses* begin after the beginning of bk. II. Some doubt would remain as to whether the *Discourses* were begun before 1513, but this seems improbable for various reasons, and also for the fact that among the allusions to events which occurred during or shortly before the composition of the work, there are none which refer to events before 1513. Almost at the same time as this book of mine was being written and printed in the first Italian edition there appeared the notable contribution by F. GILBERT, *The composition and structure of Machiavelli's 'Discorsi'*, in *Journal of the History of Ideas*, vol. XIV (1953), pp. 135–56. In this article a thesis is put forward based largely on structural arguments but much influenced by the well-known testimony of Nerli, to which it would be wrong in my view to attach importance and belief in every detail (see the explanation I give of it in ch. 16, note 17, which seems to me to be reasonable). Gilbert's thesis is that the work on republics referred to by M. in the *Prince* is a different work from the *Discourses*, and was assimilated by M. into the *Discourses* between 1516 and 1517. I must confess that this hypothesis also occurred to me when I first considered the question, but I quickly rejected it for reasons which space forbids me to explain here, and which seem to me obvious. I would simply say that while M. in the *Discourses* refers to the *Prince* as 'the treatise on the Prince' or 'the treatise on principalities', he does not say in the *Prince* that he has written a treatise on republics but merely that he has 'spoken of them at length'; and this description suits the *Discourses*, which are not a treatise. He could hardly have referred in that way to a 'treatise' still in a somewhat embryonic state. Furthermore, looking at the probable genetic process, one can understand a compact treatise like the *Prince* emerging from a volume of commentaries like the *Discourses*, but not the hypothetical compact treatise on republics (for which we have no shred of evidence let alone a text) dissolving into a volume of commentaries. This seems to me an important consideration which has not been sufficiently taken account of by those who have written on the subject since this book was published. The most important are H. BARON, *The 'Principe' and the puzzle of the date of the 'Discorsi'*, in *Bibliothèque d'Humanisme et Renaissance*, XVIII (1956), pp. 405–28, and G. SASSO, *Intorno alla composizione dei 'Discorsi' di N.M.*, in *G.S.L.I.*, CXXXIV (1957), pp. 482–534, and CXXXV (1958), pp. 215–59. The latter, both in these articles and in his volume *Niccolò Machiavelli* quoted in the preface to the present English edition, supports all the arguments which I have myself advanced. The indefatigable H. BARON has recently taken up again

this problem of the composition of the *Discourses* and the *Prince* in his art. *Machiavelli: the republican citizen and the author of the 'Prince'*, in *English Historical Review*, April 1961, pp. 217–253; his ingenious argument does not give us the necessary proofs, but simply adds fresh and hardly necessary conjectures. The onus of proof lies firmly with the proposer.

[11] *Discourses*, Introduction to bk. I (these words are also missing in Blado's edition; see note 7 above); *Opp. MC.*, p. 56.

[12] *Discourses*, bk. I, ch. XVII; ed. Blado, f. 21; *Opp. MC.*, p. 85 ff.; TOFFANIN, p. 397.

[13] *Discourses*, bk. I, ch. XVIII; *Opp. MC.*, p. 88. A little further on, considering 'the difficulty or impossibility of maintaining a republic or instituting a new one in cities that are corrupt', he concludes that 'it would be necessary to bring it more towards a tyranny than a popular state'. For the genesis of the *Prince*, and especially for the role to be assigned to ch. XVII, and to the following ch. XVIII which continues the argument, as the point of departure of this famous book, cf. G. SASSO, op. cit., pp. 213–20.

[14] *Prince*, ch. XVIII; *Opp. MC.*, p. 34.

[15] *Prince*, ch. XXVI; *Opp. MC.*, p. 51, on which my quotation is based.

[16] TOFFANIN, p. 386.

[17] This letter was published in *Lett. fam.*, p. 300 ff., with serious lacunae, and in complete form by VILLARI, vol. II², p. 566 ff. The original autograph is in B.N.F., *Carte Machiavelli*, V, 26.

[18] The autograph of this famous letter is unfortunately not known. In Barberini MS. LVIII, 47, it is dated 10 October; but this is obviously an error, as is shown by the precise references to it in M.'s letter of 19 December and Vettori's of 24 December (see notes 21, 22). The mistakes must be due to a correction made by the copyist on the basis of a corrupt reading in the text, which I have emended for the first time (see following note). The Ricci copy has the correct date: 10 December.

[19] The MSS. and all the editions, including the critical text given in *Opp. MC.*, p. 884 ff., read 'throughout September', but this is obviously an error (which has so far gone unnoticed), because the migration of thrushes begins in October, it does not end in September, and because M. could not write on 10 December that he had 'up to now been snaring thrushes', if he had only done it, as the texts say, 'throughout September'. My correction, therefore, is certainly right.

[20] This is one of Tommasini's usual wild theories (vol. II, p. 102 ff.; cf. *Rendiconti della R. Accademia dei Lincei*, vol. IV, 1900, p. 322), which is rightly rejected with historical arguments by F. CHABOD, *Sulla composizione de 'il Principe 'di N.M.*, in *Archivum Romanicum*, vol. IX (1927), p. 330 ff., and also by M. Casella (cf. *Opp. MC.*, pp. LXVII, 2; and especially the critical note to his ed. of the *Prince* and other works of M., Rome-Milan, 1930). Casella also contradicts Meinecke's supposition (1923) that the work went through various phases of augmentation at different times. The first edition of the *Prince* is that published in Rome by Blado, 1532; for this and the Giunta edition, see GERBER, II, 23–30.

[21] Letter from M. to Vettori, 19 December, in *Lett. fam.*, p. 311; see above note 18. In this letter he gives an account of the sermon by Fra Francesco da Montepulciano, and jokes about it, concluding: 'These things so frightened me yesterday

that I was supposed to go and see Riccia this morning and I didn't go; but if I had been going to see Riccio, I am not sure that I would have been put off' (see ch. I, n. 32).

²² This letter from Vettori to M., 24 December 1513, was published with lacunae in *Lett. fam.*, p. 315 ff., and in complete form by VILLARI, vol. II², p. 570 ff.

²³ See the excellent study, based almost exclusively on the *Prince*, by F. CHIAPPELLI, *Studi sul linguaggio del M.*, Florence, Le Monnier, 1952.

²⁴ Letter from M. to Vettori, 5 Jan. 1513/14, published in *Lett. fam.*, p. 320 ff., with some lacunae, and almost complete in *Opp. MC.*, p. 888 ff.; *Lett. L.*, p. 97 ff.

²⁵ Letter from Vettori to M., 18 Jan. 1513/14; this too has lacunae in *Lett. fam.*, p. 323 ff., but is complete in VILLARI, vol II², p. 573.

²⁶ Letter of 18 January, cit.

²⁷ Letter of 4 Feb. 1513/14, published in *Lett. fam.*, p. 329, with the usual omissions on moral grounds; complete in *Opp. MC.*, p. 889 ff. It begins: 'I came back yesterday from the country . . .' The letter is a reply to Vettori's of 18 January.

CHAPTER 15

¹ Letter from M. to Vettori, 4 Feb. 1513/14, in *Lett. fam.*, p. 329 ff.

² Letter of 23 Nov., 1513, in *Lett. fam.*, p. 300. In the passage quoted by me, corrected on the autograph, *Lett. fam.* has *amoreggiare* (to make love) instead of *a motteggiare* (to joke).

³ Letter of 10 Dec. 1513, cit. in ch. XIV, note 18.

⁴ Letter of 24 Dec. 1513, cit. in Ch. XIV, note 22: 'If you go to see Cardinal Soderini on some occasion, no one will mind. Piero has his mind made up, and I do not think he would care to be visited especially by you, and if you did not call on him, I do not believe you could be accused of ingratitude; for I have made some enquiries, and I do not find that he or his people have done you so much favour that you need to feel any special obligation to them. You did not get your job from them, you began employment three years before he became gonfalonier, and in the affairs in which he employed you, you served him faithfully, and you did not receive any extraordinary reward for it.'

⁵ Letter from M. to Vettori, 5 Jan. 1513/14, cit. in ch. XIV, note 24. This aphorism which must have been familiar to M. was also inserted by him in his *Life of Castruccio*; cf. *Opp. MC.*, p. 672. See F. P. LUISO, *I detti memorabili attribuiti a Castruccio Castracani da N.M.*, in *C. C. degli Antelminelli: Miscellanea di Studi storici e letterari*, Florence, 1934, pp. 232 ff., 257.

⁶ Letter of 4 February, cit.

⁷ Letter from M. to Vettori, 25 February, published with lacunae in *Lett. fam.*, p. 337 ff.; complete in *Opp. MC.*, p. 891 ff.; omitted out of modesty from *Lett. L.*

⁸ Letter from M. to Vettori, 16 April 1514, in *Lett. fam.*, p. 341 ff.

⁹ *Opp. U.*, p. 1146.

¹⁰ Letter from M. to Vettori, 10 June, in *Lett. fam.*, p. 355 ff.; *Opp. MC.*, p. 822 ff.; 'I have not come to see you, because I was held back for the reasons which you now make clear to me, and which I had already imagined for myself.'

[11] Both M.'s request for an answer and Vettori's reply have been lost. They must have been written between 16 May and 10 June, the date of M.'s letter which refers to this correspondence.

[12] Letter of 10 June, cit.: 'I received two of your letters in the country where I am staying with my family . . .' I have many doubts about the reply to these letters, which M. said he had forgotten in the country when he came into Florence whence he intended to despatch it. Sant 'Andrea was on the road to Rome and very near the post where the horses were changed; so that M. had no need to wait until he went to Florence to send off letters. But I am most doubtful because, after he had promised in his letter of 10 June to send that reply, he never did, as is evident from Vettori's letter of 27 July (*Lett. fam.*, p. 357). So, he either never wrote that reply, or it was so expressive of his strong feelings that he decided not to send it; which amounts to the same thing.

[13] Letter from Vettori to M., 27 July, cit.; VILLARI, vol. II², p. 579; *Opp. MC.*, p. 892 ff.

[14] Letter from M. to Vettori, 3 Aug. 1514, in *Lett. fam.*, p. 360 ff.; *Opp MC.*, p. 893 ff.

[15] Several months before, in his letter of 18 Jan. 1514, cit., Vettori had written: 'I have seen you in love sometimes and realized how strong your passions were'.

[16] This sonnet was sent by M. to his friend with his letter of 31 Jan. 1515 (*Lett. fam.*, p. 391 ff.; more fully and correctly published in *Opp. MC.*, 894 ff.).

[17] See above, ch. XIV, note 20.

[18] In fact, Vettori's letter to M. on 15 December, cit. infra, begins: 'After a long silence, I have received three letters from you in the past two days. . . .'

[19] Letter from Vettori to M., 3 Dec. 1514, in *Lett. fam.*, p. 361 ff.; VILLARI, vol. II², p. 579 ff.

[20] Letter from M. to Vettori *ex Percussina* 4 Dec. 1514, in *Lett. fam.*, p. 364.

[21] Letter from M. to Vettori, 10 Dec. 1514. In *Lett. fam.*, p. 367 ff., this letter, which I shall call *A*, is published with the date 20 December, which is the date on the copy (not 'draft' as some have said) in B.N.F., *Carte Machiavelli*, VI, 57², and on other copies. But there must certainly have been a mistake at the outset, for Vettori wrote on the 15th to say that he had already received this letter. The date of this letter of Vettori's cannot be altered, because it is confirmed by another letter of M.'s written on 20 December (*Lett. Fam.*, p. 385), which I shall call *C*. Besides, it is unlikely that M., who was so anxious to gain the Pope's favour, would have waited until the 20th to answer his questions; and it is evident that *C* was not written on the same day as *A*, but after an interval of time. There is also a third letter from M. published with the date 20 December (*Lett. fam.*, p. 381), which I shall call *B*, which is an appendix to the letter of 10 December (*A*), and it is quite clear from the text that it could not have been written on the same day, but only after further reflection. In his letter of 15 December Vettori says that he has received three letters from M. in two days; and these were the one in Latin recommending Tafani, one in reply to the Pope's questions (*A*), and finally the one, now lost, in which M. asked for the blue woollen material. The 'enclosed' mentioned in *C*, is *B*.

[22] Letter from Vettori to M., 15 Dec. 1514, in *Lett. fam.*, p. 365 ff.; VILLARI, vol. II² p. 581.

²³ Cf. above, note 21 (letter *B*).

²⁴ Cf. above, note 21 (letter *C*).

²⁵ Letter from Vettori to M., 30 Dec. 1514, in *Lett. fam.*, p. 387 ff.; VILLARI, vol. II², p. 583.

²⁶ Letter from Vettori to M., 15 December, cit.

²⁷ The papal decision was communicated to Giuliano on 28 Feb. 1515; cf. C. GUASTI, *I Manoscritti Torrigiani . . .*, Florence, 1878, p. 67 ff. But M. knew about it and wrote of it to Vettori on 31 January.

²⁸ Letter from M. to Vettori, 31 Jan. 1514/15, published in *Lett. fam.*, p. 391 ff., with a large lacuna; complete in *Opp. MC.*, p. 894 ff.

²⁹ C. GUASTI, op. cit., p. 67.

³⁰ It should be noted, however, that Vettori came back to Florence on 15 May 1515 (see the documents published by Reumont in his ed. of F. VETTORI, *Sommario della storia d'Italia dal 1511 al 1527*, cit., p. 280); this removed the need for correspondence between M. and Vettori.

³¹ The letters from M. to Vernaccia which precede the date at which we have arrived in our account, are: 26 June 1513, in *Lett. fam.*, p. 245 ff. ('I was deprived of my office and in danger of losing my life, which God and my innocence have preserved . . .'); 4 August 1513, ibidem, p. 266 ('. . . Marietta gave birth to a daughter, who died after three days . . . I am well in body, but ill in every other respect . . .'); 20 April 1514, ibidem, p. 345 ff.

³² *Lett. fam.*, p. 395; *Opp. MC.*, p. 896.

³³ *Lett. fam.*, p. 396; *Opp. MC.*, p. 896.

³⁴ Letter from M. to Vettori, 20 Dec. 1514 (it is the letter referred to in note 21 as letter *C*).

³⁵ G. PIERRACCINI, *La stirpe de' Medici di Cafaggiolo*, cit., vol. I, p. 256. GIOVIO (*Illustrium virorum vitae*, Florence, 1551, p. 95) says that it was commonly rumoured that Lorenzo wished to conquer Lucca and Siena, extend the boundaries of his state from the Adriatic to the Mediterranean, and have himself made King of Tuscany.

³⁶ Published in *Lett. fam.*, p. 298 ff. The original autograph, long lost sight of by biographers and editors of M.'s works, is in A.S.F., *Carte Strozziane*, ser. 2, 86, f. 32. It appears to be a fragment, or more probably a postscript to a letter to Vettori. Alvisi attributes it to Aug. 1513, which is too early for it to contain such an informed opinion on the habits and government of Lorenzo, which had begun in the middle of August! Besides, M. was at that time in the country immersed in the *Discourses* and the *Prince*, and between 26 Aug. and 10 Dec. his correspondence with Vettori was, as we have shown, interrupted. I would rather attribute it to M.'s stay in Florence in Feb.–March 1514. In *Lett. fam.* Alsivi stated that he took it from the Ricci apograph, but it is not there, as Lesca pointed out in *Lett. L.*, p. 254. This is what probably aroused doubts in the minds of Villari and Tommasini and made them overlook this important document, whose authenticity I am now able to confirm from the autograph. The reading of the text in *Lett. fam.*, which is reproduced in *Lett. L.*, contains some minor inaccuracies, and has *lo proviamo* (p. 299, third from last line) where the autograph reads *l'observiamo*.

³⁷ Dedicatory letter of the *Prince* (I follow the text of *Opp. MC.*).

³⁸ *Lett. fam.*, p. XIV.

[39] A. VERDI, *Gli ultimi anni di Lorenzo, duca d'Urbino*, Este, Pietrogrande, 1905, p. 34, also places the dedication of the *Prince* to Lorenzo 'towards the end of 1516'. VILLARI, vol. II⁴, p. 255, would even put it after the conquest of Urbino (Sept. 1517). But it is evident that the dedication precedes his investiture with the dukedom (8 Oct. 1516), because the dedicatory letter does not address him with the title of Duke, and uses Magnificence not Excellence. This is a point which earlier biographers and critics appear to have overlooked. It seems strange too that, dedicating the book to Lorenzo, M. could have refrained, when speaking of Borgia's conquest of Urbino, from mentioning the recent conquest of the city by Lorenzo. On the other hand, it is probable that the dedication is later than Lorenzo's election as captain-general of the Florentines. One may assume that the anthology of poems entitled *Lauretum*, edited by Carlo Aldovrandi, was printed for this latter occasion (cf. A. M. BANDINI, *De Iunctarum tipographia*, Lucca, 1741; G. SANESI, *La vita e le opere di Donato Giannotti*, Pistoia, Bracali, 1899, p. 13, attributes the anthology to the second half of 1515, Bandini to 1516). It contains poems by old humanists like Ugolino Verino, and also by younger men who include some of M.'s friends, like Luigi Alamanni and Donato Giannotti. There is also some contribution from the Dazzi jokingly referred to in M.'s sonnet to Giuliano. There is no poem in it by M., and I wonder if he, who was so anxious to gain the favour of the 'Medici princes', did not present the *Prince* to Lorenzo on this occasion when others were offering him poems. A *Lauretum* was presented to Lorenzo also in 1514, but it cannot be the anthology we know in print; it must have been an earlier MS collection, which perhaps inspired the later and more important presentation.

[40] *Lett. fam.*, p. 396 ff.; *Opp. MC.*, p. 897.

[41] Letter from M. to Paolo Vettori, 10 Oct. 1516, in *Lett. fam.*, p. 397 ff.; *Opp. MC.*, p. 897.

[42] Cf. TOMMASINI, vol. II, p. 1372.

[43] *Lett. fam.*, p. 398 ff.; *Opp. MC.*, p. 897 ff. In the same letter he wrote: 'Bernardo and Lodovico are growing up, and I hope, on your return, to find a job for one of them with your assistance.'

CHAPTER 16

[1] The only source for the text of this poem is the Giunta edition of 1549 (cf. GERBER, II, 79), in which it already has the longer title, *Asino d'oro*, under the influence of the works of Apuleius and Firenzuola. Two contemporary documents (referred to below) which mention the poem and its contents, show that 'golden' is a spurious addition. I am sorry to rob the Academy of Xylographers, who according to Leopardi have three golden asses; one of them, Machiavelli's, is just an ordinary ass. I cannot agree with L. F. Benedetto (*Le operette satiriche di N.M.*, Turin, Utet, 1920), who maintains that the *Ass* was begun in 1512, which I find unacceptable, among other reasons, because of the reference to 'his labours without reward', etc.

[2] Cf. the letter which Biagio Buonaccorsi, who evidently remained M.'s friend throughout his misfortunes, placed before a copy he made of the *Prince*, in *Opp. U.*, p. 397.

³ Ch. I., lines 113–114:   Ch'un dei più destri giuochi che far sappi
                            e trarre un paio di calci e due corregge.
[One of the smartest tricks that he can play is to administer a couple of kicks and a pair of farts].

⁴ Ch. I, line 103 ff. In these quotations from the *Ass* I have followed the edition in *Opp. MC.*, p. 817.

⁵ Ch. III, line 76 ff.

⁶ Ch. V, line 76 ff.

⁷ Letter from Giuliano Brancacci to Francesco Vettori, 3 March 1518, of which large extracts were published from Riccardiano MS 2240 by TOMMASINI, vol. II, p. 324. Brancacci relates that M. had said of certain merchants: 'It will happen to them as it did to me with the *Ass*—they will have to pay the expenses. I am off to Genoa for them to talk to the Doge about the affairs of David, and to tell him that it is more a case of theft than of bankruptcy for David to take the cloth and send it away and then clear off himself. Niccolò degli Agli and I agreed that he was right, and told him he should make sure that the blows on the Ass and the pack-saddle fell on David's creditors . . .'

⁸ Published in *Lett. fam.*, p. 401 ff.; and more correctly in *Opp. MC.*, p. 898 ff. (for instance, in the passage referred to, this ed. has *Fiandra* (Flanders) where *Lett. fam.* has *Francia* (France)).

⁹ Guidi Mazzoni in his excellent introduction to *Opp. MC.*, p. LVIII.

¹⁰ L. PASSERINI, *Degli Orti Oricellari*, Florence, 1854; cf. A. DELLA TORRE, *Storia dell' Accademia Platonica di Firenze*, Florence, 1902, pp. 30 ff., 833 ff.; VILLARI, vol. II⁴, pp. 276–81; F. GILBERT, *Bernardo Rucellai and the Orti Oricellari*, etc., in *Journal of the Warburg and Courtauld Institutes*, vol. XII (1949), pp. 101–31. There has been much discussion as to when the meetings in the Orti began. We are concerned rather to know when M. began to frequent them, which was long after they began, and much later than some people have thought. In fact, in M.'s correspondence there is not a word, not only about the Orti, but even about the friends who attended those meetings, before the letter to Alamanni already referred to: and he would not have been sharing his leisure time between 'Riccia's house and Donato del Corno's shop if he had had anything better to do at that period. His long stays in the country between 1513 and 1516 also make it unlikely that he could then have frequented the Orti. We have to rely on conjecture and intuition. I believe that M. began to go to the Orti about the middle of 1517, or 1516 at the earliest. Although one should not place much reliance on such literary fictions, this is the year (1516) in which M. imagines the conversations in the Orti between Fabrizio Colonna, Buondelmonti, Rucellai and Alamanni. F. GILBERT, *The composition and structure of M.'s 'Discorsi'*, cit., has recently suggested that M. began to take part in the discussions in the Orti in 1515; but G. SASSO, *Intorno alla composizione dei 'Discorsi'*, cit., pp. 491–9, after careful reconsideration, finds my dating 'far more convincing'.

¹¹ Ariosto was in Rome during M.'s legation there, from 28 October to 10 December. He was in Florence on several occasions, but in 1510, when he fled from the anger of Julius, M. was in France. In 1513 Ariosto arrived in Florence on the day after M. was released from prison. See M. CATALANO, *Vita di Ludovico Ariosto*, Florence, Olschki, 1930–1, vol. I., pp. 202 ff., 333 ff., 353; vol. II, p. 392 ff.

[12] See above, note 7.

[13] Letter from Mariotto de' Bardi, Francesco Lenzi, Carlo Strozzi and Antonio Martellini to M. in Genoa, 8 April 1518, published in an appendix by VILLARI, vol. III², p. 403 ff.

[14] MACHIAVELLI, *Art of War*, dedicatory letter; J. NARDI, *Istoria di Firenze*, ed. cit., vol. II, p. 72.

[15] NARDI, op. and loc. cit. With reference to my conjecture about 'services rendered to Strozzi's literary ambitions', I would point out that of two works written by Strozzi, *Description of the plague* and a *Comedy in verse*, we have autograph copies made by M., who at the end of the comedy put the famous enigmatic phrase: *Ego Barlachia recensui* (cf. F. PINTOR's art. with this title, in *G.S.L.I.*, XXXIX, 1902, p. 103 ff.); see TOMMASINI, vol. II, p. 406. Giannotti also wrote some things for Strozzi and revised his work, for which it seems he received some favours and payment; cf. RIDOLFI, *Opuscoli*, p. 97 ff.

[16] We know this from the following passages of the *Discourses*: Bk. I, ch. 23; Bk. III, ch. 27; Bk. II, ch. 10. The *Discourses* were published posthumously in Rome by Blado in 1531 from the autograph which at that time was in the possession of cardinal Niccolò Ridolfi, a great collector not only of old Greek and Latin MSS., but also of autograph works by contemporaries; see R. RIDOLFI, *La biblioteca del cardinale N.R.*, in *La Bibliofilia*, vol. XXXI (1929). For the text, see the splendid critical note by G. MAZZONI, *Sul testo dei 'Discorsi' del M.*, in *Rendiconti Acc. Naz. Lincei*, Classe di Scienze Morali, ser. vi, vol. IX (1933), pp. 41–82; for the editions, GERBER, II, p. 7 ff.

[17] NERLI, *Commentari*, etc., Augusta, 1728, p. 138. This is the interpretation that must be put on Nerli's words: 'at their instance Machiavelli composed his book of the *Discourses* on Titus Livius and also the book of those treatises and discussions on the art of war'. Either Nerli, in spite of his own attendance at the Orti ('I was very friendly with Niccolò and all of them, and I conversed with them very often') was not well informed in this matter, or his memory failed him, or in writing this down he extended what he knew of the second work also to the first. As we have said in Ch. XIV, part of the *Discourses* were already composed when, in the summer of 1513, he began to write the *Prince*. And at that time M. was not frequenting the Orti (see above, note 10).

[18] Dedication of the *Discourses*; *Opp. MC.*, p. 55.

[19] In the chronology of M.'s works the date of *Mandragola* has till now been one of the most controversial and uncertain. Leaving aside some of the less authoritative opinions, and other extravagant proposals (recently A. RENAUDET, *Machiavel*, Paris, Gallimard, 1942, p. 109, puts it after 1523, and Tiraboschi assigned it to 1498!), TOMMASINI, vol. II, p. 384 ff., placed it between the end of 1512, the beginning of M.'s misfortune to which there is a clear reference in the Prologue, and April 1520, the date of a letter written from Rome by Battista della Palla (cit. infra) which shows that the comedy was at that time finished and their parts learned by the players, and that della Palla had already either read or heard it in Florence some time before. The action of the play takes place in 1504 (in Act I, sc. 1, Callimaco says: 'I was sent to Paris, where I stayed 20 years; and since after 10 years the Italian wars began with the descent of King Charles . . .'), but, as Tommasini, this time rightly, observed,

the date of the action has no importance for the date of composition. VILLARI, vol. II[4], p. 369 agrees with Tommasini: 'not before 1512, and not later than April 1520; but the exact year is not known'. I intend to show the exact year, but it should first be said that the *terminus non ante quem* and the *terminus non post quem* proposed by Tommasini and Villari are absolutely correct (I refrain from mentioning the works of Medin, Mondolfo and others, which are absorbed by these two). It is therefore surprising that a learned scholar like Guido Mazzoni has recently (*Opp. MC.*, p. XLVI) called the whole matter into question by proposing a chronology of M.'s comedies based on aesthetic considerations, which could not be more patently inaccurate. Believing that in order to reach the heights of *Mandragola*, M. must have 'practised a good deal', Mazzoni maintains that he progressed from the translation of the *Andria* through the *Clizia*, an imitation and in part a paraphrase of Plautus, and through the lost *Maschere*. The fact that *Mandragola* is mentioned in the *Clizia* does not seem to have worried him. In order to explain away the contradiction of the Prologue, he supposes that it is a later addition, although it is found in all the editions printed in M.'s lifetime. He does not realize either that the date of the action was placed at an earlier time in order to provide an explanation with the Italian wars for Callimaco's long stay in France, and also to permit some piquant reflections in the political passages on the past popular government. Critics are therefore divided into two camps of unequal force and numbers. More recently F. D. COLIMORE, *The Date of M.'s 'Mandragola'*, in *Modern Language Notes*, vol. LV (1940), p. 526 ff., came to the aid of the weaker side with a curious discovery. In the sonnet 'In questa notte pregando le Muse', written to Giuliano from prison (see above, ch. XIII), the Muse says to Machiavelli:

> Va' al barlazzo
> con quella tua commedia in guazzeroni.

On the basis of this reference, Colimore argues that the comedy was already written and known at that time (i.e. between 19 Feb. and 13 March 1513: though he says, I cannot imagine why, 'November 1512–March 1513'); and so those who attribute it to 1504, or at least to the period between 1504 and 1512, are right. He did not realize that the author of the 'commedia in guazzeroni' was Dazzi, whom the Muse thinks she is addressing: and for this mistake (the Muse's, not Colimore's!) Machiavelli pretends to despair and makes fun of Dazzi.

To return to the real question, it remains to be determined in which year between 1513 and April 1520 the *Mandragola* was written. First of all it is clear that the lines:

> che gli è stato interciso
> mostrar con altre imprese altra virtue
> non sendo premio alle fatiche sue.

permit us to place the *terminus non ante quem* after 1513, after, that is, his labours had had a welcome and a reward such as to prevent other attempts: the allusion to the *Prince* is clear. We are therefore in August 1515 or more likely in the middle of 1516. But is it possible to restrict even further the date of composition of the play? I think it is. No one appears to have noticed a passage in Act III, sc. 3 in the dialogue between the friar and the widow: 'Do you think the Turk will land in Italy this year?' Between the dates mentioned there was one year in which the fear of a Turkish invasion of Italy was so great that the Pope ordered special prayers to be said; and that was at the beginning of 1518. 'They said that all his thoughts were turned towards Italy', wrote Guicciardini of Selim (*Storia d'Italia*, ed. cit., vol. II, p. 197 ff.); and in May of that year in Florence, as Cambi writes (*Istoria*, cit., p. 138), there were great fears that he would launch an attack on Christendom. The widow's question was all the more pointed for being topical. On this basis the date of the *Mandragola* can be precisely determined. I would also add that in 1504 and the years following, on account of the truce between the Turks and the Venetians and the nature of the Sultan, Bajazeth II, 'a prince of peaceful character . . . and very averse from war' (GUICCIARDINI, op. cit., vol. II, p. 106), there was very little fear of a Turkish invasion—until precisely the beginning of 1518.

[20] But this is not an arbitrary title like that of other works of M. In fact, the Prologue says: 'The tale is called Mandragola.' For the early editions, see GERBER, op. cit., II, p. 70 ff.; cf. F. D. COLIMORE, *Edizioni e traduzioni della Mandragola*, in *Italica*, vol. XVIII (1941), p. 55 ff. I will add some bibliographical information. The first edition, published in Florence by a small printer with the old 15th-century fount 113R, was probably done in 1518 or soon after. The Roman edition, which also lacks precise typographical indications, was certainly printed by Calvo in 1524; cf. F. BARBIERI, *Le edizioni romane di F. M. Calvo*, in *Miscellanea . . . in memoria di L. Ferrari*, Florence, Olschki, 1952, p. 76.

[21] The 'canzone' which precedes the Prologue in all the modern editions was written and inserted in the comedy together with the 'canzonette' which precede the acts, in 1526. The text was enclosed in a letter from M. to Guicciardini on 3 Jan. 1526. This must be borne in mind, because the words of adulation addressed to 'him who governs you' are not in praise of Lorenzo de' Medici, but of Francesco Guicciardini: and the phrase 'the man who gave him to you' (in the last line) must be understood to refer to Clement VII.

[22] TOFFANIN, p. 408, supposes that in speaking of being prevented from accomplishing more worthy works, M. was referring to practical activities. But he had been prevented from doing these by quite other causes than the refusal of reward. This had been denied to his other more worthy and more serious works in writing, the *Prince* and the *Discourses*.

[23] Ch. III, line 99.

[24] LEOPARDI, *Zibaldone*, VII, 329, 3.

[25] Ch. III, line 85 ff.

[26] *Mandragola*, Prologue. It was Gaspary who said this, in his History of Italian Literature.

[27] *Mandragola*, II, 3; *Opp. MC.*, p. 702.

[28] Della Palla's letter, cit. supra, note 19, suggests that it had been read or performed before a limited audience of friends from the Orti; Della Palla, who frequented those gatherings, could not have spoken about the play to the Pope unless he already knew it. Furthermore, Giovio, whom I think we may believe in this matter, says in his *Elogia clarorum virorum*, Venice, Tramezzino, 1546, f. 55ᵛ, that when Leo X heard with what success the *Mandragola* had been performed in Florence, he wished it to be played in Rome with the same scenery and actors. There would appear to be no

doubt, therefore, that it was played in Florence before the performance in Rome discussed by the Pope and Della Palla, of which the latter wrote in his letter of 26 April, 1520.

[28a] This conjecture about the date of performance has since been accepted in an art. by A. PARRONCHI, *La prima rappresentazione della Mandragola*, in *La Bibliofilia*, LXI, 1962. This is an excellent study, especially as regards the arrangements for the play and scenic effects, although I do not feel able to agree with all the author's ingenious interpretations of the allegory. I would have far more serious reserves to make on this account to the recent art. by T. A. SUMBERG, '*La Mandragola: An Interpretation*, in *The Journal of Politics*, II, 1961, pp. 320-340.

[29] CAMBI, *Istoria*, cit., vol. XXII, p. 145. As for M.'s feelings on the death of Lorenzo, I do not see how A. RENAUDET, op. cit., p. 290, can make him 'grieved by the disappearance of two young Medici to whom he had offered in vain the chance of accomplishing a heroic task.'

[30] The exact date of death was not known even to the genealogist L. PASSERINI, *Genealogia e storia della famiglia Rucellai*, Florence, 1861, p. 145, who put it 'about 1520'. It was Tommasini who exhumed the information (if I may be permitted the expression) from the *Libro dei Morti* in the A.S.F., which records that Cosimo di Cosimo Rucellai was buried in Santa Maria Novella on 2 Nov. 1519. It is not clear from Passerini's work whether the meetings in the Orti went on under Giovanni and Palla, but Bandini says they did, and the facts prove it.

[31] I would not say definitely that the *Serenata* could not have been inspired by some other affair of Machiavelli; there is simply no evidence to suggest that it was not written for this one; not even the line: 'non è la sua età vecchia e matura' [his old and mature age is not . . .], which is perfectly compatible with M.'s 43 years. Tommasini (II, 1047) makes the extraordinary conjecture that this was the serenade which M. offered to sing beneath the window of Vettori's lady. A serenade in octaves, 33 of them, being 264 lines in all! Did he mean to put her to sleep or give her pneumonia, since it was the month of December? I would also attribute to this same affair and the same period the sonnet 'Se sanza a voi pensar solo un momento' (*Opp. MC.*, p. 869), which was written in the country ('e questi boschi pur creduto l'hanno' [and even these woods have believed it]); it was there that his loved one lived.

[32] In 1577 Giuliano de' Ricci, M.'s nephew, transcribed it, saying, however, that he had not seen 'either original or draft', but believing that he could attribute it to him 'without doubt' on the evidence of contemporaries and on the statement of Niccolò's eldest child, Bernardo, that 'he remembered having heard his father talk about it and seen it in his hands on many occasions' (TOMMASINI, I, 663). Giuliano de' Ricci noticed some difference of style, but this may be explained by the more literary nature of the work. Among the reasons that militate in favour of the attribution to M., besides the strong originality of the work, typical of Machiavelli, there is the use of the initial N[iccolò] to indicate the author, and the fact that it was written in the country, or more precisely 'while I am busy with the vine-harvest'. The attribution to M. was sustained by Bottari, who in his edition of 1730 referred to the author with a periphrasis: it was denied by Polidori in his edition, and denied too by Tommasini (I, 100; II, 349-362). Villari, however, confirmed it (II[4], 399 ff.), and Rajna supported it with his customary skill and learning in his article, *La data del*

'*Dialogo intorno alla lingua*' *di N.M.*, in *Rendiconti della R. Acc. dei Lincei*, Classe di Scienze Morali, ser. V, vol. II, 1893, pp. 203–22. Here, on the question of attribution, Rajna wrote that the *Dialogue* is 'such as to reveal to us a mind so powerful and original that, even if we were not absolutely obliged to keep within Florentine limits, we should think at once of Machiavelli'; as for the chronology, he attributes it to the Autumn of 1514, and certainly not later than 1516 nor earlier than 1514. As I have little that is original to say on the matter, I refer the reader to the works cited. I would simply add that the 'great felicity and state of tranquillity', which according to the author of the *Dialogue*, Florence enjoyed whilst he was composing it, could very well refer to the papacy of Leo X; except that the passage on the court of Rome which says: 'I am surprised that, in a place where no worthy or good things are done, you should think they would do this; for where their habits are perverse, so too must be their language', leave me in doubt as to whether M. could have written it during the reign and lifetime of Leo. The papacy of Adrian comes to mind (1522–3), which would also fit the passage about the happiness of Florence; and although I am well aware, after Rajna's demonstration, of the arguments against such a late dating if M. is indeed the author, these do not seem to me stronger than those which can be adduced again atrributing it to the time of Leo X. Whilst this translation was being prepared, a learned art. appeared by H. BARON, *Machiavelli on the eve of the 'Discourses'; the date and place of his 'Dialogo intorno alla nostra lingua'*, in *Bibliothèque d'Humanisme et Renaissance*, XXIII, 1961, pp. 449–476, in which he argues the case for ascribing it to the Autumn of 1515.

[33] *Opp. MC.*, pp. 773–6; cf. F. CHIAPPELLI, op. cit., p. 7 ff.

[34] The first edition which bears M.'s name is the Giunta ed. of 1549. In 1545 it was printed by Blado in a small collection of *novelle* and poems by Giovanni Brevio, who attributed the tale to himself. The autograph is in B.N.F., Magl. VII, 335, ff. 1r–12r, from which derive the Giunta ed. and that of Doni, *La seconda libreria*, Venice, 1551, ff. 89r–97r. Doni speaks of Brevio's theft, asserting that both Brevio's version and the Giunta edition are 'forgeries' of a text of which he possessed the original. But who can trust Doni? Cf. GERBER, I, p. 44 ff.

[35] G. MAZZONI, in *Opp. MC*, p. XLVIII; cf. p. XLVI.

[36] TOMMASINI, vol. II, p. 372.

CHAPTER 17

[1] NARDI, *Istorie*, cit., vol. II, pp. 61–63.

[2] Letter from Filippo Strozzi to his brother Lorenzo, 17 March 1519; published by TOMMASINI, vol. II, p. 1081, without considering the possibility that it might be dated in Florentine style, particularly as it was written, albeit from Rome, by one Florentine to another. VILLARI (vol. II[4], p. 281) thought it 'uncertain whether the indication of the year was according to the Florentine or the Roman style'. Yet, reading the letter, the matter becomes entirely clear. Apart from the fact that in March 1519 Lorenzo de' Medici was still alive and seriously ill (I am not sure which of these alternatives would have been less propitious for a visit by M.), the reference in the letter to the imprisonment of Giampaolo Baglioni, which occurred precisely

on 17 March 1520, is enough to prove without a shadow of doubt that the dating is Florentine style. Since Filippo habitually addressed his brother in the second person singular (*tu*), the use of the plural *voi* in this letter to congratulate those who had taken M. to see the Medici, indicates that Strozzi did not go alone. Tommasini's inferences on the subject are, as usual, very odd, and I have no doubt that Strozzi's companions in this affair were the friends from the Orti who were his strongest supporters and had close contacts with the Cardinal. The approximate date of the visit can be gathered from the date of Lorenzo's letters referred to in Filippo's reply.

³ This will be dealt with more fully below. At this point I would merely say that in a letter of the following month (April) there is reference to a 'commission to write' to be given to M., and it is spoken of as a matter discussed 'some time ago'; it does not seem possible, therefore, that the matter was not discussed some days before during the visit to the Cardinal.

⁴ We shall speak below of the first edition prepared by the author himself. Beside this edition, which is the only valid text, the autograph (B.N.F., Magl. VIII, 145 bis, prov. Strozzi) and a copy with autograph inscriptions (Bibl. Comunale, Verona) are merely of philological interest. See GERBER, part I, p. 49 ff., or the brief but clear summary of the position in *Opp. MC.*, p. 264. Our quotations are from this latter edition.

⁵ A. BURD, *Le fonti letterarie di M. nell' Arte della Guerra*', in the *Memorie Acc. Lincei*, Classe Scienze Morali, ser. 5, vol. IV, pt. 1 (1896), pp. 188–261.

⁶ *Opp. MC.*, p. 266; cf. on p. 366 the famous passage deriding the Italian princes 'before they felt the blows of the ultramontane wars'.

⁷ VILLARI, vol. II⁴, p. 313.

⁸ VILLARI, vol. II⁴, p. 306. For a critical examination of the military teachings of the *Art of War* and bibliographical indications, see *ibid.*, pp. 304–42; 579–82 (note giving account of, and strongly criticizing the book by M. HOBOHM, *Machiavellis Renaissance der Kriegskunst*, Berlin, K. Curtius, 1913). See also the full introduction by P. Pieri to the edition of the *Arte della Guerra*, Rome, Edizioni Roma, 1936 (cf. the review by P. Carli in *G.S.L.I.*, vol. CX (1936), pp. 156–60), which in part absorbs his earlier work, *Intorno all' Arte della Guerra di N.M.*, Bologna, 1927.

⁹ *Opp. MC.*, p. 265.

¹⁰ *Opp. MC.*, pp. 276, 367.

¹¹ Letter from Battista della Palla to M., Rome, 26 April 1520, in *Lett. fam.*, p. 407 ff.

¹² Letter from Filippo de' Nerli, Florence, 1 Aug. 1520, in *Lett. fam.*, p. 411.

¹³ A large number of documents concering Guinigi's bankruptcy and M.'s mission were published by TOMMASINI, vol. II, pp. 1089–95. Other documents were published by VILLARI, vol III², p. 402 ff., among them a letter from one of the merchants, G. B. Bracci, who wrote: 'As for looking into the financial condition of Michele and the account-books and other necessary things, which is not your profession, it would need either an accountant or a book-keeper.'

¹⁴ TOMMASINI, loc. cit.

¹⁵ I say this because both Villari and Tommasini give great prominence to the phrases *amice mi carissime* and *amico nostro carissimo* used below and above the letter, without realising that they are current formulae which come from the book and the

secretary not from the Cardinal. In the well-known formulary of Landino, and in others, this formula is used by superiors to inferiors. On the date of this letter from the Cardinal to M., published in *Opp. P.*, vol. I, p. LXXXVIII, see VILLARI, vol. II⁴, p. 297.

¹⁶ TOMMASINI, loc. cit.

¹⁷ *Opp. P.*, vol. VI, pp. 291–7; cf. VILLARI, II⁴, p. 294 ff.

¹⁸ Published for the first time together with the *Prince* in the Blado edition of 1532 (see above, ch. XIV, note 20) and the Giunta edition of the same year (GERBER, I, 101; II, 123 ff.). There is a MS. dated 28 Oct. 1520 (B.N.F., Palat. 537), evidently prepared for Buondelmonti and Alamanni or some other habitué of the Orti from the autograph which the author sent to his two friends on 29 August; this MS. has two apophthegms which the others do not have. On the other hand, the Laurenziano MS. XLIV, 40 has 14 apophthegms less and gives a different version of one other; leaving aside the question of the accuracy of this text, I would differ from Casella's view in *Opp. MC.*, and regard this reduction of the apophthegms as a direct consequence of the criticism expressed by Buondelmonti in his letter of 6 Sept., cit. infra, note 22; though doubt remains as to whether this reduction was effected by his critics rather than by the author himself.

¹⁹ This is expressly stated in the letter of 6 Sept., cit. infra, note 22. Speaking of the genesis of the work, my intention was to go no further than establishing the motives which inspired M. to write it and the aims he had in mind while composing it. Looking more deeply TOFFANIN, op. cit., p. 403, speaks of a new theory of fortune which M. intended to treat in this *Life*, as it were as a corrective to the negative view expressed in the *Prince*. I would hardly say it was a new theory, even if the needle of his thought, which is always oscillating between two extremes (in his famous letter to Vettori, while he was still augmenting and polishing the *Prince*, he said that 'fortune wishes to do everything') is pointing in the *Life* to a pessimistic view.

²⁰ N. TEGRIMI, *Castruccii Antelminelli Castracani lucensis ducis vita*, Modena, Domenico Roccocciola, 20 April 1496; Hain-Copinger-Reichling 15363.

²¹ See (also for full bibliography) the clear and sober discussion by Villari (II⁴, 297–303), and by Tommasini (II, 427–44); G. SIMONETTI, *I biografi di Castruccio Castracani . . .*, in *Studi storici*, directed by A. Crivellucci and E. Pais, vol. II (1893), pp. 1–24; E. FUETER, *Storia della Storiografia moderna*, trans. by A. Spinelli, Naples, Ricciardi, 1943, vol. I, p. 76 ff.

²² Letter from Zanobi Buondelmonti to M., 6 Sept., 1520, in *Lett. fam.*, p. 414 ff. The observation about the apophthegms reads as follows: 'That last part with the apophthegms and the clever and witty sayings of Castruccio . . . would be better for being shorter, because besides being too numerous, there are some of them that have been attributed to other wise men of ancient and modern times, and some others have not the spirit and greatness which one would expect from so great a man.' For the sources of these sayings and their history from Campanella to Leopardi, see the learned study by F. P. LUISO, *I detti memorabili . . .*, cit., pp. 217–60.

²³ Letter, cit. We have other private letters written to M. during his stay in Lucca, in particular one written on 30 July, by his son Bernardo, who already took a share in the harvesting and domestic duties, and one from Filippo de' Nerli, dated 1 August, in reply to a letter of M.'s, 'which, to begin with, tells a lie, because you say you

will be brief, and then send two sheets full of writing from edge to edge'; unfortunately M.'s letter is lost.

24 See the documents published by Tommasini, cit. supra.

25 *Lett. fam.*, p. 418 ff.; VILLARI, vol. II⁴, p. 344. The autograph is in A.S.F. *Carte Strozziane*, ser. I, 137, f. 214.

26 The commission given to M. for the Histories was published in *Opp. P.*, p. LXXIX.

27 See the study on 'Il salario del M. per le Istorie fiorentine', in RIDOLFI, *Opuscoli*, pp. 165–173.

28 Published for the first time in a volume entitled *Opere inedite di Niccolò Machiavelli*, London (Florence), 1760, pp. 1–44. Here the work has the title, which is also found in MS. II, IV, 309 of the B.N.F., of *Discorso sopra il riformare lo stato di Firenze, ad istanza di papa Leone X*, but this is clearly spurious and a late addition. In the contemporary MS. owned and described by Tommasini, vol. II, p. 1024 ff., it is entitled *Discursus florentinarum rerum post mortem iunioris Laurentii Medices*, translated by another hand as *Discorso per rassettare le cose di Firenze dopo la morte del duca Lorenzo*. We have already noted M.'s habit of giving Latin titles to his vernacular works, and so this must be the correct title of the *Discourse*. For an analysis of this work see VILLARI, vol. II⁴, pp. 286–292, and TOMMASINI, vol. II., pp. 200–207; to which I would add that while other biographers regard it as having been composed immediately after the death of Lorenzo, and while I have no evidence to reject this opinion outright, I consider it more likely that he was commissioned to write it by the Cardinal after M.'s visit to him, and perhaps after M. had been employed by the university to write histories 'et alia faciendum'. In addition, one must take account of what is said in the *Discourse*, that it was written while the Cardinal, 'having been in Florence in these past months' (ed. cit., p. 41), was in Rome. The Cardinal left for Rome in Oct. 1519 and returned to Florence on 13 Feb. 1520; he had a visit from M. about 10 March, left for Rome on 6 November and returned to Florence in Feb. 1521. It is therefore certain that the *Discourse* was not written before the end of 1519 or after Feb. 1521, and that between these dates the period between February and November 1520 must be excluded. Doubt remains as to whether it is to be attributed to the period between Nov. 1519 and Feb. 1520 or to the end of 1520. I have preferred the second of these alternatives for the reason already stated, though I cannot altogether exclude the first. There is reference to this *Discourse* in PITTI, *Apologia dei Cappucci* in *A.S.I.*, ser. i, vol. IV, pt. II (1853), p. 325.

29 FLAMINI, *Il Cinquecento*, cit., p. 34.

30 *Discorso*, ed. cit., p. 38 ff.

31 Letter from Filippo de' Nerli to M., Rome, 17 Nov. 1520, in *Lett. fam.*, p. 417 ff.

32 CURTIUS RUFUS, *La historia d'Alessandro Magno . . . tradotta in volgare da P. Candido*, Florence, Filippo di Giunta, 1519.

33 Letter of 15 April 1520, in *Lett. fam.*, p. 406 ff.; letter of 15 Feb. 1520/1, recently published by F. GILBERT, *An unpublished Machiavelli letter*, in *The American Historical Review*, vol. XLVII (1942), p. 292. Before Prof. Gilbert published this letter, we only knew Vernaccia's reply to it, published in *Lett. fam.*, p. 419 ff.

34 TOMMASINI, vol. II, p. 255 note. The letter in which Soderini made the first proposal to M. is lost; and Villari for some curious reason believed that the 'Raugia

proposal' was the one which the Gonfalonier did not recommend to him in his letter 'in pappafico' [in disguise], to which M. replied with his 'fantasies', mentioned above (chap. XIII, note 5).

[35] Letter from Soderini to M., Rome, 13 April 1521, in *Lett. fam.*, p. 419. The autograph is in B.N.F., *Carte Machiavelli*, V, n. 40; see RIDOLFI, op. and loc. cit.

CHAPTER 18

[1] The original of these instructions is in B.N.F., *Carte Machiavelli*, V, 164. Published in *Opp. P.*, vol. VI, p. 211 ff.

[2] Letter from Francesco Guicciardini to his brother Luigi, 22 Aug. 1512, in GUICCIARDINI, *Carteggi*, cit., vol. I, p. 90. Not only for these early relations, but for everything concerned with the friendship between M. and Guicciardini and the opinion the latter had of M., the reader should consult R. RIDOLFI, *Vita di Francesco Guicciardini*, Rome, Belardetti, 1960. Published six years later than the second Italian ed. of the present biography, this work not only shows this famous friendship from the point of view of the other partner, but has also benefited from my later discoveries and reflections on the subject. In order to avoid needless repetition in the notes, reference to this work should be taken as implied whenever the name of Guicciardini occurs in these pages.

[3] Fra Ilarione Sacchetti, quoted by Sbaraglia in the *Supplementum et castigatio ad Scriptores trium Ordinum S. Francisci a Waddingo . . . descriptos*, Rome, 1806, vol. VI, p. 356. His instructions to M. in B.N.F., *Carte Machiavelli*, V., 165; *Opp. P.*, vol. VI, p. 213 ff. The instructions of the Eight, referred to above, begin: 'Niccolò, you will go to Carpi and make sure you are there for the whole of Thursday next [16 May] . . .' On this mission, see p. Z. LAZZERI, *Un'ambasceria di N.M. al Capitolo generale di Carpi*, in *Archivum Francisc. Hist.*, vol. XVI (1923), pp. 149–66.

[4] The original of the instructions of the Consuls of the Guild (14 May 1521) is in B.N.F., *Carte Machiavelli*, V, 25; published in *Opp. P.*, vol. VI, p. 215 ff. In this document the Consuls state that they had already signified their desire to Rovaio but had received no reply. Evidently he was making difficulties, as he did with M. Writing to Guicciardini on the subject, M. pretends that he chose the preacher.

[5] On this man see R. RIDOLFI, *La vita di G. Savonarola*, vol. II, p. 223.

[6] GUICCIARDINI, *Carteggi*, cit., vol. IV, p. 56 ff.; *Lett. fam.*, p. 421.

[7] Letter from M. to Guicciardini, 17 May, in *Lett. fam.*, p. 422 ff.; *Opp. M.C.* p. 900 ff.; GUICCIARDINI, *Carteggi*, vol. IV, p. 67 ff.

[8] One might imagine that M. was here alluding to something he deeply regretted —that he could not say what he would have liked to say about the Medici in his *Histories*, and therefore had to conceal it or cover it up in some way; but when he wrote this letter he had not yet reached the point in his writing where this embarrassment might have made itself felt.

[9] The original autographs are in B.N.F., *Carte Machiavelli*, V., 110, 111. The letters were published in *Lett. fam.*, pp. 426–9, and recently by Palmarocchi in GUICCIARDINI, *Carteggi*, vol. IV, pp. 59–61 (though Palmarocchi has got them and their replies in the wrong order; they should follow one another in this order; nos. 72, 74, 73, 76).

[10] For some curious reason Palmarocchi reads: '*Uno* vi mando a posta *che pare* balestriere [instead of 'Però vi mando a posta el presente balestriere', which is quite clear in the autograph]; and where the original reads: 'né anche sendo solito a fare tale ufficio sanza el ducato', a witty reply by the lawyer Guicciardini to M. asking for an opinion, Palmarocchi misses the sense and reads: 'nè anche sendo solito a fare tale ufficio sanza *che 'l diciate*'; and further on he reads *pezzo* where the original has *piego*.

[11] Letter from M., 18 May, in *Lett. fam.*, p. 429 (incomplete); *Opp. MC.*, p. 902 ff.; GUICCIARDINI, *Carteggi*, cit., vol. IV, p. 61 ff.

[12] In Palmarocchi's ed. there occur at this point the words *mi ricordo* in square brackets; in the original they are crossed out.

[13] GUICCIARDINI, *Carteggi*, cit., vol. IV, p. 60 ff.

[14] GUICCIARDINI, *Carteggi*, cit., vol. IV, p. 63. *Lett. fam.*, p. 432; *Opp. MC*, p. 903 ff.

[15] Letter of 1 May, cit.

[16] Letter of 18 May, cit.

[17] Autograph draft of M.'s letter to cardinal Giulio de' Medici, bearing no date, but written, as is clearly evident from the text, on the Monday evening (20 May) from Modena; preserved in B.N.F., *Carte Machiavelli*, I, 51; published in *Opp. P.*, vol. VI, p. 216 ff.

[18] Letter to Cardinal de' Medici, cit.

[19] Letter to Cardinal de' Medici. cit.

[20] For all this chapter, and especially for the correspondence between M. and Guicciardini, see my *Vita di Fr. Guicciardini*, cit., pp. 142–5, where it may be seen what business Guicciardini and M.'s host had in common—which adds further to the piquancy of this Carpi correspondence.

CHAPTER 19

[1] *Istorie fiorentine*, proem.

[2] For analysis and criticism of the *Histories*, cf. VILLARI, II[4], pp. 419–97, and especially E. FUETER, op. et ed. cit., vol. I, pp. 79–83, with whom I agree when he says, contrary to the opinion of others, that M. did not systematically despise the truth, but paid less attention to it whenever poetic inspiration rather than his political prejudices carried him away; though I disagree with him when he states that M. purposely mingled the true with the false so that the false should also appear true. This great historian of historiography has the merit of having pointed to a quality which M. alone possessed among his contemporaries: 'a wide view and the gift of recognizing the great links in history and of placing individual facts in the framework of a general development' (p. 81). For the text of the *Histories* see the masterly introduction to his critical ed. by P. Carli; cf. also Casella's note in *Opp. MC.*, p. 376, and Carli's observations on the subject in his *Rassegna machiavelliana*, in *G.S.L.I.*, vol. CII (1933), p. 282 ff. For the editions of the work, GERBER, II, p. 35 ff.

[3] B.L.F., *Med. Pal.*, 230; cf. TOMMASINI, vol. II, p. 454 in note. The most common verson of the tercet quoted in the text, as it is found in various MSS. and printed editions of the late 15th and early 16th centuries, is the following:

Tu che con questo libro ti trastulli
Guarda colla lucerna non s'azzuffi
Rendimel presto e guardal da' fanciulli.

Biondo's *Decades* were acquired by Niccolò's father on 26 Aug. 1485. See his *Libro di Ricordi*, cit., p. 207.

[4] Printed on 16 Aug. 1521, by the heirs of Filippo di Gunta; GERBER, II, 44. M. at once sent a copy together with a letter to cardinal Giovanni Salviati, son of Jacopo and of a daughter of Lorenzo the Magnificent, who made a great name for himself in the history of Florence and of the Church. The Cardinal replied on 16 Sept. 1521, after having read the work, with a long and very kind letter, in which he praised it and thanked M. for having let him see it before anyone else in Rome: 'and I am not a little obliged to you for having sent it to me immediately, and for being the first in Rome to see so fine a work, which is truly worthy of your talents, experience and wisdom. I urge you to continue to conceive and compose some work or other, and to bring honour to our city with your abilities'. The letter was published by TOMMASINI, vol. II, p. 1088.

[5] R. RIDOLFI, *Opuscoli*, p. 62.

[6] The most complete and up-to-date biographical work on this political writer is at present my own 'Sommario della vita di Donato Giannotti', in RIDOLFI, *Opuscoli*, pp. 55–164.

[7] Letter from Donato Giannotti to Marcantonio Michieli, 30 June 1533, published by L. A. FERRAI, *Lettere inedite di Donato Giannotti*, in *Atti del R. Istituto veneto di Scienze, Lettere ed Arti*, ser. IV, vol. III (1884–5), 'p. 1570 ff. The editor, however, who is known in other respects for his modest critical abilities, saw in this account 'a proof . . . to be added to the accusations of Donato Giannotti's enemies who said that he readily followed and sought the friendship of great and powerful men, and so was inclined also to exaggerate the closeness of his connections with men of high birth and great fame'. He did not stop to think that when Machiavelli was writing his *Histories* 'for florins' he was neither great nor powerful among his fellow-citizens, nor of great fame: he was poor, unhappy, and despised by many, and some called him a house-pest or a shop-pest; and at the time of this letter, six years after his death, his reputation had not yet begun to rise. Furthermore, when Giannotti knew him, he was not a butcher or a baker, but a lecturer in Greek at Pisa; and when he wrote those words, he had occupied the same office held by M. There are also other proofs of M.'s friendship with Giannotti, the most important of which is that Giannotti possessed the autograph of the *Histories* and perhaps other things besides of Machiavelli. In one of his letters he relates a witticism of Niccolò, which is not recorded by others, and he must have heard it, as he says, from M. himself. See R. RIDOLFI, *Opuscoli*, pp. 62–65, from which the information in this brief note is taken.

[8] Letter to Francesco Vettori, 25 Dec. 1521; the autograph original is in the collection of Mr. O. R. Barrett in Chicago. An English translation of it was published by F. GILBERT, *An Unpublished Machiavelli Letter*, cit., p. 290 ff. Vettori was at that time holding the highest office in the Republic, and M. may have come into Florence for the Christmas festivities and to see his friend the Gonfalonier, who was as ever miserly with his favours. That he was in Florence for a short time only is indicated clearly by the signature to the letter: 'Niccolò Machiavelli, in the city'.

[9] BERNI, *Orlando innamorato*, book III, canto 7.

[10] The autograph draft is in B.N.F., *Carte Machiavelli*, I, 79. It begins: 'Our magnificent and illustrious Signori, considering (*he then wrote and crossed out*: on the order and advice of the most excellent monsignore) that no law and no order is more praiseworthy in the eyes of men or (*he first wrote*: nor) of God than that whereby a true, united and holy republic is established. . . .' Villari (II[4], 354), after having correctly given the first words of this *incipit*, then goes curiously astray. No less curious is Tommasini's (II, 449 note) assertion that only the handwriting is M.'s (yet it is a draft, not a copy!), and he follows this up with a typically groundless hypothesis that it was composed by a certain Francesco Ricci. Although much later, there is also the notable assertion of PITTI, *Apologia de' Cappucci*, in *A.S.I.*, vol. IV (1843), pt. II, p. 326: 'There is also the proclamation in M.'s hand . . . beginning: *Our magnificent and illustrious Signori . . .!*; and he goes on to reproduce a long extract from it. Although I do not think that this was the proclamation ordered by the Cardinal for publication on the 1st of May, it is clear that M., perhaps at the Cardinal's request, wrote that draft.

[11] Published in *A.S.I.*, vol. I (1842), pp. 420–32; the opinion on M.'s proposal is on p. 429.

[12] JACOPO PITTI, *Istoria fiorentina*, in *A.S.I.*, vol. I (1842), p. 124 ff.

[13] NARDI, *Istorie fiorentine*, ed. cit., vol. II, p. 71.

[14] The proceedings against Niccolò Martelli, 'at Civitavecchia on 17 June 1526', were published by C. GUASTI, *Documenti della Congiura fatta contro il cardinale Giulio de' Medici nel 1522*, in *G.S.A.T.*, vol III (1859), p. 239 ff. Some doubt might arise that the Niccolò Machiavelli named by Buondelmonti was the other one, son of Alexander; but there are decisive arguments against the suggestion: our Machiavelli, not the other Niccolò, was the friend of Buondelmonti, who in a matter of this nature and danger would have been more likely to confide in someone close and in some way obliged to him. Besides it must be remembered that it was our Machiavelli, not the other Niccolò, who frequented the Orti, from whose habitués Boundelmonti had drawn the principal conspirators. But what removes every trace of doubt is that the Niccolò denounced by Martelli was a poor man, whereas Niccolò, son of Alexander, was rich. All the historians, early and modern, state that M. came out of these proceedings without the slightest shadow of suspicion, except, as Nardi (vol. II, p. 72) writes, on account of his close association with the Orti: 'so that for the thoughts and actions of these young men even Niccolò was not without suspicion'. NERLI, *Commentari*, cit., p. 138, acutely observes that 'in conspiring they did not consider well what Machiavelli had written for them in his *Discourses* about conspiracies; for if they had, either they would not have done it, or if they had done it, they would have proceeded with more caution'.

[15] B.N.F., cod. Magl. VII, 59. f, 74r. The reading of cod. VII, 271. f, 115r is as follows:

> La notte che morì Pier Soderini
> l'anima andò de l'Inferno alla bocca;
> gridò Pluton: Ch'Inferno? anima sciocca,
> va' su nel Limbo fra gli altri bambini.

¹⁶ Among those who denied the authenticity of this epigram is Passerini (MACHIAVELLI, *Opp. P.*, p. XXVII; P. LITTA, *Famiglia Soderini*). VILLARI, vol. I⁴, p. 650 ff., admits its authenticity, but justifies it as a joke 'in bad taste possibly'. I do not see the bad taste, only the joke, in which the flavour belongs to a fairly common-place kind of humour (cf. TOMMASINI, vol. I, p. 38 note: C. CANTÙ, *Storia degli Italiani*, vol. III, p. 83), but one which is not displeasing in this particular epigram.

¹⁷ These words of Ricci are quoted by VILLARI, loc. cit.

¹⁸ Letter from Roberto Pucci to M. 'at home', 8 June 1522, in *Lett. fam.*, p. 434. Roberti Pucci was then Gonfalonier, and when he wrote this affectionate letter to M., Totto was *in extremis*. Biographers have remained unaware of the biographical content of this letter; and so G. LESCA, *Lettere machiavelliane inedite*, cit., could imagine that Totto died away from Florence.

¹⁹ *Istruzione a Raffaello Girolami quando ai 23 di ottobre partì per Spagna all'Imperatore*. Passerini and Milanesi, republishing the document in *Opp. P.*, vol. VI, p. 375, corrected the name of the addressee to that of Raffaello de' Medici, pointing out that Raffaello Girolami was not sent to Charles V until 1529. But their emendation is wrong, because Raffaello Girolami did go to Spain in October 1522, and with him, oddly enough, was Raffaello de' Medici. But the suggestion is totally unfounded that the instructions were addressed to Raffaello de' Medici, who had already been to the Emperor in Spain on a previous occasion in 1519, and therefore had no need of instructions. Nor can it be insinuated that the document refers to this earlier embassy of Raffaello de' Medici, which also took place late in October, because it contains certain historical allusions which cannot refer to 1519. The truth of the matter was re-established by Tommasini, vol. II, p. 245 ff. The instructions are important because they are an authentic gloss by M. himself on his own legations, and provide the key to understanding many things in his correspondence. In particular it helps us to understand a device he frequently used: 'And as it would be odious to put your opinion in your own mouth, the following terms are used in letters: Considering therefore all that which has been communicated to you, men of good judgement here believe that such and such a result will occur . . .' If I am not mistaken, the origin of these important instructions may be readily conjectured. A servant of Raffaello Girolami had wounded a brother of his who appears to have been working for Machiavelli. On 14 Oct. 1522, M. wrote from the country to his brother-in-law Francesco del Nero asking him to persuade Girolami to use his good offices. It is evident that Girolami did so, and that when he wrote to M. or spoke to him about it in Florence where Niccolò went on the 15th or 16th, he told him of his forthcoming journey to Spain, asked him for his instructions, and was quickly obliged within seven or eight days. The brief letter referred to above, published by A. BOSELLI, in *La Bibliofilia*, vol. XXVII (1925), pp. 215–18, shows us M. completely pre-occupied with his pastime of bird-catching: 'I should like to bring thirty thrushes, and I fear I may not be able to.' This letter and another published by F. NOVATI, *Una letterina inedita e sconosciuta di N.M.*, cit. sup., evidently escaped Lesca and do not figure in *Lett. L.*

²⁰ Published for the first time in the appendix to the collection of *Lettere di Niccolò Machiavelli . . .*, Cosmopoli, 1769.

²¹ C. GUASTI, op. cit., p. 145 ff.

[22] As I have observed above, there is a big gap in M.'s correspondence in these years. There is a curious and obscure letter written by him on 26 Sept. 1523 to Francesco del Nero, who was, as we have said, administrator of the Studio, apparently asking him for payment of the salary due to him for the *Histories*. It was written, like almost all the letters of this period, 'from the country', and so appropriately and somewhat sadly he concludes with: 'And I will remember you to the chickens' (*Lett. fam.*, p. 435).

[23] A. NIFO, *De regnandi peritia*, Naples, Caterina di Silvestro, 26 March 1523 (GERBER, III, p. 7 ff.); VILLARI, vol. II[4], p. 169 ff.; TOMMASINI, vol. II, p. 137. We do not know whether M. knew of the plagiary before it was printed (although, *pace* Tommasini, it seems to me very unlikely), nor when he knew of the printed edition, nor how upset he was by it; but the suggestion that he might have been pleased at seeing himself plagiarized in this way, naturally without any mention of his name, seems to me to be pure Tommasini.

[24] As I have recently shown, after the publication of the Italian editions of this biography, the work incorrectly entitled *Descrizione della peste del 1527* (Description of the plague of 1527) is to be attributed to this period. It was written in epistolary form and in an elaborate Boccaccesque style by Lorenzo Strozzi to M. during the plague—to be exact, in May 1523. As M. made a copy of it in his own hand (and perhaps others too), some misguided editors published it in various editions of his works (see e.g. *Opp. U.*, p. 694 ff.), where it is obviously completely out of keeping with the rest. Cf. R. RIDOLFI, *Schede per l'epistolario del Machiavelli . . .*, cit., p. 237–8.

[25] *Lett. fam.*, p. 435. The fragment here quoted is the only part of this letter preserved to us by the copy of Giuliano de' Ricci, who simply summarized what went before, as it seemed to him of little importance. For catching beccafichi Niccolò had made snares in the Poggio farm, referred to in his second will as 'machia becaficorum'. A letter of 6 Aug. 1524 addressed to M. 'in the country at Sant'Andrea' by a certain 'ser Piero', is preserved in a group of replies to M. which belonged to the Bargagli Petrucci and have recently been acquired by the B.N.F. (*Nuovi acquisti*, 1004, f. 96); the letter has so far not been published.

[26] This is evident from the elaboration of the text in the corrections made on the first draft of the *Histories* (in B.N.F., *Carte Machiavelli*, I, 82) and from a comparison of this draft with the definitive text. This was pointed out by Villari, vol. III, p. 228 ff., and supported with some examples. For other comparisons between the two texts, with passages selected on a different basis, see TOMMASINI, vol. II, p. 1128 ff. Comparison can now be carried out completely on the excellent and monumental critical edition of the *Florentine Histories* by P. Carli, who published in an appendix (vol. II, pp. 225–304) the text of the valuable autographs with a complete philological apparatus.

CHAPTER 20

[1] Some research on this person was done by TOMMASINI, vol. II, p. 414 note. Jacopo di Filippo Falconetti, called 'il Fornaciaio', belonged to the councils of the Signoria when he was dismissed from his office and banished for five years. But it was a

pleasant exile, because he was ordered to reside in his house in Santa Maria in Ver-
zaia outside the San Frediano gate, where he had a famous garden, a farm and a kiln,
which must have earned him a great deal of money. He was recalled on 13 Jan.
1524/5; and this date, taken together with that of a letter of Nerli, which we shall
refer to presently, permits us to establish the cause and the date of the celebration.

[2] G. B. BUSINI, *Lettere a Benedetto Varchi*, cit., p. 84.

[3] This letter from Vettori to Del Nero was published by Tommasini, vol. II,
p. 1148. Its date is 5 Feb. 1523, that is 1524 by ordinary reckoning. The Florentine
historians speak of this solemn embassy 'of obedience'. Vettori himself in his *Sommario della storia d'Italia dal 1511 al 1527*, cit., p. 349, tells how one day the Pope sent
for these ambassadors together with Jacopo Salviati and Piero Ridolfi, and asked
them what method he should adopt for the government of the city. Ten of them
advised him to send Ippolito to Florence under the guidance of the Cardinal of
Cortona; and three, Roberto Acciaioli, Francesco Vettori and Lorenzo Strozzi, spoke
against this proposal, urging the Pope to leave the government of the city to the
citizens themselves.

[4] The letter is sent from Rome, where Barbera, who was by then the widow of
Tommaso Raffacani (perhaps the nephew of the writer of carnival songs?), had
moved. It is dated 5 July 1544 and was published in part by me in *Rivista storica
degli archivi toscani*, vol. I (1929), p. 202 ff.: 'I have to trouble Your Excellency again
over that business of mine at Prato; because once more those Corsini of yours are
bothering me, and Your Excellency knows what has happened in the past. . . . Now
again, I am told by Giovanni Filippi, known as 'il ballerino', who lives in a poor
cottage which belonged to my Tommaso, those Corsini are troubling me. So I beg
Your Excellency to stop this matter for the love you bore the good memory of
Niccolò Machiavelli and for my sake too; because, messer Lorenzo, their trouble-
making almost drove me out of Florence, I would ask you to see that they do not
try also to get me out of Rome.' It is worth noting, without wishing to draw any
conclusion from the fact, that Marietta, Niccolò's wife, was a Corsini († 1553). It
appears that Barbera was a Salutati; cf. TOMMASINI, vol. II, p. 1048; C. SALUTATI,
Epistolario, ed. F. Novati (I.S.I.), Rome, 1891–1911, vol. IV, p. 621 note. If the poems
mentioned by Tommasini, loc. cit., were written by her, they certainly do not serve
to distinguish her among the poetesses of her day, though they do distinguish her
among the women in general. It was another advantage she had over the good
Marietta.

[5] VASARI, *Vita di Bastiano, detto Aristotele da San Gallo*.

[6] See the first note to this chapter.

[7] This intention seems to me obvious, as everyone knew about his affair with
Barbera. It would seem otherwise impossible that a man of his wit would stir up this
wasps' nest unintentionally. Another argument, but a very weak one, in support of
this hypothesis, might be that he did not put on his *Andria*, which he must have
already written at that time, or the imitation of the *Aulularia* which was attributed
to him. The manuscript of the latter, once owned by Bernardino di Giordano (in
whose house the performance of *Mandragola* took place), would appear to have
come into the hands of Gelli who borrowed a good deal from it for his *Sporta*;
Lasca wrote:

Il Gello
che fece anch'egli una commedia nuova
ch'avea prima composto il Machiavello;

[Gelli, who also wrote a new comedy, which Machiavelli had first composed].
I have already noted (chap. 16, n. 19) that G. Mazzoni, in spite of documentary
evidence and the text itself of *Clizia*, states that this play was written before *Mandragola*, which in turn he puts as early as 1504, basing himself on aesthetic criteria.
The first edition of *Clizia* was printed ten years after M.'s death, in 1537; for this
and the other editions, see GERBER, II, p. 77. The autograph of the comedy has not
come down to us. Gerber cites only two copies, which have over-generously been
raised to the dignity of apographs (cf. *Opp. MC.*, p. 624); but a short time ago, six
years after the second Italian edition of this biography, a fine presentation copy with
an illuminated border carrying the Ridolfi and Strozzi arms was found in Colchester
library. It was probably presented in 1525 by M. himself to Lorenzo Ridolfi, on
the occasion of his marriage to Maria di Filippo Strozzi. See R. RIDOLFI, *La Clizia
del M.*, in *Il Veltro* (Rome), IV (1960), fasc. 12, pp. 5–8; and especially B. CORRIGAN,
An unrecorded manuscript of M.'s 'La Clizia', in *La Bibliofilia*, LXIII (1961), pp. 73–87.

[8] MACHIAVELLI, *Opp. MC.*, p. 870. Other poems of his written for Barbera, ibidem,
p. 869.

[9] It is the song which precedes the third act, *Opp. MC.*, p. 672.

[10] This hypothesis was first put forward in the well-known study by G. TAMBARA,
Intorno alla Clizia di N.M., Rovigo, 1895.

[11] GIANNOTTI, *Della Republica Fiorentina*, in *Opere politiche e letterarie*, Florence, Le
Monnier, 1850, vol. I, p. 228. Giannotti speaks of this performance of the comedy in
order to criticize the bad behaviour of the young people who were present.

[12] GIANNOTTI, op. and loc. cit.

[13] VASARI, op. cit.

[14] Nerli here used the first line of Politian's *Stanze per la giostra*: 'Le gloriose pompe
e i fieri ludi.'

[15] Letter from Filippo de' Nerli, 22 Feb. 1525, published in *Lett. fam.*, p. 436 ff.
It begins: 'Fornaciaio and you, and you and Fornaciaio have made the fame of your
splendours travel not only throughout Tuscany but also over Lombardy. Go on then
and do not despair! I have heard about the garden being levelled to make the stage
for your comedy...' The date of this letter is common style; see the following note
concerning another letter of Nerli, which is linked with this one, not only by its
subject, but also by a precise reference.

[16] Letter from Filippo de' Nerli to Francesco del Nero, 1 March 1525, in VILLARI,
vol. III[2], p. 434. The date of this letter, and with it that of the performance of *Clizia*,
were assigned by Villari and historians of literature to 1526, in the belief that Nerli
used the Florentine style of dating. But I have decisively and irrefutably proved that
he used the common style, not only on the basis of elements from Giannotti's biography but with firm chronological arguments taken from Nerli's correspondence
files; see RIDOLFI, *Opuscoli*, p. 71 ff. It is abundantly confirmed in any case by the
biographical information on Fornaciaio given above in note 1. There is no doubt
that Nerli did not behave in an altogether agreeable way with M.; but Villari
dramatizes too much the pungent tone of some of his letters to M. This is to be

attributed above all simply to a typical Florentine mordacity, to the habit evidently existing between them of treating and writing to one another in a facetious manner, and perhaps also to inability on Nerli's part to accept some of his friend's passions and eccentricities. There is no doubt—and it is clearly expressed in his *Commentari*—that he was a great admirer of M., and is considered by historians as his most faithful disciple. Cf. R. RIDOLFI, *Per l'epistolario del M.*, cit.

[17] Letter from Francesco Vettori to M., 8 March 1525, published in *Lett. fam.*, p. 437 ff. The letter is dated 8 March 1524, and although Vettori like all Florentines who were not permanently resident in a city where another system of dating obtained, used the Florentine style, one might here be tempted to ascribe this one to the common style, and attribute the letter to his stay in Rome on the occasion of the solemn embassy of which I spoke above. But this hypothesis must be resolutely discarded on grounds which emerge from Vettori's correspondence. Besides, it is apparent for several reasons that the writing of the *Histories* could not have reached the death of Lorenzo by March 1524.

[18] Letter of 11 March 1524/5 published by TOMMASINI, vol. II, p. 1149; on the date of the letter see the preceding note.

[19] See above, chap. XIX, note 4.

[20] DESJARDINS, *Négociations diplomatiques*, cit., vol. II, p. 840.

[21] A.S.F., *Carte Strozziane*, 1st ser., 157, ff. 105–108.

[22] See, for example. Busini's opinion in *Lettere al Varchi*, cit., p. 89 ff., and also the incident reported there. But one should read especially the fine, strongly worded letter of 24 May 1525 from Jacopo to his son, which shows particularly what sort of man he was and what authority he had over the Cardinal. Here is part of it: 'Monsignor, I hear that you have a very badly behaved household, and that without any respect whatever your servants talk of nothing but wickedness and sodomy and every kind of evil, in public and in everyone's hearing. I would remind you that you are going to places where such things are regarded as an abomination and great scandal, and that you are considered better than you are. And so I beg and pray you, for the honour of God and the sake of your own soul, to discipline yourself and your household so that at least it does not give a bad example; and I assure you that the affairs of the Church are in such a state that her priests and prelates by doing the very best they can and not by following such ways will have great difficulty in saving the Church. I pray you, I order you by the authority which a father has over his sons, to attend to this and all other things which concern the honour of God . . .' (A.S.F., *Carte Strozziane*, 1st ser., 157, ff. 245–6). It is clear that the writer of such advice would never have proposed to his son, as he did at that time, that he should take M. as his secretary, if his behaviour had been reprehensible.

[23] DESJARDINS, op. and loc. cit.

[24] A.S.F., *Carte Strozziane*, 1st ser., 157, f. 245.

[25] It is certain and obvious that M. presented his *Histories* to Clement VII during his visit in May 1525. As the above quoted letters of Vettori assure us, M. was only waiting for a sign from Rome to set out; and when at last he went in May 1525, it is impossible to imagine that he went without the book. Tommasini, believing that Sadoleto's letter of 6 July 1525, cit. infra., referred to the *Histories* and not to the Romagna militia, argues that M. had gone to Rome, not to present his book, but

summoned by the Pope *proprio motu* for the affairs of Romagna. This conjecture is wild and improbable; but, as if this were not enough, Tommasini appears to have believed that, when he left, M. forgot his book either in Florence or at San Casciano! He goes on to suggest that M. remedied his forgetfulness by taking it on another visit to Rome, of which we have no evidence and for which there is no room; and he puts this between 'the letter of 6 July sent him by Cardinal Sadoleto . . . and another letter of Francesco del Nero to M. of 27 July'. According to Tommasini, he must have gone to Rome when in fact he was in Faenza waiting for the Pope's reply!

[26] See the entry from the *Registro della spesa privata di Clemente VII dal 1523 al 1526*, preserved in A.S.R., and quoted by TOMMASINI, vol. II, p. 769.

[27] On Tommasini's (vol. II, p. 378) curious idea that M. did not go to Rome of his own accord to present his book, but was summoned by the Pope 'as a theorist of war', see note 25 above.

[28] The Brief was published by TOMMASINI, vol. II, p. 1150.

[29] GUICCIARDINI, *Opere inedite*, cit., vol. VIII, p. 263. A letter from Agostino del Nero to M., 'in Romagna', dated 26 June 1525, is to be found in the Bargagli Petrucci group of letters recently acquired by the B.N.F., cit. sup., f. 98.

[30] Letter from Francesco del Nero to M., 27 July 1525, in *Lett. fam.*, p. 439 ff.: 'Filippo Strozzi writes to say that he has spoken with His Holiness about the increase of your salary, and finds him well disposed . . .'

[31] GUICCIARDINI, *Opere inedite*, cit., vol. VIII, pp. 266-9. It ends: 'If this is to go ahead, I will devote all my thought and action to it; and if it is to succeed, Your Holiness must do the same; either you should not begin it, or you should go into it with your mind firmly made up to help in everything that is needed, to overcome all difficulties, and to regard it as more important than anything else.' The edition cited above dates the letter 19 June, and reads *destinato* at one point where the autograph has *obstinato* (con l'animo obstinato di aiutarla . . .)

[32] GUICCIARDINI, *Opere inedite*, cit., vol. VIII, pp. 270-4.

[33] We have information of this letter from one of Sadoleto to M. of 6 July 1525, published in *Lett. fam.*, p. 438 (where, as in other editions, the date is given as 8 July; but the Ricci apograph, from which they all directly or indirectly derive, has 6 July), of which I shall speak below.

[34] It is the first of two sonnets about Clement (BERNI, *Poesie e Prose*, ed. E. Chiorboli, Florence, Olschki, 1934, p. 76), and was written in 1525. It begins:

> Un papato composto di rispetti,
> di considerazioni e di discorsi,
> di pur, di poi, di ma, di se, di forsi,
> di pur assai parole senza effetti . . .

[A papacy composed of respects, considerations and talk; of yets and thens and buts and ifs and maybes; of many words that end in nothing.]

[35] *Opere inedite*, cit., vol. VIII, p. 281.

[36] *Opere inedite*, cit., vol. VIII, p. 283.

[37] Letter from Sadoleto to M., 6 July, cit. (for the date, see note 33 above).

[38] *Opere inedite*, cit., vol. VIII, p. 287.

[39] TOMMASINI, vol. II, p. 791. With one of his curious misunderstandings, Tom-

masini, believing that this plan was suggested to the Pope by Jacopo Salviati, states that Guicciardini also excused himself with Salviati for having brought it to failure, and quotes certain words written by him in a letter of 11 December on an entirely different subject.

[40] M., writing to Guicciardini on 3 August, asks him to greet his wife and tell her that he did not fail, immediately he reached Florence, to carry out the embassies of respect with which she had charged him.

[41] Letter from Guicciardini to M., 7 August 1525, published in *Lett. fam.*, p. 444 ff.: 'If you honour the superscriptions on my letters with "illustrious", I will honour yours with "magnificent"; and so with these reciprocal titles we will give one another pleasure, which will turn to grief when in the end we all, I repeat all, find ourselves with nothing to our credit'.

[42] Published in *Lett. fam.*, p. 440. Note the following words in this letter: 'I wrote to Rome as necessary, and I have not since heard anything from there on the subject' —on the subject, that is, of the Militia proposed by M.

[43] Letter of 3 Aug. 1525, in *Lett. fam.*, p. 441 ff.

[44] Letter of 3 Aug., cit.

[45] GUICCIARDINI, *Opere inedite*, cit., vol. X, p. 100 ff.

[46] Letter from Filippo de' Nerli to M., Modena, 6 Sept. 1525, in *Lett. fam.*, p. 455 ff.

[47] See note 30 above.

[48] The decision is summarized thus in a document published by me for the first time (RIDOLFI, *Opuscoli*, p. 171).

[49] For the difference of value between gold ducats and 'studio' florins, see RIDOLFI, *Opuscoli*, p. 167 ff.

[50] Instructions, letters patent and other documents concerning this mission are preserved in B.N.F., *Carte Machiavelli*, V, 47–49; VI, 85. They were published in part in *Opp. P.*, vol. VI, pp. 220–4.

[51] Letter from M. to Guicciardini, 17 Aug. 1525, in *Lett. fam.*, p. 452. The recipe for these pills (of which M. writes: 'I never took more than two once a week, and when I feel heavy in the stomach or the head'), noted at the foot of the letter is as follows:

bitter aloes	dr.	$1\frac{1}{2}$
carmen deos (*sic*)	,,	1
saffron	,,	$\frac{1}{2}$
myrrh	,,	$\frac{1}{2}$
betony	,,	$\frac{1}{2}$
pimpernel	,,	$\frac{1}{2}$
Armenian bole	,,	$\frac{1}{2}$

On the components of this recipe see especially TOMMASINI, vol. I, p. 644 note. He suggests reading *Camedrios* in place of *Carmen deos*; VILLARI (II[4], 527) suggests instead *Cardam[omum] Dios[coridis]*.

[52] Letter from bishop Lodovico Canossa to Francesco Vettori, 15 Sept. 1525, in VILLARI, vol. III[2], p. 432 ff.

[53] This date derives from the letter from Canossa to Vettori, cit., which reads: 'he told me he intends leaving tomorrow morning to come to you'.

[54] Letter from M. to Guicciardini, 17 Aug. 1525, cit.

[55] This letter from M., published in *Lett. fam.*, p. 458 ff., bears no date; but as it is a reply to one of Guicciardini's written on a 13th, and as 13 Sept. can be excluded because M. was then still in Venice, there are good reasons for supposing it to be 13 October; in which case M.'s answer belongs between the 16 and 20 October.

[56] GUICCIARDINI, *Storia d'Italia*, ed. cit., vol. III, p. 424.

[57] TOFFANIN, p. 412.

[58] This letter, published in *Lett. fam.*, p. 461 ff., also bears no date, but this is suggested by the information of Morone's capture, of which firm news reached Florence on 21 October. The letter must have been written a few days later.

CHAPTER 21

[1] FRANCESCO BERNI, *Poesie e Prose*, cit., p. 84 ff.

[2] Letter from M. to Guicciardini, 19 Dec. 1525, in *Lett. fam.*, p. 466 ff.

[3] *Paradiso*, VI, 133 ff. It is quite clear that M. was once again quoting Dante from memory, because he has substituted an entirely different line for line 134, writing 'della qual cosa al tutto fu cagione/Romeo, persona umile e peregrina', instead of 'Ramondo Berlinghieri e ciò gli fece/Romeo', etc.

[4] Letter from Guicciardini to M., 26 December, in *Lett. fam.*, p. 468 ff.

[5] Re-reading it, one is tempted to think that Guicciardini was not very happy about it. He could not have been very pleased to hear the author say of himself to the audience of Faenza:

> In ogni parte
> del mondo ove il sì suona
> non istima persona
> ancor che facci el sergieri a colui
> che può portar miglior mantel di lui.

[For translation see p. 171].

The President wore a finer garb than he, and M. very often acted as his 'servant'. But Guicciardini must have been consoled when his friend sent him, together with the four songs to be sung between the acts, the opening song 'Perchè la vita è breve', which, if it was not to substitute the Prologue, must at least have toned it down; and it also contained praise for Guicciardini himself. Cf. chap. XVI, note 21.

[6] In the letter which I have attributed to 20 October (*Lett. fam.*, p. 458 ff.; see above, chap. XX, n. 55) M. wrote to Guicciardini about the performance of the comedy: 'While you are pressing on up there, we here have not been sleeping, because Lodovico Alamanni and I have dined these evenings with Barbera and talked of the comedy, so that she offered to come with her singers to be the chorus between the acts, and I offered to write the songs for the acts'.

[7] Letter from Guicciardini to M., 26 December, in *Lett. fam.*, p. 468 ff.

[8] Cesena, Girolamo Soncino, [between Dec. 1525 and Jan. 1526]. It is the edition described by Allacci, 896; Gerber, II, 72. That Soncino was the printer of the presidential proclamations may be seen from those published at that time. Some are preserved in the Guicciardini Archives; cf. R. RIDOLFI, *Gli Archivi delle famiglie fiorentine*, cit., p. 191.

[9] All the early editions of *Mandragola* have in fact the Prologue but not the songs between the acts, which remained for a long time unpublished among Guicciardini's correspondence. The President was not in time to insert them in the Soncino edition. But perhaps between 1572 and 1573 the heirs of Francesco Guicciardini gave the letter with which the songs were enclosed to Giuliano de' Ricci, together with 18 other autograph letters of M. Ricci, who was descended from the Secretary *ex filia*, transcribed them in his well-known apograph; and it was fortunate he did so, as the originals were later lost. As is evident from the text of the letter of 3 Jan. 1525/6, only the words of the songs were enclosed; M. proposed to bring the music with him when he came to Faenza, but he never went, and perhaps it was never written. If it was written, TOMMASINI, vol. I, p. 101 ff., believes that M. wrote it himself. The only grounds for this opinion would be the visit M. paid when passing through Constance to the famous musician Ysaach whom he had known in Florence, and the recommendation made to his son Guido, in a letter we shall quote presently, to learn music. Simply on the basis of these indications it seems to me likely that Niccolò knew and loved music; I would hesitate to say that he composed any without firmer evidence.

[10] Letter from M. to Guicciardini, 3 Jan. 1526, in *Lett. fam.*, p. 470.

[11] Letter from M. to Guicciardini, 3 Jan. 1526, cit.

[12] GUICCIARDINI, *Opere inedite*, cit., vol. VIII, p. 355. The information which precedes and follows in the text regarding this important commission given to G., is taken from other letters in the volume cit. and from the work by P. GUICCIARDINI, *Scritti inediti di Francesco Guicciardini sopra la politica di Clemente VII dopo la battaglia di Pavia*, Florence, Olschki, 1940. The author of this work very kindly gives me credit in his introduction for my discovery of these important writings and other unpublished Guicciardini material. I should like, though somewhat belatedly, to thank him in return for having contributed so much and in so many ways to the progress of studies on his famous ancestor.

[13] Letter from Guicciardini to Colombo, *Opere inedite*, vol. VIII, p. 375. It is understandable, therefore, how G. could write to M., as he did on 26 December, about his invitation and the comedy without any dissimulation whatever, since he had expressed to Colombo barely two days earlier his dissatisfaction at seeing the Pope inclined to make an agreement, which, if made, would render his presence in Rome unnecessary.

[14] Letter from Giovanni Manetti (not Mannelli, as Villari has it: vol. II⁴, p. 532 note) to M., Venice, 28 Feb. 1526, in *Lett. fam.*, p. 473 ff. The original of this letter is in B.N.F., *Carte Machiavelli*, V, 19. Manetti acted as prompter at the performance of *Mandragola*, which gave him this occasion to write. In his letter he also asks M. for 'a sonnet or *capitolo* in praise of a lady'. I do not know whether M. obliged him. It seems rather unlikely that he would send a poem expressly written for the purpose, although it would not be the first time that verses of this kind were composed without the direct inspiration of love. The inspiration in this case would have come from three pairs of smoked roes which Manetti sent to the greedy poet.

[15] SANUTO, *Diari*, vol. XXXII, coll. 458, 466. The first performance, which was interrupted by the great crowd of spectators, took place on 13 Feb. 1521/22; the second on 16 Feb.

[16] Letter from Donato Giannotti to Marcantonio Michieli, cit.; cf. RIDOLFI, *Opuscoli*, p. 62 ff.

[17] I have already written at length about the extracts and summaries compiled by M. at the time of the first *Decennale* (see chap. IX, note 2). The extracts digested into a more advanced, but still summary version, might be those *Frammenti storici* (in *Opp. P.*, pp. 77–127), which are perhaps a draft of parts of book IX of the *Histories*; I also spoke of these at the end of the note to chap. IX, cit. The words written by M. to Guicciardini in his letter: 'I am now starting to write again and I vent my feelings by accusing the princes . . .' (chap. XX, n. 58) must refer to this re-elaboration of the extracts or to some fragmentary part of book IX which has not come down to us, if we except the fragments known under the title of *Nature di uomini fiorentini* (in *Opp. MC.*, pp. 729 ff.) which are already stylistically perfect. It is true that GERBER, I, p. 19, puts among what he calls the preparatory works for the '*Decennale* in prose' not only the *Frammenti storici* but also the *Nature di uomini fiorentini*. But it must be added that this latter work was obviously written after 1508, and by that time, his thoughts of history writing were probably dormant. Besides, the method of dating used by Gerber, which cannot be applied to the *Frammenti*, of which we do not have the autograph, is far from infallible.

[18] *Opp. P.*, vol. II, p. 138.

[19] Letter from M. to Guicciardini, 15 March 1525/26, in *Lett. fam.*, p. 476.

[20] Now lost. We know of it through the reply of Strozzi, 31 March 1526, published in *Lett. fam.*, p. 482 ff.

[21] Letter from Filippo Strozzi to M., 31 March 1526, cit.

[22] Letter, cit.

[23] *Opp. MC.*, p. 872. Tommasini makes wild conjectures about this epigram, among them the suggestion that the figure of Argos represents Clement VII.

[24] Letter from M. to Guicciardini, 4 April 1526, in *Lett. fam.*, p. 285 ff.

[25] The report is published in *Opp. P.*, vol. VI, p. 364 ff. For a modern judgement, see that cited by VILLARI, II[4], p. 536 note. The document preserved in B.N.F., *Carte Machiavelli*, I, 66, must be of a slightly later date.

[26] Letter from Francesco Guicciardini to his brother Luigi, 27 April 1526, in TOMMASINI, vol. II, p. 1157 ff.: 'Machiavelli has left with orders to make the necessary provisions and officers, and begin the fortifications in the manner which you will learn from him . . . Machiavelli was the one who proposed this affair, so you must treat him well during this visit and help him in any way necessary, for he has well earned his reward . . .'

[27] Letter to Guicciardini, 17 May, in *Lett. fam.*, p. 487.

[28] 'One of my sons', writes M. in his letter to Guicciardini of 17 May, cit., and Villari is no more precise. But this son could only be Bernardo, because Lodovico was then in the Levant, Guido and Piero were boys. The document which established the office of the *Cinque Procuratori* was written by M. himself; it is published from the autograph in *Opp. P.*, vol. VI, p. 360.

[29] No record of any allocation or payment to M. for this service has been found.

[30] *Lett. fam.*, pp. 490–4.

[31] Letter from M. to Guicciardini, 17 May 1526, cit. Guicciardini's reply, dated

22 May, *Lett. fam.*, p. 489, reassured M. that the Pope was firm in his support of the office of the Curators of the walls, and he agreed with him *de rebus universalibus.*

[32] These words of Guicciardini were first published in my *Vita di Francesco Guicciardini*, cit., p. 245. Until then only Acciaioli's reply, quoted in the preceding note, was known.

[33] A.S.F., *Carte Strozziane*, 1st ser., 137, f. 212; *Opp. U.*, p. 1214 ff. The heading of the letter is missing in the copy, and we do not know to whom it was addressed, but there are good reasons to suppose it was sent to Bartolomeo Cavalcanti, to whom the other letter from M. on the same page is addressed (this one, which lacks the ending, was published by TOMMASINI, vol. II, p. 1251). It is likely that Cavalcanti copied or had copied the two or more letters he received from M., to circulate them among his friends. Furthermore, with regard to this letter of 13 July, it is evident from the following words that it was sent to a man of letters: 'And may this serve as a reply to one I had from you in Latin, which was read to the Lieutenant. . . .' Villari not only makes M. go into the field so late that Vettori's letters of 5 and 7 August must have reached him whilst he was travelling, but he has him come back to Florence immediately after his mission to Cremona, that is in mid-September, whereas he did not return until the end of October after having remained in the field for about four months on end. In a letter from Roberto Acciaioli to Guicciardini, Amboise, 7 Aug. 1526, published by VILLARI, vol. III², p. 452, we read: 'I am glad that Machiavelli has given orders to drill the infantry, and would to God that what he has in mind might be achieved; but I fear it may be like Plato's Republic—it was impossible ever to find anybody who created one in practice according to his precepts. So it would seem to me better that he go back to Florence to do his job of fortifying the walls, for the times are such that there will be need of them . . .'

[34] BANDELLO, *Novelle*, I, 46. The incident is narrated in the Prologue to this tale which was dedicated and sent by the author immediately afterwards to Giovanni de' Medici; and it is the tale told at table by Niccolò. There would seem no reason for suspecting its authenticity, even though L. DI FRANCIA, *Alla scoperta del vero Bandello*, in *G.S.L.I.*, vol. LXXVIII, pp. 290–324, LXXX, pp. 1–94, LXXXI, pp. 1–75, shows with some cogent examples that one cannot rely too much on Bandello's veracity. In this case, however, it appears a good deal easier to doubt the authenticity of the tale attributed to M. than that of the incident narrated. Cf. V. OSIMO, *Il Machiavelli e il Bandello*, in *G.S.L.I.*, vol. LIV (1909), p. 86. Lodovico Domenichi in his *Nobiltà delle donne*, printed in Venice by Giolito in 1549, five years before the first edition of Bandello's novelle (Lucca, Busdrago, 1554), writes: 'Signor Giovanni de' Medici used to say . . . that between him and Niccolò Machiavelli there was this difference; Niccolò knew how to write things well and he knew how to do them'. It is hard to say whether these military experiments of M. had anything to do with the commission to 'drill the infantry' (see note 32 above).

[35] Letter from Jacopo Fornaciaio to M., 5 Aug. 1526, in *Lett. fam.*, p. 495 ff.; VILLARI, vol. III², p. 445. It appears from Vettori's letter to M. of 5 August in TOMMASINI, vol. II, p. 1242, that Barbera possessed the cypher used by M. for corresponding with his Florentine friends.

[36] Letter from Vettori to M., 5 Aug. 1526, cit. (it was first published, incompletely, in *Lett. fam.*, p. 496 ff.), and other letters from V. to M. of 7 and 24 August in *Lett.*

fam., pp. 499 ff., 508 ff. But see now R. RIDOLF, *Schede per l'epistolario del M.* (II)... in *G.S.L.I.*, CXXXVIII, cit, pp. 552 ff.

[37] Letter from Vettori to M., 24 August, cit. In a letter of 17 August, now lost, M. had discussed three ways of pursuing the war; one of these was to carry the war into the Kingdom of Naples. In his reply V. discusses these proposals. In a letter dated 26 September from Filippo Strozzi to Vettori (TOMMASINI, II, 1245), we read: 'today I took Machiavelli's letters to His Holiness and he read them all calmly, and then at last he said that the recommendation about attacking the Kingdom did not please him'. He approved instead the third of the three proposals, that is, to attack Milan from two sides.

[38] We have two of his letters to M., of 11 Aug. and 18 Sept. 1526, *Lett. fam.*, pp. 506 ff., 511 ff.; and one from M. to him, published by Tommasini, vol. II, p. 1251 ff. M.'s letter is incomplete at the end, and bears no date, though this may easily be conjectured, from references in the text, as around 6 Oct. 1526. Another letter from M. to Cavalcanti is the one of 13 July 1526 referred to above (note 32).

[39] GUICCIARDINI, *Opere inedite*, vol. IV, p. 361.

[40] The instructions from Guicciardini to M. are published without date (but it is clear they were written on 9 September) in *Opp. P.*, vol. VI, p. 224 ff.

[41] VILLARI, II[4], p. 544, states that after this mission to Cremona M. returned to Florence, where he reported verbally and then 'gave a written account of the true state of affairs'. As we shall see, however, he stayed in the field for almost a month and a half more. As for the written account, this is nothing more than the letter to Cavalcanti referred to above in notes 32 and 38, of which Villari had found an incomplete and inaccurate version in old editions of M.'s *Opere*. Even when he saw it more completely in print, he persisted in regarding it as 'a written official report' (op. cit., p. 545 note), as if an official report could begin with 'My dear Bartolomeo' and contain jokes! We may cite here the autograph of a plan for attacking Cremona drawn up by M. on 13 September, published by Tommasini, vol. II, p. 1247 ff.

CHAPTER 22

[1] Preserved in a copy in A.S.F., *Carte Strozziane*, 1st ser., 137, f. 212 (see chap. 21, notes 32, 38, 41); first published as a letter 'to a friend' (*Opp. U.*, p. 1219 ff.); republished by Tommasini, vol. II, p. 1251, more fully and with the name of the proper addressee.

[2] This appears from Jacopo Salviati's letter to M., 5 Nov. 1526, in *Lett. fam.*, p. 517 ff.

[3] Letter from Guicciardini to M., 12 Nov. 1526, in *Lett. fam.*, p. 518 ff.; cf. Salviati's letter quoted in preceding note.

[4] Letter from Guicciardini to M., 30 Oct. 1526, in *Lett. fam.*, p. 513 ff.

[5] Letter from M. to Guicciardini, Florence, 5 Nov. 1526 (another letter from M. to G. from Modena is now lost), published in *Lett. fam.*, p. 515 ff., where the beginning should be corrected to read: 'Signor Luogotenente. Di Modana si scrisse a V.S. una lettera...' A sample of the terrible reproaches made by G. against Nerli may be read in *Opere inedite*, cit., vol. IV, p. 187 ff. Closely related to the matters

discussed in this letter and in the one cited in the preceding note, is a letter from Nerli
to M. of 1 November, which I discovered after the publication of the Italian editions
of this biography. Cf. R. RIDOLFI, *Schede per l'epistolario del M.*, cit., p. 232 ff.

[6] Letter from Guicciardini to M., 12 November, cit.

[7] The original instructions, dated 30 Nov. 1526, were published in *Opp. P.*, vol.
VI, p. 226 ff.; cf. TOMMASINI, vol. II, p. 866 note.

[8] Letter from M. to the Eight, Modena, 2 December, in *Opp. P.*, vol. VI, p. 228 ff.;
cf. GUICCIARDINI, *Opere inedite*, cit., vol. V, p. 9 ff.

[9] Letter from M. to the Eight, Modena, 3 December, in *Opp. P.*, vol. VI, p. 230 ff.
But on 5 December Filippo de' Nerli wrote to the Cardinal of Cortona: 'Niccolò
Machiavelli left this morning and will come by daily stages'. This information is
confirmed by other letters from Nerli to Guicciardini; cf. the extracts published by
TOMMASINI, vol. II, p. 857 note.

[10] In the register the last letter in M.'s hand is dated 26 January. Cf. VILLARI, vol.
III², p. 445 note.

[11] Letter to the Eight, Parma, 7 February, in *Opp. P.*, vol. IV, p. 233 ff. He left
Modena on the morning of the 6th, two hours before dawn, with an armed escort
given him by the governor Filippo de' Nerli, who informed Jacopo Salviati of their
journey. On the same day Nerli also informed Guicciardini who had written asking
him to urge M. to hurry. See the extracts from Nerli's correspondence, quoted but
not utilized by TOMMASINI, vol. II, p. 857 note.

[12] The letter from Guicciardini to the Cardinal of Cortona of 5 February begins:
'This morning I received your letter of the 31st, and was glad to hear that Machiavelli
is coming here, because besides the fact that he will return entirely informed of the
nature and method of the assistance which can be expected from here, I shall profit
from his coming by getting him to tell the Duke and the Marquis what is needed',
etc. One should not be surprised that a decision of the Eight should be announced
so long before it was in fact taken, because affairs were dealt with in the Palazzo dei
Signori after they had been decided on by the Cardinal in the Medici household.
The instructions for this mission, dated 3 February, were published in *Opp. P.*, vol.
VI, p. 232 ff.

[13] See above, note 11.

[14] Letter to the Eight, 7 February, cit.

[15] Letter from Guicciardini to the Cardinal of Cortona, 7 and 8 February, in *Opere
inedite*, cit., vol. VIII, p. 215 ff.; letter from M. to the Eight, 7 February, cit. sup.
note 11. SANUDO, *Diari*, vol. XLIV, col. 71, records: 'Messer Niccolò Machiavelli
arrived here today, sent from Florence to confer with the Duke about the affairs of
the war, and this evening they spoke together at length.'

[16] *Opp. P.*, vol. VI, p. 235 ff. Tommasini (II, 874), instead of *in costà* proposes
reading *in costa*, 'according to the autograph', as if M. and his contemporaries used
accents as we do in modern times!

[17] *Opp. P.*, vol. VI, p. 238 ff. On the same day Guicciardini wrote to Rome to
Datario, which was the same as writing to the Pope, praising M.'s work (he who
was never satisfied with anyone!): 'Machiavelli is still here and in the letters he has
written he has done good work; I do not know what he will do on his return; but
if friendship avails, you will not be disappointed in anything he writes.' The last

letters written by M. to the Eight from Parma appear to be those of 16 and 18 February, published in *Opp. P.*, vol. VI, pp. 239–42. In his first letter from Bologna on 4 March he excuses himself for not writing for some time, and relies on the daily letters sent by the Lieutenant.

[18] L. STAFFETTI, *Il cardinale Innocenzo Cybo*, etc., Florence, Successori Le Monnier, 1894.

[19] Letter from M. to the Eight, Bologna, 18 March, in *Opp. P.*, vol. VI, p. 248 ff. He wrote other letters to the Eight from Bologna on 4, 5, 12 March, published ibid., pp. 242–7; then on 23, 24, 27, 29, 30 March, ibid., pp. 250–6.

[20] Letter from M. to the Eight, Imola, 2 April: 'As soon as the enemy moved from San Giovanni, the Lieutenant sent me here to arrange the billetts for the troops who are to come' (*Opp. P.*, vol. VI, p. 256 ff.). I do not understand how C. RICCI, *Gli Spagnuoli e i Veneziani in Romagna* (cit. by Staffetti, op. cit.) can state that Guicciardini went to Imola while M. stayed in Bologna with Cybo.

[21] Letter to the Eight, 2 April, cit.

[22] Biographers and genealogists know nothing of this last child of M. He was certainly born after the death of his uncle whose name he was given († 1522), and probably at the beginning of 1526 or the end of 1525, as he was still out to wet nurse, although they were about to take him back. He must have died soon after. Other children of Niccolò also died young, one on 14 June 1506, another on 15 Feb. 1510 (see above, chap. 9, note 30; chap. 11, note 41). So as not to miss even the last crumb of these domestic minutiae of M.'s family, I would add that early in March 1527 'Niccolò Machiavelli's servant girl is ill', with suspected plague, according to the record for that year of the 'Ufficiali del contagio'.

[23] Very detailed information about Lodovico and the penalties inflicted on him, all for violence and quarrels, is to be found in C. AMICO, op. cit., p. 614. The first was on 11 May 1525 for having beaten a notary; the second on 16 June 1525 for wounding someone; the third for a fight over a whore. We have a letter from him to his father, written on 14 Aug. 1525 from Adrianapoli, full of anger, threats and proposals of revenge; and another from Ancona, dated 22 May 1527, which must have reached his father shortly before his death. Lodovico died fighting in the siege of Florence for the free republic; at least in this he was not unworthy of his father.

[24] Guido took orders, for which his father may have intended him, if we interpret in this sense his reference to his recent friendship with Cardinal Cybo, 'which will be useful to you'. Guido cultivated literary studies, and we have an original comedy, another translated from Terence, and various other writing of his, all mediocre and unpublished. On him and Piero (1514–64) see the more detailed information given by AMICO (op. cit., pp. 612 ff., 614 ff.), who also published (p. 667 ff.) a *Discorso* by Piero to Duke Cosimo on the way to drive the French and Spanish out of Tuscany and to establish a Tuscan fleet. He was following in his father's footsteps.

[25] *Lett. fam.*, p. 519 ff.

[26] *Lett. fam.*, p. 521 ff.

[27] Guicciardini wrote from Forlì to Cardinal Cybo on 8 April, and M. wished to be remembered to his new patron: 'Machiavelli is Your Excellency's good servant, and commends himself to you and kisses your hand'; STAFFETTI, op. cit., p. 68.

[28] *Opp. P.*, vol. VI, p. 261 ff.

²⁹ Letter from M. to Vettori, 14 April 1527, in *Lett. fam.*, p. 523 ff.

³⁰ It is worth noting that Guicciardini, who was never satisfied and always ready to criticize and reprove everybody, Pope, cardinals, governors, had nothing but praise for M. in these last days. See the passage quoted in note 17 above, in which —and it is an extraordinary thing for him—he speaks of *friendship* between him and M. This does not mean that he became converted suddenly to M.'s theories. Ten years later, narrating in his *Storia d'Italia* the sack of Rome by Bourbon, he was to write the following page which renews and reaffirms the spirit of his famous *Considerations* on the *Discourses* of M., written in 1530 (GUICCIARDINI, *Le cose fiorentine*, published for the first time by R. Ridolfi, Florence, Olschki, 1945, p. xxiii ff.): 'By which [i.e. the poor resistence put up by the defenders], as on many other occasions, it was shown to those who through ancient examples have not yet learnt modern affairs, how different the force is of men trained to war from that of new armies made up of assembled rabble, and of the popular multitude'. The fact is that both men spoke a different language, and each had some reason on his side, for one spoke of present reality, the other of reality in general, one about the present, the other about the future (ed. cit., vol. IV, p. 123). In the particular case in question, where the polemic against M. seems to me obvious, the example was inapposite and did not justify that critical observation, because the defenders of Rome had been 'collected hastily together from the cardinals' and prelates' stables, from the artisans' shops and from the inns': it is Guicciardini himself who says it; and this was not the militia that M. wished to create! For Guicciardini's views and feelings about M., see R. RIDOLFI, *Vita di F.G.*, cit., p. 325 ff.

³¹ Letter from Guicciardini to the Eight, Forlì, 16 April, *Opere inedite*, cit., vol. V, p. 409 ff.

³² Letter from M. to Vettori, Forlì, 16 April 1525, published in *Lett. fam.*, p. 524 ff. His last letter from Forlì to the Eight was on 13 April, published in *Opp. P.*, vol. VI, p. 262 ff., in which he gave encouragement to his fellow-citizens with these words: 'It is said that men must make a virtue out of necessity; but if necessity is added to virtue, then virtue must increase greatly and become insuperable. Your Lordships and this city have so far with your virtue alone defended and saved Lombardy and Romagna; it is impossible that now, when necessity is added to virtue, the city should not save herself.' On the expression 'loving more than his own soul' (here applied not only to Florence but also to Guicciardini!), people have, as usual, talked a good deal of nonsense, and far more than a proverbial phrase warrants.

CHAPTER 23

¹ See above, chap. I, note 35. As I have said, there is no certainty that the person represented by this bust is M.; there are notable similarities, but also some dissimilarities. It might be objected too that in this portrait, made, as is supposed, some months before his death, the face appears so much older than that of the Loeser bust, which according to tradition derives from the death mask, and so must be later. But this objection is not very substantial, because, even if we admit that the Loeser bust does derive from the mask, it is a well-known fact that after death the features

elax with the slackening of the facial muscles. Besides, in these posthumous portraits one must also take into account the work of the artist responsible, which may be influenced by the suggestions of relatives of the deceased.

² *Opp. MC.*, p. 778 ff. The *Esortazione*, which was first less aptly called *Discorso morale*, is published there for the first time from the autograph preserved in B.N.F., *Carte Machiavelli*, I, 76. The handwriting suggests that it was composed in the last years of M.'s life. In spite of the light, which especially since De Sanctis has been driving away the dark clouds of prejudice surrounding M., they were still so powerful that not only could Villari (II⁴, 414) see in the *Esortazione* 'a certain veiled irony', but even Croce could call it 'a frivolous joke'! But cf. ALDERISIO, p. 199.

³ Letter from M. to Vettori, Brisighella, 18 April 1527, in *Lett. fam.*, p. 527 ff.

⁴ The letter of Guido Machiavelli was published in *Lett. fam.*, p. 526 ff.; republished by VILLARI, vol. III², p. 477 ff.

⁵ To encourage citizens to bring supplies into the city, the Signoria had ordered that victuals and wood could come in duty-free, wine and oil at half-duty; CAMBI, *Istorie*, cit., vol. XXII, p. 303.

⁶ Letter from Guido Machiavelli, cit.

⁷ Letter from Guido Machiavelli, cit.

⁸ In the margin of his instructions, cit. sup. chap. XXII, note 12, there is the following note: 'He left on the said day (3 Feb.) at the 24th hour, and came back on 22 April, that is 80 days.' For Guicciardini's return see his *Opere inedite*, cit., vol. V, p. 417 ff.

⁹ Letter of 24 April, in GUICCIARDINI, *Opere inedite*, cit., vol. V, p. 417.

¹⁰ *Opere inedite*, cit., vol. V, p. 427 ff. He wrote these things to Datario for him to read them to the Pope, but the Lieutenant also told the Pope directly what he thought. See, for example, his last letter from Brisighella, dated 19 April (GUICCIARDINI, *Opere inedite*, cit., vol. V, p. 415 ff.), in which the reproval is not tempered by reticence: 'I would speak graver words if respect did not prevent me.'

¹¹ VARCHI, *Istoria fiorentina*, ed. L. Arbib, Florence, 1838–41, vol. I, p. 106.

¹² F. VETTORI, *Sommario della Storia d'Italia*, cit., p. 378.

¹³ Soon after the publication of the second Italian edition of this book, I came across a letter written to Machiavelli on 26 April 1526 by the captain Guido Vaina, who had been sent to Poggibonsi by Guicciardini. This letter is more important than might appear at first sight (Villari saw it, but did not use it), because it confirms what I cautiously suggested above about M.'s functions as commissioner with the papal army, and it tells us that on that day or the next he must have been at Figline. A note in his hand on the outside of a letter from Alessandro Del Caccia to Guicciardini sent from Figline on 25 April, also suggests that M. was on the road from Florence to Figline or about to leave Florence on that day. Nevertheless, as it is not possible to be absolutely sure about this, I have not altered the substance of what I wrote in the Italian editions. Cf. R. RIDOLFI, *Spigolature machiavelliane*, cit.

¹⁴ *Opp. P.³* vol, VI, p. 265 ff. Francesco Bandini has signed after M. (for once!). It is likely that there were also other Florentines with M., who were leaving the Medici Pope's army after the departure of the Medici from Florence and the change of government. From the letter we gather that M. would be leaving the next day or the day after that for Livorno with the galleys carrying the Marchesa of Mantua, or with

one of Doria's brigs, if it left before them. In order to show what relations existed before (according to him) between M. and the great Genovese admiral, TOMMASINI, vol, II., p. 1256 ff., publishes what he thinks is a 'commission from Andrea Doria to N. Machiavelli', and accompanies it with his usual weird conjectures and incredible mistakes. He proposes to date it from Naples, 'between the end of March and the middle of April 1527', at which time (as everybody knows except this author of a book of more than 2,000 pages on M.) Machiavelli was with the papal army between Bologna and Florence. The commission ordered him to go to Rome to report to 'the Very Reverend Monsignor De' Medici', that is, according to Tommasini, the young Ippolito. As is known, Ippolito at that time was styled 'Magnificent', not 'Very Reverend Monsignor', which applies to cardinals; and furthermore, he was not in Rome but in Florence under the guidance of the Cardinal of Cortona. In any case it is doubtful whether the commission was issued by Andrea Doria; in the text there is reference to a brother by the name of Giovanni, and Andrea had no brother of that name.

[15] There is a very curious *lapsus* (if that is the right term) on Tommasini's part in this connection. He conjectures (II, 895 ff.) that Guicciardini had sent M. to Doria to get him to put a galley at the disposal of Filippo and Clarice Strozzi, and received a negative reply in M.'s letter of 22 May; he then says (II, 897) that Clarice came by sea from Civitavecchia to Pisa, arriving on 11 May—which is quite correct. He goes on (II, 899): 'It seems that M. returned from Civitavecchia with Strozzi. Perhaps he accompanied Clarice to Florence'! In other words, M. had gone about 20 May to ask for a galley to bring Clarice to Livorno, which had arrived there on the 11th; and M. would appear to have accompanied her to Livorno and then to Florence while on the 22nd he was still in Civitavecchia!

[16] BUSINI, op. cit., p. 85: 'Messer Piero Carnesecchi, who came with him from Rome with one of his sisters, says that he heard him sigh many times, when he heard that the city was free. I think he was regretting his conduct, because in fact he greatly loved liberty; but he regretted having involved himself with Pope Clement.'

[17] *Mandragola*, act II, sc. iii.

[18] BUSINI, op. cit., p. 84: 'He tried hard to get back his post with the Ten; Zanobi and Luigi supported him strongly.'

[19] Tarugi was first secretary of the Otto di Pratica (Eight) from 8 June 1525, and the instructions for M.'s second mission to Guicciardini were signed by him (MARZI, op. cit., p. 317; TOMMASINI, II, 906. For the decision regarding Tarugi's appointment, see VILLARI, vol. III², p. 479).

[20] VARCHI, *Storia fiorentina*, ed. cit., vol. I, p. 171; cf. p. 158.

[21] BUSINI, op. cit., p. 84

[22] BUSINI, op. cit., p. 9: 'I heard Machiavelli say he was giving away what was not his to give, and joke about his foolishness'. Perhaps rather than to the later explicit consent of the Pope, Busini's words refer to the ambiguous statement in Guicciardini's letter to the Eight (*Opere inedite*, cit., vol. IX, p. 14): 'His Holiness has sent me word to write to Your Lordships on his behalf that you should take that course in your affairs. . . .'

[23] From what one may now conjecture, M., who may have been suffering from chronic appendicitis or a gastric ulcer (for some years, riding especially for long

periods and in haste seems not to have suited him 'on account of some infirmity of his'), died of acute peritonitis caused by taking some of his famous pills (see above, chap. XX, note 51) during an attack of pain. G. PIERI, in *Policlinico* (Sez. Pratica), XXXVII (1930), p. 704 ff., argues for appendicitis. He quotes a communication from Dr. Baccarani about clinical results from M.'s pills; but if the medicine was innocuous, it certainly could not have been so to a patient suffering from appendicitis, if taken in larger doses than usual.

²⁴ BUSINI, op. cit., p. 84 ff. This 'famous dream' was well known to some contemporaries, so much so that Giovio clearly refers to it in his *Elogia* to show us a M. sneering at God on the point of death. But record of it was then lost, as though it were not worth writing down. Some written record must, however, have been seen by the Jesuit p. Stefano Binet (1569–1639), who related it as we have told it here. VILLARI, vol. III⁴, p. 562, recently followed also by ALDERISIO, p. 219, with that mania deprecated by Balbo 'for defending everything and everybody', rejected the account as late and not confirmed by contemporaries—as if Busini and Giovio, who were his contemporaries, did not confirm the dream and its substance in such a way that there seems no doubt of its authenticity. The theory that this 'late' account was made up from material in *Mandragola* (act IV, sc. i) and the *Discourses* (but if it was not this one, which was the comic and ironical dream he told on his deathbed?) is no more reasonable than the conjecture that M. possibly developed on a suitable occasion ideas referred to in those writings, which were habitual to him in humorous conversation.

²⁵ Letter from Piero Machiavelli, Niccolò's son, who was then thirteen, to his maternal uncle Francesco Nelli, a lawyer in Pisa. I cannot refrain from mentioning the ridiculous mistake made by Tommasini, who thought he could identify this fra Matteo with a certain Matteo Canigiani who was beheaded for murder in 1529 (VARCHI, op. cit., vol. II, p. 260) and mentioned by Busini (op. cit., p. 36) as 'a great fool'. But this man was never a friar (although Busini mentions him after a friar, it was easy to see that he was not one, because friars do not have farms and lands mentioned in the text); and even if he had been a friar, it can be reckoned that there were never less than a few dozen fra Matteos in Florence. The worst is that other biographers followed Tommasini's almost incredible error. Furthermore, Tommasini took it upon himself (though by now we know how much reliance to put on his judgement) to state that Piero's letter is a forgery. The reasons he adduces are without substance, and apart from the one about fra Matteo, whose weight we have just tested, they show how little he knew about the life and customs of the time. I would make bold to say that if the document had come down to us in a late copy, I would have considered it authentic for its manner, expression and sincerity, and for certain details which only the close associates of M. could understand and the curiosity of modern historians appreciate. As for the handwriting which is tremulous, uncertain and very different from autographs of Piero in later life, it merely proves the extreme youth of the writer of the letter. I do not believe in forgeries unless I can see an adequate reason for them. If it were a forgery, it would have been made at the time or soon after; and who can have wished then to invent the letter? Perhaps M.'s children to create a document showing the religious death of their father or grandfather? But even admitting that they needed such a document, was it necessary to

have one of this particular kind? If at all, one might imagine a forgery of a more likely kind, and suppose that someone in later years chose to make a sort of imitation copy for sentimental reasons or financial gain. There are instances of such copies made in the 16th century, like the one of the famous letter from Savonarola to his Father preserved in the Gondi archives (SAVONAROLA, *Lettere*, ed. R. Ridolfi, Florence, Olschki, 1933, p. XXII). But in this case the document though diplomatically false, is historically authentic. It must be added that Tommasini's strange opinion was not followed by any worthy scholars; and if it was not rejected with arguments as I have tried to do here, it was allowed to lapse. Villari, in his first edition, not having any doubts about the authenticity of the letter, was induced to consider false the account of the somewhat irreverent jokes made on his death-bed, for he regarded as contradictory in the account what was merely a contradiction in the personality of Machiavelli. In his later edition he came into line with Tommasini's statement.

²⁶ A.S.F., *Libro dei Morti* (*Medici e Speziali*), 249, f. 128: 'Niccolò di . . . Machiavelli, on the 22nd [June] buried in Santa Croce.'

CHAPTER 24

¹ G. CAPPONI, op. cit., vol. III, p. 191.

² The privilege to Blado to print the *Histories*, *Prince* and *Discourses* was given by Clement VII in a brief dated 22 Aug. 1531, which was published at the beginning of the *editio princeps* of the *Histories*. In another brief of 20 December 1531, 'considering it just that the works of the said Niccolò should be printed in his own city', and as Blado had already been able to sell the greater part of the copies he had printed (the sale would seem to have been very rapid), he allowed the Giunti to print freely, with the agreement of Machiavelli's heirs, 'Historiarum et de Principe et Discursus libros'. This second brief was published by TOMMASINI, vol. II, p. 550 note. After the prohibition of Paul IV (1559) and the Council (1569), negotiations were already in progress in 1572 to have M.'s works republished with the usual expurgations, and Giuliano de' Ricci in his Apograph could write with satisfaction of his Author: 'and now with the assent of the Superiors he will return to the world'.

³ Machiavellianism is dealt with at great length by TOMMASINI, vol. I, pp. 3–75; vol. II, pp. 749 ff., 922 ff., 953 ff. See also F. MEINECKE, *Die Idee Staatsräson in der neuren Geschichte*, Munich-Berlin, 1925.

⁴ E. PISTELLI, *Profili e caratteri*, Florence, Sansoni, 1921, p. 67 ff.

⁵ G. CAPPONI, op. cit., vol. III, p. 190.

⁶ If I am not mistaken, the first to use this expression was Macaulay in his famous essay (*Essays*, London, 1864, vol. I, p. 30). *L'énigme de M.* is the title of a lecture given by H. Hauvette at the Institut de France on 23 Nov. 1934.

⁷ See also P. CARLI, in *G.S.L.I.*, vol. XLIX (1932), pp. 133–46 (important review of Alderisio's book). Much insistence has been placed in recent times on the contradictions and dualisms of M., but more on those in his theories than in his personality, especially by A. RENAUDET, op. cit., who speaks of 'the dualism of a hard positive intelligence and the imagination of a visionary and poet' (p. 175). In this he seems to me not far from the truth (even if this view is described as 'traditional'

by G. SASSO, *Recenti studi sul M.*, in *Rassegna di Filosofia*, vol. I (1952), p. 140 ff., who uses the term in a sense which neither I nor the Italian language are prepared to give it: 'traditional' judgements can also be 'acute', and often are); but one should not confuse these and other antitheses of M. with certain supposed paradoxes of his thought and teaching, such as the one dear to Renaudet of the 'princely hypothesis' theorized about in the *Prince* as opposed to the 'republican hypothesis' of the *Discourses*. In this case, if one studies the genesis of these works, there is no contradiction. But if Renaudet and others saw dualisms and contradictions which do not exist, one cannot deny, without denying M.'s own words which confess them, the contrasts which govern his passionate and impulsive character, and which must, like his poetic and artistic nature, find their reflection in his political writings.

[8] *Istorie Fiorentine*, book VIII (*Opp. MC.*, p. 621); I do not know whether Macaulay (op. and loc. cit.) had this passage in mind when he wrote of M. 'two characters altogether dissimilar are united in him'. I do not know why, but Villari could not bear the idea of two opposite natures combined in M.!

[9] E. GARIN, *La Filosofia* ('Storia dei Generi Letterari Italiani'), Milan, Vallardi, 1947, p. 176 ff.

[10] F. ERCOLE, *La politica del M.*, Rome, Anonima Romana Editoriale, 1926, p. 61.

[11] F. ALDERISIO, p. 89 ff., and especially p. 100 ff. His conclusions must be tempered with the opinions expressed by Carli in his excellent review, cit. sup.

[12] B. CROCE, *Etica e politica*, cit., p. 252. L. RUSSO, p. 7, also writes that M. turns a deaf ear to the moral problem.

[13] G. GENTILE, *Economia ed etica*, cit. by ALDERISIO, p. 109 note.

[14] On this subject the most important work is ALDERISIO's, pp. 173–201; but he makes apologetic comments which go too far beyond the mark and rightly provoke some of Russo's (p. 202) bitter sarcasm.

[15] B. CROCE, *Etica e politica*, cit., p. 227.

[16] Besides the well-known passages from his Carpi correspondence with Guicciardini, I give other examples from letters of M. and his correspondents: M. to Vettori: 'I did not hear the sermon, for I do not follow such practices' (*Lett. fam.*, p. 314 ff.); F. Vettori to M.: 'On feast days I go to mass and I do not do as you do who sometimes miss it' (*Lett. fam.*, p. 303; cf. p. 455).

[17] G. CAPPONI, op. cit., p. 190.

[18] See above, chap. XXIII, note 2.

[19] I am sorry, but I cannot share the opinion of RUSSO, p. 202 ff., that the famous words 'one must speak of so great a man with reverence' are 'an ambiguous ceremonial phrase'. Rather than by his maturer years (the Carpi letter is later), that phrase was suggested by the platform from which he spoke, and which made him change his expression. It is certain that M. had no liking for Savonarola; some hidden reverence, perhaps. M.'s character was such that one should not give too much weight to certain facetious expressions in his private letters.

[20] *Opp. MC.*, p. 265.

[21] ALDERISIO, p. 102.

[22] *Discourses*, I, 12.

[23] Modena, Tipi del Commercio, 1869.

[24] See above, chap. 10.

INDEX

1953